Second Edition

The Philosophic Roots of Modern Ideology

Liberalism, Communism, Fascism

DAVID E. INGERSOLL
University of Delaware

RICHARD K. MATTHEWS
Lehigh University

Prentice Hall, Englewood Cliffs, New Jersey 07632

Library of Congress Cataloging-in-Publication Data

Ingersoll, David E., (date)
    The philosophic roots of modern ideology : liberalism, communism,
fascism / David E. Ingersoll, Richard K. Matthews.—2nd ed.

    p. cm.
    Includes bibliographical references.
    ISBN 0–13–662644–0
    1. Political science—History. 2. Liberalism—History.
3. Communism—History. 4. Fascism—History. I. Matthews, Richard
K., (date). II. Title.
JA83.I55 1991
    320.5′09—dc20   89–72173
                                                          CIP

Editorial/production supervision and
    interior design: Mary A. Araneo
Cover design: Ben Santora
Manufacturing buyer: Robert Anderson

© 1991, 1986 by Prentice-Hall, Inc.
A Division of Simon & Schuster
Englewood Cliffs, New Jersey 07632

Printed in the United States of America

10 9 8 7 6 5 4 3

ISBN 0-13-662644-0

Prentice-Hall International (UK) Limited, *London*
Prentice-Hall of Australia Pty. Limited, *Sydney*
Prentice-Hall Canada Inc., *Toronto*
Prentice-Hall Hispanoamericana, S.A., *Mexico*
Prentice-Hall of India Private Limited, *New Delhi*
Prentice-Hall of Japan, Inc., *Tokyo*
Simon & Schuster Asia Pte. Ltd., *Singapore*
Editora Prentice-Hall do Brasil, Ltda., *Rio de Janeiro*

Josy W. Ingersoll, for her patience and understanding; Jamie and Michael Deiner for their toleration of an all too often irascible student of ideas.

Deborah Jean and Zachary Daniel Matthews, who provide the support for my wings.

The surest way to corrupt a youth is to instruct him to hold in higher esteem those who think alike than those who think differently.

Nietzsche

Contents

7 SOVIET MARXISM   166

8 THE POLITICAL THOUGHT OF MAO ZEDONG   193

Preface
to Second Edition

Recent, dramatic events in the realm of political ideology demand that a new edition of our earlier book be written. This edition deals specifically with three crucial milestones: (1) the rise of Mikhail Gorbachev, (2) the eclipse of Deng Xiaoping, and (3) the resurgence of Islamic fundamentalism. Each of these occurrences has already produced important, sometimes tragic, political effects that need to be understood within an ideological context. More important, all have the potential to change profoundly the world of politics.

This book is designed as an overview for readers who have little or no knowledge of three basic idea systems of modern times. Given that purpose, we have constantly found ourselves in the frustrating position of oversimplifying, ignoring interesting side issues, and avoiding topics that in a longer work would surely be essential. What follows is original scholarship in the sense that the emphases and interpretations are dependent to a large extent on our own backgrounds and interests. We have, however, often relied heavily on the work of other scholars and will be happy if we have provided a partial synthesis of their work. In trying to accomplish this, we are acutely conscious of at times seeming to "parrot" the work of others—if this occurs too often we are sincerely apologetic. Along the same lines it is difficult to sort those interpretations that are ours and those that have resulted from the hard work of others. We have benefited tremendously from the writings of scholars in these areas—many of whom we have never met. Our simple hope is that we have assisted in their endeavors by presenting these idea systems in a form whereby they can be more easily understood by beginning students. Our fondest hope is that this work will stimulate readers to explore these idea systems in all of their complexity and richness, and that they will see the importance of ideas in themselves as well as in relation to what too often passses for the "real world."

Much of the intellectual groundwork for what follows is to be found in David E. Ingersoll's 1971 book *Communism, Fascism, Democracy.* This new book contains interpretations that are radically different from the former book, treats numerous topics not covered in the earlier work, and benefits from the major contributions and insights of coauthor Richard K. Matthews. We should also acknowledge that our treatment of American liberalism—particularly regarding Thomas Jefferson—is largely based on Matthews' *The Radical Politics of Thomas Jefferson.*

A final explanatory note concerning the use of footnotes and bibliography seems in order. We have used footnotes sparingly, and we have appended a brief bibliography to each chapter. This is in keeping with the nature of the work, which purports to provide an overview of an extremely complex subject matter and to stimulate students to explore further on their own. To that end it seemed desirable to avoid copious footnoting while leading the student directly to the primary sources and to other, more detailed works in the field. We are certain there are many excellent books that are absent from the bibliography, either because of a lack of knowledge or because of space limitations. We hope that the ones that are included will be sufficient to assist the student in the pursuit of further knowledge.

We would like to acknowledge the contributions, both direct and indirect, of the many persons who have made this book possible. Our students at the University of Delaware and at Lehigh University have contributed, often unwittingly, through their reactions to ideas we have presented and techniques we have attempted to use—our respective classrooms have often served as experimental laboratories. Pam DeMond, Ginger Carroll, Pat Trayner, Susan Smith, Marlene Bartholomew, Susan Yacone, Matilda DiDonato, and Dorothy Windish have provided typing assistance at various stages. The following scholars have read and commented on the manuscript, and we have benefited both from their critiques and from their encouragement: C. B. Macpherson, Paul Pfretzschner, James Lennertz, Ronald Hill, Yaroslav Bilinsky, Mark Miller, Norman Girardot, Ray Wylie, Jim Reid, Greg White, Andrew Davison, Andrew Zlotnick, and most especially, Don Barry. We also wish to thank the Prentice Hall reviewers for their helpful comments: Mary Ellen Fischer, Skidmore College; Andrea R. C. Helms, University of Alaska, Fairbanks; Richard Hofstetter, San Diego State University; Isaac Kramnick, Cornell University; Frank M. Lewis, University of Toledo; Daniel J. O'Neil, University of Arizona; Andrew Raposa, Westfield State College; Peter C. Sederberg, University of South Carolina; John B. Taylor, Washington College; Joel G. Verner, Illinois State University; and David M. Wood, University of Missouri.

Despite all this assistance, there are, no doubt, errors of omission and commission in what follows; if so, they are our responsibility.

D.E.I.
R.K.M.

Acknowledgments

Displayed quotations in the text are from the following sources:

Opening
Quote
Walter Kaufman, ed., *The Portable Nietzsche* (New York: The Viking Press, Inc., 1954; renewed 1982 by Viking Penguin, Inc.), p. 91. Reprinted by permission of Viking Penguin, Inc.

Chapter 1
John Stuart Mill, *On Liberty* (Baltimore, Md.: Penguin, 1974), p. 95.

Chapter 2
Thomas Hobbes, *Leviathan,* C. B. Macpherson, ed. (Baltimore, Md.: Penguin, 1968), pp. 189–90.

Chapter 3
James Madison, *The Federalist,* Jacob E. Cooke, ed. (Middletown, Conn.: Wesleyan University Press, 1961), p. 374. © 1961 by Wesleyan University.

Chapter 4
John Dewey, The Public and Its Problems (Chicago: The Swallow Press, 1954), p. 149. Reprinted with the permission of Ohio University Press.

Chapter 5
Karl Marx, "Theses on Feurerbach," in *The Marx-Engels Reader, 2nd ed.,* ed. Robert C. Tucker (New York: W. W. Norton & Company, Inc., 1978), p. 145.

Chapter 6
V. I. Lenin, "What Is to Be Done?" in *The Lenin Anthology,* Robert C. Tucker, ed. (New York: W. W. Norton & Company, Inc., 1975), p. 19.

Chapter 7
Mikhail Gorbachev, *Perestroika: New Thinking for Our Country and the World* (New York: Harper & Row, Publishers, 1987), p. 35.

Chapter 8
Mao Zedong, *Selected Works of Mao Tse-tung,* 4 Vols. (Peking: People's Publishing House, 1960), Vol. 1, p. 28.

Chapter 9   Herbert Marcuse, quoted in *Dissent, Power, and Confrontation,* Alexander Klein, ed. (New York: McGraw-Hill Book Company, 1971), p. 37.

Chapter 10   Benito Mussolini, "The Doctrine of Fascism," in *Social and Political Philosophy,* John Somerville and Ronald E. Santoni, eds. (Garden City, N.Y.: Doubleday and Company, 1963), p. 427.

Chapter 11   Adolf Hitler, *Mein Kampf,* trans. Ralph Manheim (Boston: Houghton Mifflin Company, 1971), p. 296.

Chapter 12   Imam Khomeini, *Islam and Revolution: Writings and Declarations of Imam Khomeini* (Berkeley, Calif.: Mizan Press, 1981), p. 275.

Chapter 13   G. W. F. Hegel, *Reason in History* (Indianapolis: Bobbs-Merrill, 1977), p. 27.

1

The Origins
of Political Ideologies

*No one can be a great thinker who does not recognize that as a
thinker it is his first duty to follow his intellect to whatever
conclusions it may lead. Truth gains more even by the errors of one
who, with due study and preparation, thinks for himself than by
the true opinions of those who only hold them because they do not
suffer themselves to think.*

John Stuart Mill

THE CAVE: THE ILLUSION AND THE REALITY
OF EDUCATION

Think of Plato's Cave. Perhaps the most powerful and frightening of all metaphors in Western political philosophy, it is an insightful allegory about the potential of domination and oppression, but ultimately about education and liberation.

Plato ingeniously compares the effect of education, and the lack of it, upon people to the following situation: Imagine a place where humans are living in an underground, cavelike dwelling. The cave contains a way out and up to the sun, but it is rather far removed from the people. They have been here from birth; their necks and legs are in bonds, so that they remain in place and can see only what is directly in front of them. Light inside the cave is provided by a fire burning somewhere behind and above them. Between the fire and our contented prisoners, somewhere behind and on a higher level, there is a path across the cave and along this a low wall has been built. It is similar to the screen at a puppet show in front of the performers who display their puppets above it. Imagine also that these puppeteers carry all kinds of objects, statues of people and animals, so that the figures are above the screening wall. Imagine also that some of the puppeteers are talking while others are silent.

In such a situation, our prisoners could see only the shadows that the fire casts upon the wall of the cave in front of them. Moreover, they would believe that the sounds they hear are coming from these shadows. Since they can see neither their own bodies nor the bodies of the other people, they inevitably assume reality to be nothing else than the shadows and sounds of the puppeteers and their artifacts.

"Preposterous!" you say. "How could such people be either so stupid or so foolish as to be tricked by shadows on the wall?" And yet Plato claims this is precisely the human condition. We are all born into a type of comfortable slavery where it is extremely difficult for us even to become aware of our slavery, our ignorance, let alone become capable of discovering the difference (assuming there is a difference) between truth and illusion.

Continuing his tale, Plato asks us to imagine what would happen if one of the prisoners, suddenly released from bondage, turned around and looked into the light of the fire. Would that person not be temporarily blinded by the light? It would be impossible to see either the shadows or the things that produced them. Even though reality was now closer in that the person was at least looking in the right direction, one would be frightened, disoriented, and in considerable discomfort. The world of comfortable illusions has been shattered: The fire has been seen. Yet our observer is in a state of confusion. Undoubtedly, one would prefer to retreat to the prior condition, having one's back securely pressed against the wall. The desire to return to bondage is so strong that Plato claims that the prisoner may have to be dragged, by physical force, out of the cave and into the sunlight—the entire journey producing considerable physical pain and mental anguish. Once out of the cave, our prisoner again is incapable of seeing or understanding the simplest things even though surrounded by the light of day. Slowly, the eyes adjust, the senses become aware of their new surroundings, and the prisoner begins to differentiate among things in this new world. In time, even the sun itself will become an object of attention and comprehension. Although this odyssey is no easy task, it too is part of becoming human. We all long for the comfort and security of a world filled with few questions, readily comprehensible answers, and universally accepted, seemingly correct values—the original paradise of the prisoners in the cave. Yet such a situation is both an illusion and, if paradise, the paradise of fools.

Originally, we said that Plato's allegory of the cave was a story of domination and oppression as well as education and liberation. It is appropriate to explain these terms and why they are important in Plato's tale. Domination is a peculiarly human condition of self-enslavement where individuals (mis)perceive their condition to be one of freedom. In Plato's story, the people in their original state think they are free; they think that they understand the nature of their world. As external observers of this situation, we, the readers, are aware of the more genuine reality. Nevertheless, the prisoners continue to hug their chains, believing that they are experiencing reality. Education is a slow, often painful process of exposing individuals to the truth, and the first step in that process is a recognition of the incomplete nature of the shadow world. In their original confines the prisoners had *a* way of looking at the world, and, at least for them, this manner of viewing reality made sense. However, it made more sense to view the situation from outside the confines of the cave. As the angle of vision was enlarged, so too was the freedom of our prisoner–cum–fully conscious human being. Liberation and education are thus intimately connected. In the experience of becoming educated, our prisoner is being liberated from a condition of ignorance.

Plato's ultimate goal in *The Republic*, as well as his purpose in using the allegory of the cave, is to describe the process whereby human beings come to know the objective Truth—to contemplate, to the extent they are capable, the sun. Our concern in what follows is not with Plato's search for the sun, but with the initial process of breaking the shadowlike chains of conventional wisdom, believing that such a questioning process is the beginning of education and liberation.

Finally, we stated that the allegory of the cave is also a story of oppression, that is, direct, obvious physical control of people over others. This aspect is not as readily apparent in Plato's allegory. It occurs when the prisoner, anxious to return to the comfort and security of the chains, is forcibly dragged out of the cave and into the sunlight.

Who might want to do this? Who is capable, either through force, persuasion, or influence, of leading others out of the cave? It is logical to assume that this person would have to possess knowledge of the way out of the cave if that person is to lead others to the sun. This person, then, would have to be a philosopher!

Since earliest times, political philosophers have often provided society with warnings of potentially disastrous courses of action. Like those of the mythical figure Cassandra, prophesies of doom, although true, are fated to fall on deaf ears. Plato's allegory, as we understand it, contains such a portent. It warns against the inevitable attempts of humans—*armed with their vision of the truth*—who feel compelled, for *our* own good, to drag by force their fellow humans out of the cave and into the "light." Each of the ideologies examined in this book contends that it understands reality and it knows what is best for humanity; each is militantly committed to help us see the light. Even though Plato believed that finding one's way out of the cave is an important part of being human and that other humans called philosophers will play a crucial role in this undertaking, he also knew that the process is extraordinarily difficult and exceedingly dangerous.

Still, like it or not, all of us either have been, or presently are, in a position similar to the prisoners in Plato's cave. From our first days, we have been taught by well-intentioned puppeteers—parents, teachers, religious leaders, politicians, authority figures—what is best for us. What we must attempt to accomplish is to be able to differentiate between shadows and puppets, truth and illusion, so that we will be in a better position to understand the differences among what various people believe to be true, just, beautiful, and good.

What Is Ideology?

Contemporary students of modern idea systems have been unable to agree on a common definition of the term *ideology*. Some see an ideology as a rather loosely organized folk philosophy encompassing the totality of ideals and aspirations of a people. Others describe it as a weapon to be used in a battle, a club designed to flatten opponents. There are perhaps as many definitions of ideology as there are definers. The following discussion is offered with little hope of clearing up the confusion surrounding this term (desirable as that clarification may be), but to indicate initially what seem to be some of the salient differences between ideologies and other types of idea systems. First, some distinctions between classical political philosophy, modern (scientific) political theory, and ideology are in order.

The classical tradition of political philosophy, beginning with Plato, and more recent efforts to develop meaningful political theory share the conviction that it is their task to make correct statements about the existing environment. Their initial endeavor is to use whatever means available (in contemporary times this is primarily the scientific method) to establish a body of statements that provide accurate descriptions and predictions of human behavior. These statements may then be tested by reference to the observed facts of human behavior and judged to be more or less accurate. The ideal of modern political theory and surely a major goal of classical political philosophy is the development of propositions that, taken together, would provide descriptions of politics and political activity. To use the traditional terminology, the propositions in such a system must correspond to the known facts of existence and the system as a whole must cohere, that is, one proposition must not contradict another.

Although both political philosophy and modern scientific theory seek accuracy, both the scope of their individual activities and their ultimate intentions are different. Traditional political philosophy attempts to construct philosophic systems that are all-inclusive, explaining every dimension—including explicitly moral judgments—of human behavior. Modern scientific approaches to political analysis, however, do not attempt to be as comprehensive as the grand theorists. Rather, they restrict their endeavors to more specific, empirically testable questions and they explicitly desire to avoid judgments of value.

Another important difference between the classical tradition and modern analysis is that the classical philosopher felt compelled to go beyond mere description, to propose remedies for perceived insufficiencies in the environment. Thus a Plato, while developing a theory of human nature and social interaction based upon his observation and insight, believed it necessary to set forth an ideal society wherein human beings would achieve their ultimate potential. As he saw it, his task was both descriptive (to explain how humans *do* live) and prescriptive (to explain how humans *ought* to live); he sought both to explain and to reform existing conditions.

Ideology's Distinguishing Features

In many respects an ideology has more in common with traditional political philosophy than it does with modern political theory. An ideology also attempts a meaningful analysis of the existing environment so as to discover real truths concerning humanity. Although its analysis is frequently far less rigorous and less systematic than modern political theory or political philosophy, this is not always true. Marxism, for example, is certainly systematic and attempts to be quite rigorous. Whatever the case, a major distinguishing feature of the type of ideology we will be discussing, as opposed to modern political theory, is its desire for massive changes in the existing environment. Based upon its picture of humanity as it *should* be, this brand of ideology usually finds fault with the existing conditions and demands change in the immediate future. These ideologies are, by definition, action oriented; they provide a picture of a better life for humans (a *goal culture*) that will develop once the existing structure is altered.

Ideologies share with much of political philosophy the desire to significantly alter the world to conform to their conception of a goal culture, whereas modern political theory does not concern itself with this prescriptive dimension, that is, what ought to be. Despite this common desire for change and a concern with the human situation as it ought to be, this kind of ideology is rather easily distinguished from traditional philosophy. Indeed, it can be argued that what is often called the Age of Ideology came about as a reaction to classical philosophic thought and its apparent lack of concern with the processes by which change could be effected. Karl Marx put it quite nicely: "The philosophers have only *interpreted* the world; the point is to *change* it." A focal point for our ideologue is the realm of action, as opposed to the classical political philosophers who tended to spell out utopian ideals and used rationalism to convince others of the truthfulness of their vision.

Our ideologue, furthermore, is more concerned with the issue of time: When will the change occur? Immediacy frequently is crucial. These ideologies demand not simply change, but change now! While humans are surely capable of working toward a better society for their sons and daughters, the revolutionary fervor found in many ideological movements is more easily sustained if adherents believe utopia is attainable within their own lifetime. It is possible, however, to have an ideology that advocates gradual change in pursuit of the goal culture—democratic socialism and much of the tradition of liberalism are examples. Lastly, it is also true that ideologies may be highly supportive of the existing state of affairs—the status quo. The term *ideology* can be used to describe individuals and movements that actively advocate keeping things as they are. Still, it is our belief that a fundamental trait shared in varying degrees, to be sure—by the ideologies discussed in this book is a desire for *change*, frequently massive change. Imagine Plato, determined to see his ideal republic become a reality, as the leader and organizer of a mass movement of Athenians bent on revolution. Platonism might then qualify for inclusion in our discussion. Of course, this was not the case.

Many reasons can be cited for the extreme *action orientation* that characterizes modern ideologies. Such ideological movements are similar to the religious crusades of the Middle Ages. Adherents believe their ideal state to be possible (indeed, sometimes inevitable) on earth rather than in some heavenly kingdom. Ideological movements can be seen as political outgrowths of the tremendous optimism generated by the Industrial Revolution, an optimism that believed humanity for the first time in history was capable of truly controlling its environment. Undoubtedly, such ideologies are part of the rise of masses of people to political consciousness and participation, making them essentially twentieth-century phenomena. Whatever the reasons behind the revolutionary orientation of these modern ideologies, there is little doubt that we are dealing with a phenomenon quite different from the political thinking of the classical philosophers. Some of the preconditions for an ideological movement will be discussed throughout this book, but first it is necessary to explore some other general characteristics of change-demanding ideologies.

As systems of ideas based on certain assumptions concerning humans and their relationship to the world, ideologies in general perform at least three functions: (1) They simplify the view of the world; (2) they demand action either for (when out of power) or against (when in power) change; and (3) they attempt to justify the course of action taken as well as the view of the world established. Each of these functions is dependent upon and gains support from the other two; therefore, it must be kept in mind that none of these can be understood, in the final analysis, in isolation from the other. Still, a discussion of each function will be helpful.

1. To simplify:

Ideologies attempt to make verifiable statements about reality by specifically focusing on human beings, and their relationship to other humans, as well as to the past and future world. Although ideologies are often backed by political philosophy, ideologies are usually (here Marxism may be the exception) neither as detailed nor as sophisticated as philosophic systems. Since their goal is to make an increasingly complex world more readily understandable, ideologies tend to suspend the intellectual intricacies of the grand philosophical systems of an Aristotle or a Hegel, and make simple—if not simplistic—observations about the world. Consequently, the ideological system need not be terribly concerned with logical coherence. Moreover, empirical verifiability based on rational thought processes is of secondary importance; what matters is not so much "what is," as what people *believe* to be the situation. So strong is this emphasis on belief, or faith, that one of the more common contemporary definitions of ideology is *belief system*.

Because of their desire to enlist mass support, ideologies in general are less concerned with logical niceties than are traditional political philosophy and modern political theory; earlier we listed logical coherence and a reliance on human rationality as two major characteristics of both. Relying greatly on faith and belief, ideology is much less bothered by logical inconsistencies within the system of ideas. Indeed, it can be argued that for purposes of attracting dedicated followers, inconsistency is desirable in that it requires total belief. If individuals cannot rationally understand a system of ideas but nevertheless choose to become members of the movement, they can accept additional, even contradictory, changes in the idea system. Total belief in the validity of an ideology, however contradictory it may seem to another person, can produce a creature who will carry out any action that seems necessary to ensure success. Political ideologies, then, should be evaluated more in terms of their success in persuading individuals to embrace them rather than in terms (important to both political philosophy and modern political theory) of either accuracy or logical coherence.

In their attempt to simplify reality, ideologies make statements about the political world that are often presented in critical black-and-white terms of what is "right" and what is "wrong" with humanity, the world, and the future. In addition, change-oriented ideologies usually locate some fatal flaw(s) in the world that their converts must struggle to overcome. For Karl Marx it was alienation and the oppression of the proletariat by a capitalist economic system. For Adolf Hitler it was modern materialism and the unnatural domination of the Aryan race by the "Jewish menace." For James Madison it was the rise of sociopolitical factions and the difficulty of governing masses of people without creating either tyranny or anarchy. And, tied to the fatal flaw is usually a body of "sacred literature" that followers are expected, more or less, to embrace: the *Communist Manifesto, Mein Kampf,* The Constitution of the United States.

2. To demand:

With their stress on action rather than mere comprehension, ideologies demand certain courses of behavior from their adherents. Toward this end, ideologies generate goal cultures, that is, ideal visions of conditions under which human beings can truly fulfill themselves. These goal cultures serve as guideposts toward which humanity must move. When the ideology is out of power, it demands active, continuous pressure—sometimes lawful, but not necessarily so—to bring about a change in the status quo. When the ideology is the status quo, it attempts to use its position to maintain its following and to help it move toward the appropriate goal, if that goal has not been as yet fulfilled.

3. To justify:

One of Plato's more brilliant, but often forgotten, observations concerning humanity is his comment that people can love the beautiful. In the present context, we understand Plato to mean that all humans want to think of themselves as good, or just, or beautiful beings. How they define the good, the just, or the beautiful is subject to heated debate and sometimes armed conflict. Indeed, in many ways this very conception is at the heart of every ideological system. In spite of this subjective aspect, Plato's insight is of paramount importance to under-standing ideologies: It shows, however defined, the motivating factor behind the clarion call for action.

To understand—or, more appropriately, to empathize with—each ideology, it is crucial to keep foremost in mind the fact that each of these ideologies believes that it alone knows the beautiful, it alone knows what is best for humanity. People do not want to believe themselves the creators of evil; rather, we all want to be thought of as agents of good. Difficult as it may appear at first, it is important to realize that Marx, Lenin, Madison, Jefferson, Mussolini, and Hitler all believed that their systems were best for those for whom they were addressing. Thus armed with their vision of the beautiful, each ideology uses its vision to justify and to support its own and its members' action.

In terms of this book, then, an ideology is any more or less systematic set of ideas about human nature, history, society, economics, government, and the relationships among these things. Each of these sets of ideas, moreover, explicitly or implicitly makes certain assumptions about reality, and on the basis of these assumptions demands action in support of its position. Once these assumptions are granted, or, as is more often the case, left unexamined, there is little left to debate: The conclusions drawn from the initial premises normally follow given the traditional rules of logic. It is important, then, both to expose and to examine the postulates upon which each of these ideological systems is constructed. To aid us in this endeavor certain crucial questions will be asked of each idea system, questions that relate to people, history, society, and political economy. Among these questions are the following:

1. What is the ideology's concept of humanity? Is the nature of the species fixed? Is it variable? Evolutionary? Are people emotional and passionate creatures who must be led to fulfill themselves? Or are they both reasonable and sensitive beings who could be free and human only if allowed self-government? Are people selfish? altruistic? self-interested? Are they a combination of each?
2. What is society? Is it an artificial creation inevitably in conflict with individual self-interest? Or is it a natural and beneficial by-product of human development?

3. What is government? Is it a necessary arbitrator of competing interests? Is it the very embodiment of God's rational presence on earth? Or is it the agent of oppression of the ruling class? And if government is either necessary or desirable (a proposition anarchists would challenge) who should rule? People of property because they are more rational and have a greater stake in society? Or an all-powerful, mystically selected leader whose presence guarantees the destiny of a race?

4. What is the relationship between politics and economics? Are these separate, independent arenas in which people can find a meaningful existence if the political can be kept out of the economic? Or do these two areas automatically intertwine to the point where it becomes utter nonsense to talk about the one without the other?

5. What is history? Does history proceed through recurring cycles? Or is it more of a linear progression? Are people the fated pawns of inevitable laws of history? Or does individual will and volition play a crucial part in human development?

Each of the idea systems examined will provide specific answers to these questions. Before discussing reasons for and approaches to studying these ideologies, we must briefly examine some of the factors that permit many people to call this the Age of Ideology.

MASS MOVEMENTS

If, as has been argued, the ideologies to be discussed are distinctive in their demand for and ability to bring about change in the existing state of affairs, they must develop a vehicle for effecting that change. While a discussion of the highly complex phenomena of revolutionary change is not possible within these brief confines, the enlisting of mass numbers of people in pursuit of a new society is such a central part of the Age of Ideology that it cannot be overlooked.

There have been numerous attempts to define the conditions that are conducive to the development of revolutionary movements. Classical Marxism contends that the major factor in revolutionary development is an ever-increasing discrepancy in the amount of wealth in modern society—the rich get richer and fewer, the poor poorer and more numerous, and the latter eventually revolt. Other theories contend that the inability of political leaders to respond to demands arising in the society results in a decline in support for the regime and provides the preconditions for revolution. Still others assert that the inability of a society to fulfill the ideals of its culture produces a tension between those ideals and actual practice, leading to growing dissatisfaction with the existing conditions. We know also that the revolution of rising expectations, whereby the lot of once poverty-stricken groups in society is significantly improved, does not automatically produce contentment but can lead to demands for greater improvement. Whatever theory or combination of theories is correct, most students of the phenomenon would agree that a vital element in producing revolutionary change is the development of an ideology that coordinates the various dissident elements in the unstable society, gives direction to their frustrations, and provides leadership for their cause.

Why do people become members of a revolutionary movement? Is there a particular type of individual who is attracted by a mass movement? Does the content of the ideology really matter or is the relief that a person apparently feels in joining a mass movement of prime importance? These are but some of the important questions that the student of mass movements must ask; the answers, unfortunately, do not come easily. There does seem to be agreement that converts to an ideology experience a tremendous feeling of exhilaration, a discovery of a new, more important identity when they enter the ranks. There is evidence that people who see their status in the present society declining are prime recruits. The petite bourgeoisie, the shopkeepers and small merchants in Nazi Germany whose status was severely shaken by the depression of the 1930s, provided one of the important groups for the Nazi movement. Others have theorized that people who are unable to succeed in the existing society are a major source of potential revolutionaries. Because of this inability to succeed, they experience overwhelming feelings of personal guilt, which can be relieved only by attacking the society; if it is the existing society and its values that are wrong, the unsuccessful person need feel no guilt. In joining a revolutionary movement the individual renounces the old self and all the failures attached to it to become a member of a group and attain a new identity. Most observers agree that this "giving up of self" is a prime characteristic of a revolutionary and that the selflessness often produced by membership is a truly remarkable phenomenon. Hannah Arendt in her classic study *The Origins of Totalitarianism* puts it this way:

> The disturbing factor in the success of totalitarianism is rather the true selflessness of its adherents: it may be understandable that a Nazi or a Bolshevik will not be shaken in his conviction by crimes against people who do not belong to the movement or are even hostile to it; but the amazing fact is that neither is he likely to waver when the monster begins to devour its own children and not even if he becomes a victim of persecution himself, if he is framed and condemned, if he is purged from the party and sent to a forced-labor or a concentration camp. On the contrary, to the wonder of the whole civilized world, he may be willing to help in his own prosecution and frame his own death sentence if only his status as a member of the movement is not touched.[1]

If this is the case—if it is the emotional catharsis that accompanies group membership that is most important—one must ask whether the

[1]Hannah Arendt, *The Origins of Totalitarianism* (New York: Meridian Books, 1958), p. 307.

content of the ideology really matters at all. Would, for example, our "true believer" be as eager to join a revolutionary communist group as he would a fascist movement? We know that some of the world's most committed anticommunists are former party members whose "god" failed. Further, Hitler at one time asserted that communists were the easiest people to win over to the doctrines of Nazism, implying that the capacity for belief was more important than the actual goals of the movement. While there may be some truth to these assertions, in all probability the content of the ideology establishes certain limits for the potential revolutionary. It is a bit difficult, for example, to conceive of a well-established capitalist joining a movement that vows to destroy capitalism or a Jew embracing the Nazi doctrine of anti-Semitism, although such situations have occurred. A person's culture and the values the person holds dear probably should not be antithetical to the goals of the revolutionary movement. Of course, it may be easier to convert a true believer to another ideology once that individual has developed the capacity for total belief in any set of ideas. Whatever the case, this discussion is not meant to support the notion that all people committed to ideological goals are somehow demented or emotionally sick—surely idealism is a prime motivating force in the development of a revolutionary movement.

Leadership Roles

Even if we can support the concept of a true believer who gives up everything in life to be a member of a revolutionary group, there are important figures active in ideologies who, while totally dedicated to the cause, are also quite aware of more pragmatic goals. As mentioned earlier, most ideologies seem to have a priesthood or a small circle of leaders who can manipulate the ideology to conform to environmental changes as well as formulate revolutionary strategy. While the truly modern element of contemporary ideological movements is their ability to enlist masses of people in the cause, the leadership role of a small cadre of adherents is nevertheless quite essential.

Lenin's concept of the role of the Communist party in fomenting and carrying out a revolution is probably the best example of the relationship between leaders and masses. Although Lenin did not believe it would be possible to have a coup d'état staged by a small group of dedicated Bolsheviks, and insisted that mass support was a prerequisite for successful revolution, his manipulation of Marxist ideology to give it immediate appeal to the Russian peasant clearly showed that the followers were being used by the leadership elite. Moreover, the tendency of revolutionary movements to develop one individual as the personification of the movement (Hitler, Mussolini, Lenin, Mao Zedong) generally gives that person great latitude in interpreting the ideology. Perhaps the safest summary of ideological movements is to say they are essentially modern phenomena, potentially involving masses of dedicated people, and they seem to be an essential element in producing revolutionary change. While the content of the ideology seems to be important in eliciting mass support, we are not, from the ideological perspective, quite sure just how much it matters.

Here, then, are some indications of the problems involved in the study of idea systems, as well as some reasons that show why such a study is worthwhile. The phenomena of the revolutionary personality and the general subject of the role of mass movements, while they are very important aspects of the investigation of idea systems, are subjects that are somewhat tangential to our main topic.

Why Study Ideologies?

Anyone who attempts to write a brief survey of the intellectual foundations of three major modern ideologies will probably be greeted by great cries of laughter from a whole host of sincere students and colleagues. The complexity of the subject matter is such that one is open to all sorts of possible criticism. The expert on the development of Marxian thought will immediately declare the task impossible, students of Nazi Germany will deem it superficial, committed liberals will assert that it is unneeded, and the pragmatist will scream that it is worthless, for ideas have little effect in the real world of action. While all of these criticisms may be in part correct, and some finally just, the fact remains that a general knowledge of a subject matter is better than no knowledge at all.

What follows is an attempt to provide that general knowledge of three major systems of political ideas of modern times: liberalism, communism, and fascism. What is desired is a presentation that is simple but not simplistic, and which makes no claims to be comprehensive, yet satisfactorily explains central themes. Such a purpose is easily stated, but even a superficial examination of the existing literature will indicate how difficult it is to achieve. There are, for example, almost as many ways of approaching the thought of Karl Marx as there are Marxian scholars. Many people believe that fascism is best seen as a phenomenon peculiar to the period between World Wars I and II and is hardly contemporary, or that it is impossible to speak, in general, of either liberal or democratic thought because both are diverse and changing traditions.

A further complication is the common identification of these systems of ideas with particular nation-states. When the average American speaks of communism, the referent normally is the Soviet Union or China, while fascism brings forth dark images of the Holocaust and Nazi Germany. Yet it is quite appropriate to see these nation-states as highly imperfect attempts to realize sets of ideals that transcend the political systems that invoke them. That is, these states attempt to apply the ideas advanced in the ideology, but the ideology itself exists independently of them. One of the underlying assumptions of this book is that the three idea systems are capable of being profitably studied as systems of ideas—regardless of their applications in the "real world." Obviously, when a major contributor to the development of an ideology is also the head of a political system, as in the case of a Lenin, a Mussolini, or, in a certain sense, a Madison, the ideological contributions may have a quite direct effect in political action. Even so, Lenin's contributions to Marxism may be studied as an effort to keep Marx's thought and vision relevant in a new historical context. In the same light, Madison the politician may be separated from Madison the theoretician and his contributions in each area judged separately, even while we realize that they were very much interrelated in his personal life.

Although the complex question of the relationship of ideas to action is beyond the scope of this book, a few tentative remarks on that subject are in order. It is extremely difficult if not impossible to prove a cause and effect relationship between ideas and action. When someone declares he or she acted in a particular way because the principles of Marxism-Leninism commanded it, how are we to respond? Obviously, the person could simply be lying, using the ideological argument as a rationalization to disguise the real reasons for action. Again, the person could be deluding himself or herself, being unaware of the actual motivation for action—a German SS officer exterminating Jews for the good of the Fatherland while actually giving vent to his own latent anti-Semitism. Most often, the real reasons for any action are so complex that it is impossible to single out any particular factor that triggered the action. Having said all this, it still seems obvious that idea systems do affect human behavior in some way, even if the exact relationship cannot be conclusively proven. The persistence of the Soviet Union in retaining for many years the obviously incorrect genetic theories of Lysenko because they supported the ideological goal of producing a new proletarian generation, the absurd tenacity of Hitler in following minute details written in *Mein Kampf,* the radical democrat's enduring belief in the essential goodness of the common person in spite of much evidence to the contrary are but some examples of the effects of ideology. When we recognize the tremendous impact particular cultures and values have upon individual development we cannot doubt the importance of ideas in influencing action. This, then, is an initial reason for studying ideologies—they seem to have a good deal to do with influencing human behavior, and perhaps a knowledge of the ideology will assist us in predicting and explaining that behavior. There are, however, other reasons for exploring idea systems, which can be mentioned briefly.

As already indicated, it is worthwhile to study systems of ideas irrespective of their effect in producing action in the real world. The three ideological systems under discussion are all attempts to say meaningful things about humans and their environment. Thus, we may judge the accuracy of their descriptions. Are humans, as Karl Marx believed, inevitably in a condition of alienation under a capitalist system? Does the fragmentation and depersonalization of a modern liberal democratic society produce human beings who are stunted in their growth, unable to be truly human, as Mussolini would have us believe? Are these accurate portrayals of reality? Does the democrat's belief in humanity's capacity for self-governance ring true in light of the discoveries of modern psychology and sociology? Whatever the ultimate answers to these questions may be, their descriptions of humans and the human condition may be subjected to tests of their validity and found either sufficient or wanting. Since each of the ideologies ultimately seeks converts, their ability to make correct statements about reality may be influential in their achieving the desired mass support.

The Competition for Hearts and Minds

The final reason that can be advanced for this type of study is that all three systems are in present-day competition for the "hearts and minds" of humanity. Whether stated in terms of the "free world" versus "atheistic communism" or "fraternal socialist states" against "imperialistic capitalism," the war for converts has waxed and waned ever since the turn of the century. This makes the task of the student of ideologies extremely difficult. While the ultimate objective must be the understanding of ideologies, the student is already either disposed toward or committed to one of them. The classical problem that social science faces in separating personal value judgments from impartial (or "value free") investigation is thus particularly difficult in the study of idea systems. Can a person who believes that one particular ideology is better than another temporarily free himself or herself of that bias to attempt to understand another? This book tries to do precisely that, and it supplies specific suggestions as to how this might be attempted.

Ultimately, of course, we will fail in this attempt, for impartial investigation is seldom achieved, and in this area it seems an impossible ideal. Yet the attempt must be made, for the reflexive anticommunist and the unthinking anticapitalist both do a disservice to human intelligence by not attempting to understand the phenomena they are trying to combat. Indeed, they weaken their own cause by knowing little of their enemy. Even the most committed liberal democrat must admit that some sort of vaguely defined communism has been attractive to many people during the past century, just as an avowed communist must realize that people continue to flock to and die under the banner of liberal democracy. The intelligent response to such facts is to ask why; to attempt to understand what it is in these idea systems that accounts for their continuing viability. The end product of such an attempt at understanding may well be a renewed dedication to fight the enemy, but the combat will be more effective with a knowledge of the opponent's strengths and weaknesses. It is for this reason that this book devotes a larger amount of space to the presentation of communist thought than to fascism or liberalism. It will be read primarily by those who believe that liberal democratic ideas are, if not absolutely correct, at least the best possible in an imperfect world. It is this person who must attempt to understand the appeal of communism, must evaluate its view of humanity and the world, and must decide whether its criticisms of democratic liberalism are just.

Why, one might ask, include liberal democracy, or for that matter fascism and Islamic fundamentalism at all? Primarily because it is only by comparing and contrasting these different portrayals of reality that one can come to an understanding of each. As the following discussion will show, they are related in many ways. Finally, we have a vague suspicion that our "committed democrat" is not as fully aware of the strengths and weaknesses of liberal democratic ideology as is possible, and knows little of the phenomena of either fascism or Islam and their relationship to liberalism.

Here, then, are some reasons for studying ideologies as well as an initial indication of some of the difficulties to be encountered. Additionally, by way of introduction, one must justify the discussion of only liberalism, communism, and fascism and the exclusion of numerous other systems of ideas. Moreover, we must point out some of the difficulties in identifying these three ideologies. One of the most widely used textbooks in this field treats four "isms" as relevant in today's world (communism, fascism, capitalism, and socialism). To these one might add conservatism, individualism, libertarianism, or even African socialism. Granted that these labels are somewhat vague and many of the ideas overlap, it should be possible to come up with some relatively concrete definitions of these phenomena. Surely they are relevant in today's world if only in the sense that people habitually describe themselves as being a conservative or an individualist. What distinguishes the three idea systems under consideration here from these numerous other isms? Initially our three isms seem more inclusive; one may be described as a conservative democrat or a conservative communist. More important, liberalism, communism, and fascism constitute relatively systematic attempts to describe humanity and human nature and to set forth goals for their achievement. Even in the case of liberal democratic thought—perhaps the most ill-defined of the three systems—there have been and presumably will be continued attempts to integrate core liberal democratic ideas into a coherent system of thought. Thus, they may be studied as comprehensive attempts to develop political philosophy and may be subjected to the traditional tests of that discipline. In the end, perhaps it is only a question of how one categorizes various idea systems. One can, for example, make a good case for setting forth a general category of socialist thought, then conceive of communism as the left wing or most radical brand of socialism. Similarly, fascism could be seen as a radical modern manifestation of traditional organic political philosophy and treated as merely a part, albeit an important part, of a long tradition. Disregarding limitations of space and time, perhaps the major justification for speaking only of liberalism, communism, and fascism is that they seem to the authors to be the most important political idea systems of the twentieth century, and they form a theoretical base for many other ideologies. We believe that they constitute a kind of theoretical matrix within which the more "contemporary" ideological debates take place. They provide, in other words, the basis for twentieth-century ideological warfare. Finally, if this is the Age of Ideology, surely these are the most important, if only by a count of worshipping adherents.

We have discussed some of the reasons why a study of ideologies is both important and difficult. Before moving to a presentation of the three idea systems, we want to reemphasize a few crucial points.

Why Tolerate Unpopular Ideas?

Earlier in our discussion, Plato, through the allegory of the cave, served as our guide in explaining why it was necessary for humans to break the chains of conventional wisdom and see the "shadows" on the wall of the cave for what they were—imperfect copies of a more fundamental reality. However, as we noted, in Plato's mind this was but the initial step in an arduous process of discovering objective truths (the puppets themselves, and ultimately the sun), which he believed were universally correct. Proper education, at least for some, would lead to the discovery of ultimate reality. Sure of his truth (or, at least, the appropriate process for discovering it), it became Plato's task to instruct others as to the true nature of reality. We make no such claim for what follows. Rather, it is our belief that the processes of education and liberation are most effectively accomplished—at least in the beginning—through an examination of alternative views of reality. In a sense, we will be examining differing perspectives of the shadows on the cave wall, always holding out the possibility that one perspective, or a combination of them, may provide at least a glimpse of the sun. This is, we understand, somewhat of a liberal bias in that it presupposes no "objective truth" to be communicated to the reader, no absolute knowledge to be conveyed. Plato, in that he presupposes the existence of such truth, is therefore an inadequate guide for the remainder of our journey. A far better one is the liberal British philosopher John Stuart Mill (1806–1873), who with extraordinary effectiveness describes the desirability of trying to understand ideas that may seem foreign or are unpopular.

Mill on Toleration

By the middle of the nineteenth century, England was well into the Industrial Revolution: Industry, business, and finance were developed; a working class was evolving; and a fear of what Mill and the French student of democracy Alexis de Tocqueville called the "tyranny of the majority" was commonplace. Beyond the reaches of the coercive power of government to control the opinions and beliefs of its citizens, Mill was alarmed by the potentially threatening power of public opinion to stifle, if not silence, the flowering of divergent viewpoints and lifestyles. Out of the social context of this modern, industrialized world, Mill, in the second chapter of his classic book *On Liberty*, stated what has become the cornerstone of the liberal-democrat's arguments for toleration and freedom of expression:

> If all of mankind minus one were of one opinion, mankind would be no more justified in silencing that one person, than he, if he had the power, would be justified in silencing mankind.[2]

Mill begins his defense of free thought and open discussion with these ringing words; he follows this with a fourfold argument for toleration of unpopular ideas: (1) The opinion that is being suppressed may possibly be true. Of course, those who are attempting to suppress the opinion deny its truth, but they themselves may be wrong. Hence, Mill concludes that any silencing of discussion is an assumption of infallibility. The history of the famous Italian astronomer Galileo Galilei is illustrative of Mill's point. In 1633, when papal authorities forced Galileo to recant his support of Copernicus's heliocentric theory of the universe, they simultaneously attempted to rob humankind of the opportunity to exchange falsity for truth.

Mill's first case, then, assumes the unorthodox opinion to be the correct view. But what if the new opinion is in error? On this point (2) Mill maintains that, although the opinion may for the most part be incorrect, it may nevertheless contain a portion of truth. It is rare, he

[2]John Stuart Mill, *On Liberty* (Baltimore, Md.: Penguin, 1974), p. 76.

argues, that an opinion is wholly true or wholly false. It is therefore important to allow the less correct opinion to see the light of day, to challenge and to refute the erroneous portion of that view, and thereby allow humankind the chance to accept and to embrace the grain of truth it may contain. Mill reasons that truth is often found in a delicate balance between two or more contrasting positions. Pushing his argument to its extreme, Mill claims that (3) even if the commonly held opinion is not only true, but the whole truth, unless it is continually and vigorously challenged and tested, it risks the danger of being held in the manner of prejudice, rather than the end result of a rigorous thinking process based on rational grounds. And, if this occurs, it is but a matter of time until (4) "the meaning of the doctrine itself will be in danger of being lost or enfeebled." In place of a vital truth, humanity will have unwittingly substituted a dead dogma. So grave are the consequences of losing the dynamic process of critical dialogue, Mill argues, that if none is present the society should appoint an advocate of the minority view.

> So essential is this discipline to a real understanding of moral and human subjects, that if opponents of all important truths do not exist, it is indispensable to imagine them, and supply them with the strongest arguments which the most skillful devil's advocate can conjure up.[3]

Mill argues that we, as individuals, should struggle to identify and to empathize with those opinions we initially find unacceptable so that we may test our own truths and determine if our rejection is based on reason or prejudice. Mill urges us to emulate Cicero—philosopher, politician, and the greatest of all Roman orators.

> What Cicero practiced as the means of forensic success, requires to be imitated by all who study any subject in order to arrive at the truth. He who knows only his own side of the case, knows little of that. His reasons may be good, and no one may have been able to refute them. But if he is equally unable to refute the reasons on the opposite side; if he does not so much as know what they are, he has no ground for preferring either opinion.[4]

Become a "True Believer"

In the wisdom of Plato and Mill (strange bedfellows, some would say), we find reasons for attempting to liberate ourselves from the ghosts of our past, warnings about the perils of the education/indoctrination

[3]Ibid., p. 99.
[4]Ibid., p. 98.

process, and guidelines on how to proceed in this Herculean journey to humanness.

Although it is no small task to attempt to walk the line between Plato's warning of indoctrination and Mill's guidelines for open inquiry, this is precisely the position taken by this book. Although our presentation of each ideological system is inevitably skewed by the authors' individual backgrounds and personal beliefs, we will strive to present in as persuasive and favorable a manner as possible each of the ideologies under discussion. It is the reader's task not only to attempt to understand the systems presented but also to empathize with and to become, at least a few hours a week, a "true believer." Specifically, this means you must try to be Karl Marx when communism is the focus of the discussion, James Madison when American liberalism is under examination, and Benito Mussolini when Italian fascism is being presented. To be sure, this is hard. And, yet, we too are persuaded by the powerful imagery of Plato's cave and the compelling logic of Mill's arguments for free discussion. Like Aristotle, we believe people are political, are uniquely human, when they use their capacity of *logos:* reasoned speech. Therefore, we will consciously attempt to provide an atmosphere where you will be able to carry on a rational dialogue about political ideology, where you will be able to present many of the arguments *for*, rather than against, each of the ideologies presented. If this position is openly embraced and practiced for each ideology, the critical perspective will take care of itself; for in the final analysis, each ideology is the refutation of its competing system. Once again, it may not be the case that any one of the systems contains the whole truth, for Mill may indeed be correct when he argues that the truth may be contained in a delicate balance of the cases presented.

SUGGESTED READINGS

ARENDT, HANNAH, *The Origins of Totalitarianism.* New York: Meridian Books, 1958.

BELL, DANIEL, *The End of Ideology: On the Exhaustion of Political Ideas in the Fifties.* New York: Collier Books, 1962.

FREIRE, PAULO, *Pedagogy of the Oppressed.* New York: Continuum Press, 1982.

FREIDRICH, CARL J., ed., *Totalitarianism.* New York: The Universal Library, 1964.

KONTOS, ALKIS, ed., *Domination.* Toronto: University of Toronto Press, 1975.

KRAMNICK, ISAAC, and FREDERICK M. WALKINS, *The Age of Ideology: Political Thought, 1750 to the Present.* Englewood Cliffs, N.J.: Prentice Hall, 1979.

LACLAU, ERNESTO, *Politics and Ideology in Marxist Theory.* London: New Left Books, 1977.

MACPHERSON, C.B., *Democratic Theory: Essays in Retrieval.* Oxford: Clarendon Press, 1973.

MANNHEIM, KARL, *Ideology and Utopia.* New York: Harcourt Brace and World, 1936.

MILL, J.S., *On Liberty.* Baltimore, Md.: Penguin, 1974.

2

Liberalism

And because the condition of Man . . . is a condition of Warre of every one against every one; in which case every one is governed by his own Reason; and there is nothing he can make use of, that may not be a help unto him, in preserving his life against his enemyes; It followeth, that in such a condition, every man has a Right to every thing; even to one anothers body.

Thomas Hobbes

Although *liberty* is obviously at the root of *liberalism*, it is not, nor has it ever been, precisely clear what is meant by liberty, for the word has had different meanings to different people. Liberalism is a rather diffuse system of ideas and values that has had associated with it such widely divergent thinkers as Thomas Hobbes, James Madison, and John Stuart Mill. Since there appears to be considerable liberty in the very use of the word liberalism, it is important to identify those common characteristics that are embraced by most of its proponents.

As American liberals we automatically tend to assume that everyone is in favor of liberty or freedom, and we are sometimes surprised to discover that such is not the case. When the Tory party in early nineteenth-century England first attached the Spanish label *liberales* to their opponents, they meant it in a bad sense: The Tories were directly linking the opposition with a foreign political movement, thereby suggesting that there was something un-English in their new ideas. This illustrates the historic fact that in its beginning liberalism played a revolutionary, sometimes destructive role in Europe by challenging, altering, and often smashing the values, customs, habits, and opinions of the traditional culture. In short, liberalism was received originally by some segments of European society with as much enthusiasm as the notion of communism in our age.

In this section we will take an extended look at liberalism. We hope to show the radical character of the doctrine as it first appeared in the realm of ideas by contrasting it to the ethos of preliberal society. A historical approach to liberalism will accomplish this and will help to clarify the distinction, too often overlooked, between liberalism and democracy. The simple truth of the matter is that mankind first devised a liberal society that, with the pressure of time, developed into a liberal-democratic society. We will then attempt to indicate the historical background and theoretical framework of what we believe to be a second, distinct brand of liberal thought—we shall call it *alternative liberalism*. This will set the stage for a more exhaustive treatment of these two traditions as they were imported into the American political environment. Before doing that, however, we must briefly look at the environment from which the modern age of liberalism emerged.

PRELIBERAL SOCIETY AND THE RISE
OF LIBERALISM IN RELIGION AND SCIENCE

During the greater part of the Middle Ages, Europe operated under a social system known as *feudalism*. The word itself developed from the Germanic *fehu-od*, referring to property in land. Founded upon an agriculturally based, locally oriented economic system, feudalism established pockets of interconnected communities where hierarchy, order, and harmony were the valued goals. The system itself involved a complex series of interrelationships, obligations, and bonds among individuals. This produced communities that were rigidly structured, hierarchically organized, and, for a very long period of time, quite stable. This land-dominated system had a profound organic and natural orientation pervading it. It valued the good of the ordered community, where individuals had neither independent rights nor independent meaning. Tied to these attributes was the omnipresent sense of tradition: People rarely conceived of questioning the feudal order because it appeared both to be ordained by God and to have been in existence from the beginning of time. Given the cohesiveness of this complex, hierarchical system where each person had a place and everything had its own unique function, to question any single part was to threaten the entire structure.

In spite of its incredible stability for centuries, feudalism eventually gave way to the onslaught of modernity, particularly liberalism. Over the course of decades the rise of a capitalist economic system coupled with the deliberate political action of an increasingly powerful, increasingly centralized state brought down the old tradition-bound, community-oriented society and established in its place the modern market society erected upon a radically individualistic concept of human nature.

The feudal tradition lacked any notion of the individual separated from special functions within the overall structure of society. Moreover, any particular person was such a small, insignificant part of this system that sacrifices at the altar of the common good were easily made. Nevertheless, in religion, science, and political theory the idea of *individualism* broke through these traditional norms of thought. A brief look at Martin Luther and René Descartes will help clarify the role of individualism in smashing the remnants of the feudal order in religious and scientific thinking. A fuller discussion of Thomas Hobbes will expose the modern epoch's interest in economic and political individualism.

Luther and Descartes

On October 31, 1517, the day Martin Luther nailed his 95 theses on the church door at Wittenberg, he simultaneously sounded the beginning of what was to become the death knell for the whole prior tradition. In spite of his reactionary political beliefs, Luther's actions called into question not only the position of the Church in the realm of religion but also the entire traditional society. Under the religious practices of the day, salvation could be attained only through the mediation of the Church's earthly representative. To Luther, authentic religious experiences could have no intermediary; the relationship between God and the individual was extremely personal, and no outside party could interfere. Luther also attacked the notion that the scriptures were under the total interpretive jurisdiction of the clergy. He reasoned that since the pope and his lieutenants were human, they could err in matters of theology. Each individual, therefore, had to be free to understand God's word in an individual manner. Similarly, Luther called the monopoly control of the sacraments by the Church "oppressive," in that it denied each believer's "right" to full participation in the exercise of religion. At the foundation of Luther's theology was the "priesthood of all believers," which held that grace was a gift from God given freely to each individual on the basis of faith alone. As individuals, each stood alone before God. In this regard, all people were equal.

Luther's egalitarianism, like his freedom, however, was solely an inner matter. The same individual still was subject to the system of wordly powers, was still a tiny fragment of a social hierarchy that Luther accepted as both natural and necessary, given the chaos of the fallen world of humanity. Nevertheless, Luther set into motion certain ideas that in time would ripen in the political realm. After all, if a person as an isolated individual must stand alone before God, why should that person kneel before an earthly lord?

The rise of individualism is also evident in the scientific philosophies prevalent at that time. Even though Galileo's verification of Copernicus's hypothesis dramatically altered human knowledge about the universe, it is in the ideas of Francis Bacon (1561–1626) that the scientific spirit found its modern beginnings. Bacon believed that science had given humanity the means to create, literally, a new world. The desire to control, command, subdue, and dominate nature through the use of science is at the heart of the Baconian dream. "For man by the fall fell at the same time from the state of innocency and from his dominion over creation. Both of these losses however can even in this life be in some part repaired; the former by religion and faith, the latter by arts and sciences," Bacon declared.[1] Through the abandonment of prejudice, the adaption of experimentation and cooperative investigation, humanity could turn away from superstitious cosmology and return to the idyllic state prior to humankind's Fall: The objective of human knowledge is "a restitution and reinvesting (in great part) of man to the sovereignty and power (for whensoever he shall be able to call the creatures by their true names he shall again command them) which he had in his first state of creation."[2]

In René Descartes (1596–1650), scientific knowledge as power is again a central theme as he too encouraged humanity to "make ourselves

[1]Francis Bacon, "The New Organon," in *The Works of Francis Bacon*, J. Speeding, R. L. Ellis, and D. D. Heath, eds. (New York: Hurd and Houghton, 1869), Vol. 4, pp. 247–48.
[2]Ibid., Vol. 3, p. 222.

the masters and possessors of nature."[3] However, in Descartes the emphasis on individualism is explicitly evident. Starting from the philosophic premise that everything must be questioned, he attempted to ground his theory on a more certain base than did past thinkers: *"Je pense, donc je suis"* ("I think, therefore I am").[4] With these famous words, Descartes plays the role of a god as he places himself (and all thinking individuals) at the center of a world in which he—as an isolated individual—is both discoverer and creator. No longer a mere fragment in a larger, more important whole that is governed by the mystical laws of an unknowable God, humans were now conceived of as creators of their own selves, their own world, and owing allegiance only to their individual selves.

Thus in religion and science, individualism combined with rationalism to confront traditional society with some very threatening ideas. As the economic arena began to witness the breakup of the traditional moral rules against profit, commercialization, and usury, the final vestiges of the feudal order toppled to earth. Secularization, individualism, rationalism, and power are all central themes in the political theory of the English philosopher Thomas Hobbes (1588–1679), who developed what can perhaps be called the first modern theory in political science. For our purposes, Hobbes's view of human beings in their most natural condition illustrates most graphically the individualistic liberal conception of the nature of humankind. Hobbes developed a theory of the role and function of politics that most would call distinctly illiberal—indeed, perhaps totalitarian. In spite of this, the boldness and clarity of his thought, along with the economic basis of his prescriptions, makes him particularly important in the history of individualistic liberalism. Quite simply, he laid the groundwork for those who were to follow.

Thomas Hobbes: Individualistic Roots of Liberalism

The Value, or Worth of man, is as of all other things, his Price; that is to say, so much as would be given for the use of his Power . . . . And as in other things, so in men, not the seller, but the buyer determines the Price. For let a man (as most men do,) rate themselves as the highest Value they can; yet their true Value is no more than it is esteemed by others.[5]

As in any philosophical endeavor, Hobbes attempted to take a fresh

---

[3]René Descartes, *Discourse on Method*, tr. Laurence J. Lafleur (Indianapolis: Bobbs-Merrill, 1950), p. 40.

[4]Ibid., p. 21.

[5]Thomas Hobbes, *Leviathan*, C. B. Macpherson, ed. (Baltimore, Md.: Penguin, 1968), p. 151–52.

look at humans and human nature. As we shall see in later chapters, Karl Marx described the evolution of humanity from a condition he called primitive communism, and Benito Mussolini asserted that people were by nature social animals. In a similar fashion Hobbes tried to envision what human relationships would be if no governmental power was present. He was the first in a series of political theorists who attempted this feat using an intellectual device called the *state of nature.* State of nature theories tried to use the human mind to imagine an environmental setting with people unencumbered by politics, acting in ways that were basic to their very nature. Although some thinkers who used this intellectual device to describe this natural condition had a tendency to write as though this state actually existed in human history— somewhere back before civilization—this was not an attempt at a theory of history but simply a method of discovering how people would act in their most basic condition.

What did Hobbes view as the qualities basic to human nature? In *Leviathan,* a book containing the most complete formulation of Hobbesian politics, Hobbes began his analysis on a sure-footed, Cartesian-like base. He advised his readers to follow his example and *"Nosce teipsum, Read thy self."*[6] Hobbes believed that this political theory was so reasonable that if people would but look inside themselves, they would agree with Hobbes's premises on human nature and would have to accept his conclusions on how to deal with this fact of life. From his individualistic starting point, Hobbes proceeded to deduce political rights and obligations. Explicitly rejecting all prior attempts to erect a political theory based upon an externally imposed sense of purpose, order, or harmony to the universe, Hobbes elected to construct his theory on a secure, scientific foundation of empirical observation. He closed the door on the feudal ethos by attacking the classical notions of justice. In response to the feudal norms of exchange based on equality of value and equality of benefit, Hobbes scoffingly responded: "As if it were Injustice to sell dearer than we buy; or to give more to a man than he merits."[7] Fully aware that the opposite situation is the reality to be shunned, Hobbes declared that, as in all matters, the market mechanism determined what is genuinely the just value of anything. Hobbes sharpened his assault on the tradition of an ordered and just universe by boldly declaring that "no law can be Unjust." In Hobbes's world, humanity is the creator of all things.

By observing the actions of both himself and others, Hobbes believed he had uncovered the basic traits of human nature. All humanity is moved by appetite and aversion. Some appetites and aversions are

[6]Ibid., p. 82.
[7]Ibid., p. 208.

innate, but most are acquired; they are subject to alteration, and are different in degree and character in different people. Moreover, our appetites are incessant, keeping people in constant motion: "Life itself is but Motion, and can never be without Desire, nor without Feare, no more than without Sense."[8] In order to stay in motion, everyone needs some amount of power, and Hobbes believed that this naturally resulted in a situation where the power of every individual—by definition— resisted and hindered the power of every other person. My power, then, is always relative to, and in conflict with, the power of others. Hobbes further believed that the desire for power, although necessary to the life of each individual, was limited in most humans, but limitless in some. From this he concluded:

> So that in the first place, I put for a generall inclination of all mankind, a perpetuall and restlesse desire of Power after power, that ceaseth onely in Death. And the cause of this, is not alwayes that a man hopes for a more intensive delight, than he has already attained to; or that he cannot be content with a moderate power: but because he cannot assure the power and means to live well, which he hath present, without the acquisition of more.[9]

Given this universal competition for power, which, as must be recalled, is power over others, Hobbes asked, somewhat rhetorically, what human interaction would be like if there were no governmental power to keep people in check. In one of the most famous passages ever written in the history of political theory, he described the natural condition of humanity in the prepolitical state of nature.

> In such condition, there is no place for Industry; because the fruit thereof is uncertain: and consequently no Culture of the Earth; no Navigation, nor use of the commodities that may be imported by Sea; no commodious Building; no Instruments of moving, and removing such things as require much force; no Knowledge of the face of the Earth; no account of Time; no Arts; no Letters; no Society; and which is worst of all, continuall feare, and danger of violent death; And the life of man, solitary, poore, nasty, brutish, and short.[10]

Two things are particularly worth noting in this quotation. First, Hobbes indicated that he assumes, above all else, that people do not want to die. Second, he has given an additional indication of the kind of society he implicitly holds in his mind as being the model of, and for, human interaction: a society pervaded by industry, agriculture, and commerce.

[8]Ibid., p. 130.
[9]Ibid., p. 161.
[10]Ibid., p. 186.

To this point, we have spelled out Hobbes's premises on human nature: (1) people are inevitably involved in a power struggle with others, and (2) they want to avoid death. Hobbes found these premises to be factually true and assumed his readers would be in agreement. Hobbes also introduced into his argument the idea of natural right: He claimed that all people have rights simply by virtue of their humanness; neither providence nor society grants them. These are rights that individuals have in the state of nature, where there is no political power to protect people from each other. To Hobbes, the most fundamental right of nature was "the Liberty each man hath, to use his own power, as he will himselfe, for the preservation of his own Nature; that is to say . . . of doing any thing, which in his own Judgement, and Reason, hee shall conceive to be the aptest means thereunto."[11]

Social Contract

In the state of nature, this right is fully operative; any individual can "do anything" to anybody: "It followeth, that in such a condition, every man has a Right to everything; even to one anothers body." Furthermore, Hobbes believed that all possessed this right and, in that sense, they were equal. Hobbes's postulate on human equality was similar to the rest of his theory, not based on an ethical principle but rather on empirical reality. Hobbes reasoned that all people are equal in that they are capable of killing each other. Even if one individual is particularly gifted with natural power, Hobbes assumed that others are capable of forming a temporary alliance to "do in" the strongest. So even though we are equal in terms of natural right, it is a useless situation since it results in a condition of war of all against all.

Hobbes paired his natural rights argument with a notion of natural law where humans, with the aid of reason, can discover certain general rules of conduct that will help them preserve themselves. Because all want to avoid death, it is natural that people are forbidden to do anything that is destructive of their own lives. In addition, they must look for a reasonable way out from under the condition of war in the state of nature, for that situation is intolerable. Through reasoning, Hobbes uncovered two fundamental laws of nature that all individuals should embrace: (1) "to seek Peace" and (2) "to lay down this right to all things; and be contented with so much liberty against other men, as he would allow other men against himselfe."[12] Briefly, Hobbes thought it reasonable that individuals would find it to their personal advantage to give up their right to everything provided others reciprocated. They

[11]Ibid., p. 189.
[12]Ibid., p. 190.

would, in effect, form a *social contract* with each other and relinquish their claim to everything. And yet, given what we know about human nature, only a fool would uphold the contract without some mechanism to enforce the agreement.

The Hobbesian solution came in the form of a self-perpetuating, authoritarian government that possessed virtually unlimited power over its subjects. It must be understood that the social contract was among individuals—not the individuals and the sovereign. It was the function of the government, the Leviathan (which means *monster*), to enforce—by whatever means it deemed necessary—the contract among these individual power competitors. Individuals give up and transfer all natural rights save one: the right to self-preservation. Because this was the factor that originally led them to create a contract, it would make no sense to give up this right. But even here there are qualifications concerning the right of rebellion. People were, for example, obligated to give up their lives in defense of the state as long as the sovereign remained in clear command.

It is through this mechanism of a social contract that humans learned to control some of the effects of their contentious nature. The desire to invade one another was still present, the war of all against all would continue to rage, but now the energy would be channelled into more socially constructive outlets: industry, commerce, agriculture—activities that produce what Hobbes called "commodious living." Government's function, then, is to establish rules of conduct that will allow people the liberty to pursue their own self-interest while prohibiting certain other types of behavior. This leads to another crucial aspect of Hobbesian politics. Hobbes, in spite of his intentions, seems not to be describing a universal human condition valid across time and place, but rather is analyzing a particular type of society with its particular mode of human interaction and its particular conception of man: bourgeois society with market relationships conducted by modern consumers. No wonder we find Hobbes so painfully convincing—he is describing us!

Possessive Market Society

Hobbes's political theory was constructed to confront the economic and social reality of seventeenth-century England. Given his depiction of "commodious living" and the human desire "to live well," it is obvious that he was analyzing an economically advanced civilization. However, through his description of power—and the relationships among people—it is also clear that he was describing a society where power was constantly and continuously being exchanged. People have always desired power over others, and since individuals have contracted not to kill one another, an individual may still gain power over others provided that person can get others to transfer—in exchange for something, for example, money—their power to that person. "The Value, or Worth of a man, is . . . his Price; that is to say, so much as would be given for the use of his Power . . .," Hobbes declared. In order to heighten the contrast between this particular type of society with other economically based societies, the political analyst C. B. Macpherson has called Hobbes's society a "possessive market society." It differs from those societies where social arrangements both for work and rewards for work were distributed by those in authority. It also differs from a society of independent producers where only goods are exchanged. In contrast with these societies, a possessive market society has a market in human power, that is, a market in labor. Macpherson describes the situation in this way:

> If a single criterion of the possessive market society is wanted it is that man's labour is a commodity, i.e., that a man's energy and skill are his own, yet are regarded not as integral parts of his personality, but as possessions, the use and disposal of which he is free to hand over to others for a price. It is to emphasize this characteristic of the fully market society that I have called it the *possessive* market society. Possessive market *society* also implies that where labour has become a market commodity, market relations so shape or permeate all social relations that it may properly be called a market society, not merely a market economy.[13]

Possessive market societies, of which capitalism is the most developed form, emphasize the degree of economic penetration into the very fiber of human relationships. Virtually every aspect of social interaction is conceived in market terms; the market is the measure of all things.

Many of the central concepts of what will become liberal thought are present in the Hobbesian view of human nature and the origin of the state even though, as we have noted, his "solution" to these problems of natural man can hardly be called liberal. The innate individualism, radical freedom, natural rights, relative equality, and emotion-based motivation are all part of the human condition. Furthermore, we see society and government formed as a creative act of human intelligence—institutions designed to serve the selfish interests of individuals, and both society and its institutions are conceived of as being *artificial*—human constructs. Only out of an urgent sense of necessity do people agree to live together, and only as long as the Leviathan is present is order maintained.

This is quite a different picture of human nature and society than that which will be presented by communism, and it differs greatly from fascism as well. Still, what is significant is that Hobbes has shown us a rather dark side of the liberal tradition. People, although naturally free,

[13]C. B. Macpherson, *The Political Theory of Possessive Individualism: Hobbes to Locke* (Oxford: Clarendon Press, 1962), p. 48.

independent, and equal, are forced to establish institutions that limit their behavior in the name of self-preservation. The prospect of a return to the state of nature is so menacing that all are willing to subject themselves to tremendous limitations in the name of order.

Finally, the Hobbesian view of people as dominated by passion, always attempting to maximize their own self-interest, even if it is at the expense of other's rights, is an early indication of one of the central themes and major problems in liberal democratic theory. We shall meet this problem later in the form of the conflict between majority rule and minority rights as well as in a discussion of democratic elitism. In Thomas Hobbes, then, we find perhaps the first, most certainly the boldest, expression of the modern, individualistic liberal concept of man. Given his concept of the natural human condition, his conclusion as to the necessity of a powerful sovereign seems to follow inexorably. If, however, Thomas Hobbes outlined the theoretical basis for the liberal conception of human nature, it received its most famous modern embodiment in the hands of John Locke.

John Locke

The Lockean view of the state of nature contains many of the same elements we observed in Hobbes, but there are also significant differences worthy of note. People are seen as distinctly individual, free, equal, and possessed of certain natural rights, by John Locke as well as Hobbes. In Hobbes's theory, all of these attributes were deduced from empirical observation in an effort to give his approach the weight of scientific rationality. However, in Locke, God is introduced as a central factor in politics, giving Locke's theory a far more palatable flavor than Hobbes's secularism. John Locke (1632–1704) was an English philosopher, physician, and student of politics who is widely regarded as the founder of liberal democratic thought. In Locke's thought, all people possess certain natural rights—which they hold prior to, and independent of, either government or society—by virtue of the fact that all people are created by God. This common, divine origin is also the reason why people are equal. It is not surprising, then, that seventeenth-century readers found Locke's political theory far more appealing than Hobbes's.

Following Hobbes's lead, Locke also used a state of nature argument to make his case. At times, his description of the state of nature sounds rather idyllic, even though he eventually comes around to a position reminiscent of Hobbes: "To avoid this State of War . . . is one great reason of Mens putting themselves into society, and quitting the State of Nature."[14] In this passage, Locke considered the state of nature to

---

[14]John Locke, *Two Treatises of Government*, Peter Laslet, ed. (New York: New American Library, 1960), p. 323.

be a state of war, and he assumed people would like to remove themselves from this condition. Even so, Locke argued that there were moral imperatives present in the state of nature that required humans, even without the presence of government, to respect the rights of others, including their mutual right to acquire property. In a sense, it seems appropriate to speak of a primitive, protocommunity in the state of nature with God acting as the creator and sovereign.

Locke found this theological connection helpful in the economic basis of his argument as well. He believed that God had "given the Earth to the Children of Men, given it to Mankind in common."[15] From the two additional assumptions that (1) every individual has "a right to . . . [self-]Preservation" and (2) "every Man has a Property in his own Person [which] . . . no Body has any Right to but himself," Locke deduced an individual's natural right to property.[16] By approaching this issue from a theological angle, Locke could not ignore the feudal restrictions on property accumulation. He specifically discussed two natural law restrictions on this individual property right: (1) an individual must leave enough property for others to use (after all, the earth was given, by God, to people in common), and (2) an individual must not allow anything to spoil (God's grant was to make use of the earth, not to allow it to "rot"). Having respected these prohibitions, an individual could claim *exclusive* property rights over anything with which he or she mixed their labor. Here, long before Karl Marx, we have presented one of the earliest arguments on behalf of the relationship between property and human personality. As a person invests labor in something, part of the self is placed in that object; this expenditure of personal energy gives the person rights of ownership that are independent of, and prior to, civil society. Indeed, individual property rights are part of providence's plan for humanity. In an ingenious manner Locke continues his argument on these rights, demonstrating how people not only have the right to individual accumulation of property but also how humanity has circumvented the natural law restrictions on property accumulation and substituted the right—and obligation—of *unlimited* property accumulation, all as part of divinity's design.

The Invention of Money

Locke's argument proceeds along two stages. Originally, a person could accumulate only as much property as could be used personally, without spoilage and with sufficient property remaining for others. However, with the invention of money, Locke argued that humanity

[15]Ibid., p. 327.
[16]Ibid., pp. 327–28.

unanimously agreed to alter the rules of the original situation. At this point Locke is introducing the notion of a *tacit agreement* among people in the state of nature. They agree to the usage of money as a medium of exchange. In addition to functioning as a medium, money serves an even more valuable purpose of allowing people a mechanism to avoid the natural law prohibition against spoilage: Gold and silver do not spoil. Of course, goods still could not be permitted to spoil, but with the invention of money this burden shifted from the producer to the consumer. As for the second limit of allowing sufficient property for others to use, Locke explicitly argued that when people agreed to use money they simultaneously and unanimously agreed to the right of "disproportionate and unequal Possession of the Earth."

> This I dare boldly affirm, That the same Rule of Propriety (*viz.*) that every Man should have as much as he could make use of, would hold still in the World, without straitning any body, since there is Land enough in the World to suffice double the Inhabitants had not the *Invention of Money*, and the tacit Agreement of Men to put a value on it, introduced (by Consent) larger Possessions, and a Right to them.[17]

Furthermore, as succeeding generations continue to use money to serve their needs, they reaffirm their commitment to the right of individual, unlimited accumulation.

Locke's Views of Property

Before examining Locke's argument for limited government, two final points concerning his view of property must be examined. First, throughout his analysis of humanity in the state of nature, Locke assumes that it is natural for them to sell their labor to others: One may sell to another "for a certain time, the Service he undertakes to do, in exchange for Wages he is to receive."[18] When this exchange takes place, the laborer also transfers any property claim over the goods produced to the buyer. Therefore, to Locke, property ownership can be established through both direct, personal labor, or through indirect, purchased labor.

> Thus the Grass my Horse has bit; the Turfs my Servant has cut; and the Ore I have digg'd in any place where I have a right to them in common with others, become my *Property*, without the assignation or consent of any body. The *labour* that was mine, removing them out of that common state they were in, hath *fixed* my *Property* in them.[19]

[17]Ibid., p. 335.
[18]Ibid., p. 365.
[19]Ibid., p. 330.

The second point concerning property is Locke's assumption of qualitatively different levels of rationality in people. Immediately after arguing that God gave the "World in common to all Mankind," he refines his position, asserting that given the "penury" of the human condition, God "commanded" people to labor on the earth. Labor then, is critical not only to human survival but also to the human soul. In the next paragraph of his famous *Second Treatise*, Locke further qualifies the commonality of this grant by stating: "He gave it to the use of the Industrious and Rational . . .; not to the Fancy or Covetousness of the Quarrelsom and Contentious."[20] Some people are industrious and rational; others are quarrelsome and contentious. The former act in accordance with natural law, the latter against it. Thus, it follows that the former should be rewarded for their good work, and money makes this possible. By permitting the industrious and rational to accumulate more property than they individually can use, Locke grants them not only material rewards but also the right to infinite accumulation. The virtue of this system of added material incentives for the industrious, Locke argues, is that all of humanity benefits from their efforts.

> There cannot be a clearer demonstration of any thing, than several Nations of the *Americans* are of this, who are rich in Land, and poor in all the Comforts of Life; whom Nature having furnished as liberally as any other people, with the materials of Plenty, i.e., a fruitful Soil, apt to produce in abundance, what might serve for food, rayment, and delight; yet for want of improving it by labour, have not one hundredth part of the Conveniences we enjoy: And a King of a large fruitful Territory there feeds, lodges, and is clad worse than a day Labourer in *England*.[21]

Here, Locke presents an early form of the "trickle-down theory." By rewarding those who are industrious, the whole society benefits as the fruits of the labor of those at the top make their way down to those at the bottom. The industrious and rational will employ the less industrious and less rational, so that the most efficient use of labor is achieved.

We have quoted Locke extensively because his arguments establish the basis for a capitalist market society against a society where there are no private property rights. A person at the top of the social stratum of a society where land is still held in common is—given Locke's materialistic criteria—worse off than a person at the lowest point in a market society.

Finally, Locke extends this bias in rationality among people into his arguments on governing society. Those who have demonstrated their rationality by owning property (and by virtue of their ownership also

[20]Ibid., p. 333.
[21]Ibid., pp. 338–39.

have a stake in the maintenance of social order) may also participate in the governing of society. Those who possess nothing but their labor may not participate in the governing of society. The former may vote; the latter may not. Because the laborers nevertheless are still subject to the laws of society, even though they cannot participate in the making of those laws, they are said to be *in*, but not *of*, civil society. If at some point the laborer is able to acquire property, that person also will be admitted into the ruling class.

Dramatically, Locke has turned the arguments of traditional society concerning unlimited property accumulation on their head. What in the feudal tradition was once considered morally reprehensible behavior is, in a market society, now virtuous. In like manner, the old arguments in favor of traditional government have been jettisoned, to be replaced by Lockean limited government.

By returning to Locke's state of nature and the transition from it into civil society, it becomes possible to recognize some of the differences between Locke and Hobbes that result in Locke's more benign conception of the role of government. Locke spoke not merely of one social contract in the tradition of Hobbes, but of two agreements, one appropriately called a *contract* and the other more of a *trustee relationship*. The initial contract was called the *contract of society*, whereby people agree to relinquish the total freedom of the state of nature and to establish a society. The society as an entity then proceeds to the establishment of a disinterested third party, absent from the state of nature. This action, resulting from the second agreement, is the origin of government. However, the type of agreement here is substantially different from the earlier contract of society. Initially, it is not properly called a contract, for the two parties to the agreement (society and government) are not equals, each possessing certain rights. Government possesses no rights whatsoever, thereby making the agreement process simply one of society's imposing obligations upon the government.

The designation of a *trustee relationship* is used by Locke to describe this situation since, in a trust arrangement, the manager of the trust operates solely in the interest of a client (in this case the society) and possesses no legal rights in the relationship. To speak of governmental rights in the Lockean political philosophy is simply incorrect. Government has no rights; it simply incurs obligations.

In addition to this, the agreement to constitute a government is not made by unanimous decision, but by a majority of the property owners who are, after all, the fully rational members of society. From civil society the government is given certain powers to perform limited duties, such as providing for defense of the community and contributing to the general welfare. The extent of the powers granted government is a subject of continuing controversy among students of Locke's philosophy, and it will become a major concern of our future discussion. For the moment, however, the important fact is that the society, which by *majority rule* establishes a government, may also remove it by a negative majority vote. Further, if a government is overthrown in this fashion there is no Hobbesian-like fear of a return to a chaotic state of nature, for the contract of society remains intact, and only the majority-initiated government is replaced.

The majority (of the men of property), not the individual, becomes then the central unit in Lockean politics. To be sure, Locke does grant the majority of civil society the power to *un*make government, and with this power they will be able to hold the government accountable to their wishes. In Hobbes there is no such grant: The Leviathan is checked by itself alone.

The Lockean notion of a dual agreement that occurs in the process of leaving the state of nature introduced an important element in the liberal tradition. In the Hobbesian state there was a one-to-one relationship between the political system (sovereign) and the individual member of the state. While for Hobbes, people did retain the right of self-preservation as individuals, there was no intermediary body to act as a mitigating force or as a check on state power. In the Lockean system there is a three-tiered relationship: The individual is at one and the same time a private person, a possible member of a societal majority, and the subject of a limited government. With such a scheme, Locke provides for a clear differentiation between the general and the particular, or, better, between the *public* life and *private* life. There is a sphere of human existence that is not subject to political action, namely, the area encompassed by Locke's notion of individual rights, that is, those areas that the majority decides are not appropriate subjects for governmental policymaking.

A Plea for Toleration

In *A Letter Concerning Toleration* (1689), Locke drew this crucial public versus private distinction in terms of provinces where governments may or may not intervene. In this letter Locke argues that in its very essence religion is a subject of belief rather than of science or reason; humanity, therefore, could never be absolutely certain of the truthfulness of any particular interpretation of Christianity. In light of this uncertainty, then, Locke argues that government may not interfere with any individual's religious beliefs. Furthermore, he calls for toleration not only by government but also by all people to respect other's beliefs. Here Locke establishes two essential liberal values: toleration and a separation of the public from the private. The public-private dichotomy eventually develops the groundwork for the creation of civil rights, that is, rights individuals have that neither the state nor society may interfere with. In the United States this idea of civil rights finds its clearest expression in the first ten amendments to the United States Constitution, usually called the Bill of Rights.

As we shall see in the subsequent discussion, the exact delineation of these areas of appropriate governmental and societal concern is one of the most crucial problems of the entire liberal democratic tradition. For present purposes, however, the Lockean distinction between public and private spheres provides another direct contrast with Marxism and fascism. As we shall see, in both of these ideologies all individual action is seen as the appropriate concern of the state or society.

Under fascism, the individual achieves fulfillment as a human being by contributing to national greatness, thus making all actions the direct concern of the state. Under the "transfer culture" of modern Marxism, the individual is viewed as a builder of socialism and all of that person's activities are public matters. And in pure communism any distinction between public and private or, for that matter, self and other ceases to exist.

HOBBES AND LOCKE RECONSIDERED

In both Hobbes and Locke the one feature of human existence that stands out most noticeably is individuality. People are viewed as atomic units, rather sufficient unto themselves and interacting with other individuals primarily in pursuit of their own selfish interests. True, there are differing degrees of this individualism expressed by the assorted members of the liberal school. Where Hobbes saw people as completely self-contained entities, contacting others only when they desired similar things, Locke saw at least a minimal connection between people because they are all subject to the constraints of the natural law of God. Despite these differences, the liberal tradition of Hobbes and Locke can only be characterized by its emphasis on radical individualism; people exist, prior to the establishment of society, as self-contained individuals.

We should immediately anticipate a great difference between British liberalism and the other two ideologies we will be discussing. To the fascist, for example, people are viewed as human in their natural condition insofar as they are members of the group or the race. Their interaction with that group defines in large part their very existence. To a Marxist, "natural" humans are gregarious, members of a community governed by shared values; humanity's major difficulties are economic. In British liberalism the individual is supreme. Further, people possess certain rights—natural rights—that are granted them by the very nature of their humanity. These rights are not dependent for their existence upon their recognition by a state, or by any other human institution, but are inherent in human nature itself. To some members of the liberal tradition, people possessed the right to acquire anything they wanted, even a right to another person's body. Such unlimited rights were, however, constrained by the fact that all other individuals possessed them. Despite differences in physical and mental ability all human beings were similarly endowed with these natural rights, leading to a position of relative *equality*. People were equal to the extent that they all possessed the right to a great many things. Granted, I have the right to attempt to take away property that you have acquired, but you have a corresponding right to defend that property from any attack. Thus, we may say that the British liberal tradition viewed people in the state of nature as relative equals, whether that equality derived from a common parenthood in God or from the ability of one individual to deprive others of their rights. Implicit in this notion of equality is the fact that all possess the *freedom* necessary to secure their natural rights. While at times that freedom may be constrained by the presence of other people or by certain natural laws of God, in general, humans are endowed with the freedom to secure the objects they desire.

Here then is a brief sketch of the attributes of humanity in its natural condition: free to pursue ends; relatively equal; possessed of rights that are not subject to the authority of any other human being; and, above all, dependent only upon themselves, or God, for their existence. Of particular note in the liberal concept of the natural human condition is what modern social theorists would call the lack of *shared values*. There is no natural human community which sets up standards of behavior for the individuals in it. Indeed, a community or society is conspicuous by its absence in early liberal thought. Even Locke, whose view of the natural state is somewhat less individualistic than other liberals, believed that people merely shared a common origin through their creator and were governed by natural laws that were difficult to apply to particular cases. This lack of shared values is underscored if we look more carefully at individuals in the state of nature and, in particular, at the forces motivating their behavior.

Self-interest Motivation

People are motivated largely by a selfish desire to acquire things. They are interested primarily in satisfying their desires, in fulfilling the needs that their emotions dictate. Throughout the liberal tradition there is an emphasis on the emotional basis of human motivation, and a consequent deprecation of human rationality as a major force in governing behavior. People are dominated by their own selfish interests, and reason serves the function of instructing them how to secure those desires most efficiently. This orientation is nicely summed up by the Scottish philosopher David Hume, whose view of reason was that of a "scout" for the more basic human passions. Obviously the most prevalent way these passions find their expression is through the acquisition of objects taken from the environment, and all of the individualistic liberals were most concerned with the notion of *private property*. Given what we know of the relative equality of people combined with the freedom they possess, it follows that the liberals thought that humans had a right to acquire property for their own selfish interests. Indeed, it is probably correct to assert that British liberalism as a whole was preoccupied with humans as economic beings. The mere mention of Adam Smith's name among their number indicates that. Inventing the labor theory of value, which we will encounter again in Marxian thought, the liberals argued that, when people mixed their labor with an object in the environment, the object became an extension of the person and therefore could be legitimately owned by that person. Indeed, there is much in liberalism that viewed property as the natural expression of human potential and an indication of personal creativity. Given all of this, it is appropriate to speak of a natural right to the unlimited acquisition of property in the state of nature. The state of nature, therefore, is hardly an idyllic setting, and instead is definable as a state of war.

Conflict arises because selfish interest leads people to desire the same objects, and there are simply no rules of the game to determine whose interest in a thing is more legitimate. Insofar as all people had a natural right to acquire anything, it was inevitable that their desires would lead them to concentrate on similar objects, producing disagreement as to legitimate ownership. As long as an unlimited right existed, people could not feel secure in their possessions or, for that matter, in their own continued existence. It is this conflict in the state of nature that leads people to use their reason to discover ways by which their selfish interests may be better served and which leads them out of the state of war and into society. Although Hobbes and Locke disagreed over the desirability of holding the government accountable for its actions, they did not disagree over the necessity for a strong, authoritarian sovereign who possessed virtually unlimited power—when so endowed by the people.

Locke's political theory contained within it a theological dimension that undoubtedly made it more appealing than Hobbes's more naked statement. But in the final analysis, it is the similarity of the two theories, rather than any minor differences, that is important. Both theorists, beginning from the assumption of a capitalist society with aquisitive humans as its component, erect political structures designed to fit the needs of this radically individualistic, highly competitive society. This again emphasizes the fact that in terms of its origin, there is not much democracy in liberalism. Indeed, it is only by looking to Jeremy Bentham and James Mill that we can see why, and how, liberalism decided to become democratic.

LIBERALISM BECOMES LIBERAL DEMOCRACY

Thus every part was full of vice, yet the whole mass a paradise.[22]

As we have seen in the discussion of Hobbes and Locke, liberalism arrived on the scene at the same time as did capitalism, providing an explanation of and a justification for this new economic system. By rewarding those individuals who use their reason and industry in pursuit of personal gain, everyone in the society benefits. As the noted satirist Mandeville put it, Private vice becomes a public virtue. Be that as it may, it was also clear that not all members of civil society had equal rights: Only the fully rational, those who owned property, were permitted to vote. As decades passed and class divisions began to harden in this economic universe, it seemed unlikely that those people who composed a clear majority of society were going to remain satisfied being ruled by the propertied class. Hence, out of a sense of practical power politics, liberal theorists began to make a case for extending the franchise to all males.

In 1818 Jeremy Bentham proposed that the franchise should be extended to all males of mature age, and of sound mind, who shall have been resident either as householders or inmates, within the district or place in which they are called upon to vote. Shortly thereafter, James Mill, John Stuart Mill's father, made a similar argument for universal male suffrage. Mill's position is straightforward: The vote gave political power; and, given human nature, every person needed the vote for self-protection. In his 1820 *An Essay on Government,* Mill describes the human condition in bold terms reminiscent of Hobbes.

> That one human being will desire to render the person and property of another subservient to his pleasures, notwithstanding the pain or loss of pleasure which it may occasion to that other individual, is the foundation of government. The desire of the object implies the desire of the power necessary to accomplish the object. The desire, therefore, of that power which is necessary to render the persons and properties of human beings subservient to our pleasures is a grand governing law of human nature. . . . The grand instrument for attaining what a man likes is the actions of other men. Power . . . therefore, means security for the conformity

[22]Bernard Mandeville, *The Fable of the Bees,* 2 vols. (Oxford: Clarendon Press, 1924).

between the will of one man and the acts of other men. This we presume, is not a proposition which will be disputed.[23]

Given this, "one person, one vote" was logically necessary in order to keep these invading individuals at bay. In spite of his own logic, Mill was willing to exclude many groups in society, for example, women, from voting. Nevertheless, Mill presents the case for democracy. Hence, it now becomes appropriate to speak of liberal democracy.

In concentrating on the thought of Thomas Hobbes and John Locke we have obviously ignored other important members of the British liberal tradition. John Stuart Mill, for example, is far more eloquent on the subjects of human nature and individual liberty than is Locke. Adam Smith provides a more incisive picture of humans as economic animals than does Hobbes, and David Hume has no peer in discussing the effect of human passions. Still, Locke and Hobbes provide us with most of the basic presuppositions of modern individualist liberal theory as well as pointing to a great many problems that troubled their successors. There is little doubt as to the effect of British liberalism on the development of an American democratic tradition, for the writings of its major representatives were read and digested by most of the Founding Fathers. We will attempt to describe that impact in the following chapter. Before doing that, however, we must point to the existence of another line of thinking that is appropriately called "liberal"—and which we chose to call *alternative liberalism*.

LIBERALISM: AN ALTERNATIVE VISION

It is in the open air, under the sky, that you ought to gather and give yourselves to the sweet sentiment of your happiness. Let your pleasures . . . be free and generous like you are. . . .

But what then will be the objects of these entertainments? What will be shown in them? Nothing, if you please. With liberty, wherever abundance reigns, well-being also reigns. Plant a stake crowned with flowers in the middle of a square; gather the people together there, and you will have a festival. Do better yet; let the spectators become an entertainment to themselves; make them actors themselves.[24]

Up to this point the discussion of liberalism has been restricted to that form of the phenomenon that is intimately connected with capitalism. There exists a second branch of liberalism which, realizing that

[23]James Mill, *An Essay on Government*, Currin V. Shields, ed. (Indianapolis: Bobbs-Merrill, 1955), p. 56.

[24]Jean Jacques Rousseau, *"Letter to d'Alembert,"* in *Politics and the Arts*, tr. Allan Bloom (Glencoe, Ill.: The Free Press, 1960), pp. 125–26.

there are large political and social costs of modern market societies, tries to construct a more egalitarian political community that is less subject to the never-ending competitiveness of the market. The political theorist who gave the clearest early expression to this alternative liberal ideology was the French philosopher Jean Jacques Rousseau (1712–1778). We will later explore the American manifestation of alternative liberalism in the thought of Thomas Jefferson. For the moment, however, let us examine in some detail Rousseau's effort to formulate a different vision of liberal society.

Rousseau's State of Nature

The third of the great political philosophers to employ a state of nature metaphor to help convince his audience of the validity of his position, Rousseau consciously constructed a portrait of humankind prior to government that strives to be both critical of, and superior to, the models of Hobbes and Locke. While the latter two theorists' views of the state of nature were imaginative constructions of what "civilization" would look like if the government were missing, Rousseau presented a historical, evolutionary description of humanity from prehistoric times to the relative present. In other words, Rousseau described how natural humans evolved into social beings, and then moved to civilization, while Hobbes and Locke restricted their discussion to people who were already civilized. By pushing back humanity's starting point thousands of years, Rousseau critically exposed many of the unexamined assumptions of the other two philosophers, questioned their conclusions, and presented an alternative political solution to the problems of his day.

Rousseau's chronicle of human evolution, titled *Discourse on the Origin of Inequality*, begins with a description of the life of our protohuman ancestors. Asocial, amoral creatures blessed with sufficient food and natural shelters, they lacked any reason for interaction among themselves. Having very simple needs which the natural environment easily met, these creatures were lazy, contented, and peaceful. Rousseau believed that they operated on two principles of motivation: self-preservation and compassion. Naturally, these primitives did everything necessary to survive. Given the low, animal level of wants and the relative bounty of nature, this did not require struggle for scarce resources. But in addition to self-preservation, these creatures displayed compassion because they did not like to witness the suffering of any of their number. Although the first principle—self-preservation—would always take precedence over the second, conflict between the two would rarely occur.

Over a period of years, these primitive needs began to change, and it became necessary for these creatures to expend additional energy to meet the new, superfluous wants. As Rousseau put it, "The first man who made himself clothing or a dwelling, in doing so gave himself things that were hardly necessary."[25] Taking on a force of its own, a dynamic situation developed between human *needs* and *wants.* As these creatures began to want new objects and to work to secure what they desired, they become incapable of being satisfied or fulfilled, always desiring additional, more sophisticated things. Out of this process developed the need for other people; thus, humans became social creatures. Originally *a*social, they evolved and needed other humans in order to survive. Rousseau, in contrast to Hobbes and Locke, believed humanity to be a developing species changing over time. More important, humans are the only species who had the potential to participate knowingly in their own evolution!

At first, temporary hunting and gathering associations were sufficient to meet the needs of humanity. Eventually, psychological needs developed, more permanent relationships were required, and families were formed. Believing this stage to be the happiest in history, Rousseau lamented its passing and noted the transition into civil society caused by the creation of protocapitalist property rights.

> The first person who, having fenced off a plot of ground, took it into his head to say *this is mine* and found people simple enough to believe this, was the true founder of civil society. What crimes, wars, murders, what miseries and horrors would the human race have been spared by someone who, uprooting the stakes or filling in the ditch, had shouted to his fellowmen: Beware of listening to this imposter; you are lost if you forget that the fruits belong to all and the earth to no one![26]

To be sure, prior to the invention of property rights that allowed individuals to exclude others, there occurred random, sporadic outbursts of violence, but this was the exception. With the creation of property, the generally peaceful existence of precivilized humanity came to a close and a constant, systematic, all-pervasive competition and exploitation of people by one another began.

> But from the moment one man needed the help of another, as soon as they observed that it was useful for a single person to have provisions for two, equality disappeared, property was introduced, labor became necessary; and vast forests were changed into smiling fields which had to be watered with the sweat of men, and in which slavery and misery were soon seen to germinate and grow with the crops.[27]

[25]Jean Jacques Rousseau, *The First and Second Discourses,* tr. R. D. Masters and J. R. Masters, R. D. Masters, ed. (New York: St. Martin's Press, 1964), p. 112.

[26]Ibid., pp. 141–42.

[27]Ibid., pp. 151–52.

Rousseau's account of human history reached the point where Hobbes and Locke began their arguments. As economic inequality and class divisions developed between those who own and those who do not own property, a general condition of war prevailed. Pressed by necessity, the rich devised a clever scheme to deceive the rest of the people into establishing a state to protect the property of the rich. In Rousseau's view, "Destitute of valid reasons to justify himself . . . the rich, pressed by necessity, finally conceived the most deliberate project that ever entered the human mind."[28] The project was the creation of a *social contract* designed to protect the rich from the poor in the name of justice for all. Presented with the contract creating government, Rousseau argued that, "All ran to meet their claims, thinking they secured their freedom."[29] The modern state, then, is the product of a fraudulent contract; and as such, it must be overthrown in order to establish a legitimate community.

The Social Contract

Rousseau begins his most famous work, *The Social Contract* (1762), by reminding us of both our past and the predicament of the present with this enigmatic observation: "Man is born free, and everywhere he is in chains. One believes himself the master of others, and yet he is a greater slave than they."[30] Here, Rousseau is exposing the self-deceptive nature of modern life. People think they are free, yet they are not. The modern person is a creature of alienation, an alienation that is self-inflicted and self-endured. Individuals agreed to establish a state believing it would bring them freedom; instead, they established class inequality and the rule of the rich for themselves, but with the appearance of rule of all by all. Among the first of all modern political theorists to understand alienation, Rousseau was aware of the awesome power of domination when individuals enslave themselves—all under the guise of autonomy or freedom. If the present situation was unacceptable, what prerequisites were necessary to create a legitimate community? Since neither fraud nor force can be resorted to, Rousseau had to create a condition in which all willingly and knowingly consent to live together. His prescription is threefold, involving property, factions, and individuals.

Recognizing the disruptive effect of class division among people, Rousseau argued that a moderate equality of property is necessary to a harmonious society. "It is therefore one of the most important functions

---

[28]Ibid., pp. 158–59.

[29]Ibid., p. 159.

[30]Jean Jacques Rousseau, *The Social Contract*, tr. and ed. Charles M. Sherover (New York: New American Library, 1974), p. 5.

of government to prevent extreme inequality of fortunes; not by taking away wealth from its possessor, but by depriving all men of the means to accumulate it; not by building hospitals for the poor, but by securing the citizens from becoming poor."[31] The role of government was to help combat the creation of antagonistic class relationships by passing legislation, for example, income and luxury taxes, property laws, designed to redistribute wealth. "No citizen shall ever be wealthy enough to buy another, and none poor enough to be forced to sell himself," Rousseau argued.[32] In this specific prescription involving "citizens" who either "buy" other citizens, or must "sell" themselves, Rousseau showed clearly that his concern was with the lack of freedom created by capitalist economic relations where one class of citizens bought the services and freedom of another class of citizens.

Anticipating Karl Marx, Rousseau was alarmed at the condition of wage-slavery by which modern citizens were oppressed. To guard further against class conflict, Rousseau argued that everyone in society needed to own a *limited* amount of property. Calling this right to property "the most sacred" of all rights, Rousseau's position was that small ownership gave every individual an alternative to working for someone else. Limited property was instrumental in securing freedom; freedom remained the ultimate goal, but without the economic security provided by property, freedom could not be achieved.

Having dealt with the economic impediments to the creation of a legitimate society, Rousseau next turned his attention to the divisive effects of factions. The equilibrium he desired can be achieved by one of two policies: (1) ban all factions, or (2) create so many factions that they check each other so that no one faction will become too powerful. In effect, Rousseau was arguing that the economic and social prerequisites to community were necessary, but insufficient by themselves. The most critical factor was the individual. While specific public policies could be invoked to handle the evil effects of property and factions, legislation could not bring about the type of change in individuals that Rousseau believed was essential to community.

In his *Social Contract* Rousseau introduces a figure called "the Legislator," even though he actually does not legislate. Without legislative power, it is not surprising that the Legislator was described by Rousseau as having "an authority that is mere nothing." And yet, the Legislator is to play the most important role in the development of community by helping individuals change their perceptions of themselves. The Legislator is to "transform," to "change human nature," to "alter man's constitution." Given this task of transforming humanity, it becomes

[31]Ibid., p. 271.
[32]Ibid., p. 85.

clearer why legislation itself will not help: What is needed is a change in the internalized forms of control. The Legislator's function, then, is to lead individuals to a stage of self-awareness where they come to understand both their individual selves and their common history. Rousseau's model of man is not static; humanity changes, and will continue to do so. Thus, the Legislator's task is to assist in this process of self-enlightenment.

> It is a grand and beautiful sight to see man emerge from obscurity somehow by his own efforts . . . rise above himself; soar intellectually into celestial regions; traverse with giant steps, like the sun, the vastness of the universe; and—what is even grander and more difficult—come back to himself to study man and know his nature, his duties, and his end.[33]

Exactly how Rousseau's charismatic leader will achieve this transformation need not detain us. Indeed, it remains the subject of much scholarly controversy. What is important is that for individuals to be free they must rule themselves. Obedience to a law one prescribes for one's self is Rousseau's definition of freedom. Under this standard of consciously self-imposed laws, Rousseau rejected the possibility of representative government. Indeed, representative forms of government are usually among the most corrupt forms because the citizenry believe that they are free. From Rousseau's perspective, the citizens of a representative government would be free only during the moment they voted for their representatives; as soon as that was accomplished, they would return to slavery because they allowed others to run their lives for them. For Rousseau, then, any form of government short of a direct, participatory democracy is an insult to and denial of humanity. Hence, by actively participating in the political life of society, by making the laws they themselves will obey, all individuals achieve freedom—after all, they are only obeying themselves.

Individual *participation* is crucial. Yet Rousseau's chronicle of human evolution must be kept in mind. As creatures, our development began as isolated, atomistic beings who owed no obligations to others even though there existed a natural repugnance to see others suffer. Eventually, we became social creatures whose need for others was more psychological than material. Rousseau's human, then, is a social-individual. Above all, the Legislator must enlighten individuals to both the social and individual components of human existence. Society is not an artificial creation of individuals as portrayed by Hobbes; it is material and necessary to human development. Once individuals come to view themselves as extensions of others, they will be able to participate actively in the creation of the general will. The *general will* is in the best interests

---

[33]Rousseau, *First and Second Discourses*, p. 35.

of society and *every* member of that society. Prior to transforming themselves from their bourgeois mentality, the citizens do not recognize this. However, after the transformation, individuals consciously construct public policies, recognizing both the individual and the social dimensions of their actions. Rousseau believed that a community of social-individuals will achieve such a level of coordination, that any individual from the community could be called upon to articulate the general will. As Rousseau put it, this individual will merely "give expression to what all have previously felt."

In Rousseau, then, we are presented with an alternative view of liberal democracy. It is liberal in that it begins with a view of people as radical individuals in the state of nature who have the liberty to pursue whatever their limited imaginations desire. As humanity develops, people become social beings who still need freedom in order to lead a fully human life. Rejecting capitalism as antithetical to equality, freedom, and community, Rousseau argued for a simple one-class society where the citizens would own sufficient property to sustain themselves and where it would not be possible for a capitalist system to develop. Rousseau, then, is a liberal democrat in a dual sense: He conceives of democracy as a kind of society where everyone must have an equal chance to develop; and democracy is an electoral mechanism whereby individuals—not their representatives—discuss and vote on public policy. Although Rousseau's theory was constructed to fit a small city or territory, Thomas Jefferson created his own alternative vision of liberal democracy, which in many ways was similar to that of Rousseau but designed to confront the needs of an entire continent.

Conservatism

In our examination of the historical roots of the liberal tradition we have devoted much of the discussion to a description of the individualistic liberalism of Hobbes and Locke rather than to the "alternative vision" presented by Jean Jacques Rousseau. This is, we think, appropriate for two reasons. The first is that Rousseau's vision of an alternative form of liberal democracy is just that—a vision. It lacks the clarity and detail of presentation that we found in the individualist tradition. Moreover, in the eyes of many commentators—some quite sympathetic—Rousseau's writings are filled with inconsistencies and ambiguities, being at one moment inspired by the possibility of a truly liberal democratic community and in the next rejecting it as an impossible utopian ideal.

The second reason is that the individualistic liberalism of Hobbes and Locke had a far greater impact on early modern thought, particularly in the United States. As we shall see, it is the individualistic liberal tradition that is to provide the philosophical framework for the conception of human nature and political institutions that were embodied in the American Constitution. And, undoubtedly because of that embodiment, it is that tradition which was to become the "mainstream" tradition in American political thought. Rousseau's alternative liberalism does not, however, cease to exist; it too had an advocate in early American thought in Thomas Jefferson. Having said all this, it will be appropriate in the following chapter to chronicle the future development of liberal democratic thought as it moves across the Atlantic to the United States.

Before doing that, however, we must briefly mention the existence of a political tradition generally called *conservatism*. As should be obvious from both the title of this book and the subject matter of the ensuing chapters, our primary concern is with the broadly defined tradition of liberalism. Nevertheless, a discussion of conservatism, however brief, seems necessary at this point if only to outline its central ideas and to show its development alongside of, and its compatibility with, liberalism.

Conservatism, in its specifically political context, is a relatively modern phenomenon, gaining its official usage in England in the 1830s. It developed into a political movement in reaction to progressive forces in Europe. The noted sociologist Karl Mannheim draws a useful distinction between two meanings to conservatism. The first he calls *traditionalism:* It reflects the almost universal tendency in humans to "cling to the old ways." Largely an unconscious character trait, traditionalism need not have a specific, political component. Indeed, since traditionalism is a rather subjective factor, it is possible to have a traditionalist who is also a political progressive; that is, a person who desires political innovation but prefers the status quo in his or her private life. Political conservatism, in contrast, is the conscious choice to stick to the status quo. In a sense, it is traditionalism become self-conscious of itself, and then specifically imposed on politics. Mannheim's point is twofold: first, to create terms that help to separate private inclinations or dispositions from political movements, and second, to demonstrate the ubiquity of humanity's resistance to change and the resultant widespread appeal of conservatism. It should be obvious, then, that in a very important sense conservatives are associated with every political ideology; it is appropriate to speak of conservative Marxists, like Leonid Brezhnev, as well as conservative liberals, like Milton Friedman. This being said, we will nevertheless turn to Edmund Burke as our principal spokesperson for this conservative movement inside the liberal democratic tradition.

Edmund Burke

Born in Dublin, Ireland, in 1729, Burke spent almost 30 years of his life as a member of Parliament in the British House of Commons. While contemporary conservatives still consider him to be a profound political thinker of a deservedly high reputation, Burke himself disdained abstract theorizing about politics. Instead, he preferred to deal with specific, concrete situations where it would be possible for him to bring tradition and history to bear on the issue. His most celebrated work, *Reflections on the Revolution in France and on the Proceedings in Certain Societies in London Relative to That Event* (1790), reflects this attitude, for the latter part of the title shows Burke's concern not with hypothetical speculations on revolution in a foreign country but rather the political impact of a foreign revolution on England.

Burke believed that humanity can realize itself only in history and only through conventional institutions, that is, institutions that have withstood the rigorous tests of time. "For man," he writes, "is a most unwise, and a most wise, being. The individual is foolish. The multitude, for the moment, is foolish, when they act without deliberation; but the species is wise, and when time is given to it, as a species it almost always acts right."[34] Tradition—the collected history of custom, opinions, prejudice, and wisdom—is the appropriate vehicle for achieving justice, even though it cannot be the ultimate standard of justice. Blind obedience to precedent would be as foolish a practice for humanity to follow as it would be for humanity to turn its back on the past; change, slow and gradual, is also a part of history and Burke advocates prudential development through social reform based on the lessons of history.

Society is an organism; it is both ordered and hierarchical in nature. The purpose of society is to help promote the good of the community and of every individual who comprises it. Burke understands the community to be larger than the sum of the individuals who live in it. It is much more than a loose collection of atomized units. "In a state of rude nature," he wrote, "there is no such thing as a people. A number of men in themselves have no collective capacity. The idea of a people is the idea of a corporation."[35] Men do not enter civil society in order to protect their natural rights. Like Thomas Hobbes, Burke argued that upon entering civil society individuals give up all such claims.

> Society requires not only that the passions of individuals should be subjected, but that even in the mass and body as well as in the individuals, the inclinations of men should frequently be thwarted, their will controlled, and their passions brought into subjection. This can only be done *by a power out of themselves;* and not, in the exercise of its function, subject to that will and to those passions which it is its office to bridle and subdue.[36]

Although Burke rejected *natural* rights, he nevertheless argued that

---

[34]Edmund Burke, *Works*, 16 vols., Rivington Edition (London: F. C. & J. Rivington, Publishers, 1803–27), Vol. 10, pp. 96–97.

[35]Ibid., Vol. 6, pp. 210–11.

[36]Burke, *Reflections on the Revolution in France*, Connor Cruise O'Brien, ed. (Baltimore, Md.: Penguin, 1969), p. 151.

contemporary humans, now that they are born into civil society, have certain *inherited* rights.

> Men have a right to live by that rule [of law]; they have a right to justice; . . . They have a right to the fruits of their industry; and to the means of making their industry fruitful. They have a right to the acquisitions of their parents; to the nourishment and improvement of their offspring . . . Whatever each man can separately do, without trespassing upon others, he has a right to do for himself; and he has a right to a fair portion of all which society, with all of its combinations of skill and force, can do in his favor. In this partnership all men have equal rights; but not to equal things. He that has but five shillings in the partnership, has as good a right to it, as he that has five hundred pounds has to his larger proportion. But he has not a right to an equal dividend in the product of the joint stock.[37]

Here it plainly can be seen how easily Burke employs economic terms to discuss political concepts. Burke the bourgeois theorist is fully compatible with Burke the conservative: While Burke was in favor of traditional English society, by the time he began his political career, England was already capitalist, and that Burke should see this as the natural, good, and traditional society is understandable. The example of Burke, moreover, helps to demonstrate how individualistic liberalism and conservatism easily blend together since conservatives accept as an unquestioned presumption the presence of a capitalist market as the base of the good society.

Burke, then, sees society as an organized, structured entity. All political power in society is, as in John Locke, a trust. As a trust, it is possible—though usually highly undesirable—for citizens to revolt against their government. "Governments must be abused and deranged," Burke wrote, "before [revolution] can be thought of; and the prospect of the future must be as bad as the experience of the past."[38]

An important aspect of the trust is Burke's idea of a mixed and balanced constitutional government. Burke conceived good government as being composed of three groups: the monarchy, the aristocracy, and "the people." Although "the people" play a central role in Burke's theory, the term should not be understood as applying to very many individuals. On one occasion Burke numbered them as roughly 400,000, comprising the upper property holders in Scotland and England: "the great peers, the leading landed gentlemen, the opulent merchants and manufacturers, the substantial yeomanry." Yet even the people are incapable of self-rule; they are to serve as a counterbalance to the court. The core of good government resides with the natural aristocracy who,

[37]Ibid., pp. 149–50.
[38]Burke, *Works*, Vol. 5, p. 73.

by birth, custom, and habit, know how to rule wisely on behalf of all. Given their economic status and social conditioning, the aristocracy serves as the bulwark of liberty between the pressures of monarchical despotism and of popular tyranny. In addition to the political functioning of these groups, Burke discusses the role of the British parliamentary system in terms of good government.

Burke's position on the role of parliamentary representation complements the above position. It is the duty of a member of parliament to watch out for the good of the society as a whole. Burke explained his model of representation thusly to his own constituents at Bristol:

> Your representatives owes you, not his industry only, but his judgement; and he betrays, instead of serving you, if he sacrifices it to your opinion.
> . . . If government were a matter of will upon any side, yours, without question, ought to be superior. But government and legislation are matters of reason and judgement, and not inclination. . . .
> . . . Parliament is not a *congress* of ambassadors from different and hostile interests; which interests each must maintain, as an agent and advocate, against other agents and advocates; but parliament is a *deliberative* assembly of *one* nation, with *one* interest, that of the whole; . . . You chuse a member indeed; but when you have chosen him, he is not a member of Bristol, but he is a member of *parliament.*[39]

Since representatives are not instructed delegates who represent specific interest groups, but are members of parliament who must reason for the whole, it is not essential that all individuals or groups have the vote. Burke called this idea "virtual representation." Although this form of representation is possible in a homogeneous society, Burke thought it had practical limitations. For example, he flatly rejected the claim that the Americans had virtual representation in parliament: they were too far removed from England and had fundamental interests at odds with it. Still, with the theory of virtual representation the issue of suffrage becomes one of minor import because, in theory, all groups—whether or not they have the vote—are represented by all members of parliament.

Like other political thinkers, Burke was willing to see society as a kind of contractual arrangement, and he discussed the relationship among three groups of people, two of which are not living. Here the notion of society as an organic, historic community is again evident.

> Society is indeed a contract. . . . It is to be looked on with other reverence; because it is not a partnership in things subservient only to the gross animal existence of a temporary and perishable nature. It is a partnership in all science; a partnership in all art; a partnership in every virtue, and in all perfection. As the ends of such a partnership cannot be obtained

[39]Ibid., Vol. 3, pp. 19–20.

in many generations, it becomes a partnership not only between those who are living, but between those who are living, those who are dead, and those who are to be born. Each contract of each particular state is but a clause in the great primaeval contract of eternal society, linking the lower with the higher natures, connecting the visible and invisible world, according to a fixed compact sanctioned by the inviolable oath which holds all physical and all moral natures, each in their appointed place.[40]

The role of the United States Constitution in the American political system is an excellent example of Burke's notions of good government and social obligation. Although many years have passed since the Constitution was ratified, it continues to be the fundamental law of the land. The American people can alter it, but it requires significantly more effort than majority rule. Moreover, as time passes, it rightly becomes increasingly difficult to alter the basic principles contained in it because of the *presumption* against tampering with an institution where the weight of time and experience continually reestablish the wisdom contained therein. In a 1782 speech on reform, Burke could almost have been speaking about the American Constitution today when he stated:

> . . . our constitution is a prescriptive Constitution; it is a Constitution, whose sole authority is, that it has existed time out of mind . . . It is accompanied with another ground of authority in the constitution of human mind, presumption. It is the presumption in favor of any scheme of government against any untried project, that a nation has long existed and flourished under it. . . . A nation is not an idea only of a local extent, and individual momentary aggression, but it is an idea of continuity, which extends in time as well as in numbers, and in space. And it is not the choice of one day, or one set of people, not a tumultuary or giddy choice; it is a deliberate election of ages and generation, it is a Constitution made by what is ten thousand times better than choice.[41]

Edmund Burke, then, not only demonstrates how conservatism and individualistic liberalism are compatible but he also presents us with the rudimentary outlines of conservatism: Society is an organism; good government is based on order, structure, and a natural aristocracy; the aristocracy, with *noblesse oblige*, rules on behalf of all; custom and tradition, not momentary insight, are to guide decision making; and humankind should *conserve* the best of the species by paying careful attention to the wisdom of the past.

Many of the tendencies associated with conservatism are evident in the American political tradition. Within the broadly defined tradition of liberalism there is a real concern with the value of stability. Further, as we shall see, James Madison's conception of the role and function of

---

[40]Burke, *Reflections*, pp. 194–95.
[41]Burke, *Works*, Vol. 10, pp. 96–97.

a representative is in many respects similar to that of Burke's, and Thomas Jefferson's preoccupation with a cohesive political community might be seen as an expression of a fundamental conservative value. To make sense of such observations, however, we must return to our primary concern—the liberal tradition, primarily as manifested in the United States.

SUGGESTED READINGS

BARKER, SIR ERNEST, ed., *Social Contract.* New York: Oxford University Press, 1960.

BERLIN, ISAIAH, *Four Essays on Liberty.* New York: Oxford University Press, 1969.

GOUGH, JOHN, *The Social Contract.* Oxford: Oxford University Press, 1936.

KRAMNICK, ISAAC, *The Rage of Edmund Burke: Portrait of an Ambivalent Conservative.* New York: Basic Books, 1977.

LASKI, HAROLD, *The Rise of European Liberalism.* London: George Allen and Unwin, 1936.

MACPHERSON, C. B., *The Political Theory of Possessive Individualism.* Oxford: Oxford University Press, 1962.

O'CONNOR, D. J., *John Locke.* Baltimore, Md.: Penguin Books, 1952.

PETERS, RICHARD, *Hobbes.* Baltimore, Md.: Penguin Books, 1956.

POLANYI, KARL, *The Great Transformation.* Boston: Beacon Press, 1957.

SARTORI, GIOVANNI, *Democratic Theory.* New York: Frederick A. Praeger, 1965.

TAWNEY, R. H., *Religion and the Rise of Capitalism.* New York: Mentor Books, 1947.

WOLIN, SHELDON, *Politics and Vision: Continuity and Innovation in Western Thought.* Boston: Little, Brown and Co., 1960.

3

Liberalism in America

Had every Athenian citizen been a Socrates; every Athenian assembly would still have been a mob.

James Madison

"In framing a government which is to be administered by men over men, the great difficulty lies in this: You must first enable the government to control the governed; and in the next place, oblige it to control itself."[1] These two quotations from James Madison sum up a central dilemma of the individualistic liberal democratic tradition. Once one accepts the notion that all people ought to have a voice in their governance, the task becomes one of devising a process of decision making that will translate the legitimate wishes of popular majorities into public policy. As we have seen in British liberalism, however, considerable difficulty lies in attempting to define the word *people*. Originally, the "people" was restricted, as in the writings of John Locke, to include men of property. It took considerable time, until around the middle of the nineteenth century, for liberal theorists to conceive of giving the vote to all white males; it required even more time for theorists to think of including blacks and women. If it is appropriate to view a society as being a legitimate liberal democracy only at the point where it moved from the idea of universal suffrage to the reality of universal suffrage by actually extending the franchise, then it becomes impossible to discuss liberalism becoming liberal democracy in America until well into the twentieth century.

In addition to that problem there is the historical fact that the preliberal government, like the Greek *polis*, seemed inherently unstable, quickly degenerating into either mob rule or dictatorship. The task then was one of developing a stable political system in which the inherent rights of individuals and minorities were protected and, at the same time, was capable of responding to the expressed wishes of majorities of its citizens. The examination of these questions as they were debated and resolved in their American context will occupy a large portion of this chapter. Following that discussion we will examine the thought of Thomas Jefferson as an American representative of the tradition of alternative liberalism initiated by Rousseau. Before addressing ourselves to these issues, however, we must briefly examine the political and social context of America in the late-1700s, largely as a means of discussing some of the presuppositions of a liberal democratic society.

THE AMERICAN CONTEXT: "BORN EQUAL"

The equalitarian premise of British liberalism was very much part of the intellectual tradition in the American colonies. The removal of overt distinctions between classes (titles and so forth) and the influence of

[1]James Madison, © 1961 by Wesleyan University. Jacob E. Cooke, ed., *The Federalist* (Middletown, Conn.: Wesleyan University Press, 1961), p. 349.

British libertarian rhetoric had produced a situation where political equality was taken to be the basic presupposition of all government. One need not delve too deeply into American history to recall that this notion of political equality was more often honored in rhetoric than in practice—all were created equal except black slaves, women, nonproperty holders, and so on. Nevertheless, the acceptance of the concept of political equality as an ideal, if nothing else, is an important presupposition for any regime that deems itself democratic.

America's egalitarian genesis has been an often-noted feature of its unique history. As long ago as the 1835 publication of the classic *Democracy in America,* Alexis de Tocqueville emphasized this point: "The great advantage of the Americans is that they have arrived at a state of democracy without having to endure a democratic revolution; and that they are born equal, instead of become so."[2] Indeed, de Tocqueville went so far as to maintain "that the equality of conditions is the fundamental fact from which all others seem to be derived, and the central point at which all my observations constantly terminated."[3] What de Tocqueville found significant was that America did not have to go through the kind of economic and cultural revolutionary ferment that had rocked European society. The American colonies fought a lengthy war against the British Empire over the right of self-determination, but they did not suffer the throes of a social revolution. In terms of our prior discussion of feudalism, this egalitarian origin means that the United States did not pass through the feudal stage of development; it did not have to spend decades battering down the legal and psychological barriers to egalitarian thought. Lacking a feudal experience, America also lacked the community or corporate memory of the feudal era. The American experience seemed to be, quite simply, the fulfillment of Lockean liberalism in an isolated political environment, isolated, that is, from the counter ideological pressure located in Europe.

Moreover, America was founded by men and women who fled from the feudal ethos of Europe, and they brought with them the liberal ideology of John Locke. Locke's thought, then, developed in both Europe and America. In Europe, however, liberalism had to contend with other world views: feudalism and socialism to name but two. And, if we can use England as an example, the early British liberals (Bentham, Mill, and others) had to battle constantly against a conservative monarchical establishment. Consequently, liberalism in Europe underwent important changes as it adjusted itself to the political environment there. The American situation was different. Here there was no need of compromise

---

[2]Alexis de Tocqueville, *Democracy in America,* 2 vols. (New York: Schocken Books, 1961), Vol. 2, p. 122.
[3]Ibid., Vol. 1, p. lxviii.

for there were, at that time, no major competing ideologies. As a result, any thought that did not fit into the broadly defined Lockean-liberal perspective was considered *un*-American. At least one additional factor helped produce the peculiar American experience with liberalism. America was blessed with vast expanses of "free" land. Given this economic base, an individual could become a property owner with relative ease. And, for a considerable period of time, no obvious class division developed in America as in Europe. Rather, the division existed between large property owners and small property owners, not between propertied and propertyless. All of these factors helped produce a cultural environment in which the individualism of Lockean-liberalism flourished to the point of myopia: The "American Way" is considered, by Americans, to be the *only* way.

Participation: A Basic Value

The liberal ideal of participation in government was also present in the American environment. Many citizens had indeed participated in government and, more importantly, felt they ought to participate in making decisions that affected their lives. Although many people viewed government with a good deal of suspicion, it was not thought of as the prerogative of some ruling class, elected or hereditary. Again, it is too easy to generalize from the active political participation that characterized the propertied classes in places like Virginia—we simply do not know the extent to which a common laborer, for example, participated in political decision making. However, in the minds of those who were to have the greatest influence on the making of the American political system, the concept of participation in public affairs was a basic value.

Similarly, the notion that the ideas of another person ought to be tolerated even though they were deemed wrong was a major value, at least in intellectual circles. Again, much of what was practiced in the colonies did not live up to this ideal, as evidenced in a good deal of religious persecution. Still, the principle existed and eventually was to become incorporated into the Constitution. One might go on to speak of other factors that made the climate conducive to some sort of liberal regime. A large land space, a relatively homogeneous English tradition, a country removed from the immediate presence of major military powers—all of these things contributed to produce an environment that made experimentation with liberal government possible.

One of the scholarly fads of recent years has been an attempt to draw up a list of preconditions necessary for the establishment of a stable democratic government. Thus we are told that there must be a rather well-developed industrial economy, widespread literacy, a homogeneous culture, toleration of political opposition, and so on. Whether the construction of such lists is helpful in predicting the possibility of a viable liberal democratic regime is a subject that need not concern us here. What is important from an ideological perspective is that the values held by the Founding Fathers of the American political system in general conformed to those of the liberal tradition. There is no doubt that the imperfect application of those values had important, even horrifying, consequences for individuals—if one, for example, happened to be either female or black. Perhaps it is better to look at the values embodied in the various American political documents as ideals to be achieved rather than statements of reality; as such, the entire American political tradition can be seen as an attempt to achieve these ideals.

JAMES MADISON AND THE CONSTITUTION OF 1787

The American Declaration of Independence of 1776 provided an eloquent statement of the ideals and aspirations of a democratic society. The now-familiar themes of equality, freedom, government by consent, and the right of resistance to arbitrary authority formed the ideological framework for the American revolution. But such a statement of ideals, however lofty, did not provide a solution to the type of problems in democratic theory of which we have been speaking, nor did it establish a workable framework of government. Having operated under the mainly ad hoc rules of the Articles of Confederation for almost a decade, the young nation had reached a point where few people were satisfied with the governance of the country, and committed liberals began to despair of the possibility of having an enduring liberal regime in America.

Thus, the Constitutional Convention of 1787 provided an opportunity to reconstruct the government along more viable lines, and a group of bold men made sure that that opportunity did not pass. The Convention has become many things to many people: To the patriot, it is the birthplace of the American form of liberal democracy; to the student of political coalitions, it is a fascinating study in political bargaining; to those interested in political ideas, it provides a forum for the discussion and resolution of enduring problems in democratic theory. We cannot delve into all of the personalities attending the Convention nor discuss the ideas they presented—one must tread lightly in the preserve of American historians. But if we are forced to find a figure who approximated an authoritative interpreter of the principles embodied in the Constitution there is little doubt that James Madison must be the choice. The Madisonian conception of the nature of the American system as articulated at the Constitutional Convention and later formalized in *The Federalist* papers provides the closest thing to an authoritative interpretation that we possess. Following numerous other writers on American political thought, our presentation will largely be confined to Madison's interpretation, particularly as it is developed in *Federalist No. 10*. Before moving to that detailed presentation, however, let us note some of the effects on popular thinking wrought by the Articles of Confederation.

The American revolution was fought in the name of resistance to arbitrary authority and in defense of the traditional rights of Englishmen. Naturally the symbol of that capricious authority became the English monarchy. Whether that was a correct assessment of the situation or not is unimportant in this context, but it did produce a widespread distrust of a powerful head of state. This fear of monarchy was, of course, reflected in the postwar Articles of Confederation, which provided for little effective national leadership, much less a powerful head of state. In the language of democratic theory, the prime fear was tyranny by one individual or by a minority, and the resulting political arrangements reflected that apprehension. Experience with the Articles of Confederation, however, convinced many of those who gathered at Philadelphia that the prime threat to the American experiment lay not in a tyrannical individual or minority but in the capricious moods of majorities. This distrust of uneducated, moblike majorities fit in nicely with the aristocratic attitudes of many of the Founding Fathers, and it provided some balance to the question of controlling unwarranted authority. The central problem of American liberalism then became, at least in Madison's eyes, the establishment of a popularly based government that would avoid the excess of tyranny whether imposed by a minority or a majority. It was this problem that Madison addressed in *Federalist No. 10*, justifiably the most famous analytical writing to emerge from the constitutional period.

The Federalist papers were written by John Jay, Alexander Hamilton, and James Madison as individual newspaper pieces designed to convince the people of the state of New York to support the recently completed Constitution. While their major purpose was persuasion, the papers also provided a defense of the philosophical presuppositions and institutional framework provided for in that document. In particular, Madison's tenth paper addressed itself directly to the classic political problem of tyranny, and it claimed to have found a "Republican remedy for the diseases most incident to Republican Government."

Madison's View of Humanity

Madison began his discussion by presupposing the desirability of some form of popular government. There is little in the way of systematic analysis of other possible governmental types. It is simply asserted that a government that denied a significant, albeit indirect, degree of popular sovereignty would be incompatible with the character of the American people. Indeed, there seemed to be almost universal agreement that some sort of popular government was what was needed, but the problem lay in devising one that would avoid the difficulties of past democratic regimes. Madison's analysis of all past experiments with democratic governments indicated that they were constantly subject to instability. The most common cause of this instability was a majority of the citizens who, for whatever reason, attempted to impose their will upon the rest of the society and in the process deprived them of their rights. Simply stated, prior democratic forms had a marked tendency to degenerate into mob rule. Sensing its inability to govern, the mob would then elevate a single person to assume dictatorial powers in the name of the people, and once that happened that particular democratic experiment was finished.

The cycle of tyranny of the majority leading to dictatorial rule and the consequent loss of freedom was all too familiar to students of the history of democracies. Some even contended that it was impossible to create a stable and enduring democratic government. This tendency of a group of citizens, whether a majority or a minority of the whole, to seize power and deprive other citizens of their rights was the cardinal difficulty with democracies; a solution to the problem would have to be found before the system could work. One must take note of a distinctly Hobbesian attitude in Madison's analysis of human nature. Human passions are such that, in the absence of constraints, people will naturally seek to dominate one another. As Madison boldly stated, "Ambition must be made to counteract ambition . . . But what is government itself but the greatest of all reflections on human nature? If men were angels, no government would be necessary."[4]

People are not angels. They must be held in check, or they will tyrannize each other. Here Madison notes an interesting characteristic of humanity. As an individual, isolated from other individuals, people are reasonable, timid, and cautious creatures. However, an individual inevitably comes into contact with other individuals, and behavior changes. "The reason of man, like man himself is timid and cautious, when left alone; and acquires firmness and confidence, in proportion to the number with which it is associated."[5] When this occurs, as it must, passion—not reason—rules. In one of the most uncharitable observations ever penned on human nature, Madison—in the quotation cited at the beginning of this chapter—eloquently captures the essence of the situation. It bears repeating: "Had every Athenian citizen been a Socrates; every Athenian assembly would still have been a mob." Even Socrates, historical

---

[4]Madison, *The Federalist*, p. 349.
[5]Ibid., p. 340.

symbol of the wisest and most just individual, will turn into a member of a tyrannical mob when he becomes associated with like-minded individuals.

The Problem of Factions

Political philosophers or constitution-makers must take this concept of humanity into account or their efforts will be for naught. This made the constitution-makers' task even more difficult in that popular governments were most susceptible to this disease that Madison called *faction*. Democracies, to a greater extent than any other governmental form, permitted the individual liberty that led to the development of factions. Liberty was the air that spread the fire of faction, but to remove that air would be to deny the basic premise of liberal government. Popular sovereignty would mean little if there were no liberty to form and articulate opinions. One cannot, then, solve the problem of factions by removing the liberty that permits them to exist, for, as Madison observed, the cure would be worse than the disease. Madison advanced and rejected one other possible cure for the causes of faction. Factions would not exist if it were not for the diversity of human interests, which forces people into competition for dominance. In theory, then, we could remove the cause of faction by insuring that all the citizens have similar opinions, passions, and interests. If everyone agreed on everything there would be no need for any group to attempt to dominate another. Madison dismissed this cure quickly by declaring that diverse interests are a necessary part of human nature and that it would be impossible to give everyone the same opinions. Again, we must stop and note that Madison raised a very important point, and, although his answer is consistent with his own philosophical premises, more modern democratic theorists pay a great deal of attention to the possibility of "giving everyone the same opinions." In an age where control of information and the use of propaganda are everyday realities, the possibility of controlling or heavily influencing the opinions of an entire society is not so easily dismissed. Indeed, we shall see that, at times, some ideologies attempt to do precisely that. Consistent with the premises of his individualistic liberal heritage, however, Madison rejected the possibility, and he despaired of finding a cure for the causes of faction.

Factions are ubiquitous and contentious. Madison found a correlation between factions and economic interests, as did Karl Marx less than a century later.

> From the protection of different and unequal faculties of acquiring property, the possession of different degrees and kinds of property immediately results: and from the influence of these on the sentiments and views of

the respective proprietors, ensues a division of society into different interests and parties.[6]

To Madison, then, the "most common and durable source of faction has been the various and unequal distributions of property." Unwilling to deal politically with the distribution of property, Madison accepted the inevitable socioeconomic consequences.

> Those who hold, and those who are without property, have ever formed distinct interests in society. Those who are creditors, and those who are debtors, fall under a like discrimination. A landed interest, a manufacturing interest, a mercantile interest, a monied interest, with many lesser interests, grow up of necessity in civilized nations, and divide them into different classes, actuated by different sentiments and views. The regulation of these various and interfering interests forms the principle task of modern legislation.[7]

At first glance, the antagonisms resulting from property differences seem to be the sole cause of domestic unrest. But on closer examination, it can be seen that to Madison the root of human antisocial behavior runs far deeper. Beyond property divisions are other causes of animosity. In one of his bolder statements on this point, Madison wrote:

> So strong is this propensity of mankind to fall into mutual animosities, that where no substantial occasion presents itself, the most frivolous and fanciful distinctions have been sufficient to kindle their unfriendly passions, and excite their most violent conflicts.[8]

MADISONIAN GOVERNMENT:
AMBITION COUNTERACTING AMBITION

Given that the causes of faction are latent in human nature, the only possible solution to the problems that factions generate is to attempt to control their evil effects. While human nature cannot be substantially changed, it might be possible to devise a set of institutions that would work to counter these tyrannical tendencies. It is in its proposed system of control of factions that the greatness of the Madisonian solution is to be found. Initially, Madison dismissed in a rather cavalier manner the dangers of minority factions. These present no difficulty because their evil designs can be controlled by the principle of majority rule. If a minority of citizens band together to seek to deprive others of their

[6]Ibid., p. 58.
[7]Ibid., p. 59.
[8]Ibid., p. 59.

natural rights, the vast majority of citizens will realize the threat and deny the minority access to power. One can call this a summary treatment of the problem, for it presupposes initially that the majority of citizens will recognize a threat when presented. It further assumes that access to political decision-making organs is the only means by which one group can oppress another.

In the discussion of theories of democratic elitism in the next chapter, we shall encounter the question of minority faction presented in a much more graphic manner. However, for Madison, the ability of the majority to control the minority through the ballot box was a sufficient control over a factional minority. Disposing of that, he then addressed himself to the classical problem of majority tyranny. It is obvious that the control of the vote that blocked minorities will have no effect here, for majorities can elect their leaders to positions of power. This being the case, Madison had to rely on other devices; his solutions fall into three general categories. First, there is a reliance on a particular type of political and economic environment; second, there is the introduction of a concept of representation; third, there is the development of a series of institutions that will make it difficult for a tyrannical majority to assume political power. Let us examine each of these aspects of the Madisonian solution.

Restraints on Majority Tyranny

It was a commonplace assumption in classical theory that the democratic form of government was best suited to small states. In that the translation of popular preferences into public policy was one of the major goals of that type of regime, it was understandably thought that the most accurate presentation of the people's views would occur if citizens gave voice to their own thoughts. This type of *direct democracy,* while guaranteeing that the people's views were accurately portrayed, necessarily limited the size of the state. While notions of including some scheme whereby certain people were elected to represent the views of other citizens had been advanced, the conventional wisdom held that democracies or republics should be small, the ideal being a modern variation of the Greek *polis.* As we shall discuss briefly, Madison's idea of a republic involved such a scheme of representation as one of its essential elements, but his real break with the tradition came with his advocacy of a very large territory and population.

Turning the classical position around, Madison argued that one of the major causes of instability in prior republics was that their small size made it easy for a tyrannical majority to form and gain control of the government. In the close quarters of a small state it was easy for human passions to become embroiled at a moment's notice and for the wrath of the majority to be unleashed upon innocent citizens. If the physical area of the state were much larger and its population more numerous, the formation of a majority faction would be a far more difficult enterprise. While the majority in one area of the state might be engulfed by a factional impulse, the spread of such views might well be contained by the sheer size of the country. Furthermore, given what he knew about the diversity of human passions, Madison argued that a large number of citizens would tend to produce a whole series of small interest groups, thereby making it very difficult to form a majority that was bent on depriving others of their rights. The diversity of human interests would at worst lead to the formation of numerous minority factions that could then be controlled through majority voting rules. In *Federalist No. 10* Madison wrote:

> Extend the sphere, and you take in a greater variety of parties and interests; you make it less probable that a majority of the whole will have a common motive to invade the rights of other citizens; or if such a common motive exists, it will be more difficult for all who feel it to discover their own strength, and to act in unison with each other.[9]

Rather than attempt to prevent the formation of these self-interested and potentially factional groups, governments ought to encourage them, for the effect of many interests was to ensure that no one group could gain sufficient power to be tyrannical: "Society itself will be broken into so many parts . . . that the rights of individuals . . . will be in little danger from interested combinations of the majority," Madison observed.[10] The existence of a multiplicity of factions would have the effect of achieving a balance or equilibrium, thereby mitigating against the possibility of a majority faction.

Here, then, is the Madisonian notion of an *extended republic*. We must stop and note both how well the argument flows from his premises and the ingenuity of the solution. People are selfish and power-seeking by nature, and those drives have historically led to the downfall of regimes based upon popular sovereignty. Instead of attempting to change people so that they behave in a more benign fashion (an improbable task at best), let us take these selfish motives and use them to produce a situation where they cancel each other; the private selfish vices will produce public selfless virtue. This is a clear statement of the idea that twentieth-century political theorists call *pluralism*. Because of the inability of any one group to dominate the other, there will be plural centers of power within the society and these will tend to balance each other to produce a society that is both stable and enduring.

[9]Ibid., p. 64.
[10]Ibid., p. 351.

Madison accomplished this feat without removing the freedom that permits factions to form, thus ensuring that individuals will at least have the opportunity to pursue their own selfish interests. Finally, with an eye toward future discussion, it should be remembered that Madison thought the major source of faction was the human desire for economic goods. It is well known that competition for scarce resources is a major cause of conflict in any state, and as Karl Marx observed, the state was designed primarily to protect economic privilege.

Recognizing the economic basis of most factions, Madison proposed to control their detrimental effects by encouraging the formation of a great number of factions and putting them in competition with one another. We have, then, in the political realm, the equivalent of some form of economic laissez faire, whereby Madison assumed that multiplicity and competition lead to equilibrium and ensure that no one group gains ascendancy. Indeed, the entire system is designed to avoid the political equivalent of monopoly in much the same way as classical economic theory sought to accomplish the same end in the economic arena. As a preliminary observation, then, we should note that the Madisonian political system—like both the Hobbesian and Lockean systems—seems to be most compatible with some form of laissez-faire capitalist economy where the state plays the role of umpire to competing factions. We shall explore the relationship between political systems and economic systems at a later point in the discussion; for the moment let us move on to the concept of representation, the second device that Madison proposed for controlling factions.

Control Through Representation

It should be noted that Madison carefully distinguished between the terms *democratic* and *republican,* specifically calling his proposed regime a *republic.* To his mind a republic differed from democratic forms in that it was larger both physically and numerically, and that it included a scheme of representation. This distinction has largely been lost in modern times, where we tend to think of all democracies as possessing some scheme of representation. The term *representative government* is very close to the Madisonian republic. Whether or not it is appropriate to call Madison's system democratic is an important question that we will confront shortly. For the present, let us examine further the Madisonian notion of republican government.

In *Federalist No. 39* Madison defines "a republic to be . . . a government which derives all of its powers directly or indirectly from the great body of the people."[11] A few things should be said about this

---

[11]Ibid., p. 251.

definition. Although power must ultimately come from "the people," it may be authorized by indirect methods. As will become clear, Madison tried to keep the relationship between the people and the government as indirect as possible. Second, just who comprises the category of "the people" is not readily apparent. What at first appears to be a rather open and popular basis of government eventually turns out to be rather restrictive. Perhaps more important, it is also evident that Madison tried to keep suffrage as limited as political reality would permit. In a similar manner, Madison's proposed system of representation was designed to serve functions other than mere reflection of popular opinion; he saw it as an additional curb on potentially tyrannical factions.

In many respects the term *representative* contains built-in ambiguity. Common language as well as philosophical tradition employs it with two rather different meanings. On the one hand, a representative can be viewed as a person whose task is to discover the preferences of those whom he or she represents on a particular matter and to cast votes in accordance with the wishes of a majority of those constituents. In this meaning the representative is seen as the accurate *reflector* of the constituency, simply a device to collect, synthesize, and report opinions. Modern technology might well be capable of replacing this type of representative with a computer programmed to record and transmit majority preferences.

The other meaning of the word has the representative standing, as it were, in the place of the constituents and making decisions deemed in the best interests of those represented, as well as the total community. Here the representative is seen as the *trustee* of the constituents, exercising judgment to the best of his or her ability, as each of them presumably would do in a situation of direct democracy. In this meaning of the word, it is quite possible that the representative will act contrary to the opinions of a majority of the constituents, feeling perhaps that he or she has more information, possesses a broader vantage point, or simply knows better.

These are two rather different notions of what it means to be a representative, and presumably any conception of representative democracy will vary depending on the meaning given to the initial term. The most common resolution of this difficulty is to use the word with both meanings; in effect, to assign two separate, and perhaps contradictory, roles to the legislator. Where the representative is normally the transmitter of majority opinion, at times we expect that person to assume the role of statesman and to ignore constituent wishes if they are believed to be wrong. It is in performance of this role that one can write about "profiles in courage," whereby a representative is politically defeated as the result of a principled stand. In the Madisonian scheme, the legislative role occasionally is seen in this dual fashion, but, most importantly, the representative in the statesman role is seen as providing a check against majority tyranny. Madison is rather explicit about the matter:

> The effect of the first difference [representation] is, on the one hand to refine and enlarge the public views, by passing them through the medium of a chosen body of citizens, whose wisdom may best discern the true interest of their country, and whose patriotism and love of justice, will be least likely to sacrifice it to temporary or partial considerations. Under such a regulation, it may well happen that the public voice pronounced by the representatives of the people, will be more consonant to the public good, than if pronounced by the people themselves.[12]

Clearly, there will be times, perhaps quite a few, when the Madisonian legislator will be expected to ignore the temporary or partial considerations of the people represented, thereby denying the supremacy of popular will. One of the reasons for the complexity of the process of elections described in the Constitution as well as the staggered terms of office and length of term is to provide for some distance between the representative and the constituency. Perhaps given sufficient time to think the matter over, the constituents will realize that an act in frustrating popular will was the best course of action after all. Still, representatives must eventually submit themselves for reelection and too many such acts of courage will surely lessen their chances of reelection.

Control Through Institutions

The Madisonian concept of representation is often called an antidemocratic device, and in a sense that is correct. If we use a more majoritarian definition of democracy there is little doubt that this legislative role is designed on occasion to frustrate majority will. Still, Madison could argue that it is but a temporary check on majorities and ultimately consistent with the principles of popular sovereignty, for the constituents have the last word at election time. It is rather difficult to speak of the Madisonian conception of the legislator *in vacuo* (in a vacuum) for it is part and parcel of the elaborate framework of institutions devised to provide additional safeguards against tyranny. Insofar as this third general category of mechanical or legal checks involves the entire structure of the United States Constitution, our discussion must, of necessity, be limited, but we can hardly ignore the political framework that was to make the whole system function correctly.

We have seen that the effect of Madison's first defense against tyranny (it is sometimes called the size principle) was to produce a society in which varied interest groups were free to pursue their designs while

---

[12]Ibid., p. 62.

ensuring that no one group could achieve sufficient dominance to become tyrannical. The framework of legal rules and governmental institutions advanced in the Constitution was designed to implement the size principle by providing access to major interests while assuring that there were appropriate checks on all the groups concerned. In a sense the entire Constitution, with its elaborate *federal* system, *separation of powers,* and *checks and balances,* is but a political reflection of the size principle discussed earlier. Presupposing a multiplicity of interests, we must now give these interests access to political power so that they may press their claims effectively and, correspondingly, have sufficient power so that they may block potentially tyrannical actions by other groups.

The initial device designed to accomplish this was the constitutional document itself. It granted to the government certain enumerated powers, restricting governmental involvement to only those activities explicitly or implicitly granted to it. Equally important, the Constitution expressly prohibited the government from taking certain action. As the supreme law of the land, the Constitution would prescribe the powers and limitations of the government. The Supreme Court was to become the ultimate arbiter of claims regarding the powers and limitations set forth in the document. This firmly established the principle of limited government and ensured a legalistic framework of operation. It has often been said that every matter in the United States eventually becomes a legal issue, and this may well have been intended—firmly established legal remedies for the resolution of conflicts. The other two major institutions of the federal government—the presidency and Congress— were specifically designed to give representation to large interest groups within the country. The president, although supposedly "above faction," was also viewed as particularly responsive to the propertied classes, and the power of veto provided a means to check the excesses of the legislative branch. This is readily apparent if we recall the method of election of a president as it was originally detailed in the Constitution, wherein that person was to be chosen by a group of electors who were acting as representatives of their respective states.

Given the close proximity of the legislative branch to the people and remembering Madison's concept of humanity, it is natural that Madison should fear this branch. In order to further control the most popular branch, he divided the legislature into two houses. Further, the division of the legislative branch into an upper and a lower chamber, each with similar but not identical powers, gave access to other interest groups. Representation in the Senate was by states, thereby ensuring that the interests of large populous states would not overshadow those of the smaller ones. Granted, the existence of relatively independent states would have dictated some sort of federal arrangement in any case, but if we assume with Madison that certain types of interests can be geographically defined, (that is, by state boundaries), the Senate affords them an important voice. The House of Representatives served as the voice of the people, and through the requirement of frequent elections it was presumably closest to the everyday wishes of the population. The House of Representatives was the only *directly elected* institution in the entire Madisonian scheme, and it was designed to provide representation for more populous urban areas.

Thus, these three major institutions—the executive, judicial, and legislative, the latter being further divided into two—are separate, each with unique powers, but they are also interconnected through the necessity of gaining the acquiescence of other branches before public policy can be formed. In certain instances, of course, it is possible for the will of one branch to dominate over another—as in the case of overriding a presidential veto—but the general principle is nicely summed up by the old phrase of "checks and balances." To add an additional impediment to the force of faction, Madison utilized a federal system of government. This meant that not one but 14 governmental systems—each with its own system of competing branches of power, checking and balancing each other—had to be gotten through if any fundamental issue was to become law.

Other Devices

In a similar fashion the practice of staggering elections and terms of office acted as another check against potentially factional majorities. While members of the House of Representatives are elected every two years and presumably reflect rapid changes in public opinion, control of the Senate and of the presidency requires a minimum of four years. It would take that long for a majority bent on tyranny to assume control of sufficient magnitude to put their design into effect. If we include the Supreme Court—whose members are to serve, with good behavior, for life—as a check on tyranny, presumably a majority could be frustrated for as long as it took a certain number of old justices to die or retire. It must be emphasized, however, that these are only structural limitations on majority power; in the real world a Supreme Court that did not somewhat follow the election returns would undoubtedly endanger the legitimacy of the institution.

Similarly, in a system that is to some extent based on the self-interest of representatives in being reelected, a senator would be foolish to ignore completely a powerful shift in popular will among constituents, even though that senator was not up for immediate reelection.

It is probably impossible to achieve an absolute veto over legislation strongly desired by a majority over a long period of time without sacrificing the idea of popular sovereignty. Minimally, what Madison was trying to achieve with both institutional checks and balances and other mechanical devices was *delay*—a period of time in which members of a majority faction might rethink their actions and change their behavior. In this context we should note the emergence of a slightly more optimistic side to the Madisonian view of human nature.

Earlier it was stated that Madison's assumptions concerning the essential selfishness of human beings were in line with Hobbes's view. Although this remains true, Madison was sophisticated enough to see that there were different types of selfish interests, some more disruptive for political systems than others. He was particularly impressed with how rapidly some popular passion could infect a majority and result in some precipitous action that upon further reflection would have led even selfish people to avoid. We know that Madison was influenced by the political writings of David Hume (much of *Federalist No. 10* is borrowed from Hume's work) and that a major focus of Hume's thought was a distinction between *calm* and *violent* passion. Although both types of passion were based upon individual self-interest, the latter was more volatile and temporary while the former looked to long-range selfish concerns. The violent passions of people might tell them to try to take away the natural rights of members of the community for some offense against popular opinion, but their calm passion would warn that on some future occasion they too might be subject to the wrath of some new irate majority. Note that both of these passions are based upon selfish interest, but they would lead to quite different kinds of behavior. If institutional checks and balances could produce a delay in which tempers were allowed to cool, long-range self-interest, or as Madison called it, "enlightened self-interest," might prevail.

One of the reasons why many of the Founding Fathers were preoccupied with processes of education was an attempt to ensure that citizens would adopt this long-range view of their interests. While Madison paid perhaps too little attention to such matters of habit and education in *The Federalist,* one of the later obsessions of the leadership of the country was the production of a well-educated citizenry. Some commentators argue that if Madison had been more concerned with developing democratic habits in the populace and with ensuring the existence of a liberal value structure, he need not have been so concerned with institutional checks on majority tyranny. Whatever the case, the institutional checks were at least intended in part to encourage the ascendancy of enlightened self-interest.

MADISON'S REMEDY: LIBERAL OR LIBERAL DEMOCRACY?

"In the extent and proper structure of the Union, therefore, we behold a Republican remedy for the diseases most incident to Republican Government."[13] These words, from the concluding paragraph of *Federalist No. 10* are Madisonian shorthand for summarizing the entire endeavor of the Founding Fathers as well as their claim to fame. We have attempted to describe the "extent and proper structure" remedies of the Madisonian republic using the threefold distinction of *size, representation,* and *mechanical checks.* Madison's system is brilliant. Through the structure or design of the system itself, all but the most intense factions will automatically be thwarted. A mechanical system of government, employing nonhuman factors wherever possible, was "the remedy" to factions. Hobbes's *Leviathan* relied too heavily on humans; less subject to human frailty, Madison's system attempted to employ nonhuman factors. Through an extended republic, itself divided into several states composed of numerous counties, each component with a degree of power, Madison hoped to create equilibrium. The division of the government into three branches, each one step further removed from the people, provided an additional safeguard. Limited suffrage and a trustee model of representation were additional checks. Thus, Madison strove to build a machine-like system, a structure of government that would automatically divert and diffuse factions. Furthermore, the system would check itself by not allowing its human operators to become too powerful. Madison created an ideal, self-perpetuating Leviathan that would provide the prerequisite social stability for the attainment of commodious living.

Two questions remain unanswered: (1) Does Madison meet his own standards of a "republican remedy"? (2) Can this system be considered democratic? To address the first query, the answer appears to be the affirmative. Madison desired a government based upon the principle of popular sovereignty, which avoided the tyrannical excesses of past forms of popular government. But it must be remembered that in Madison's conception of a republic, popular sovereignty could be exercised either "directly or indirectly" by the "great body of the people." Madison's reliance primarily on indirect controls, therefore, remains consistent with his definition of republican government. However, this facet to Madisonian government is more problematic when examining its claim to being democratic. Still, in permitting individuals the liberty to acquire property, form interest groups, and press demands on government, the system had to be capable of accommodating the constantly changing desires of people while avoiding the excesses of instability. To form a stable and enduring republic, Madison believed it would be necessary

[13]Ibid., p. 65.

to compromise the basic principle of popular sovereignty to the extent necessary to ensure that people did not abuse each other's rights. Yet the question remains whether the constraints he instituted were sufficient to prevent tyranny. Or did they so constrain majority will as to violate the basic principle of popular sovereignty?

Criticisms of Madison's System

Many individuals, particularly after the constitutional system had been in operation for a period of time, believed that Madison's efforts to check majority faction had not been successful. He had, it was argued, made no provision whatsoever for the development of the political party system that emerged early in the history of the republic. That being the case, even if one granted that his system controlled the development of *natural* majority factions, it did not stop the formation of the *artificial* majority factions produced by political parties. Indeed, Madison was one of the initial founders of the Republican (now Democratic) party. Parties were capable of forging temporary alliances among quite disparate minority factions for the purpose of securing control of the political structure, whereupon they went about achieving their minoritarian goals at the expense of the rights of others. Although this type of faction was not the natural majority type that Madison so feared, it was equally capable of tyrannical action.

This general position was most eloquently advanced by John C. Calhoun, the major spokesman for southern interests in pre–Civil War days. In the name of further defense of individual and state's rights, Calhoun argued for an extension of the control mechanisms on majorities, largely by giving any major interest group (states, sections) veto power over any legislation affected by it. Such a position would have further diminished the power of the national political system and greatly expanded the sphere of private action. Whatever the details of Calhoun's proposals, he is an excellent representative of those who believed that Madison correctly identified the major problem of majority faction but that his control devices were only partially effective and would have to be supplemented.

On the other side of the coin, many individuals, some of whom we shall meet in the next chapter, asserted that Madison had been so preoccupied with the potential of majority tyranny that he produced a system that so constrained majorities that it made a mockery of the principle of popular sovereignty. From this perspective, the sociological and political checks against majorities made it very easy for a small group of people to frustrate legitimate majority desires, thereby producing a government by minority. Minimally, the minority in control of the political system at any particular time could deny legitimate popular claims, but it also could produce the opposite of Madison's great fear—that is, tyranny by the minority.

Finally, in somewhat of an extension of the foregoing argument, there are those who contend that Madison achieved precisely what he intended. From this vantage point, Madison was a Virginia aristocrat, terrified of the possibility of majority power over the propertied interests of his class, yet sufficiently sophisticated to realize that some form of popular government was inevitable in America. As such, he devised an ingenious system that gave some power to popular majorities, sufficient to permit them to "blow off steam" and to believe they were actually governing, while making it virtually impossible for them to achieve enough control to initiate basic change in the capitalist economic system.

Controversy surrounds the Madisonian claim of having found a "republican remedy" to the unrest of factions. Needless to say, we are as yet in no position to evaluate these varying interpretations of the Madisonian enterprise. However, the types of questions raised here do comprise a loose conceptual framework for the debate concerning the nature and success of the American "democratic" experiment, a debate that continues to this day. Thus, the final question regarding Madison can at last be asked: Is he a democrat?

Madison's View of Suffrage

As we have already noted, Madison carefully separated himself from democratic movements of the past. He found them unstable and preferred his republican system, which required only "indirect" control from "the great body of the people." Just who, then, comprised "the great body of the people"? We can get some idea by examining Madison's view of suffrage.

Like many liberals of his day, Madison recognized the importance of the franchise question and was concerned with the impact nonproperty holders might have if given the vote. At the Constitutional Convention, Madison argued for a property qualification for electors to the House of Representatives: "the freeholders of the Country would be the safest depositories of Republican liberty." When the issue of voting for the Senate arose, he again advocated that "Landholders ought to have a share in the government, to support" their "invaluable interests." The voting pattern must be drawn up, he stated, "to protect the minority of the opulent against the majority."[14]

Although no property qualification for voters or officeholders appears in the body of the Constitution, a motion was carried at the

---

[14]*The Records of the Federal Convention of 1787*, 3 vols., Max Ferrand, ed. (New Haven, Conn.: Yale University Press, 1966), 2:203, 1:432, 143–44.

Convention instructing a committee to fix property qualifications for voting. Failing to agree upon the nature of the qualifications to be imposed, delegates to the Convention dropped the issue. The Convention established a few guidelines and returned the question to the individual states. Madison knew that by giving the states the power to establish voting standards the result would probably be that not even all white males would have suffrage since many states would impose property qualifications for voting. At the time of the Constitutional Convention, then, Madison was no democrat: He did not accept the equal right of every human to participate in the governing of society. Some years later, however, he had a change of heart.

While correcting and expanding his own Convention notes from other recently printed accounts of the Constitutional Convention, Madison in 1821 recorded a modest—but highly significant—change in his views on suffrage. Commenting on his Convention speech of August 7, 1787, he noted: "These observations (in the speech of J.M. See debates in the Convention of 1787 on the [7] day of [August]) do not convey the speaker's more full and matured view of the subject, which is subjoined. He felt too much at the time the example of Virginia."[15] Now more than three decades after arguing his freeholder's position, Madison explicitly rejected any voting conditions that would, either then or in the future, exclude the mass of society from political representation.

In this 1821 revision of his Convention position, Madison warned: "Allow the right [of suffrage] exclusively to property, and the rights of persons may be oppressed. . . . Extend it equally to all, and the rights of property or the claims of justice may be overruled by a majority without property, or interested in measures of injustice."[16] Madison reviewed several qualification schemes on which suffrage could be based, but he rejected property qualifications on the grounds that "It violates the vital principle of free Government that those who are to be bound by laws, ought to have a voice in making them. And the violation would be more strikingly unjust as the lawmakers become the minority."[17] Nevertheless, Madison ended up endorsing a system very similar to his original 1787 position: "Confining the right of electing one Branch of the Legislature to freeholders, and admitting all others to a common right with the holders of property, in electing the other Branch." This system will suffice, he argued, until "the non-freeholders should be the majority."[18] Recognizing the inevitability of the majority eventually

[15]Madison, quoted in *Mind of the Founder*, Marvin Meyers, ed. (Indianapolis: Bobbs-Merrill, 1973), p. 502.

[16]Ibid., p. 503.

[17]Ibid., p. 506.

[18]Ibid., p. 507.

becoming nonfreeholders, Madison was forced to accept the inevitable. In tones and logic similar to James Mill, Madison endorsed white male suffrage:

> Under every view of the subject, it seems indispensable that the Mass of Citizens should not be without a voice, in making the laws which they are to obey, & in chusing the Magistrates, who are to administer them, and if the only alternative be between an equal & universal right of suffrage for each branch of the Government and a confinement of the entire right to a part of the Citizens, it is better that those having the greater interest at stake namely that of property & persons both, should be deprived of half their share in the Government; than that those having the lesser interest, that of personal rights only, should be deprived of the whole.[19]

Hardly a ringing exultation in support of democratic principle, the above passage does, nevertheless, show that Madison recognized the necessity of individualist liberalism becoming liberal democracy. The answer to our question, then, is twofold. At the time of the Constitutional Convention, Madison cannot be considered a democrat: an individualist liberal to be sure, but not a democrat. Some time in the first quarter of the nineteenth century, however, Madison "backed into liberal democracy" as he recognized the impossibility of denying the vote to the ever-growing propertyless class.

We have attempted to present James Madison as the primary spokesman for the individualistic liberal tradition of Hobbes and Locke in the early years of the United States. It should now be clear that his enterprise involved much more than merely "fitting" that tradition to the unique conditions that prevailed in America. His "republican solutions to the evils inherent in republican government" constituted a real and lasting contribution to the ongoing dialogue concerning the appropriate nature of a liberal democratic society. Finally, Madison's scheme, because of its embodiment in the Constitution, in many ways set the context for the aforementioned dialogue, at least in its American context. In effect, Madisonian politics became, in the words of George Beam, "usual politics," and triumphs and failures, critiques and proposals for reform in the American system have been generally advanced within the intellectual context formulated by Madison.

We shall rejoin that dialogue in the following chapter where the American liberal democratic experiment is considered in a more modern context. Before doing that, however, we must examine the early American variant of the alternative liberal tradition discussed earlier—the alternative liberalism of Jean Jacques Rousseau. If Madison's system is properly seen as embodying the individualism of Hobbes and Locke, we

[19]Ibid., pp. 508–9.

believe it is in the thinking of Thomas Jefferson that the spirit of Rousseau finds its American home.

JEFFERSON'S SELF-EVIDENT TRUTHS

> We hold these truths to be self-evident: that all men are created equal; that they are endowed by their Creator with certain inalienable rights; that among these are life, liberty, and the pursuit of happiness; that to secure these rights, governments are instituted among men, deriving their just powers from the consent of the governed; that whenever any form of government becomes destructive of these ends, it is the right of the people to alter or to abolish it.[20]

Those heady, opening words of the *Declaration of Independence* contain both a brief summary of the evolution of liberalism and present a unique addition to liberal ideology. Concepts of equality and rights go back to the time of Thomas Hobbes, and the ideas of consent of the governed and the right to overthrow government can be traced to John Locke. What is new to more modern political thought is Thomas Jefferson's introduction of the concept of "happiness" as a standard by which to evaluate governments. In the preceding quotation Jefferson argued that if a government does not protect people's life and liberty, people have a right to overthrow it. More importantly, he argued that if government does not allow people to pursue happiness—an abstract and ethereal notion itself—people again have the right to revolution. With the introduction of happiness, then, Jefferson introduced a higher standard for government to strive for, and he began to describe a view of American liberalism that was not attached to private property.

In the *Second Treatise* on government, John Locke argued for rights to "life, liberty, and estate." But Jefferson demanded more. Although he too thought some amount of property was necessary to freedom and happiness, he did not think individuals had natural rights to property. Moreover, Jefferson did not believe that property acquisition was what individuals should pursue throughout their life. Instead, happiness is the end for which we were created. Jefferson's clear preference of happiness over property is evident on at least one other important occasion. While serving as the American Minister to France, Jefferson was asked to review an early draft of the *Declaration of the Rights of Man*. Jefferson bracketed the words "right to property" and substituted the phrase "search for happiness." Throughout Jefferson's life he argued that it was happiness—not property—to which individuals have an equal, natural right.

[20]Thomas Jefferson, "The Declaration of Independence," in *The Portable Thomas Jefferson*, Merrill D. Peterson, ed. (Baltimore, Md.: Penguin, 1975), p. 235.

Jeffersonian Government

Thomas Jefferson was never pleased with the United States Constitution of 1787. Although his reaction to it was usually cool, on a few occasions he voiced open hostility to it. Throughout his life Jefferson drafted several model constitutions that present a clearer view of his idea of what a democratic government would look like and how it would function.

Initially, Jefferson argued that suffrage was the most important single issue to democratic government. In an early draft of a model constitution for Virginia, Jefferson appeared to limit suffrage to males who owned one-fourth of an acre in town, or twenty-five acres of land in the country. However, at another point in the same constitution, Jefferson wrote that every person who never owned fifty acres of land, would be entitled to an appropriation of fifty acres. In effect, then, Jefferson thought of land as being instrumental in securing both economic and political freedom: political, in that it gave all white males the vote; economic, in that, like Rousseau, land gave individuals the freedom to reject wage-labor relationships if they chose to.

In addition to equal and universal white manhood suffrage, Jefferson—unlike the other Founding Fathers—wanted to create a public space where citizens could actively participate in politics. He believed politics was an activity that all should engage in as part of living a fully human life. Rather than an activity for a propertied few, Jefferson thought politics to be a noble activity in which all had a right and duty to participate. In hopes of creating an arena, a public space, for citizen participation, Jefferson argued the case for *ward-republics.*

"Divide the counties into wards of such size as that every citizen can attend . . . and act in person," suggested Jefferson. The local wards should have control of all local matters, for example, education, police, law. Jefferson called the ward-republic "the wisest invention ever devised by the wit of man for the perfect exercise of self-government" and constructed a scheme of government where these local units play a crucial role. The design is a four-tier, pyramid structure: The national government forms the peak and is "entrusted with the defense of the nation, and its foreign and federal relations"; the next level, the state governments, are concerned with "the civil rights, laws, police and administration of what concerns the state generally"; the lower quarter confronts "the local concerns of the counties"; and the base, composed of the ward-republics, "direct[s] the interests within itself."[21] At the base, every official position is an elective one. Each division of the pyramid functions as a republic; each is dependent on the next subordinate level for its authority and guidance.

[21]Ibid., pp. 556–57.

The elementary republics of the wards, the county republics, the state republics, and the republic of the Union, would form a graduation of authorities, standing each on the basis of law, holding everyone its delegated share of powers, and constituting truly a system of fundamental balances and checks for the government. Where every man is a sharer in the direction of his ward-republic, or of some of the higher ones, and feels that he is a participator in the government of affairs, not merely at an election one day in the year, but every day; when there shall not be a man in the state who will not be a member of some one of its councils, great or small, he will let the heart be torn out of his body sooner than his power be wrested from him by a Caesar or a Bonaparte.[22]

Division and subdivision "until it ends in the administration of everyman's farm by himself," then, is the mechanism by which political freedom is guaranteed. As in Rousseau, mere periodic elections are insufficient for a democratic society: "Every day" individuals must be a "participator in the government of affairs," Jefferson wrote. The ward-republics provided the proper mixture whereby "the whole is cemented by giving to every citizen, personally, a part in the administration of the public affairs." Certainly, with his advocacy of requiring each citizen to give his vote *viva voce*, and his insistence on dividing "the counties into wards of such size that every citizen can attend . . . and act in person," Jefferson's views are in harmony with the ancient Greek conception of politics and citizenship.[23]

Purpose of Ward-Republics

The ward-republics are to fulfill a fourfold function: (1) to check the petty tyrants at home, (2) to maintain the revolutionary spirit of 1776, (3) to provide a base for general education, and (4) to ensure a space where the citizens could become proficient in the art of politics. This last function, often overlooked in Jefferson, has two distinct, but complementary, parts. The first, already discussed, deals specifically with the creation of a public space for the daily activity of local politics. The second, elaborated next, concerns Jefferson's desire to provide for every generation the opportunity to create its own political community.

Hannah Arendt firmly grasped the importance of both aspects of the fourth function of the ward-republic in Jefferson's governmental system. She observed:

[Jefferson] knew, however dimly, that the Revolution, while it had given

---

[22]Thomas Jefferson, *Writings of Thomas Jefferson*, 20 vols., Albert E. Bergh, ed. (Washington, D.C.: The Thomas Jefferson Memorial Association, 1903–04), Vol. 6, pp. 543–44.

[23]Jefferson, *Portable Jefferson*, pp. 556–57.

freedom to the people, had failed to provide a space where this freedom could be exercised. Only the representatives of the people, not the people themselves, had an opportunity to engage in those activities of "expressing, discussing and deciding" which in a positive sense are the activities of freedom.[24]

The "fresh start" Jefferson and his contemporaries had been given in the American experience must somehow be passed on to each succeeding generation. Each generation must be allowed to begin anew. Each generation must redefine its goals and ideals; each must recommit itself to one another. Jefferson believed it essential to a democratic community that each generation can "depute representatives to a convention, and to make the Constitution what they think will be the best for themselves."[25] Jefferson recognized the necessity of recreating the constitutional congresses and conventions of the 1770s and 1780s: A mere reshuffling of the government would not do. Using the mechanism of the small ward-republics, Jefferson argued that all citizens could thereby be incorporated into the political processes of legislation and governance.

Through ward-republics, "the voice of the whole people would be thus fairly, fully, and peacefully expressed, discussed, and decided by the common reason of the society."[26] This participation alone, argued Jefferson, would make a "true democracy." Anything short of this process allows for the rule of the dead from beyond the grave.

The creation of a public place is intimately linked with the maintenance of a spirit of revolution in the society at large. In the foreground of several revolutions, Jefferson appeared to have found the experiences refreshing. His letters on revolution conveyed a sense of catharsis, of cleansing, of providing an opportunity to begin again. The year 1787 produced two of Jefferson's more famous observations on this topic. Eager to calm James Madison over the recent rebellion in Massachusetts, he wrote,

I hold it that a little rebellion now and then is a good thing, and as necessary in the political world as storms in the physical.[27]

And to William Smith, once more on Shays' Rebellion, he explained,

God forbid we should ever be 20 years without such a rebellion . . . We have had 13 states independent 11 years. There has been one rebellion. That comes to one rebellion in a century and a half for each state. What

[24]Hannah Arendt, *On Revolution* (New York: Viking Press, 1963), p. 238.

[25]Jefferson, *Portable Jefferson*, p. 560.

[26]Ibid., p. 561.

[27]Ibid., p. 417.

country before ever existed a century and a half without a rebellion? . . .
The tree of liberty must be refreshed from time to time with the blood
of patriots and tyrants. It is it's natural manure.[28]

Revolution, then, became a central principle to maintaining a vital,
democratic community. The ward-republics were to play the primary
role in maintaining a public space for humans to govern themselves.
Once again it was Hannah Arendt who accurately compared Jefferson's
ward-republics to the Paris Commune, the Soviets, and Räte. In a sense
the ward-republics were created to institutionalize revolution. But to
keep revolution a permanent part of American life, Jefferson also introduced an additional principle, "the earth belongs to the living."

Property: Economic and Political Freedom

Toward the final days of his tenure as U.S. Minister to France, in
the fateful year 1789, Jefferson sent James Madison one of the more
illuminating of his countless letters. Caught up, no doubt, in the excitement of the impending revolution in France, Jefferson took the
opportunity to speculate openly on the nature of obligations between
generations of humans. Specifically, can one generation of society bind,
either legally or morally, the succeeding one? Jefferson considered this
question both *sui generis* and important.

Echoing the style of the *Declaration of Independence*, Jefferson presented two self-evident truths: (1) "that the earth belongs in usufruct
to the living" (that is, the earth may be used but cannot be harmed)
and (2) "that the dead have neither powers nor rights over it."[29] From
these truths, Jefferson concluded that a new generation owes *no obligation*
to its predecessor. Whenever a member of society dies, the control over
the portion of land which that individual had a right to use while living
reverts to society. Inheritance laws may be socially established, but in
the absence of such laws, appropriation is based on first occupant.
Jefferson's point is that it is positive law, not natural right, that creates
property rights. "But the child, the legatee, or creditor takes it, not by
any natural right, but by a law of the society of which they are members,
and to which they are subject," Jefferson declared.[30]

This position—terminating control over land holdings with the
death of each individual—Jefferson extended to the passing of each
generation. Moreover, he also extended the principle beyond the boundaries of property; it included the repayment of any debts, public or

---

[28]Thomas Jefferson, *The Papers of Thomas Jefferson*, 20 vols., Julian Boyd, ed. (Princeton, N.J.: Princeton University Press, 1950–82), Vol. 12, pp. 356–57.

[29]Jefferson, *Portable Jefferson*, p. 445.

[30]Ibid., P. 445.

private, as well as all positive laws—even the Constitution of 1787. Jefferson's principle, that "the earth belongs to the living," is, as he put it, "of very extensive application and consequence." Lest the full impact of his principle be misread, he posed to Madison the following hypothetical case as an example. Jefferson asked: What would be the obligation of the present generation of Frenchmen if Louis XIV and Louis XV had contracted 10,000 Swiss millards of debt on behalf of the nation? Would either the lands, or the revenues from them, be due to the creditors? He responded negatively. Realizing that this notion flew in the face of tradition and the "common sense" of the day, Jefferson stated that the payment of debts by succeeding generations was a matter of "generosity and not of right."[31] It also followed that if the nation decided to end "perpetual monopolies," compensation was similarly a matter of generosity. A fiscal conservative, Jefferson thought this principle a way of avoiding the crippling accruement of large national debts, usually incurred as the result of war. Each generation was responsible for its own monetary matters; if one generation contracted debts it could not pay, the succeeding generation (calculated by Jefferson on the basis of mortality tables to evolve every nineteen years) was under no compulsion to pay them. Furthermore, by making this principle public policy, (that is, known to the world), both borrowers and lenders were liable for observing these rules, or suffering the consequences.

In the nineteenth year, all the laws and constitutions of society are to be automatically terminated. Quite simply, this means that approximately every twenty years, if not sooner, society must reaffirm or construct anew all of its statutes and institutions. The doctrine of tacit consent made popular by John Locke would not suffice; Jefferson wanted to institutionalize revolution in order to keep the Spirit of 1776 perpetually alive.

Happiness: The Ultimate Good

Although Jefferson's principle extended to every legal facet of society, its impact on property is particularly important. While much of the liberal tradition followed Locke, who viewed property as a natural right and its accumulation as the fulfillment of human endeavors, Jefferson did not. His vision of humans and of mankind's goal was much grander. Happiness is the ultimate good. More importantly, every person has a natural right to it. Property is merely an institution created by society to help people gain "life, liberty, and the pursuit of happiness." Hence, property laws could and should be altered at least every nineteen years to ensure that goal.

[31]Ibid., p. 450.

Politically, Jefferson struggled to change the property laws in his home state of Virginia by drafting legislation that put an end to the last feudal holdovers of *entail* and *primogeniture.* Entail and primogeniture guaranteed that the eldest son would inherit the father's estate *in toto,* and thus perpetuated large land holdings. Inequality of property was viewed by Jefferson as the root of "numberless instances of wretchedness." Everything that is "practicable" must be done to equalize property relations.

> I am conscious that an equal division of property is impracticable. But the consequences of this enormous inequality producing so much misery to the bulk of mankind, legislators cannot invent too many devices for subdividing property, only taking care to let their subdivisions go hand in hand with the natural affections of the human mind.[32]

He noted the impracticality, not the impropriety, of equality. Although he did not believe that it was politically possible to redistribute property equally, Jefferson did, as we have seen, argue that every male must be given some amount of property, at least fifty acres, to live. Small property holdings then become the instrument for ensuring economic freedom; copious land becomes essential for democratic communities.

Jefferson believed that free land would provide for economic freedom; as long as individuals had the option of meeting their needs on their own land, they could freely choose to leave the land and enter into a wage-labor situation that was not automatically based on exploitation.

> [In America] . . . every one may have land to labor for himself if he chooses; or, preferring the exercise of any other industry, may exact for it such compensation as not only to afford a comfortable subsistence, but wherewith to provide for a cessation from labor in old age.[33]

With the option of sustaining themselves on their farm, American laborers, unlike their European counterparts, could enter into a wage contract that was not exploitative. Land guaranteed economic freedom, and it was imperative for a democratic community.

From this brief discussion of property some of the implications of Jefferson's political theory manifest themselves. First, there is no natural right to property; such rights are social grants, created to aid people in the pursuit of life, liberty, and happiness. Insofar as economic freedom was necessary to a fully human life, every citizen had to be guaranteed the option of owning a small farm. To ensure further economic as well

---

[32]Jefferson, *The Papers of Thomas Jefferson,* Vol. 8, pp. 681–82.
[33]Jefferson, *Portable Jefferson,* p. 538.

as political freedom, Jefferson advanced his principle that "the earth belongs to the living." Once implemented, this principle would guarantee the required periodic alterations in property laws so essential to maintaining a society where all have the chance to pursue, if not always find, happiness. C.B. Macpherson has observed:

> [Jefferson's] justification of property rests, in the last analysis, on the right to life at a more than animal level: freedom from coerced labour and arbitrary government are held to be part of what is meant by a fully human life. At the same time this justification is an assertion of the right to the means of labour: the whole point is that by working on his own land or other productive resources a man can be independent and uncoerced.[34]

Jefferson's View of Humanity

Much like Rousseau, Jefferson believed that every person was an evolving creature whose human essence could flourish if placed in an appropriate environment. A social creature destined to live with other humans, all people possessed a moral sense, a sense of justice, which allowed them to rule themselves: "Man was created for social intercourse; but social intercourse cannot be maintained without a sense of justice; then man must have been created with a sense of justice," Jefferson wrote.[35]

As a scientist, Jefferson required empirical evidence to support his view of humankind. Observing the American Indian, it was as if Jefferson had discovered a state of nature that led him to his views on the human essence. He argued that the Indians could regulate themselves without the interference of traditional governments because they were moral agents who, in addition to using their moral sense, were receptive to community pressures, for example, loss of esteem, expulsion, and, in extreme cases, execution, carried out by the person who was harmed.

Imperfect as these correctional devices may appear, Jefferson reported that crime among Indian tribes was low. This is not to say that the Indian communities were leaderless. Chiefs held "power" through their ability to continually earn the respect of fellow tribe members, thereby influencing their actions. Furthermore, tribal society lacked bourgeois property rights; consequently, it suffered from no artificial class distinctions.

Confronted with the presence of a harmonious community without the presence of a Leviathan, Jefferson rhetorically queried "whether no

[34]C.B. Macpherson, *Democratic Theory: Essays in Retrieval* (Oxford: Clarendon Press, 1973), p. 135.

[35]Jefferson, *The Writings of Thomas Jefferson*, Vol. 15, pp. 24–25.

law . . . or too much law . . . submits man to the greatest evil?" On the basis of his firsthand observations, he unreservedly concluded: "One who has seen both conditions of existence would pronounce it to be the last: and that the sheep are happier of themselves, than under care of the wolves."[36] In the same vein, he also wrote: "I am convinced that those societies (as the Indians) which live without government enjoy in their general mass an infinitely greater degree of happiness than those who live under European governments. Among the former, public opinion is in the place of law, and restrains morals as powerfully as laws ever did any where."[37] This preference for a sort of social anarchism, a community of "lawfulness without laws," is not just a passing whim. Shortly after news of Shays' Rebellion in Massachusetts reached Jefferson, he dispatched a letter to James Madison in hopes of allaying Madison's fears:

> those characters wherein fear predominates over hope may apprehend too much from these instances of irregularity. They may conclude too hastily that nature has formed man insusceptible of any other government but that of force, a conclusion not founded in truth, nor experience. Societies exist under three forms sufficiently distinguishable. (1) Without government, as among our Indians. (2) Under governments wherein the will of every one has a just influence, as is the case in England in a slight degree, and in our states in a great one. (3) Under governments of force: as is the case in all other monarchies and in most of the other republics.[38]

Commenting on the forms, he easily characterized the last type as that of "wolves over sheep." Then, he candidly raised a question that he claimed plagued him: "It is a problem, not clear in my mind, that the first condition is not the best." Nevertheless, he admitted that, although the anarchism of the Indian is the optimal social arrangement, it may also be "inconsistent with any great degree of population."

As if hinting at the role of decentralization and community spirit of the ward-republics in his own theory, Jefferson carefully noted how the Indians handle the issue of size: "It will be said, that great societies cannot exist without government. The Savages therefore break them into small ones."[39] Jefferson viewed humans as social and evolutionary beings. Unlike both Hobbes and Locke, who began with arguments assuming an original sovereignty over oneself, Jefferson's theory began with sociability, not individuality. The Indians needed few positive laws because shared ideals, customs, and pasts could bind these untainted

---

[36]Jefferson, *Portable Jefferson*, p. 134.
[37]Ibid., p. 415.
[38]Ibid., p. 416.
[39]Ibid., p. 134.

humans together with bonds of affection and friendship. Coercion under these circumstances would be superfluous. And since they as individuals were naturally both social and moral, as members of a community there was, to Jefferson's way of thinking, no reason why they should behave in a contrary manner. To Madison, author of the *Federalist No. 10*, Jefferson wrote:

> I know but one code of morality for men whether acting singly or collectively. He who says I will be a rogue when I act in company with a hundred others but an honest man when I act alone will be believed in the former assertion, but not in the latter. . . .If the morality of one man produces a just line of conduct in him, acting individually, why should not the morality of one hundred men produce a just line of conduct in them, acting together?[40]

It is illuminating to compare this assertion with Madison's statement: "Had every Athenian citizen been a Socrates; every Athenian assembly would still have been a mob."

The writings of Thomas Jefferson provide an alternative view of liberal-democracy for America. Since his political theory was designed to preclude the potential difficulties of capitalism from developing, he argued for democracy as a way of life as well as a mechanism for constructing laws. Regarding the former, democracy required economic freedom and a view of people as developmental, social creatures; concerning the latter, democracy required political participation by all members of the population as a vital part of living a fully human life.

Having described Jefferson's alternative vision of a liberal-democratic society, it should be emphasized, once again, that it was James Madison's individualistic liberalism that provided the philosophic framework for the institutions of the American political system. Jeffersonian liberalism remained, to a large extent, outside the mainstream of political discourse in the United States. We shall encounter it again in the following chapter—particularly in the thought of John Dewey—but for the moment we must return to the mainstream.

SUGGESTED READINGS

BOORSTIN, DANIEL J., *The Genius of American Politics*. Chicago: The University of Chicago Press, 1953.

COLEMAN, FRANK M., *Hobbes and America: Exploring the Constitutional Foundations*. Toronto: University of Toronto Press, 1977.

[40]Thomas Jefferson, *The Works of Thomas Jefferson*, 12 vols., Paul Leicester Ford, ed. (New York: Knickerbocker Press, 1904), Vol. 5, p. 92.

COOKE, JACOB E., ed., *The Federalist.* Middletown, Conn.: Wesleyan University Press, 1961.

DAHL, ROBERT A., *A Preface to Democratic Theory.* Chicago: University of Chicago Press, 1963.

EIDELBERG, PAUL, *The Philosophy of the American Constitution.* New York: The Free Press, 1968.

HARTZ, LOUIS, *The Liberal Tradition in America.* New York: Harcourt Brace and World, 1955.

MATTHEWS, RICHARD K., *The Radical Politics of Thomas Jefferson: A Revisionist View.* Lawrence: University Press of Kansas, 1984.

PETERSON, MERRILL D., ed., *The Portable Thomas Jefferson.* New York: Penguin Books, 1977.

RIEMER, NEAL, *The Democratic Experiment,* Vol. 1. Princeton, N.J.: Van Nostrand Company, 1967.

SOLBERG, WINTON U., ed., *The Federal Convention and the Formation of the American States.* New York: Liberal Arts Press, 1958.

TOCQUEVILLE, ALEXIS DE, *Democracy in America,* 2 vols., tr. Henry Reeve. New York: Schocken Books, 1961.

4

Modern Liberal Democracy: Problems and Prospects

Fraternity, liberty, and equality isolated from communal life are hopeless abstractions.

John Dewey

Many students of American history view the Constitution of 1787 and the Madisonian political philosophy it embodied as a conservative reaction to the more majoritarian ideals expressed in the *Declaration of Independence* by Thomas Jefferson. Where the *Declaration* recognized equality, freedom, and the supremacy of popular will as the ultimate goals of government, Madison's system compromised on equality, attempted to restrict freedom through competition, and placed severe checks on the power of popular majorities—all in the pursuit of stability. One need not agree with such an assessment of the enterprise of the Founding Fathers to recognize that the overall pattern of development of the American political system since 1787 has been toward increasing majoritarianism. The expansion of the franchise led the way. Slowly but surely, all segments of the populace—nonproperty owners, blacks, and women—were granted the vote, so that universal suffrage became the hallmark of twentieth-century American democracy.

We have already noted that the early development of a political party system provided focal points for groups interested in attaining power, and to a certain extent mitigated the balance which Madison thought would be achieved through a multitude of diverse interest groups. Although American political parties remain rather weak in contrast to their highly disciplined European counterparts, the existence of a two-party system did make it possible for majorities to gain access to the government. However imperfect the American political system of the final quarter of the twentieth century might be, it functions in a far more majoritarian fashion than its eighteenth-century ancestor. Structural changes such as the popular election of senators and the evolution of the role of the presidency gave greater power to the people at the expense of states and propertied interests. The extent of that evolution toward majoritarianism and some reactions to that process comprise much of the subject matter of this final section on liberal democracy. To some degree we must delve into American political history to explain the ideological changes that accompanied the evolution of the institutions after 1787. To avoid extensive historical discussion, however, let us concentrate on the changes in the presidency as a sort of case study.

It has been noted that the presidency was in part designed to ensure that the person who occupied the office was above politics. The election of a president was left to an Electoral College of presumably distinguished people appointed by the states; they would gather and choose the best person for the office. George Washington, the first to hold the office, was somewhat successful in retaining the image of nonpartisanship, but the advent of the party system made this an impossible task. Further, despite the rhetoric advocating a nonpartisan leader, the method of election of the president ensured that, to a certain extent at least, he would be the representative of minority interests. Insofar as the members of the Electoral College were appointed by the legislatures of the varying states, and those legislatures were dominated by property owners, it is appropriate to view this office as a further check against majorities. The next 150 years in the history of the institution were marked by a sporadic but continual movement toward majority control.

The first major change is commonly seen as occurring with the election of Andrew Jackson in 1828 as a self-styled "man of the people." While the nature and extent of Jacksonian democracy is still a matter of some controversy, there is little doubt that the representation of the office as being responsive to popular wishes marked a significant change from the intention of most of the Founding Fathers. Once begun, the pattern of greater and greater influence of popular majorities on the presidency became a dominant theme in the development of American democracy. The facts of expanding presidential leadership in response to popular wishes and societal needs are familiar even to those with only a superficial knowledge of American history. Some examples are Abraham Lincoln's assumption of near-dictatorial power as commander-in-chief during the Civil War, Theodore Roosevelt's active leadership in foreign and domestic affairs, Woodrow Wilson's role as an international force in World War I, and Franklin D. Roosevelt's aggressive behavior on the economic and military fronts. One could cite others, but these examples make it clear that the American presidency in the twentieth century, largely as a result of foreign and domestic crises, became the prime focus of popular opinion, and as such became increasingly responsive to the wishes of popular majorities.

Changes in this one institution reflect in a graphic manner an alteration in the concept of the entire governmental enterprise in America and parallel a changing view of the nature of liberal democratic government itself. Largely through the expanded scope of presidential action, the traditional individualistic liberal ideal of limited government gradually eroded.

THE RISE OF MAJORITARIAN LIBERALISM

Recall that the entire American experiment with liberal democratic government was initiated in a period of profound fear of the power of states. Drawing on the ideas of classical British liberalism, the Founding Fathers produced a system intended to ensure that the individual possessed a large sphere of action that was not subject to governmental involvement. To use the standard terminology, speech, religion, assembly, movement, and economic activity were areas largely removed from political interference. It was this emphasis on the essential privacy of individual action that made the American experiment consistent with the highly individualistic ideals of the mainstream liberal tradition. However, the system was also predicated upon the assumption that individuals and groups would press their demands upon the government in an attempt to produce policies that maximized their private interests. In a real sense there was a built-in conflict between the liberal emphasis on highly limited government and the realization that groups would attempt to use the system for their own aggrandizement.

The Madisonian solution of an extended republic with built-in checks and balances and a system of representation was in part intended to assure that there would be no governmental action unless there was a broad consensus on a particular matter. In his pursuit of protection from the dangers of majority and minority tyranny, Madison produced a political system that reinforced the individualistic liberal ideal of limited government by making it quite difficult for majorities to form on any issue. If the multiplicity of interest groups and the checks and balances performed their function of balancing competing interests, there would be little in the way of a mandate for action of any sort on the part of the political system. That being the case, the scope of government would not only be limited by law but also by the absence of a widespread call for action of any type. It was in this way that the Madisonian system reinforced the inherent individualism of the tradition, for it tried to ensure a large private sphere of interaction. The gradual evolution of the presidency toward majoritarianism, combined with the other democratic changes mentioned earlier, in many respects undermined the check-and-balance functions of the system.

Although there is currently a good deal of disagreement as to the extent of majoritarianism in America (as will be obvious from the ensuing discussion of democratic elitism), let us for the moment accept the statement that changes in institutions as well as advances in communications made it easier for cohesive majorities to form and ensured that government would be more responsive to them. If that was the case, what were the consequences for the traditional liberal democratic conception of government? Two of the immediate and far-ranging consequences were that the sphere of private action dear to individualist liberalism was inevitably diminished and that the entire question of the extent of legitimate majority action arose once again.

Avoiding Instability and Revolution

In order to discuss the shrinking area of private action in a system with growing majoritarian tendencies, we must recall several points made earlier in this book. It was stated that all governments, irrespective of their ideological goals, had to satisfy certain minimal demands that arose from the citizenry if they were to avoid instability and revolution. No series of demands sought by large numbers of citizens could be ignored by any political system for a long period of time without risking social upheaval. As we shall see, in the transfer culture of communism, and in fascism as well, concerted attempts are made to control the types of demands advanced by the citizenry. Thus in both types of regimes (fascist and communist) there is extensive use of propaganda and censorship in an effort to mold popular opinion and give the leadership the widest possible latitude to pursue their goals. If the types of demands placed on the political system could be limited at their source, societal instability could be avoided. In democratic governments, however, this type of control of opinions cannot be openly attempted, for one of the basic presuppositions of democratic philosophy is that individuals must be free to develop and pursue their interests.

This is the same problem in a somewhat different form that Madison raised when he discussed and dismissed the possibility of limiting factions by giving all members of the population the same opinions. If the liberty that permits the development of myriad demands on government cannot be abridged, we must then be prepared for a constant clamoring among groups in the society who wish to secure the passage of legislation beneficial to their interests. Realizing this, Madison erected the types of checking devices discussed in the previous chapter. Since the growing majoritarianism of the American system meant a more rapid translation of popular wishes into public policy, it was probably inevitable that government would expand its scope of action so as to be able to respond to those demands. Indeed, if it did not respond to them, it would be constantly risking instability. Faced with such a situation, one would naturally expect governmental legislation to satisfy the demands of significant portions of the population whenever these demands arose. Thus, whenever the informal and customary control mechanisms of the private sector seemed insufficient to solve problems or to contain conflict, a demand was inevitably pressed on the political system to solve the problem through political rules, that is, to pass laws. As soon as this occurred, government had, in effect, turned a matter formerly private in nature into a subject of public policy. To clarify this process, let us refer in an admittedly superficial way to the Depression crisis in 1929.

Although the American government had been involved in the economic sector to a considerable extent prior to the onset of the Great Depression, the myth that the free enterprise system contained a self-control mechanism through supply and demand was still very much part of the conventional wisdom. Ever since John Locke had declared that property was something inherent in the individual and subject to only minimal regulation by government, the notion of a free market economy had been something of an individualist liberal dogma. Faced with the crisis of the Depression and the apparent inability of the informal market mechanisms to solve that crisis, the political system was immediately bombarded with demands that it step in and legislate the Depression out of existence. It could not help but respond to those demands if it valued the continued existence of not only a particular government but the entire form of government. Note that we are not discussing whether governmental actions during the Depression solved that particular economic crisis. We are only saying that the political system had little choice but to take some sort of action.

One can duplicate this example in many other areas. A decline in the cohesiveness of the family structure leads to demands that the government support the children of unstable or broken families; a decline in the status of religious institutions as keepers of the public morals leads to demands that laws be passed prohibiting deviant behavior or controlling the types of books people are allowed to read. All of these actions have the effect of greatly increasing the scope of public action and reducing the area that was formerly private.

Again, we must insert a caveat to the effect that the transference of a particular subject matter from the private to the public sphere does not necessarily mean that the freedom of the individual to do as he or she wants is greatly lessened. The informal control mechanisms of religious institutions can be just as restrictive of individual action as any formal law, and local committees formed to ban books can keep them off the shelves as effectively as any governmental edict. What is important here is that we are chronicling a distinct change in the conception of the appropriate role and function of political institutions. The highly limited government of the liberal tradition of Hobbes, Locke, and Madison is a thing of the past in America. The emergence of something that we shall call *majoritarian liberalism* lends a quite different character to modern American liberal democratic thought.

Before exploring that theme, however, it might be helpful to take a brief excursion outside of the American context to explore the effects of increasing majoritarian pressures on other liberal democratic systems. England provides a good example, for it did not possess the type of antimajoritarian structures instituted by Madisonianism.

Majoritarianism in the British Tradition

We have already mentioned that in England, James Mill and other early individualistic liberals had, however grudgingly, accepted the extension of voting rights to all males—and women were soon to follow. The implications of the extension of the franchise were, however, considerably different in England (as well as in some Continental democracies) from that in the United States. The absence of Madisonian checks designed to mute the potential power of majorities have made non-Madisonian liberal systems much more responsive to the wishes of majorities in the twentieth century. In England the rise of the mass-based Labor party provided a vehicle for the transference of majoritarian preferences into public policy.

Moreover, the English tradition of responsible parties (highly centralized and disciplined, in contrast to their American counterparts) ensured that, upon election, the preferences expressed in the parties' programs were transferred into public policy. Checking and the balancing of competing interests engendered by the Madisonian system in the United States provided no barrier in England. For this reason many critics of the American system, who believe that it is insufficiently responsive to majoritarian preferences, cite England as an alternative model of a stable liberal democratic regime. John Dewey, whom we will meet later in this chapter, exemplified this position when he argued that Madisonianism had produced a condition whereby competing interest groups precluded both the possibility of achieving and the possibility of conceiving a truly *public* interest in America.

In this context we should also mention that responsiveness to majoritarian preferences has frequently led not only to increasing governmental policymaking in areas heretofore considered "private" (the welfare state, for example), but in the eyes of many it has loosened, if not broken, the traditional tie between individualistic liberalism and capitalist economics.

In England, for example, the Labor party has successfully led periodic drives to nationalize important segments of the economy. While this need not necessarily be the case, as the reign of Margaret Thacher makes clear—it is perfectly possible for majorities to prefer capitalist economic systems and to oppose welfare-state legislation—this fact has important theoretical consequences, for it may provide a bridge between majoritarian democratic decision-making processes and socialist economics.

As we shall see in our discussion of communist thought, some Marxists early in the twentieth century (called "revisionists") viewed the extension of the franchise in places like England and Germany as providing the possibility of peacefully legislating a socialist economic system, rendering the violent revolution that Karl Marx foresaw unnecessary. If majorities desiring socialism possessed power they could use the political system to evolve into a socialist society. In the majoritarian liberal tradition of the twentieth century, we have one of the possible bases for a doctrine of *democratic socialism*.

We shall address that point in our later examination of the thought of John Dewey. For the moment, however, let us return to our discussion of the question of majoritarianism in the United States.

MAJORITARIAN LIBERAL DEMOCRACY IN AMERICA

The idea that government ought to play a more positive role in the lives of its citizens developed only gradually in the United States. If one wanted to attach a date to its emergence, one could point to the latter part of the nineteenth century, when the political system became actively involved in the protection and control of the economy, or to the expansion of functions that occurred during World War I, or to the aforementioned Great Depression. The date one might choose is somewhat immaterial. From the point of view of Madisonian liberalism the significant fact is that the one hundred years between 1850 and 1950 marked a profound change in the processes of American government.

Although the core values of the liberal tradition remained relatively intact, certain of their number were given greater emphasis while others moved to a lower position in the value hierarchy. We have already noted that the trend toward majoritarianism had a great effect on the individualistic liberal conception of limited government. Instead of viewing the political system as an umpire, balancing the competing claims of private interest groups, the majoritarian liberalism of the twentieth century envisioned government as an active force in producing a better life for its citizens. The impartial third party of Lockean theory is replaced by attempts to institute a modern welfare state. Perhaps the most important value change that occurred in the evolution from individualistic majoritarian liberalism was in the status of the individual.

We began our discussion of the tradition initiated by Hobbes and Locke by emphasizing that the idea of the free, relatively isolated individual was the one concept shared by the first liberal theorists. While that value is retained by American majoritarian liberalism, its force is considerably altered. Inevitably, as government began to expand its sphere of activity, it generated rules that necessarily constrained the freedom of individual action. To use a rather crude example, the freedom of the unscrupulous businessperson to advertise a product falsely is reduced to the extent that he is required to be at least somewhat truthful in claims for his or her product. The old notion of caveat emptor (let the buyer beware) is replaced by the legal responsibility of the producer not to sell unsafe products.

Note that there is no need to attach any sort of moral judgment to these changes in values; we are simply attempting to describe an evolution in the conception of the individual. One may heartily approve of governmental legislation to prohibit shoddy business practices or one may feel such action is interfering with individual rights; the fact is that freedom to act is being constrained. It should also be noted that governmental legislation to limit individual action was very much a part of individualist liberal democratic thought. Humans, after all, limit themselves merely by becoming members of a society. The controversy arises regarding the appropriate scope of legislation by political systems that call themselves liberal democratic regimes.

The Tension Between Liberty and Equality

Paralleling the reduction in importance of the unconstrained individual in majoritarian liberalism is the rise in importance of the old democratic value of equality. Indeed, some commentators see a necessary interrelationship between the value of liberty and equality or note a tension between these two cardinal values of the mainstream tradition. Minimally, one can assert that equality was the most ill-defined and limited of the values of individualistic liberalism. Recall that Thomas Hobbes saw people as equal only in the negative sense that they all possessed the ability to kill one another. The major question involving the interrelationship between the values of liberty and equality, however, arose in the economic area.

Beginning around the turn of the twentieth century, people began asking how one could be free without the means to exercise that freedom. To use an obvious example, a person residing in the United States possesses a theoretical freedom or right to leave that country for any other place in the world. That theoretical freedom does not, however, put the money in his or her pocket that will permit the exercise of this right. Isn't a person similarly situated, but who possesses the means to exercise the abstract right of free movement, actually more free than one who does not? Stated in a slightly more complex way, people were beginning to see that economic inequalities conferred greater power on some of their number and that the abstract values of liberty and equality meant little without the ability to fulfill them.

Similarly, the theoretical equality between black and white, male and female, is little more than meaningless rhetoric if minorities and females are systematically denied the opportunity to achieve at least some degree of economic equality. To return to our initial point, however, governmental legislation that is designed to achieve at least some degree of economic equality, or laws that attempt to ensure that blacks and women will be treated equally both in fact and in theory, will undoubtedly constrain the freedom of other members of the community. This is precisely what is meant by the tension between freedom and equality. When my ability to discriminate on the basis of race, religion, or sex is abridged through the action of government, my personal liberty is limited. While all right-thinking individuals would applaud such legislation on the grounds that such discrimination deprives others of their rights, from the individualistic liberal point of view, it does reduce freedom. The response from majoritarian liberalism would simply be that the classical value of freedom is meaningless without relative equality. The hallmark, then, of the American majoritarian liberalism of the twentieth century is the attempt to use the political system to ensure greater degrees of equality or, at least, equality of opportunity.

With the advent of majoritarian liberal democracy, a split in the ideology occurred over the meaning of both the liberal and the democratic components. The early liberals argued on behalf of those market freedoms necessary to allow individuals to pursue their own self-interest, even if this meant, as it usually did, that one person's gain was another person's loss. When the class inequalities produced by capitalism became obvious, other liberal theorists argued that the freedom that was necessary to human fulfillment was not market freedom but the *equal effective right* of individuals to develop their own capacities.

Similarly, liberal theorists disagreed over the nature of democracy. One group believed that democracy was essentially a *political mechanism* for electing government. It was important in that it allowed individuals to protect themselves from each other as well as the government. Since this viewpoint espoused the market freedoms associated with capitalism, it desired a minimum amount of governmental influence so that in the private economic arena individuals could pursue their own advantage.

The second perspective views democracy not only as an electoral mechanism but also as a *way of life*, a type of society. Placing greater weight on the principle of equality, this side believes that participating in politics is not simply an activity to be engaged in out of self-protection but rather an endeavor that is beneficial in itself, part of living a fully human life. Since every person must have an equal effective right to develop his or her own individual powers and capacities, some of the so-called market freedoms will be restricted in the interests of social well-being.

Characteristic of perhaps all developments in the realm of ideas, the creation of majoritarian liberal democracy produced a reaction to it. Combining the idea of *pluralism* found in Madison with the twentieth-century notion of *elitism*, this perspective attempts to adapt liberal democracy to the realities of modern America.

ELITE THEORY IN MODERN LIBERAL THOUGHT

We should note initially that while elitist analysis of modern liberal democratic society is directed primarily toward the United States, it has implications for all regimes as well as for democratic theory as a whole. Elitist analysis begins by attempting to assess realistically what the basic value of rule by the people really means in a complex modern society. Relying on the arguments presented by past thinkers such as Gaetano Mosca, Vilfredo Pareto, and Robert Michels as well as modern organizational theorists, these people assert that popular rule means very little indeed. It can be demonstrated conclusively that any large-scale organization, including government, is, of necessity, organized in a heirarchical fashion. That is, there are certain people, who, by the nature of the tasks they perform, possess far more power than others. Any organization can thus be divided into two groups of people—the elite who make all of the basic decisions and the mass that follows them. The reasons for such a division are many and varied. Obviously every member of a group, be it a government or a fraternal organization, cannot be expected to know all of the details involved in running the organization. In the case of political systems, people who are nominally citizens of the state are primarily concerned with earning a living for themselves and pursuing their individual interests. To expect the average person to be a full-time participant in the political process at the same time is simply absurd. The complexity of modern society thus demands that we adopt a specialization of labor whereby some people become experts in running organizations and fulfill that task on a full-time basis.

We have seen that classical liberal democratic theory confronted a similar problem and solved it by introducing the concept of representation, so that democratic governments might exist in large states. To the elitist, however, such a solution really raises more problems than it solves, particularly in complex modern societies.

A representative is, by the very nature of the position, cut off from those represented, elitists contend. The representative possesses far more information than the average constituent, pursues tasks as a professional politician, and in all probability has a broader perspective than any of those represented; in short, the concerns and position are quite different. One would not, after all, expect the chairman of the board of General Motors to submit a questionnaire to all of the stockholders of the company asking them how many cars they should build that year and then proceed to act on their recommendation. The average stockholder simply could not make an informed judgment on such a matter without spending a considerable amount of time studying the market for automobiles, that is, unless the person was willing to become an expert.

To return to political concerns, there is an even more pervasive phenomenon that colors the types of decisions that can be made. The representative's (and here we use the word to refer to any elected decision maker) position makes it possible to influence greatly even the types of questions that are submitted to the population. By posing two alternatives as the only possible courses of action in any situation, the representative can effectively preclude discussion of a third alternative that might be more desirable from the people's point of view. In effect, formidable limits can be set on the types of governmental action that can even be considered. Robert Michels, author of the "iron law of oligarchy," discussed this phenomena and argued that organization gives birth to the domination of the elected over the electors, of the mandataries over the mandators, of the delegates over the delegators. With organization inevitably comes oligarchy, Michels declared.

This, then, is the cornerstone of the elitist position. The complexity and need for expertise in modern societies ensures that popular representatives are divorced from their constituents and are capable of making—and to a certain extent must make—decisions independent of popular wishes. The choice, then, seems to be between organization (which appears indispensable) and democracy (which may be desirable). But, the elitist argues, you cannot have both.

We must note that as yet there is no moral judgment attached to such a position. From this descriptive perspective, the elitist simply asserts that, like it or not, this is the way it is, a fact of modern society. Confronted with such an argument, the defender of liberal democratic theory might admit that it is necessary to have this situation when the process of running a government is such a complicated business. Such a defender would, however, probably go on to assert that it really doesn't matter, for the representative's constituents can remove that person if they desire when the next election occurs. If a person acting in the name of the people fails in their eyes to perform his or her tasks correctly they can simply vote the person out of office. This is, in effect, the old Madisonian argument for the appropriate means of controlling minority tyranny.

Expanding on the type of reasoning used earlier, the elitist would respond that periodic elections provide no real popular control, for the choices to replace a bad representative are greatly limited. The existing elite controls the access to the political system, thereby ensuring that only candidates who possess elite values are offered as choices to the electorate. This is accomplished through the political party structure, through the necessity of having great amounts of money to wage a successful campaign, and through a series of legal rules and customs.

Further, even if a "common person" surmounted all of these obstacles and was elected to office, that person would have little power, for within the governmental institutions themselves there are additional control devices as exemplified by seniority and committee systems in Congress. These are dominated by the elite as well. Under such circumstances the only choice available to a voter at election time is between competing elite groups who possess basically the same values, which preclude the possibility of any real change in governmental policy. If this is reality, what does the phrase "government by the people" mean? Before attempting to respond to that question, we must record a further extension of the elitist argument, which makes the phrase "popular government" even more inapplicable to modern American society.

Power-Elite Analysis

Up to now we have avoided mention of any particular individual advancing the elitist position, preferring to refer to a vaguely defined group of democratic elitists. The major reason for this is that it is a most diverse tradition and sufficiently current to make it difficult to single out leading representatives. However, one person, C. Wright Mills, is most closely associated with this position, and his analysis of modern American democracy provides a further extension of the basic elitist position.

Accepting as fact the notion that complex organizations are of necessity hierarchical in structure and that a clear distinction must be made between elite and mass, Mills went on to argue that economic factors in the United States had produced a two-class society wherein even the government was powerless to effect any basic changes in policy. Let us ignore for the moment the prior argument that elected representatives are by virtue of their positions divorced from the people and assume that they actually do reflect popular desires. What real power does the average representative or senator possess? Very little if any, Mills contended, particularly regarding the basic matters such as war and peace or significant changes in the economic structure. The elected representative is at best in a middle-range power position, for the great decision-making capability lies in the hands of an economically based *power elite*, which is largely outside the control of the political system. Membership in this group is defined by birth and wealth, although it is possible for a member of the nonelite to become part of it by adopting the values of that group. Elite members go to the same schools, belong to the same social clubs, intermarry, and in general share similar values. While there may be minor disagreements among members of the elite over the everyday matters of public policy, they share a firm commitment to preserving the existing value and class structure.

Franklin D. Roosevelt is frequently cited by scholars ascribing to this position as indicative of the overall cohesiveness of the power elite. Elected to the presidency in a period of severe economic crisis and equipped with an apparent mandate for massive social and economic change, Roosevelt succeeded with a series of patchwork measures (and a war) in avoiding any fundamental change in the nature of American society. In much the same fashion, President Eisenhower drew rather unexpected applause from power-elite theorists when he cautioned against the government becoming a captive of a "military-industrial complex," which sought to use the political system for its own selfish ends.

The sum of the power-elitist argument is that the government is largely controlled by a small group of people who owe their power to their economic and social position in the society. If this be the case, there can be no true change in the system, for the members of the elite group will simply not permit any decline in their status. Government and, consequently, the representatives of the people are reduced to making relatively unimportant decisions which in the end can only serve to perpetuate the existence of the status quo.

Anticipating our forthcoming discussion, we must note that there are distinctly Marxian overtones to this type of analysis in that it sees the economic variable as crucial in determining people's actions and it relies heavily on a class analysis. Further, it might also be termed Marxian in that it views government, in effect, as the tool of a capitalist class that seeks to use the political system to perpetuate and extend class power. Whatever one chooses to term the Millsian type of analysis, from the theoretical perspective its import lies in the fact that it makes explicit a reevaluation of the concept of power in liberal democratic systems.

The Power of Money

Traditional democratic theory presupposed that by providing people with equal voting power one could keep the limited functions of government consistent with popular desires. In attempting to divorce political matters from the economic realm and by viewing the political system as an umpire between competing factions, individualistic liberalism and the Madisonian implementation of it paid insufficient attention to the power that money confers. From the power-elitist perspective, the American political system has always involved tyranny by a *minority*, which derives its power from its economic position. Attempts to implement greater economic equality through the institution of majoritarian liberalism have provided, elitists assert, nothing more than sops to the people and perpetuated a class-based capitalist economic system. Viewing the American political system as a device for perpetuating minority interests, the elitist thus calls for revolution in the system in the name of producing a true democracy. The only way the minority control of the system can be checked is through giving greater decision-making power to the people.

Similarly, the only way the norm of equality, which majoritarian liberalism purported to be trying to achieve, can actually be fulfilled is through increasing democratization of both political and economic decision making. Mills's form of democratic elitism, then, ends up as a critical analysis of existing American politics. There is present in his theory an implicit faith in the basic common sense of the average person, and in the ability of the American democratic experiment to solve all problems through increasing democratization.

Shortcomings of Elitist Analysis

Before moving to a brief discussion of the other form of the elitist responses to majoritarian liberal democracy, a position which accepts the elitist analysis of American politics but sees it as a positive virtue, we must point out some of the possible difficulties in the power-elitist position discussed thus far.

Initially, critics have contended that the elitists have been by no means able to demonstrate the existence of a distinct class of people who constitute the power elite. Indeed, even if one is able to show great similarity in background among major political and economic decision makers, does this mean that they automatically share similar values? Further, the elitist must be able to prove that there is no fundamental difference between competing elite groups, and this, so critics contend, has yet to be accomplished. If varying elite groups change their policies in an attempt to win popular support, then the elitist charge that the voter has no real choice during elections is refuted.

Other critics have contended that it can be demonstrated that numerous individuals of nonelite origins have risen to elite status with their values essentially intact, and have been able to effect serious change in public policy. Finally, critics contend there is a distressful lack of precision in the elitist argument. We are told that some ill-defined elite groups constantly use government for their own purposes at the expense of popular wishes, and that they agree on fundamental matters. But what is meant by fundamental? If it is nothing more than retention of the essentials of the existing economic system then the elite is probably reflecting public opinion accurately.

These and similar matters are the material of current controversy and dialogue among students of American liberalism. Thus it would be both presumptuous and foolhardy to attempt to resolve them here. Let us instead follow a safer path and move to a discussion of the second form of elitist reaction to the prevalent majoritarian liberal democracy of the twentieth century.

Normative Democratic Elitism

Another even more loosely defined group of individuals who merit the term *elitist* deserve brief mention if only because they form somewhat of a modern equivalent of the old Madisonian position. Impressed (perhaps depressed is the better word) by the apparent potential of the modern democratic citizen for irrational action, and distrustful of the masses' ability to support traditional democratic values in the face of crisis, these thinkers advocate elitist control of the society in the name of preserving liberal democracy. If that seems a bit paradoxical, it only serves to show again the many uses of the words liberal and democratic.

This position, sometimes called *normative democratic elitism*, can, for our purposes, be represented by the thinking of Joseph Schumpeter. In his influential book *Capitalism, Socialism and Democracy*, Schumpeter sketched the outline of his theory. His position has three main points. First, democracy is not a kind of society but simply a mechanism for selecting governments. Democracy is a political *method;* it is a certain type of institutional arrangement for arriving at political-legislative and administrative decisions. The mechanism, second, consists of competition between at least two sets of self-chosen politicians (elites). And third, the voter's role is not to decide political questions but simply to select the individuals who will decide both the questions and the answers. Thus, for Schumpeter, political participation has no intrinsic value; indeed, he did not think universal suffrage was a requisite of democratic politics. As he put it, "The electoral mass is incapable of action other than a stampede."

As an economist, it was perhaps easier for Schumpeter to view the political system as an approximation of the market, with voters as the consumers and politicians as the entrepreneurs. Schumpeter was clear, however, that this was no free market: "Party and machine politicians . . . attempt to regulate political competition exactly similar to the corresponding practices of a trade association."[1]

Concerning the will of the people, what in the market metaphor would be demand, Schumpeter described the reality of an artificially created demand. "The ways in which issues and the popular will on any issue are being manufactured is exactly analogous to the ways of commercial advertising."[2] Arguing a position reminiscent of Madison, Schumpeter summarized his position: "democracy does not mean and cannot mean that the people actually rule in any obvious sense of the terms 'people' and 'rule.' Democracy means only that the people have the opportunity of accepting or refusing the men who are to rule them."[3]

[1]Joseph Schumpeter, *Capitalism, Socialism, and Democracy*, 2nd ed. (New York: Harper & Row, Publishers, 1947), p. 283.

[2]Ibid., p. 263.

[3]Ibid., pp. 284–85.

Normative democratic elitism believes, in effect, that the mass must be protected from itself. It notes that research into the values held by members of modern democratic states shows that it is the well-educated and generally affluent minority that has the highest respect for traditional liberal democratic values. The average person seems far more prone to adopt authoritarian solutions to problems, is quick to attempt to silence dissent, and in general finds it difficult to live with individual deviation from accepted behavior.

There is a tendency in majoritarian democracies to attempt to standardize all forms of conduct and to punish any deviation from those norms. As the sphere of governmental activity expands, we have found that it establishes rules of behavior in areas formerly part of the private sphere of activity. In a majoritarian liberal democracy, what this means is that the wishes of a majority of the people gradually become the accepted standards of conduct for the entire society. What bothers the elitist is that these mass tastes seem inevitably to reflect the wishes of what they believe to be the lowest common denominator of individuals in the society. What develops is a *mass culture* composed of television programs designed to appeal to the greatest possible number of people, news programs that simplify complex events to make them understandable, architectural styles designed for broad appeal, and faddish clothing styles that reflect the changing desires of the masses. One can go on and on.

Although the phenomenon of mass culture is not in and of itself a bad thing for democracies, the elitist sees it as inevitably discouraging individual deviation from the established norms. Thus the individual who does not conform is far less successful than one who does, but the society loses the type of creative energy that seems to be generated most often by nonconformists. Put in terms of political values, mass democracy seems bent on destroying the individuality that is the core idea in liberal democratic theory. In a way we are back to the points made earlier about the tensions between liberty and equality. In pursuit of equalitarian goals, majoritarian liberal democracies tend to standardize everything, creating a society with a homogenized culture which stamps out individual liberty.

The "Irony of Democracy"

It should be apparent now why one can call this elitist position somewhat equivalent to the old Madisonian stance. Both accept as given the presence of a capitalist economic system as well as a plural society; that is, society is composed of individuals who belong to various, often conflicting, interest groups. While the basic value of popular sovereignty is not denied, the elitist recognizes that the masses under the banner of majority rule will tend toward excessive use of their power, thereby depriving others of their liberty to act as they choose. Here then is a more modern equivalent to the Madisonian tyranny of the majority, where communications advances make it quite possible to give everyone the same opinions. Far from being unhappy with the fact that modern society necessitates some type of distinction between elite leadership and mass following, the normative elitist sees the leadership group as a prime bulwark against the excesses of majorities. If the people did indeed rule as the majoritarian liberal tells us they ought, the liberal individualistic values of the tradition would soon be lost. This sober conclusion has been referred to as "the irony of democracy."

It is the irony of American democracy that the elites, and not the masses, are most committed to liberal democratic values; and, if the masses ever did actually rule, they would wipe out all vestiges of these democratic norms in favor of more authoritarian values. Voter apathy, consequently, is seen as a positive benefit since it is primarily the masses who fail to participate. There is some question whether this view can legitimately be called liberal democratic in that it explicitly relies on elite control of the masses. If one insists on a more majoritarian definition of liberal democracy, it obviously cannot be. If, however, one defines liberal democracy in more individualistic terms while retaining an overall commitment to popular sovereignty, normative elitism is probably as "liberal" as the Madisonian variety. The elitist, while recognizing the desirability of ultimate control by the people, is very happy that complex modern organizations ensure that educated liberal elites control much of the day-to-day activity of the state.

By now the reader will no doubt realize that we have come almost full circle in our discussion of liberal democracy. The normative elitist's fear of excessive majority control leading to conformity and authoritarianism is quite similar to the Madisonian concern with majority tyranny. In describing the spectrum of liberal democratic thought as it became embodied in the American political tradition, we have tried to show the full range of possibilities given the uniqueness of the American experience. However, before the discussion of liberal democracy is completed, it is appropriate to examine a final part of this diverse tradition. Although this perspective has yet to be embraced by any country, and certainly not the United States, it has had many important spokespersons. We have termed this view of liberal democratic society an *alternate vision of liberalism* and have encountered two of its early spokesmen in Jean Jacques Rousseau and Thomas Jefferson. Let us now look at twentieth-century manifestations of this alternative view of a liberal democratic society. Our primary example is the thought of John Dewey.

JOHN DEWEY AND THE LIBERAL TRADITION

John Dewey was a philosopher and educator who was quite influential in the United States in both philosophy and education during the first half of the twentieth century. Although his political thinking was perhaps less well known than his other endeavors, for our purposes he can serve as an excellent example of twentieth-century attempts to modernize the alternative vision of Jeffersonian liberalism. Dewey is particularly appropriate in this regard because his early speculations on political matters placed him squarely within the individualistic liberal tradition of Madisonianism. However, he became disenchanted with that tradition largely because of its emphasis on competition, its ties to capitalist economics, and its lack of a meaningful conception of democratic community. Consciously seeking to "update" Jefferson's legacy for a new environment, he produced a conception of democracy that placed heavy emphasis on economic equality and the need for a participatory community—two of the cardinal traits of the alternative tradition of liberalism.

In his earliest writings on politics, Dewey was operating well within the dominant tradition, referring, for example, to government as essentially an "umpire" supervising the competing groups generated from the private sector. By 1927, in *The Public and Its Problems*, however, he argued that the Madisonian solution had worked all too well—competition and checks and balances had virtually eliminated any conception of a truly *public* interest. "It is not that there is no public, no large body of persons having a common interest in the consequences of social transactions. There is too much public, a public too diffused and scattered and too intricate in composition," he wrote. In Dewey's mind this condition made the achievement of a democratic community impossible, and that fact undermined the very essence of democracy. "The clear consciousness of a communal life, in all of its implications, constitutes the idea of democracy,"[4] he observed. Finally, in the true legacy of Jefferson, he argued for a fundamental reevaluation of the very idea of democracy, particularly as it related to modern times.

The initial step in that reevaluation process seemed quite clear to Dewey. We must begin by discarding individualistic politics and the ideology underlying it as not only outmoded but simply incorrect. We must recognize the fact that natural and human events are based upon *interrelationships* and that this fact provides the basis for true human community. The recognition of the physical fact of associative behavior will provide the groundwork for developing a moral dimension of that association that will constitute a community. We must create an envi-

---

[4]John Dewey, *The Public and Its Problems* (Chicago: The Swallow Press, 1954), p. 149.

ronment—not unlike the one that Jefferson advocated in his ward republics—where participation, interrelationships, and cooperative enterprise are encouraged. The entire social environment—the political system, communications, education, socialization processes—must be transformed to support a democratic community of actively participating adults. We need not go into the details of what Dewey called the "face-to-face community," except to note that he believed such an association was possible in modern times because of tremendous advances in communication. Local communities could provide an environment that was conducive to a democratic way of life, and the symbolic interaction possible with the advent of mass communication devices would allow a less intense, but nevertheless real, national community.

Dewey attacked the fruits of Madison's labors in other areas as well, particularly with respect to the relationship between political and economic power. Recall that the individualistic liberal tradition had argued for a large private space in which human beings could pursue their essentially selfish interests. Recall also that the Madisonian tradition, following the lead of Hobbes and Locke, intimately tied its conception of democracy to capitalist economics. In Dewey's view, this conception of democracy may have been desirable in Madison's time, but by the twentieth century it had produced conditions of inequality that were incompatible with a democratic way of life.

Dewey's Political Views

Although he declared throughout his life that he was not a follower of Karl Marx (and certainly not in the authoritarian tradition of Lenin), Dewey eventually came to advocate nationalization of the means of production as the only way to overcome the inequalities that capitalist economics had produced. Perhaps reflecting his early enthusiasm for the ideas of G. W. F. Hegel, whom we will meet shortly, Dewey believed that the political system must be used to provide not only equalities of economic opportunity but also political equality. This was to be accomplished peacefully—through the ballot box. Hence, it is appropriate to view John Dewey as a modern American representative of the position we generally call *democratic socialism.*

Whatever we choose to label Dewey's views, there is no question that his ultimate commitment was to the ideal of a participatory democratic community. In his mind, democracy was the only way of life that permitted—even demanded—the constant examination of alternative courses of action, questioning of conventional wisdom, and individual and communal growth (he called it "creative intelligence") that was the essence of the human experience.

Finally, to those who would argue that the average person simply was incapable of, or not interested in, the type of active participation in decision making that he advocated, Dewey responded with a ringing defense of the capabilities of the "common man." He knew that masses of people were not inclined to participate in politics, were ignorant of political issues, and tended to support authoritarian rather than liberal democratic values. The reason for such behavior was not, in his view, some underlying "illiberal" human nature, but the result of undemocratic (even antiliberal democratic) environmental conditioning. In direct contrast to the normative democratic elitists we discussed earlier (Joseph Schumpeter was our example), Dewey argued that it was illiberal institutions and conditioning that resulted in illiberal behavior in people and that in the appropriate environment the average person was fully capable of the type of action required in a participatory democratic community.

While the political thought of John Dewey has served as our example of a modern manifestation of the alternative liberal tradition, we should note that a variety of other thinkers (and political activists) might well be regarded in the same fashion. Many of the so-called student radicals of the 1960s and 1970s articulated similar views in a less systematic way. Moreover, quite a few of the critics of "usual Madisonian politics" or the mainstream liberal tradition utilize arguments quite similar to those of Dewey in their efforts to reform liberal democracy. Nevertheless, we believe we are correct in using the term *alternative vision* to describe this tradition, for it has never achieved either the popularity or the stamp of legitimacy of the individualistic liberalism of Hobbes, Locke, Madison and their contemporary followers.

FINAL THOUGHTS ON LIBERAL DEMOCRACY

What should be evident at this point in the discussion is that historically liberalism has meant something both more specific and more complex, if not altogether different, than its common American usage. Although liberalism is often erroneously associated with social reform movements, the welfare state, and "bleeding hearts" (whatever that means), in terms of historical unfolding of the ideology it is the emphasis on the free individual and that individual's right to develop his or her full potential that is the center of liberal thought. We have argued that the broad liberal tradition can be separated into two general types—individualistic (capitalist) and alternative (noncapitalist). Each of those types has undergone numerous changes and alterations in the past four hundred years, but the two types remain, we think, clearly distinguishable.

Originally, the ideology of individualistic liberalism developed alongside of capitalism. It was believed that in contrast to the feudal economic tradition, capitalism would free humanity from the past and put an end to economic scarcity, so both individual and aggregate material needs would be met in the most efficient manner. As class divisions became more apparent and increasingly unmanageable, individualistic liberal theorists extended the franchise. First, they included nonproperty-owning white males; eventually, black males and then women were granted the vote. This extension of the franchise provided the precondition for the rise of majoritarian liberalism.

We have stated that the implementation of a more majoritarian form of the individualist tradition was more easily achieved in countries other than the United States, largely because of the strictures imposed by the Madisonian system. In America, the debate over how much majoritarianism does in fact exist or, for that matter, ought to exist, goes on.

The second tradition of alternative liberalism sprang from different roots, but its ultimate goal was and is the same as that of individualistic liberalism—the freeing of the individual so as to ensure the full development of his or her potential. These liberals, however, differ in their view of what processes ought to be used to accomplish that purpose and what values a truly liberal society ought to pursue. Lacking ties to capitalist economics, espousing a more equalitarian society, and arguing for a full participatory community, alternative liberalism provides a legitimate alternative to the dominant individualist tradition.

Finally, we must emphasize once again the values of toleration and dialogue inside of the broad spectrum of perspectives contained in liberalism. Regardless of which liberal thinker one encounters, each values the necessity of an ongoing dialogue in the search for a democratic society.

This position in favor of toleration is, at times, in marked contrast to the presentations that follow. If liberal democracy is a process in search of an unfolding and evolving truth, Marxism, German National Socialism, Italian fascism, and Islamic fundamentalism are far more certain that they have already found their path to the truth.

SUGGESTED READINGS

BACHRACH, PETER, *The Theory of Democratic Elitism: A Critique.* Boston: Little, Brown and Co., 1967.

DEWEY, JOHN, *Liberalism and Social Action.* New York: Capricorn Books, 1963.

DOMHOFF, G. WILLIAM, *Who Rules America?* Englewood Cliffs, N.J.: Prentice Hall, 1967.

GIRVETZ, HARRY K., ed., *Democracy and Elitism.* New York: Charles Scribner's Sons, 1967.

KARIEL, HENRY S., ed., *Frontiers of Democratic Theory.* New York: Random House, 1970.

LOWI, THEODORE J., *The End of Liberalism: Ideology, Policy, and the Crisis of Public Authority.* New York: W. W. Norton & Company, 1969.

MACPHERSON, C. B., *Life and Times of Liberal Democracy.* New York: Oxford University Press, 1979.

MILLS, C. WRIGHT, *The Power Elite.* New York: Oxford University Press, 1959.

RADICE, GILES, *Democratic Socialism.* New York: Frederick A. Praeger, 1966.

RAWLS, JOHN, *A Theory of Justice.* Cambridge, Mass.: The Belknap Press of Harvard University Press, 1971.

SCHUMPETER, JOSEPH, *Capitalism, Socialism, and Democracy,* 2nd ed. New York: Harper & Row, Publishers, 1947.

WHITE, MORTON, *Social Thought in America: The Revolt Against Formalism,* Boston: Beacon Press, 1957.

5
Marxism

The philosophers have only interpreted the world, in various ways; the point, however, is to change it.

Karl Marx

Karl Marx was a revolutionary—it is said he even looked like one! His mature life was spent in never-ending attempts to transcend the capitalist system that he both admired and abhorred. History is filled with figures who rebelled against existing societies and failed, their careers being relegated to mere footnotes in scholarly works, but Karl Marx and his ideas comprise no footnote in history books. If we were to speak of the number of people who have been influenced by his vision, to say nothing of those who have felt it necessary to condemn him, we would have a vast army indeed. On this scale, Karl Marx would rank among the great religious leaders of antiquity. Herein lies one of the major problems in speaking of Marx. As Robert Heilbroner has put it, Marx the symbol has come to obscure Marx the man, and Marx the revolutionary disguises Marx the thinker.[1] In more vivid terms, Michael Harrington makes a similar observation and passes along a valuable recommendation on how to begin a study of Marxism.

> For most people the first step in grasping the new and future Marx is to forget everything they have heard or read about the familiar Marx. At the same time, they must accept one of history's strangest ironies: that Marx and the Marxists made a major contribution to the misunderstanding of Marxism.[2]

Marx's own view of this enigmatic circumstance may be surmised from his comment on certain French "Marxists" who (mis)understood his thought: "As for me, I am not a Marxist." It may be impossible to discover the real man or to set forth a true picture of his ideas—getting inside another's skin is a formidable task. Yet we can attempt to separate the man from the myth, Marx from his interpreters. To begin on relatively safe ground, there is little controversy about his life.

MARX'S LIFE

Karl Marx was born in 1818 in Trier, in the German Rhineland, the eldest son of a rather prosperous Jewish lawyer. While appropriately described as bourgeois and secure, the Marx family was subjected to abuse from the periodic waves of anti-Semitism that swept most of Europe. Shortly after Karl was born, his father converted to Christianity

[1]Robert L. Heilbroner, *The Worldly Philosophers* (New York: Simon & Schuster, 1964), p. 115.
[2]Michael Harrington, *The Twilight of Capitalism* (New York: Simon & Schuster, 1976), p. 59.

and, despite the elder Marx's somewhat liberal ideas, the family enjoyed a rather safe and comfortable existence.

Karl was a very intelligent, somewhat precocious student, entering the University of Bonn in 1835 at the age of 17 to pursue legal studies. With apparent enthusiasm he entered into the life of a German university student, engaging in his share of boisterous behavior. After transferring from Bonn to the University of Berlin in 1836 he began a more intensive study of law, jurisprudence, and, eventually, philosophy. It was at Berlin that the young Marx was exposed to two major influences of his early life—Hegelianism and materialism—ideas we shall explore at greater length in the following discussion. In pursuit of an academic career, Marx completed his doctorate in philosophy at Jena in 1841. However, the academic career never materialized. Marx took a job as a reporter and later editor for the newspaper *Rheinische Zeitung*. Here, perhaps, was an early indication of Marx's desire for action and change, a bent that throughout his life was to make him contemptuous of "armchair" philosophers and academicians. At any rate, his early newspaper career ended abruptly in 1843 when the Prussian government suppressed the paper for being too radical (although thoroughly capitalist). Unrepentant, Marx moved to Paris to edit a newspaper for Prussian *emigres*, only to be expelled at the request of the Prussian government in 1845.

His years in Paris proved extremely important, for it was here he met Friedrich Engels, who was to be his lifelong collaborator and friend. Engels brought to the relationship a firsthand knowledge of the barbarities of capitalism, garnered from his study of the conditions of the British working class, as well as wit, charm, and a writing style in many ways superior to that of Marx. Their collaboration was so close that for most people Marxism has since come to mean the writings of both Marx and Engels; Marx himself referred to his work as "our theory." Marx and Engels moved to Brussels where they attempted to organize workers and became associated with a group of radicals in an organization called the Communist League. It was for this group, in the fateful year of 1848, that they wrote what has become the creed of Marxism, *The Manifesto of the Communist Party*.

The year 1848 saw revolution sweeping Europe; uprisings occurred in Berlin, Paris, Rome, Vienna, and many other cities throughout the Continent. Although the publication of the *Communist Manifesto* certainly did not cause these revolutions, it did reflect the generally radical spirit of the times. Here, many people felt, was the long-predicted workers' revolution, and, while he played at best a small role in these activities, Marx was somewhat optimistic about the prospects. Without delving deeply into history, let us merely say that the great revolution substantially failed. Alfred Meyer has stated it nicely: "Altogether, few revolutions had been expected so openly and failed so miserably as that of

1848. The Marxist image of the proletariat had turned out to be a phantom."[3]

After 1848, Marx devoted more attention to the problems of developing class consciousness among members of the working class. He returned to Cologne late in 1848 and began publishing a revised version of his old newspaper, only to have it suppressed once again. Marx was banished from Prussia in July 1849. Not welcome in Paris, the safest place seemed to be England and, although only intending to remain a short time, he spent the rest of his life in exile there.

The early years in London were particularly harsh. Although he spent over a decade as a part-time correspondent for the *New York Tribune*, Marx and his family were plagued by poverty, chronic illness, and the death of several children; they became dependent largely on Engels's money to keep them from the streets. Nevertheless, with the death of his mother in 1864, and a bequest from a Communist comrade, Marx was able to climb out from under poverty, but at this point his health deteriorated. Marx spent his days laboring at the British Museum where he sketched out, in seven lengthy notebooks called *The Grundrisse*, what appears to be the outline for his grand philosophic system. Out of this *Foundations [Grundrisse] of the Critique of Political Economy* grew his most famous published work, *Das Kapital.*

Only the first volume of his *magnum opus* was published prior to Marx's death in 1883. The remaining two volumes were published posthumously under the editorship of Engels. What is important to note is that contrary to traditional opinion about *Das Kapital,* Marx's notebooks indicate that it was but one part of an even more ambitious project dealing with a multitude of topics, which concluded with a discussion of the timelessness of great art!

Even while engaged in these intellectual activities, Marx also devoted time and energy to the immediate tactical concerns of organizing the working class; in 1864 he participated in the founding of the International Workingmen's Association, and for the next seven years remained active in its General Council. Engels outlived Marx by some twelve years, interpreting and refining the basic Marxist ideas as well as continuing his engagement with international communist activities.

Even before his death, Marx's ideas were subject to a good deal of interpretation and alteration. After his death (particularly after Engels's demise in 1895) an entire band of followers sought to update, correct, or reinterpret Marxian teachings. This trend has, of course, continued to this day with *revisionists* and *orthodox Marxists,* to name but two schools, vying for the title of true interpreters. Thus we encounter

[3]Alfred G. Meyer, *Marxism: The Unity of Theory and Practice* (Ann Arbor, Mich.: Ann Arbor Paperbacks, 1963), p. 108.

another difficulty in trying to understand Marx. Is *Das Kapital* still to be considered his definitive work? Or has *The Grundrisse* changed that consideration? Are his earlier, more philosophic writings inconsistent with his later economic emphasis? Is there a young Marx and an old Marx or are his works all of one piece of cloth? The answers to these questions will significantly affect our presentation and discussion of Marx's ideas, so some of the scholarly controversy concerning the "true" Marx must be examined.

Marx's Writings and the "Real" Marx

One of the great difficulties in having a successful revolution proclaimed in your name is that the leaders of that revolution become self-appointed authoritative interpreters of your ideas. With the Bolshevik success in Russia in 1917 all future leaders of the Soviet Union found it necessary as well as expedient to interpret Marx's ideas to fit changing times. As we shall see in Chapter 6, Lenin began the process of *authoritative* interpretation and addition to Marxian thought. It was under Stalin's reign, however, that Soviet scholars began to treat Marx's works more as rigid dogma and placed greater emphasis on certain writings.

We have referred to the *Manifesto of the Communist Party* as Marxism's "creed"; for classical Marxist scholars *Das Kapital* is its "bible." The classical Marxist view tends to emphasize the concepts of (dialectical) materialism, the labor theory of value, and Marx's theory of the state as developed in *Das Kapital.* Some would say this view greatly neglects Marx's earlier writings, which are characterized as more philosophical and humanistic, emphasizing the Marxian concepts of humanity and human alienation. Coexisting with the orthodox interpretation of Marxian thought, a small group of scholars emphasized differences between a young and an old Marx, and placed greater weight on his earlier writings; Marx the humanist-philosopher as contrasted with Marx the scientist-economist.

With the decline in Stalinist orthodoxy in the latter part of the 1950s, this interpretation of his work gained increasing acceptance, particularly in Eastern Europe. In terms of Marx's writings, the young period includes his doctoral disertation, *The Difference Between the Democritean and Epicurian Philosophies of Nature, Economic and Philosophical Manuscripts*, and the *German Ideology*—all of his works up to 1844–1845 (according to other scholars this period extends to 1847–1848). All later works, beginning with the *Communist Manifesto*, are then seen to be the product of the mature scholar.

In contrast to the classical scholars' emphasis on materialism and economics, the revisionist scholars take as central the notion of alienation as developed in Marx's early works. This controversy still rages, though in a somewhat muted form today, especially since the West has turned its attention to Marx's recently translated *Grundrisse*. As discussed previously, *The Grundrisse* casts a considerable cloud over the futurity of these heated debates on the "real Marx" in that it makes clear Marx's constancy of thought on both the humanist-philosophic issues of his early work and the scientific-economic focus of the later years.

Our presentation assumes that, while undoubtedly there are differences of *emphasis* in the young and old Marx, all of his works can be seen as a whole. The concept of human alienation, while mentioned less frequently in the later works, still is a key element in Marx's analysis of the decline and fall of capitalist systems. This does not mean that the later economic arguments are to be discarded as outmoded or that dialectical materialism is not important in Marxism. If it is necessary to take a position in this ongoing debate, the attempt here is to present both sides in the belief that some sort of synthesis is possible. We have, however, been using concepts and ideas that have not been fully explored or even defined; it is time, then, to look at the main taproot of Marxism contained in the philosophy of Georg Wilhelm Friedrich Hegel.

HEGEL'S PHILOSOPHY AND POLITICS

> For it is not *what is* that makes us irascible and resentful, but the fact that it is not as it *ought to be*.[4]

The dominant philosophic system of nineteenth-century Europe was German Idealism, and its dominant philosopher was G.W.F. Hegel. Although Marx went to considerable lengths to spell out his objections to Hegel's political theory, it is important to note his acceptance of the core of Hegel's philosophy—dialectics. As Marx neatly put it a decade prior to his own death:

> The mystification which dialectic suffers in Hegel's hands, by no means prevents him from being the first to present its general form of working in a comprehensive and conscious manner. With him it is standing on its head. It must be turned right side up again, if you would discover the rational kernel within the mystical shell.[5]

Because of the significance of Hegel to Marxism, it is essential to understand Hegel on (1) dialectics, (2) labor, and (3) politics; Marx

[4]G. W. F. Hegel, *Political Writings,* trans. T. M. Knox (Oxford: Clarendon Press, 1964), p. 145.

[5]Karl Marx, in *The Marx-Engels Reader,* 2nd ed., Robert C. Tucker, ed. (New York: W. W. Norton & Company, 1978), p. xxi.

openly embraced much of the first two and vehemently rejected the third.

It was Hegel's contention that all prior philosophic thinking was incomplete, a limited form of understanding the world, due primarily to its reliance on formal Aristotelian logic. This logical form forced people to think about their environment in a particular, highly abstract fashion. One of the central rules of formal logic, known as the *principle of noncontradiction,* held that a concept could not be both itself and its opposite at one and the same time. That is, something could not be said to be both *A* and non-*A* and convey any meaning. For example, think of red litmus paper. When red litmus paper turns blue, its here-and-now existence as red litmus paper ceases, and its existence as blue litmus paper begins. Litmus paper is either red or blue; it cannot be both at the same moment in time.

The transition from childhood to adulthood is also illustrative. In order to make logically meaningful statements about this transformation, at some point during the maturation process the human creature stops being a child (possessing the properties of childhood) and becomes an adult, thereby replacing the earlier properties with those of adulthood. In these examples, however, it makes no sense, in terms of logic, to think of red litmus paper as being potentially blue litmus paper or a child containing within it the seeds of adulthood.

This type of formal logical rule led earlier philosophical thinkers to develop systems of categorization whereby objects in the real world were abstracted into categories of genus and species; something either existed or it did not; it was absurd to conceive of both "being" and "nonbeing" at the same time. Hegel believed that this formal logic resulted in a distortion of the true complexity of both the way human thinking occurred and the movement of the real world.

Hegel was influenced by the ancient Greek philosopher Heraclitus, who believed that there was no permanent reality, except the reality of change. The universe, and everything that comprised the universe, was constantly in the process of changing, altering, of transforming. Heraclitus's famous statement of not being able to step in the same river twice is illustrative of his conception of reality: The flow of the water makes it impossible to re-create precisely the same act of stepping in exactly the same river. He also believed that all things contained within them their opposites; for example, death was potential in life, being and nonbeing were part of the whole. The only reality, therefore, was the transitional one of *becoming.* Hegel accepted this Heraclitian view of the world, and he tried to discover a process by which people could come to know their constantly changing, continually evolving world.

Hence, it was not at all absurd to think of something being both itself and its opposite; indeed the key to understanding reality was in seeing that everything in existence in some sense contained within itself its opposite or its negation. Imagine yourself *looking* at a salt crystal. As you perceive it, the salt appears white in color and cubical in shape. If you placed it in your mouth it would taste pungent; salt is neither black nor sweet. The properties of white, flat, and pungent seem to exclude their opposite of black, round, and sweet. And yet it would be impossible to *describe* salt if you could not *conceive* of the opposite properties. Without an idea of nonwhite (that is, black in this context), you could not know white. Without a conception of nonflat (roundness), you could not understand what is a plane. In order to understand any particular entity, therefore, one must be able to conceive of its negation.

It is equally important to point out the role of the thinking person in this process. For Hegel, it was the thought process between the object (salt) and the subject (you) that makes the world knowable. In a sense, you, the subject, make the salt "real" when you come to know it as a combination of a white (nonblack), cubical (nonspherical), pungent (non-sweet), et cetera, substance.

Transforming Logic

What Hegel was attempting was the transformation of the very meaning of the term *logic*. Formal or traditional logic consists of a system of rules by which we test the validity of one's own thinking. We say that a conclusion is valid if it has been reached from its premises by using the rules of logic. It was Hegel's contention that this involved a distortion of the complexity of events and that humans forced reality into an artificially contrived system. Rather than a set of rules devised to test the validity of thought processes, Hegelian logic purports to be both an actual description of those processes and an accurate reflection of events in the real world. Hegelian logic, hence, is not a logic at all, but an *ontology* or an explanation of existence. By using it we can accurately describe the true nature of reality. Since the world is constantly in transformation, the method of knowing this world of flux must also be based upon this conception of motion. Traditional logic presupposes a fixed, static world where time and motion do not operate. Hegel's dialectical method presupposes movement and change. The dialectical process is thus imbedded in the world of real events and can provide the only accurate explanation of that world. It was this belief that led Hegel to assert that he had discovered the only correct way of "explaining the world."

The dialectical process contains three basic elements, or stages, of development. Although the terms *thesis, antithesis,* and *synthesis* are often associated with his name, Hegel never used this empty schema to describe dialectics. Rather, he presented it as a dynamic unity of opposites. Hegel makes this difficult notion even more complex by using the German word *aufheben* to describe this process, for it has at least three meanings: to preserve, to eliminate, and to transcend. Hegel, moreover, intends *aufheben* to mean all three at once. To illustrate, imagine a plant. It unfolds and develops itself. To Hegel, it is *not* now a bud, *then* a blossom, but a continuous movement from bud through blossom to decay. Even in the "final" stage of decay, the plant will break down into its organic components and begin the process anew, albeit in an altered form, or the plant will begin the process again in the spring.

If we change our example from a plant to a human being, an additional aspect of dialectics becomes present. That is, like any living organism, a human "unfolds" through its various stages of development, but unlike any other temporal entity, humans alone are capable of comprehending the dialectical process itself. Since people can comprehend this, they are also capable of consciously participating in it. Humans alone have the power of determining their own subjectivity in the process of becoming a human being.

Finally, dialectics is based on a theory of internal relations. For Hegel as for Marx, everything in the world is, ultimately, interrelated to every other part of the world. Nothing—neither objects nor ideas—exists independently of, or in isolation from, anything else. Although one begins to know the world by examining discrete parts of the whole, it is crucial always to be looking for the relationship to other parts. As the process continues, people gradually comprehend more and more about additional aspects and their interrelationships. Eventually, the whole is understood. At this point, the relationships among the parts, and the parts and the whole, are "complete" in that the human person has progressed beyond the abstract perspective of entities having meaning independent of other entities. At the same time, reality never can be comprehended—in a final, ultimate sense—because the Heraclitian universe is continually unfolding. Hence, our comprehension of reality must also continue to change. Our understanding of reality, then, is both complete and incomplete: Understanding is a *process* where each new discovery unfolds new relationships and a more complete comprehension of the world.

To give an example, think of this book. In order to understand the book in an appropriately dialectical fashion, it would be necessary to understand all the relationships, both past and present, involved. That would include (1) the relationships that created and produced the book, (2) the relationships that created and continue to re-create you, and (3) the relationship between you and the book. Looking at the first aspect, it is clear that the book uses words. This presupposes a society where words have common meanings and can be used to communicate ideas. The book is printed in ink and on paper. To understand this, it would be necessary to investigate every relationship involved from writing the book, setting the type (not to mention the invention by Guttenberg), to selling the book—for a profit. This further implies a market society, workers and owners, and alienation. Although this would by no means exhaust the first category, imagine the plethora of relationships involved in the second and third categories. Higher education? Tuition? Exams? The light that enables you to see the printed words? Questions—relationships—more questions—more relationships. Where would it end? It would "end" after you had discovered and understood the whole of reality. And, by a theory of internal relations, both Hegel and Marx mean nothing less.

Hegel on Labor

This conception of human self-realization is central to the Hegelian system. What Marx also accepted in Hegel is the role of labor as the principal manner in which people realize themselves and their potential as true *human* beings. Through labor humans transform themselves from a pure, isolated subject into an object. That is, by interacting with the external world, by creating things, human beings put part of themselves in the object, thus obtaining objective status. The external world becomes a part of oneself; as people alter the external world, it is simultaneously altering them. The subject-object dichotomy apparently inherent in nature is thus transcended, or mediated—the subject (self) becomes objectified (object). In Hegel's rationalistic universe, this labor process was sufficient to provide for true self-consciousness and its corresponding freedom.

In Hegel's system, history consisted of an ongoing process of the embodiment of reason in the spatiotemporal world. Hegel used a number of words to capture a sense of the totality, the interrelated wholeness of this dynamic process: "Absolute Idea," "Spirit," "God," "Universal," "Truth." Regardless of the precise term used, for present purposes it is sufficient to say that Hegel's point is that both the world and the people who act in and on this world are becoming ever more rational, ever more free; they are also continually approaching the ideal unification of all contradictions comprised in the "Absolute Idea," "God," "Spirit," and so on. For Hegel, given the frugality of the material world, the final unification could be achieved only in thought, in ideas. For Marx, however, it had to be fulfilled in the material world: The point was not only to interpret but also to change the world.

Within Hegel's broad historical process the individual human being is constantly trying to attain consciousness of self, and the process by which one achieves this is interaction with the environment. Hegel called this interaction, *labor*. When interacting, however, humans perceive the rationality which is embodied in the external world, hence becoming more rational themselves. The process of attaining self-realization is also the path toward increasing rationality. Further, human freedom for Hegel could be achieved only when *all* people are capable of achieving self-consciousness and rationality; hence, complete rationality would be the same as "total" freedom and all people would achieve complete self-consciousness. In this scheme humans are obviously limited in their ability to achieve personal freedom by the temporal period in which they exist. If a person is living during a historical period in which little rationality is present in the world, he or she is not capable of finding true freedom. The important point here is that *all* persons must be capable of achieving freedom and no one individual may possess it at the expense of others. Thus there must be human institutions, particularly political institutions, that permit all people to achieve self-consciousness and freedom.

Prior historical epochs were limited by the degree of rationality embodied in the world and by corresponding human institutions that permitted only some to achieve "freedom" (not true freedom, of course, for all must be free in order for one to be free). Hegel spoke of an Oriental stage of human history where only one person, the Oriental despot, could achieve freedom, and a Greco-Roman stage where only a few were capable of freedom since the Greeks and Romans had slaves. In Hegel's view, the rationality embodied in the world now provided for another stage in human history, the German-Christian stage, during which, for the first time, all people could achieve rationality and freedom. Hegel's description of the French Revolution, *the* watershed political event in humanity's movement toward the creation of a free and rational political system, clearly conveys his sense of excitement and expectation that this moment in history presented:

> Never since the sun had stood in the firmament and the planets revolved around him had it been perceived that man's existence centres in his head, i.e., in Thought, inspired by which he builds up the world of reality. Anaxagoras had been the first to say that *nous* [i.e., Rationality or Reason] governs the World; but not until now had man advanced to the recognition of the principle that Thought ought to govern spiritual reality. This was accordingly a glorious mental dawn. All thinking beings shared in the jubilation of this epoch. Emotions of a lofty character stirred men's minds at that time; a spiritual enthusiasm thrilled through the world, as if the reconciliation between the Divine and the Secular was now first accomplished.[6]

[6]G. W. F. Hegel, *The Philosophy of History*, trans. J. B. Sibree (New York: The Colonial Press, 1956), p. 447.

Hegel's Political Theory

Hegel's dialectical understanding of the German-Christian stage in history divides it into the three basic constitutional components of the Family, Civil Society, and the State. The *Family* stage is characterized by relationships of love and affection existing among members of the family unit; here is an entity in which all members are freely associated under communal norms—it is a cohesive unit. The family unit generates its own negation in a component called *Civil Society.* This is characterized by a more intense individualism and competition than the family stage; brother begins to compete with brother, largely in the economic realm. The cohesiveness and unity of the Family are lost and replaced by the particular wills of individuals in competition for self-development. These two stages are then mediated by the institution of the *State,* which takes the unity and general will aspect of the Family and combines it with the best of Civil Society, that is, the individual appropriation of the environment. We thus have a society that united both particular and general will, the individual and the society, humans with their fellow humans. This reconciliation in Hegel's ideal state is accomplished by the interaction of legally recognized classes called *estates.*

The estates were the peasantry (similar to the characterization of the Family); the middle class, comprised of burghers and businesspeople (reflecting the characteristics of Civil Society); and a well-educated, duty-bound bureaucracy. Individuals would have their interests represented through their estate association. Economic equality, universal education, and an open estate system with both upward and downward mobility were further guarantees of freedom and rationality. So well run and harmonious would Hegel's pluralist state be that the role of its sovereign would be to "dot the i's and cross the t's."

In our earlier discussion of Hegel, we saw that he believed the world was becoming increasingly endowed with the rationality of the Absolute Idea, or Spirit, or God. Hegel's system, then, is *teleological.* That is, it is movement upward toward some goal. However, it is important to note that for Hegel, there is *no permanent, final goal:* As humans reach any particular level of rationality, the never-ending dialectical process will continue to unfold, providing people with the opportunity of achieving an even greater degree of rationality, freedom, and self-realization.

CRITICS OF HEGEL: FEUERBACH AND MARX

This notion of a rationally *becoming* universe had found many critics by the time Karl Marx came to study Hegel's ideas. Notable among those critics was Ludwig Feuerbach, whose criticisms of Hegel's abstractions were thoroughly assimilated by the young Marx, and whose ideas eventually led Marx to reject Hegelian idealism for something Western scholars have called *dialectical materialism.*

Feuerbach contended that the entire Hegelian system was an unconscious attempt to divert human attention from the real problems of existence. The notion of a rational "Absolute Idea" (or "God," or any of the other terms noted above) gradually manifesting itself in history was seen by Feuerbach as nothing more than the invention of an abstract entity, which was then endowed with all of the attributes missing from real human existence. What people found lacking in their lives was made part of something eternal, an attribute of the Absolute Idea. The difficulty with this form of reasoning was that it turned attention away from human beings and their predicament, and it made this highly abstract Absolute Idea the true subject of history. Humans were reduced to small elements in the overall pattern of things, where to Feuerbach they were actually the central figure in all history. The entire Hegelian system focused on such abstractions and diverted attention from the true human condition. After all, if one can find intellectual satisfaction in such a fashion why worry about the insufficiencies of everyday life? Absolute Idea, rationality, and freedom became, to use Marx's word, "opiates," abstract ideas that falsely satisfy without attempting to solve problems.

Marx thoroughly accepted this criticism of Hegel and was determined to apply Feuerbach's critical insight to the realms of politics and economics. Recall that we spoke of Hegel's triad of Family, Civil Society, and the State, which mediated the contradictions of the prior stages. It was Marx's contention that Hegel's notion of the State was exactly the same sort of abstract solution to real human problems as Feuerbach had found in Hegel's religious teaching. Civil Society in Hegel was the antipode of the cohesive Family unit in that it permitted individuals to appropriate freely objects in the environment. This process would inevitably lead to conflicts among individuals desiring similar things and eventually, if unchecked, to much *inequality.*

The major source of this inequality, recognized as such by Hegel himself, was to be found in *private property.* Private property, while an essential part of human self-development in that it permitted people to become closer to the environment, would lead to inequality because some individuals would be able to accumulate more than others. Hegel realized all this and declared that the individual, ego-dominated stage of Civil Society must be transcended in an ethical entity called the State, which would solve this inequality and provide for a truly cohesive human community. The State would be a neutral agent that would only express the general will of the entire state; it would be the personification of the will of all the members of the community.

In the eyes of Karl Marx, the Hegelian State was but another example of the insufficiencies of this abstract system. The State was a projection of all of the problems of Civil Society and provided only an intellectual solution, leaving untouched the real-world problem of inequality and lack of freedom. Further, anyone who took a clear look at the actions of existing states could readily see that they were anything but the neutral agents that Hegel envisioned. Indeed, a more appropriate description of state action would be that it served to perpetuate and enhance the existing inequalities. For these reasons Marx demanded a rejection of abstract philosophizing à la Hegel and a concentration on the real-world forces that produce the human condition. People must no longer be concerned with abstract *explanation* of the world; they must attempt to *change* it.

Rejecting Hegel's political theory and Hegel's overemphasis on ideas, Marx's concern turned to the real determining factor in all human experience; that is, he abandoned abstract philosophy to study economics. Hegel's dialectical process is thus no longer an abstract rational process, but is found to be embedded in the material world of economics and politics. Dialectics remain, but as a materialistic dialectical process, with human beings the true subjects of history. It is now time to return to the writings of Marx to uncover his view of humanity, capitalism, and, of course, communism.

Marx on the Human Condition

As individuals express their life, so they are. What they are, therefore, coincides with their production, both with *what* they produce and with *how* they produce.[7]

Marx and Engels lived and wrote during the period of European history generally called the Industrial Revolution. With the possible exception of Russia, all major European countries during the latter part of the eighteenth and throughout the nineteenth century experienced a rapid growth of industrial production, which involved the introduction of machinery, establishment of factories, and the development of a specialization of labor. This period of industrialization is properly called a revolution in that it resulted in profound changes in the values and way of life of vast numbers of people.

The artisan who formerly produced objects by hand, to be consumed or exchanged, now toiled on a production line in a factory, placing bolts in a complex piece of machinery. The introduction of mass production techniques forced individuals to become far more specialized

[7]*Marx-Engels Reader*, p. 150.

in their work and to become part of a vast production process rather than fabricators of entire objects. Individuals who once fashioned a pair of fine shoes now found themselves operating a machine that stamped out the soles for thousands of shoes, to be assembled later by other workers in the factory. There is little doubt that the Industrial Revolution produced tremendous hardships for members of the working class. History books are full of examples: twelve- and fifteen-hour workdays, women and children forced to labor under intolerable conditions, disease unchecked, and poverty everywhere. Even today, one of the best descriptions of the excesses of the Industrial Revolution is to be found in Friedrich Engels's *Condition of the Working Class in England in 1844,* an early pamphlet that greatly impressed Karl Marx.

Given these deplorable conditions it is easy to see how sensitive and sensible people could condemn the results of industrialization and the capitalist economic system that brought them about. Marx and Engels were by no means alone in their violent reaction to these conditions. Such notable figures in the history of political philosophy as Thomas Jefferson, Jeremy Bentham, and James and John Stuart Mill were openly critical of the conditions of the laboring poor. Yet, where others fought for reform within the capitalist system and sought to bring about more humane working conditions, Karl Marx believed that such conditions were an inevitable part of capitalism. The condition of the working class led Marx to the conclusion that the entire capitalist system was outdated and must be radically changed. Marx's indictment of capitalism, while undoubtedly inspired to some extent by the human suffering it produced, is far more profound. It was his contention that capitalism as an economic system denied people their own humanity—it literally dehumanized people. We can understand such a conclusion only by examining the Marxian conception of the unique role that laboring plays in human development.

Labor: Alienated Versus Unalienated

Laboring, according to Marx, is not merely a process whereby humans satisfy needs; rather, it is their existential activity. It is how people define themselves. It is the way in which they achieve their true nature. It is the species-specific characteristic of humanity. People are seen as actors capable of altering nature for their own human uses and, of course, are altered by it as in the dialectical analysis. The individual confronts the external world, enters it, and alters it by mixing with it. In this laboring process, the individual (subject) comes to realize what he or she is and to appreciate his or her potential as actor by discovering what one is not, that is, the external world, the "object." Thus, humans in the process of mixing themselves with the environment can be said to come to know, and to be themselves:

But man is not merely a natural being; he is a *human* natural being. That is to say, he is a being for himself. Therefore he is a *species being,* and has to confirm and manifest himself as such both in his being and in his knowing.[8]

What Marx argued was that humans, whether they will it or not, actively participate in their own creation. Marx viewed people as beings comprised of a variety of "tendencies and abilities," who have certain "powers and needs." When they labor (a human need), they interact with the external world (nature); they exercise and develop their tendencies, abilities, and powers. The more they interact with nature the more refined their capacities and powers may become. Marx wrote: "That man's physical and spiritual life is linked to nature means simply that nature is linked to itself, for man is a part of nature."[9]

People are also unique creatures, what Marx termed the *species being,* in that they pass along their development to both the rest of society and to the entire species. In a sense, then, as one develops (the particular) so too may all people develop (the universal). Therefore, as people learn to understand and to interact with the world, they alter both the world and themselves; and, as they exercise and develop their unique human capacities, they help refine them for all future members of the species. As Marx put it:

> For not only the five senses but also the so-called mental senses—the practical senses (will, love, etc.)—in a word, *human* sense—the humanness of the senses—comes to be by virtue of its object, by virtue of *humanized* nature. The *forming* of the five senses is a labour of the entire history of the world down to the present.[10]

Marx used the term *alienated* to describe the condition of human beings existing under a capitalist economic system. This word has become all too common in modern usage—we speak of alienated youth, voters, workers, artists, using the term to indicate some sort of vaguely perceived disenchantment with one's lot. Indeed, alienation can be and has been used to describe almost anything. For Marx, however, it had a specific meaning. As we have seen, the act of laboring is the process by which human beings attain self-realization, and the product of their labor is an integral part of that process. The sculptor who fashions a statue from a formless block of stone has endowed that stone with part of his or her person. Something of that person is there in the statue. The hallmark of a capitalist economic system is that one class of individuals (capitalists) possess a monopoly of the means used to produce things;

[8]Ibid., p. 116.
[9]Ibid., p. 75.
[10]Ibid., p. 89.

that is, they own the machines and capital necessary for production. Under such circumstances the noncapitalists (the proletariat or workers) are forced—in order to survive—to sell their labor power—the only resources they possess—to the capitalists so that they can engage in productive relations. They then work for the capitalist to produce objects that the capitalist sells for profit and pays to workers a wage for their work. The relationship between capitalist and workers is necessarily exploitive.

As we shall see more fully in the later discussion of capitalist economics, the only way a capitalist can make a profit, that is, produce capital, is by exploiting the labor force. Thus, by laboring for the capitalist workers give the capitalist additional power to be used against them and their fellow workers. Under the capitalist system, then, the product of labor (which, remember, is the only source of human development) is taken away from its fabricator (maker) and used to exploit that person because part of the profit is reinvested in the production process in order to extract ever-increasing amounts of surplus labor from the workers. Part of the worker's own being, embodied in the product, is now used against the worker. Instead of recognizing the object of creation as a part of a process of self-development, the worker sees it as an alien object, something that has become independent of its maker. The relationship between workers and the product of their labor is one of the fourfold aspects of alienation. The other three are the act of production itself, the relations of production among persons, and the relationship of people to their essence as the species being.

In a very real way, part of the laborer's self is being taken away and used to hurt that person. The product of one's creative power becomes a weapon in alien hands. Thus Marx concludes that humans are irrevocably alienated from themselves under a capitalist economic system. Further, under capitalism that joyous creative act of laboring, which is a uniquely human gift, becomes an activity to be dreaded. The act of laboring under capitalism increasingly becomes simplified and routinized so that mental fatigue gradually augments physical exhaustion. The labor process itself is alienating. Labor under capitalism becomes forced labor; time spent away from the job is considered "free time" when it should be just the other way around.

> As a result, therefore, man (the worker) no longer feels himself to be freely active in any but his animal functions—eating, drinking, procreating, or at most in his dwelling and in dressing-up, etc.; and in his human functions he no longer feels himself to be anything but an animal. What is animal becomes human and what is human becomes animal.[11]

[11]Ibid., p. 74.

Under capitalism, an individual's humanizing activity, that which makes a person free, becomes the negation of humanity: It is wage-slave labor.

Capitalism produces still a third and fourth dimension of alienation, which completes the process of negating a truly human existence. People are not only alienated from themselves, but also from their fellow human beings. This is because capitalism turns all human relationships into dollars and cents terms. People treat each other as commodities, as objects to be used and manipulated; their labor becomes something to be bought and sold. Under such a system they are related to one another only through the commodities they exchange; they treat each other as things, not as fellow humans. Human beings are forced into constant competition with one another; the things they produce come to take on an objective status and prevent human interaction.

Even members of the exploiting class (capitalists) are not free because of the cutthroat competition among capitalists, and because of the wage-slave status of the proletariat. Commodities become symbols and attain a status different from their production and use. Larger and more flashy cars, "keeping up with the Joneses," "clothes are the mark of the person"—these are the more simple modern examples of Marx's meaning. One relates to "Jones" not as a human being but as a competitor in the accumulation of status-laden products; one looks at the clothes of a person but not at the person. So all-inclusive is the apparent power of commodities of people and of things, that men and women are reduced from multitalented individuals with numerous mental and physical senses to possessive creatures with the sole sense of "having." "In place of *all* these physical and mental senses there has therefore come the sheer estrangement of *all* these senses—the sense of *having*,"[12] Marx wrote.

Alienation as Estrangement

The final aspect of alienation is the estrangement of humans from their essence as the species being. Unlike animals that "produce" from instinct for immediate survival, humans can produce independently of instinct, in freedom. In addition, humans can produce the whole of nature (the human subject is the universal), and does so according to the laws of beauty, which are also a human creation. Humans, moreover, treat themselves as "The actual, living species."[13] As the individual refines and develops, so too does the species; as the species changes and adapts, so too the individual. Humans are *social individuals.* And yet, as Marx acutely pointed out, under capitalism all of these advantages of

[12]Ibid., p. 87.
[13]Ibid., p. 75.

humans over animals are turned into disadvantages: Only humans can be alienated from their essence; only humans can help produce their own estrangement, for their alienation is, ultimately, a condition of *self-alienation.*

Marx, in an extended and rarely published passage on James Mill— taken from the notebooks he kept while working on his *Economic and Philosophic Manuscripts*—presented what can be taken as the obverse of his description of alienation contained in the *Manuscripts.* So important is this account of *un*alienated labor, that we quote the passage at length.

> Supposing that we had produced in a human manner; each of us would in his production have doubly affirmed himself and his fellow men. I would have: (1) objectified in my production my individuality and its peculiarity and thus both in my activity enjoyed an individual expression of my life and also in looking at the object have had the individual pleasure of realizing that my personality was objective, visible to the senses and thus a power raised beyond all doubt. (2) In your enjoyment or use of my product I would have had the direct enjoyment of realizing that I had both satisfied a human need by my work and also objectified the human essence and therefore fashioned for another human being the object that met his need. (3) I would have been for you the mediator between you and the species and thus been acknowledged and felt by you as a completion of your own essence and a necessary part of yourself and have thus realized that I am confirmed both in your thought and in your love. (4) In my expression of my life I would have fashioned your expression of your life, and thus in my own activity have realized my own essence, my human, my communal essence.[14]

Emphasizing both the essentiality and the communality of free, human labor, Marx closed this discussion with these words: "In that case our products would be like so many mirrors, out of which our essence shone. Thus, in this relationship what occurred on my side would also occur on yours . . . My work would be a free expression of my life, and therefore a free enjoyment of my life."[15]

Marx drew a picture of capitalist society where people are prevented from becoming human—alienation is all encompassing. Every member of society is drawn into the never-ending web of alienation. Given the Marxian definition of freedom, no single class can ever attain that status: All must be free before any one can be. Having said all this, it must now be noted that in Marx's eyes the capitalist system is, in a limited sense, a good thing. It is an essential phase of an overall historical process that will eventually result in a society where all people can realize their true potential. Capitalism is the penultimate stage in the historical

[14]Karl Marx, in *Karl Marx: Selected Writings*, David McLellan, ed. (Oxford: Oxford University Press, 1977), pp. 121–22.
[15]Ibid.

progression from a condition of impotence and limitation to one of power and freedom. In order to understand such statements, we must now explore Marx's view of this historical process and examine the role of dialectical materialism in his thinking.

HISTORY AND THE DEVELOPMENT OF CAPITALISM

Where Hegel sought to use the rationalistic Absolute Idea as the determining force in the historical process, Marx saw the central element to be ownership of the means of production and distribution of goods. He outlined five basic stages in human history: primitive community (primitive communism), slavery, feudalism, capitalism, and socialism. In each stage the determining factor is the control of the productive forces within the society, and when those means of production are owned by a particular group within the society, they will exploit some other segment of the population. Thus, slavery, feudalism, and capitalism are necessarily oppressive societies, for they ensure that one group will be able to control the means of production, thereby forcing the remaining individuals in the society to sell their labor in order to continue to exist.

In each instance there are two principal classes that exist in opposition to one another: under slavery it is the masters versus the slaves, under feudalism the lords against the serfs, and under capitalism it is the capitalists against the workers. Both the primitive community and socialism are nonexploitive in that there is community control of the means of production and therefore no particular group can maximize its interests at the expense of others. Nevertheless, in the former epoch humans are not yet free in that they are still subject to the domination of nature; in the latter epoch due to the advance of science, technology, and productive forces, humans are finally free from both human and natural exploitation.

Marx was far too sophisticated to believe that this two-class analysis (oppressors versus oppressed) was a completely accurate description of the real world at any point in history. In all real-world situations there will be a mixture of different classes. Under capitalism there will still be groups within the society whose relationship is primarily feudal, and even master-slave, but the prevailing relationship in the society can be appropriately characterized in terms of the worker versus the capitalist. Without going into a detailed description of the development of each of these conditions, let us concentrate, as Marx did, on the situation under the capitalist mode (system) of production.

Marx was one of the earliest social scientists to place great weight on the conditioning effect that economics has on all phases of human activity. While today it is commonplace to assert that human thought and action are greatly conditioned by upbringing, socioeconomic status, and the values of a particular culture, in Marx's time the general tendency was to place far greater weight on the effect of ideas in shaping human behavior. This is especially evident in the thought of Hegel where ideas and rationality primarily determine the existence of the world. To Marx the fundamental—but not sole—conditioning factor in human action is essentially economic.

The class structure of a society is a direct reflection of its distribution of wealth, which is a result of past and present ownership of the means of production. Under the three antagonistic modes of ownership of the means of production (slavery, feudalism, and capitalism), all institutions, values, morality, and religion are conditioned, if not determined, by the class structure. These institutions and values occur as the result of the ruling class's desire for continued domination, and nothing more. Under capitalism, for example, the state, far from being the neutral agency seen by Hegel, is a device used by the capitalist class to further its own interests. Religion is the "opiate of the masses" in that it is designed to provide comforting rationalizations for the oppressed classes so that they will become resigned to their lot. These institutions, part of what can be called the *superstructure,* are but reflections of the underlying *substructure* of economic relationships. Under capitalism, then, all morality is capitalist morality, religion is bourgeois religion, and the state is nothing more than an instrument of class oppression. It is in this context that Marx and Engels would later speak of the "withering away of the state" in a communist society, for the need for a state will cease to exist once the class antagonisms, which the state perpetuates, are abolished.

There remains some ambiguity as to the precise relationship between the substructure and the superstructure in Marxian thought. At times Marx and Engels speak as though the relationship is causal in nature; that is, the substructure can only affect the superstructure and not vice versa. This would deny the possibility, for example, of the political system in a capitalist country materially altering the process of allocating resources within the society. This position is commonly referred to as that of the "vulgar Marxist."

At other points Marx and Engels seemed to be saying that, while the economic substructure is the major determinant in all relationships, there is at least some interaction between substructure and superstructure and that superstructural institutions can alter the economic base.

In an attempt to clarify this relationship, Engels noted:

> According to the materialist conception of history, the *ultimately* determining element in history is the production and reproduction of real life. More than this neither Marx nor I have ever asserted. Hence if somebody

twists this into saying that the economic element is the *only* determining one, he transforms that proposition into a meaningless, abstract, senseless phrase.[16]

On other occasions, Engels used the word *codetermined* to emphasize the interdependent nature of the relationship. This notion is captured by Marx in his third thesis on Feuerbach:

> The materialist doctrine that men are products of circumstances and upbringing, and that, therefore, changed men are products of other circumstances and changed upbringing, forgets that it is men who change circumstances and that it is essential to educate the educator himself. Hence, this doctrine necessarily arrives at dividing society into two parts, one of which is superior to society.
>
> The coincidence of the changing of circumstances and of human activity can be conceived and rationally understood only as revolutionising practice.[17]

Although it appears from these sources that the relationships are clearly codetermined, for our purposes it is sufficient to emphasize the tremendous weight Marx placed on economic factors as determinants of all human activity. Many people assert that Marx's major contribution to social science was his recognition of this preponderant role that economic matters play in human affairs. However, it makes sense to follow Engels on this point:

> Marx and I are ourselves partly to blame for the fact that the younger people sometimes lay more stress on the economic side than is due to it. We had to emphasize the main principle vis-à-vis our adversaries, who denied it, and we had not always the time, the place or the opportunity to allow the other elements involved in the interaction to come into their rights.[18]

The relationship between the forces of production and the relations of production has also been the source of considerable confusion in Marx. The mode, or system, of production is the basis of every society since it determines how that society will produce the material needs of life. Marx discovered four historic modes: Asiatic (primitive communist, tribal societies), ancient (slave societies of Egypt, Greece, Rome), feudal, and capitalist. Each of these systems implies a different relationship of human dependence or independence, a relationship of domination and subordination. Each mode consists of particular *forces of production* and *relations of production*. The *relations* of production are the extratechnical

[16]*Marx-Engels Reader*, p. 760.
[17]Ibid., p. 144.
[18]Ibid., p. 762.

relationships between people in the production process, for example, the particular division of labor in society (hunters versus gatherers, or slaves versus masters), or the means of exchange (barter or money). The *relations* of production *correspond*, Marx said, to a definite stage in the development of the forces of production.

The *forces* of production are comprised of the techniques (including labor skill), technology (including tools), and the natural resources made workable by them. Another way of explaining this is that the forces of production consist of the matter and energy, both human and natural, which people have and know how to use. By using the word *correspond*, Marx again made clear the interrelatedness of the relationship between the forces and the relations of production. Marx offered no simple, unicausal explanation of history. Historical change takes place when the *forces* of production are impeded by the *relations* of production. The latter become "fetters" on the former. When this develops, class antagonisms crystalize, producing a revolution into a new mode of production. As capitalism continues to overproduce due to technological innovation, there develops a tendency for both opulence (in terms of commodities) and impoverishment (workers without the money to buy goods because the workers have been rendered superfluous). At this point, change occurs.

One final point. Although the *mode* of production is the base of Marx's analysis, and although it is comprised of both the *forces* and the *relations* of production, it must be remembered that both are creations of human beings.

The Progress of Humanity

Although Marx substantially altered Hegel's dialectical process by embedding it in the material world, he did not forsake the general notion of gradual progress in world history. Thus, each of the stages in history mentioned earlier is appropriately seen as part of a dialectical process moving toward the goal of a communist society. In another more important sense these societal stages can be viewed as part of the process of humans achieving greater and greater control over their environment. We have seen that the fundamental fact of human development is people's ability to mix themselves with the environment, to interact with it, and to change it. Indeed, it is not inappropriate to view Marx's conception of human development as involving an ever-increasing control over the natural world.

Humanity moves through varying historical stages, from a condition of scarcity to one of abundance; from a state of lack of control to one of power. Herein we can see the major difficulty Marx envisioned in his nonantagonistic stage of the primitive community. While it was a classless society in that the means of production (however primitive) were possessed by all, individuals could not labor freely because they were totally preoccupied with satisfying the basic needs of subsistence. Humans had not achieved sufficient control over their environment to enable them to develop their nature without being constrained by the simple need to survive.

If the laborer under capitalism can be said to be forced to work because of the exploitive class structure, in the primitive community human beings were in a similar sense forced to labor for their very existence. In the primitive community, despite its lack of class antagonisms, people could not achieve true self-consciousness or freedom because they were hampered by the natural environment. The dialectical process thus moved on to other stages whereby humans achieve the potential of greater and greater control over their lives. It is for this reason that the capitalist stage is particularly important and the capitalist or bourgeois class is crucial for eventual human freedom. Capitalism was particularly effective in unleashing individual human wills to exploit the environment for their own personal benefit. In so doing it provided the technology that would permit future generations to achieve a new society.

It is important to remember, however, that this discussion of the liberating tendencies of technology is, in many ways, relegated to the future, to potential freedom, since under capitalism the same technology that can liberate is being used to exploit the workers even more.

Marx's View of the Bourgeois Class

There is little doubt that Marx had tremendous admiration for the bourgeois class even while he was predicting its eventual overthrow. Under the capitalist mode of production and its corresponding ideology of liberalism, the bourgeoisie had succeeded in throwing off most of the values of traditional cultures and had further developed a technological base hitherto unknown in human history. Although this technology was based in the end on the exploitation of others (proletarians), this does not alter the fact that the capitalist system provided people with the tools at last to control their environment. Expressing sentiments worthy of a John Locke or an Adam Smith, Marx observed:

> The bourgeoisie, during its rule of scarce one hundred years, has created more massive and more colossal productive forces than have all preceding generations together. Subjugation of Nature's forces to man, machinery, application of chemistry to industry and agriculture, steam-navigation, railways, electric telegraphs, clearing of whole continents for cultivation, canalisation of rivers, whole populations conjured out of the ground—

what earlier century had even a presentiment that such productive forces slumbered in the lap of social labour?[19]

Using England as his model, Marx believed that eventually capitalism would spread throughout the world and provide the economic preconditions for a truly human existence. The internal dynamics of the system itself would force it to gradually spread around the world in search of new markets and new sources of raw materials. In doing this the capitalist system would destroy all of the traditional values and modes and provide the preconditions for a new society for all people. Yet, by unleashing individual egos in cutthroat competition and exploitation (the very thing which made it so successful), capitalism ensured its own demise. As Marx stated, "What the bourgeoisie, therefore, produces, above all, is its own grave-diggers."[20]

In pitting person against person in economic competition, capitalism denies the fundamental equality of all humans, making some superior to others while prohibiting vast numbers of others from achieving their true nature. Capitalism must therefore be transcended in a pure communist stage, which will utilize the technological expertise of the capitalist epoch to provide a "postscarcity" economic situation. Here humans for the first time in history will engage in the free conscious activity of labor for its own sake. No longer will it be necessary for human beings to struggle at a mere subsistence level as was the case in the primitive community. No longer will they be buffeted about by the forces of nature, for they now can control these forces. The inequalities and sufferings that capitalism produced will vanish once the ownership of the means of production is given to the entire community. Human relationships will once again be harmonious as people consciously move beyond their "prehistoric" forms of social organization. They will freely interact with the environment and each other in harmonious accord.

Such is the broad outline of the Marxian vision of a communist society. We shall speak at greater length of this at another point, but first it is essential to describe in detail Marx's analysis of the contradictions inherent within capitalist society, contradictions which lead to its eventual downfall.

THE CAPITALIST ECONOMIC SYSTEM: ITS DECLINE AND FALL

We have seen how the young Marx described the dehumanizing and alienating effects of a capitalist economic system. The system itself inevitably produces a vast class of nonhuman wage slaves. This philo-

[19]Ibid., p. 477.
[20]Ibid., p. 483.

sophical analysis is by no means Marx's only method of attacking capitalism; after all, anyone who asserts that the economic substructure of any society is the prime determining factor in its development must deal at length with the economic structure of that system. Marx's analysis of the decline and fall of capitalism is to be found primarily in *Das Kapital*, a work both brilliant and boring, insightful and repetitious.

The two key concepts in Marxian economics, concepts which are the building blocks for his entire analysis, are the *labor theory of value* and the *theory of surplus value*. Given what we know of Marx's regard for humans as "laboring animals," it is not surprising that he, along with most of the classical economists (Adam Smith, David Ricardo), regarded the amount of human labor involved in producing an object to be the sole source of any value that product might have. Simply, the quantity of labor *socially necessary* to produce any object determines its exchange value. By "socially necessary," Marx means the quantity of labor necessary to produce the object given the average level of labor productivity and skills existing in a country at a specific historic time. In addition, the word "quantity" incorporates within it the difference between skilled and unskilled labor: An hour of labor by a skilled worker is considered as compound labor to be measured as a multiple of an hour of unskilled labor; the coefficient of multiplication cannot be arbitrary but rather is based on the cost of acquiring the given skill.

Thus, if it takes three hours of human labor to produce a pair of shoes, and labor is priced at one dollar an hour, the shoes have a true value of three dollars; if a suit takes six hours to produce, it will be valued at six dollars. In a purely competitive capitalist system, the market value of a product is determined by the amount of human labor it took to produce it. Marx was by no means unaware of the effect of supply and demand in establishing the market price of an object, but he asserted that in the long run, for the capitalist system as a whole, that price is ultimately reducible to the true value of the product, that is, the amount of human labor in it.

Furthermore, the labor involved in a product need not be merely the direct physical labor of an individual. It can be indirect labor, such as conceiving of a more efficient design for the product or a better way of packaging it. Despite these qualifications, all value is in the end reduced to what Marx called "simple average labor," which, it seems, is somehow determined by convention.

The labor theory of value was an attempt by economists to find some common element that would provide a measure of value for products that was more objective than the fluctuations of supply and demand. The demand for a particular product is, after all, a subjective thing, subject to the taste and preferences of the individual. While most non-Marxian economists today would declare that the labor theory of value is at best an awkward way of explaining capitalist economics, Marx did succeed in using it to point out some basic facts about capitalism. Grounded in the labor theory of value, Marx's analysis led him to an amazingly acute understanding of the dynamics of capitalism and to a host of farsighted predictions.

If everything is ultimately reducible to the amount of labor necessary to produce it, and the prices of objects in the long run reflect the amount of labor in the object, Marx then asked where the capitalist's profit came from. If the price of a product is equal to its actual value, there can be no such thing as profit, at least for the system as a whole. Granted, one individual capitalist might benefit from a temporary variation between the actual value of a product and its current market price, but this is not sufficient to explain the existence of profit in the entire capitalist system. The only explanation of profit in capitalism is to be found in the monopoly of the means of production that the capitalists possess. Because they control the means of production the capitalists can force the working class to produce a profit for them.

The analysis goes like this. Labor power, like anything else, has a certain exchange value, defined in terms of the amount of labor necessary to sustain and reproduce it. The true value of an individual laborer, since he or she too is a commodity, can be seen as the amount of human labor necessary to keep that worker alive and to reproduce the worker; hence, to support a family. If it takes five hours of human labor to produce the goods necessary to keep one laborer alive (food, clothing, and so forth), then the value of the laborer is five. This is what Marx called *necessary labor*, the amount of labor time necessary to sustain one worker. Since capitalism needs an ever new supply of workers, the role of the family is to produce workers. As real wages decrease due to competition and technological innovation, the nuclear family, as the core of the *reproduction* process, must find additional sources of wages to survive. Similarly, as the rate of profit falls, the capitalist must find additional sources of workers to exploit. As if providentially planned by some invisible hand, the needs of the family and the capitalist are met as women are forced into the market to help keep their families afloat and to provide another source of exploitation for the capitalist.

The Surplus Value of Labor

Why do the workers tolerate this condition? How does it develop? Because the capitalist class possesses a monopoly of the means of production it can force the workers to labor longer than is necessary for their own existence as the price extracted for using the means of production. For example, let us say the laborer signs a contract with the capitalist to work ten hours a day; five of these ten hours are involved in necessary labor. The rest of the time is spent, in effect, working to produce a profit for the capitalist because the worker receives wages only for his necessary labor. The worker is producing five hours of extra value for the capitalist, five hours of *surplus labor,* which is the source of the capitalist's profit. Workers have no choice but to do this. If they refuse to work for the capitalist this additional period of time they have no livelihood, for the means of production are controlled by the capitalist class.

Surplus value, the difference between the actual value produced by a worker in a laboring day and the worker's necessary labor, is the source of profit in a capitalist system. It is money extracted from the worker solely by virtue of the fact that the capitalist class—backed by the power of the state—can force the worker either to accept this inherently exploitative situation or fail to survive. To be sure, the worker can choose by whom he or she will be exploited, but workers cannot choose to be unexploited. Small wonder that Marx declared all labor under capitalism to be forced labor!

The most pervasive aspect of capitalism is its emphasis on competition. Members of the bourgeois class are in constant competition with one another to maximize profit. We have seen how the only means of acquiring profit is through the exploitation of the laborer; the capitalist, then, increases profits by driving workers harder and harder, still paying them a subsistence wage. If we can say that the hallmark of capitalism is the acquisition of profit and capital by private individuals, it is now evident why Marx saw this type of system as necessarily exploitative. If the laboring class were to receive the true value in wages for their labor, capitalism would literally cease to exist for there could then be no private profit. Capitalism must have a class of "wage slaves" in order to exist! One cannot overemphasize the necessity of constant competition that capitalism generates. Individual capitalists are constantly seeking ways in which they can increase profits, and this leads them to behave in ways that will eventually ensure the demise of the entire system.

Increasing Profits at Worker Expense

Let us assume we have a capitalist operating within one industry producing a single product. While the price that product can command on the open market may fluctuate slightly from day to day, the long-range price is determined on an industrywide basis. Our individual capitalist then can attempt to increase his or her profit margin by driving workers harder to achieve greater productivity from them during the time they are at work. Marx gives several examples of how this can be done, including such things as shortening the time allowed for eating and rest periods. In doing this our capitalist makes his or her position with respect to the whole industry more attractive, producing a greater number of products at the industrywide price, thereby increasing profits. Or our capitalist can lower the price of his or her products and attempt to undersell competitors, thus capturing a larger share of the market.

Although our hard-driving capitalist now seems to be in a favorable position vis-à-vis the rest of the industry, it is really only a temporary solution. Initially, by the very nature of capitalist economics the other firms in the industry will respond to this initiative by driving their workers equally hard thereby reducing our capitalist's competitive advantage. In effect, the industrywide price is lowered so that our capitalist is no longer able to produce at a lower than industry cost.

Moreover, this process of extracting more and more from one's laborers has physical limitations; a person can be driven just so far. Still, the internal dynamics of capitalism demand that our owner increase profits so our capitalist looks for other means of doing so. This is accomplished through the introduction of labor-saving devices (machines), which make it possible to produce more products than the industrywide norm. Once, again, our capitalist is in a favorable position with respect to the industry as a whole.

In addition, insofar as machinery is capable of performing the more complex tasks involved in the production process, the capitalist can reduce the number of people employed, particularly skilled workers. The skilled technician who was essential before the advent of the machine can now be replaced by an unskilled laborer or even by women and children. As the necessary labor required for sustenance is based upon the family unit as a whole, the wages paid to such workers can be further reduced, thus adding even more to the owner's profit. A final consequence is that work becomes increasingly boring and repetitious and the laborer loses all interest in what he or she is doing; the worker becomes a mere appendage of the machine he or she operates.

Although the introduction of machinery does give the innovating capitalist a temporary advantage with respect to the rest of the industry, eventually the same forces we noted earlier will come into play and negate that advantage. In order to remain competitive other owners will have to follow the lead and replace their workers with machines, thus ensuring the increasing mechanization of the industry and a growing pool of unemployed laborers. While machines may well bring increased profit to the innovating capitalist (and even this is not certain because of the high costs of invention), it is only a temporary thing, for competition will inevitably drive the industry-wide price downward.

There are, however, further consequences for the industry as a whole that result from increasing mechanization. Machinery (Marx called it *constant capital*), like any other product, has a value equal to the amount of human labor necessary to produce it. A machine is appropriately seen as stored-up human labor and is capable of producing only as much value as human labor put into it. The "life" of a piece of machinery can be seen as a gradual process of spinning out the amount of labor in it. A machine cannot be exploited in the same way workers (*variable capital*) can. Further, the use of machines produces a great flood of products on the market and there is no one to buy them. As more and more machines are introduced, the number of unemployed workers greatly increases and even those who have jobs find their wages at the subsistence level. Thus they are unable to consume the machine-produced products. The system experiences ever more serious crises of overproduction and begins a frantic worldwide search for new markets for its products.

In addition, the ever-increasing cost of machinery makes the competitive situation of many capitalists untenable. Because of the dramatically increasing costs of constant capital, many of the smaller capitalists are simply unable to continue the struggle; they are bought out by the more affluent ones. There is an ever-increasing concentration of capital in fewer and fewer hands, and the marginal capitalists are forced into the ranks of the proletariat. Here is a second major Marxian prediction of capitalist development: it will tend inevitably toward *monopoly.*

Finally, the system has succeeded in producing a vast army of unemployed workers who are living barely at the subsistence level and have little or no hope for a better future (Marx's *Law of Increasing Misery*). It is this vast, alienated, proletarian class which is to provide the negation of the capitalist system; capitalism has sown the seeds of its own destruction. Metaphorically, Marx captured the dynamics of this process:

> Let us sum up: *The more productive capital grows, the more the division of labour and the application of machinery expands. The more the division of labour and the application of machinery expands, the more competition among the workers expands and the more their wages contract.*
>
> In addition, the working class gains recruits from the *higher strata of society* also; a mass of petty industrialists and small rentiers are hurled down into its ranks and have nothing better to do than urgently stretch out their arms alongside those of the workers. Thus the forest of uplifted arms demanding work becomes ever thicker, while the arms themselves become ever thinner.[21]

Thus, the condition of the individual continually deteriorates while the number of people suffering continually increases.

[21]Ibid., p. 216.

Beyond Capitalism

It is now evident why Marx saw the great proletarian revolution occurring in highly developed capitalist countries. Highly developed capitalist economies would inevitably produce this radical cleavage between the few remaining capitalists and the vast industrial proletariat, and the latter would gradually become aware of the fact that the only way they could improve their lot was through the overthrow of the entire system. Marx expected this revolution to be both spontaneous and violent. Although he did concede the possibility of a nonviolent revolution, perhaps in England or the United States, in general, his expectation was that the bourgeois class would fight for the existing system with all the weapons at its command. And, as long as the working class was without the vote, the likelihood of peaceful transition seemed remote. As the capitalists used more and more repressive measures to keep the proletariat in line, the workers, heretofore unorganized and impotent, would begin to see that their real enemies were the bourgeoisie and would begin to realize their collective power. In the Marxian language, they would develop *class consciousness*, a realization of their power as a unit and the firm conviction that their emancipation from slavery lay in the abolition of capitalism. Once they achieved class consciousness, the revolution would simply occur, a spontaneous uprising of the alienated.

Although Marx became somewhat disenchanted with the revolutionary potential of the proletariat after the abortive revolutions of 1848, he retained throughout his life this belief in spontaneous revolution. This is particularly important in that Marx consequently had only a somewhat vague conception of a revolutionary communist party dedicated to producing a revolution. The idea of a group of dedicated revolutionaries constantly attempting to foment revolution, to light the "spark," is not Marxian in origin but a Leninist idea that produced many changes in the classical Marxian analysis.

Finally, it must be noted that there is very little that the bourgeois class can do about all this. They may attempt to placate the proletariat in a variety of ways, but ultimately the very nature of the capitalist system will, in proper dialectical fashion, ensure its own destruction. It is this "scientific," inevitable aspect of the analysis that gives Marxian much of its revolutionary appeal. Capitalism is doomed; it is merely a question of time and volition.

Neither a clairvoyant, a soothsayer, nor a prophet, Marx was necessarily vague as to the specifics of the society that would follow capitalism. Still, the broad outlines should now be rather clear. The abolition of private property and the establishment of community control of the means of production will ensure a society where classes and exploitation cease to exist. Marx, and later Engels, talked specifically of universal suffrage and direct responsibility of leadership elements to the people through a process of referendum and recall. Any hierarchical power structure, whether based on class or expertise, was rejected. The technological base provided by the capitalist stage in history will provide humans with the means to control their environment and make scarcity and poverty a thing of the past. People will interact with their environment freely, treating each other as fellow humans all engaged in the common task of self-realization. Marx wrote:

> In a higher phase of communist society, after the enslaving subordination of the individual to the division of labour, and therewith also the antithesis between mental and physical labour, has vanished; after labour has become not only a means of life but life's prime want; after the productive forces have also increased with the all-round development of the individual, and all the springs of cooperative wealth flow more abundantly—only then can the narrow horizon of bourgeois right be crossed in its entirety and society inscribe on its banner: From each according to his ability, to each according to his needs![22]

The oppressive superstructural state of capitalism will vanish, bourgeois morality will be replaced by a truly human morality, people will labor according to their ability and be rewarded according to their needs. Simply put, Marx envisioned a community of peace, tranquility, and power over nature that would ensure true freedom for all humanity.

It is now almost a cliche to say that Marxism possesses great appeal for masses of people because it promises the equivalent of a heaven on earth. Combine this ethical vision with a doctrine that promises "scientific" inevitability and one has a most powerful ideology. We shall not attempt specific criticisms of Marxism at this point largely because the other ideologies discussed provide us with a highly critical perspective of Marxism. In the final analysis, criticisms of Marxism—and all ideologies—must deal with views of people, society, history. Only then is it possible either to evaluate it or to determine whether a world built upon such promises is possible or, for that matter, desirable.

Marxism did not, of course, die with Karl Marx. While his ideas to this day provide the building blocks for socialist and communist thought, one may now speak of Marxism-Leninism or perhaps Marxism-Leninism-Stalinism-Maoism. Marx's ideas undergo changes in the hands of his dedicated followers, changes that often make the current doctrine quite different even while it retains the broad outlines of classical Marxism. We must now look at some of those changes, in particular those made by the leader of the first successful revolution proclaimed in Marx's name—Vladimir Ilich Ulyanov, better known as V. I. Lenin.

[22]Ibid., p. 531.

SUGGESTED READINGS

ALTHUSSER, LOUIS, *For Marx.* New York: Vintage Press, 1970.

AVINERI, SHLOMO, *Hegel's Theory of the Modern State.* Cambridge: Cambridge University Press, 1972.

COHEN, G. A., *Karl Marx's Theory of History: A Defense.* Princeton, N.J.: Princeton University Press, 1980.

HEILBRONER, ROBERT L., *Marxism: For and Against.* New York: W. W. Norton & Company, 1980.

KAUFMANN, WALTER, *Hegel: A Reinterpretation.* Garden City, N.Y.: Doubleday and Company, 1966.

MANDEL, ERNEST, *Marxist Economic Theory,* 2 vols. New York: Monthly Review Press, 1971.

MARCUSE, HERBERT, *Reason and Revolution: Hegel and the Rise of Social Theory.* Boston: Beacon Press, 1960.

MCMURTRY, JOHN, *The Structure of Marx's World-View.* Princeton, N.J.: Princeton University Press, 1978.

MILIBAND, RALPH, *The State in Capitalist Society.* London: Weidenfeld and Nicolson, 1969.

OLLMAN, BERTELL, *Alienation,* 2nd ed. Cambridge: Cambridge University Press, 1976.

PANICHAS, GEORGE E., ed., *Marx Analyzed: Philosophical Essays on the Thought of Karl Marx.* Washington, D.C.: University Press of America, 1985.

TUCKER, ROBERT C., ed., *The Marx-Engels Reader,* 2nd ed. New York, W. W. Norton & Company, 1978.

6

Marxism and Leninism

Without revolutionary theory there can be no revolutionary movement.

Lenin

By the time of Karl Marx's death in 1883, his ideas had become a recognized school of thought among European radicals; there was an established international communist movement, a quite strong socialist party in Germany, and potentially serious stirrings elsewhere on the Continent. Behind the facade of a united, monolithic international movement, however, there were many debates and arguments about the real meaning of Marx's thought. Until his death in 1895, Engels, because of his status as a founding father of the movement, was able to maintain some cohesiveness to the interpretations of Marxism, yet even during this period warring factions were beginning to arise. This intellectual ferment about the true meaning of Marx's teachings was to continue even after the imposed Stalinist orthodoxy of the 1930s.

Nevertheless, the period between Marx's death and the Bolshevik success in Russia in 1917 shows, in ways not unlike that of early Christianity following the death of Christ, the varying controversies in all of their richness. Indeed, so multifaceted, vociferous, and polemical were these ongoing debates that one noted scholar of Marxism, Leszek Kolakowski, has called this era the "Golden Age" of Marxism.[1] While it is impossible to go into great detail regarding these arguments and their effects on the international communist movement, we must have some basic understanding of the contending positions if only to set the stage for Lenin's contributions.

THE DIVISIONS WITHIN MARXISM—PEACEFUL OR VIOLENT REVOLUTION?

Two major subjects dominated the Marxist debate of this period: (1) the question of violent or peaceful revolution and (2) the question of readiness of the industrial proletariat for the revolution. With regard to the first question, Marx's response depended upon specific historic context. Although Marx always noted the *possibility* of a peaceful revolution, his 1872 speech in Amsterdam perhaps best captured Marx's view on revolution:

> We are aware of the importance that must be accorded to the institutions, customs, and traditions of different countries; and we do not deny that there are countries like America, England (and, if I knew your institutions better, I would add Holland), where the workers can achieve their aims by peaceful means. However true that may be, we ought also to recognize that, in most of the countries on the Continent, it is force that must be the lever of our revolutions.[2]

[1]Leszek Kolakowski, *Main Currents in Marxism*, 3 vols. (Oxford: Oxford University Press, 1978), Vol. 2, passim.
[2]Karl Marx, in *Karl Marx: Selected Writings*, David McLellan, ed. (Oxford: Oxford University Press, 1977), pp. 594–95.

Given the class antagonisms that capitalism produced, Marx did not expect the bourgeois class to sit back calmly and preside over its own demise. Hence, Marx argued that force would probably be necessary.

The years between Marx's death and World War I produced a growing belief in the political power the working classes could achieve, now that they had the vote, through democratic processes. Even Engels, although hardly renouncing the right of the proletariat to take up arms to ensure revolutionary success, believed that significant changes were occurring via the ballot box. On this specific issue of the vehicle for revolution, violence versus suffrage, three divisions within Marxism developed: *orthodox Marxism, revisionism,* and *Marxism of the left.*

Marxism of the Center

The first position, that violence still might be necessary but that significant progress toward socialist goals was being made through legal means, is generally called Marxism of the center, or *orthodox Marxism.* The major spokesman for this position was Karl Kautsky (1854–1938), the intellectual leader of the powerful German Social-Democratic party (SPD) and a major theoretician of the time. While emphasizing the fact that Marxian political parties were indeed revolutionary in nature, Kautsky made a rather clear distinction between a party that tries to foment a revolution and one that reflects the inevitable historical progress being made toward the achievement of a socialist society. It was Kautsky's unwavering commitment to the inevitability of the revolution that led to the orthodoxy label. According to Kautsky's interpretation, Marxism was a theory and a method of historical investigation that provided people with the *only* system that was valid for understanding social phenomena. Believing Marxism theoretically complete in itself, Kautsky opposed attempts to supplement it with other philosophic doctrines—the exception being his support of the addition of Darwinism. In his efforts to popularize Marxism and to establish it as a mirror image of the natural sciences, Kautsky was chiefly responsible for creating the stereotype of "scientific socialism," that is, Kautsky's erroneous view that Marx had uncovered the universal, inevitable, objective laws of human development that, by necessity, would culminate in communism. Tied to this notion of "scientific socialism" is the (mis)understanding that moral questions are irrelevant to Marxism: Given the deterministic, inevitability of the future it is silly to discuss the question of how humans *ought* to live—they will be socialist.

Placing great weight on Marx's doctrine of the historical inevitability of a socialist society, Kautsky cautioned against trying to speed up the process of history by reckless and clandestine revolutionary activity. He advocated open and active participation in the political processes of capitalist states, fully confident that the revolution would, in time, occur. If Marx was somewhat ambiguous regarding the violence necessary for the transition into socialism, the orthodox Marxist position seems much more so. Violence, its adherents seem to say, may be necessary in order to achieve their goals, but only when dictated by history, when conditions are "ripe"; we are revolutionary, but not actively engaged in the starting of revolutions. Perhaps the orthodox position may be explained by the general optimism concerning democratic processes that existed prior to World War I. Unwilling to renounce the Marxian prediction of violent revolution, the orthodox wing of the movement is nevertheless very much in the position of not rocking the boat. They are appropriately called Marxists of the center, and perhaps their position will become clearer through an examination of the two extreme positions prevalent at the time.

Marxism of the Right

Marxism of the *right*, or more commonly *revisionism*, does not share the ambiguity of the centrists or, for that matter, of Karl Marx. With Eduard Bernstein (1850–1932), a somewhat heretical member of the German Social-Democratic party as their principal spokesman, revisionists simply abandoned the Marxian doctrine of violent revolution. While acknowledging that this was a significant revision of Marx's teaching, Bernstein asserted that the political power of the newly enfranchised proletariat made it possible to achieve most of the socialist goals by lawful means. He also rejected Marx's predictions of the increasing concentration of capital and the theory of the polarization of the classes leading to a single, worldwide revolution. He further argued that the ultimate goal of socialism was not as important as the movement involved in achieving it—the process was everything. Instead of expending all their energy theorizing about a communist society or dreaming of the violent overthrow of capitalism, true socialists should be working to improve the lot of the proletariat through trade unions and political parties. Bernstein and his allies (principally Jean Jaurès, a French socialist) thus laid the theoretical groundwork for many social democratic parties and trade union movements throughout Europe.

Still, Bernstein considered himself a dedicated follower of Marx, thinking only that he was making the doctrine compatible with changing times. Given the revisionist position, Marxism of the center perhaps makes more sense. Both the revisionists and the centrists were forced to deal with increasing evidence that the demands of the proletariat were being realized within the capitalist system. The revisionist position acknowledged that fact and went on to assert that most of the goals of socialism could be satisfied in this way, and further that a significant improvement in the lot of the workers was more important than the achievement of some abstract and far-off goal. Centrists attempted to combat the revisionist position by declaring that some, but not all, demands could be achieved in this fashion, and they affirmed the revolutionary nature of the struggle.

Marxism of the Left

As might be expected, *Marxism of the left* completes the spectrum of positions on the role of violence in producing revolution. With V. I. Lenin and, to a certain extent, German Socialist Rosa Luxemburg as its leading advocates, Marxism of the left places great weight on the antagonistic nature of the class struggle under capitalism and declares violent revolution to be absolutely necessary in the realization of socialism. The revisionist and centrist positions can be seen from this perspective as denying the true Marxian vision of a socialist society and as distorting Marx's teachings on the relationship between substructure and superstructure. The supposed gains made by the trade union movement and by social-democratic political parties are nothing but sops given by the capitalists to keep the workers in line; a fundamental change in the system can only come about through a true revolution.

Instead of allowing themselves to be used by the capitalists through participating in politics, true Marxists should be engaging in general strikes to paralyze the system, using violent activities to reveal the true repressive nature of capitalism, and constantly agitating for revolution. Left Marxism is, then, the position of the uncompromising revolutionary who is dedicated to the overthrow of the system and refuses to believe that reformist measures of any sort will benefit the movement. Indeed, those so-called Marxians who believe in progress within a capitalist system are really helping the capitalists retain their superior position, for they lead the working class to renounce the necessity for radical action and inhibit the growth of class-consciousness. Action, agitation, and revolution are the cries of the left. Their position on the second of our two major questions of this period—the readiness of the proletariat for revolution—exhibits the same traits, and it is to that question we must now turn.

The Readiness of the Proletariat

A considerable period of time had passed since Marx predicted the spontaneous mass uprising of the proletariat in highly developed capitalist states. While he attached no specific timetable to this prediction, there was a general expectation that revolution was imminent. The abortive revolutions of 1848 forced Marx to think about the problem of working toward a revolution rather than just waiting for it to happen, but his confidence in the proletariat as the class chosen by history for this task never seriously wavered. It is important to note that the entire "scientific" interpretation of Marxian thought is at stake here. A large, alienated, class-conscious proletariat was the necessary outgrowth of highly developed capitalism, and the fact that no uprising of major consequence had occurred cast Marxism's entire set of scientific propositions in doubt. As we shall see later in this chapter, Lenin and other Marxists developed an ingenious explanation for this lack of proletarian activity in developed capitalist states. However, for the moment it is sufficient to note that the entire question of the readiness of the proletariat for revolution was widely debated in the period leading up to World War I.

As might be inferred from their position on the question of violence in the revolution, orthodox Marxists retained Karl Marx's basic belief in the spontaneous uprising of the proletarian class in highly developed capitalist countries. Because of this there was no need for a revolutionary activist party; class-consciousness would naturally develop because of the inherent contradictions of capitalism, and no amount of "adventurism" or revolutionary agitation on the part of dedicated Marxists would help.

Here again we see the reliance of the orthodox Marxists on the doctrine of historical inevitability and their faith in the scientific nature of Marx's predictions. They believed that Marxian political parties should be mass-based organizations that would provide some help in increasing the consciousness of the working class, but their prime function was to work by legal means for the betterment of the proletariat. In sum, the orthodox position was that the proletariat would become ready for revolution sometime in the future as a result of the internal contradictions of capitalism, and the task of dedicated Marxians was to work through mass-based political parties to gradually increase the proletariat's consciousness and improve its lot.

The revisionist position on this question should be quite evident. Disavowing the violent nature of revolution, revisionist Marxists advocated the recruitment of the entire working class in individual countries so that workers' political power would be enhanced. By developing a strong working-class movement, workers could force the capitalists to change the very nature of the system and implement most of the goals of socialism. The question of whether the working class was ready for revolution was rather irrelevant to the revisionist. What was necessary, and immediately realizable, was the development of class solidarity in order to maximize the achievement of the workers' goals. It was in left Marxism, particularly in the thought of Lenin, that this question of proletarian readiness became particularly important and eventually led to profound alterations in classical Marxian teaching.

TWENTIETH-CENTURY RUSSIA

To explain Lenin's beliefs on the revolutionary potential of the proletariat we must introduce, for the first of many times, the subject of the peculiar position of Russian Marxists. Most of the major figures in the international communist movement prior to World War I resided in developed capitalist countries that possessed a significant urban proletariat. In their eyes Russia was generally viewed as an anachronism: a country half-Asian, half-European, backward in industrial development, and possessing only a small working class—hardly fitting Marx's model of a well-developed capitalist state. This is not to say that Marx was ignored in Russia. The Russian intelligentsia, a class of well-educated individuals cut off from participation in political affairs by the autocratic rule of the Czars, had a long tradition of radicalism, even anarchism.

The first major Russian Marxist group was formed in Switzerland by Georgi V. Plekhanov in 1883, and Marx found a ready ear among the highly alienated Russian intelligentsia. Despite this, the notion of a proletarian revolution in Russia was problematic: Out of a population of 129 million, approximately 3 million could be called proletarians, while 80 percent were peasants. This fact was to force Lenin and his followers to make many alterations in Marxian doctrine so that it fit the Russian experience, but for present purposes it also led Lenin to question the revolutionary potential of the working class.

In contrast to the orthodox Marxist position of waiting for the development of class-consciousness and the spontaneous uprising of the urban proletariat, Lenin came to believe that the proletariat in alliance with other disaffected groups in the society would require strong leadership to accomplish its revolutionary mission. Probably because of his Russian background, Lenin was not optimistic about the possibilities of a spontaneous proletarian revolution. Even in a highly developed capitalist country such as Germany it seemed that the proletariat, under the influence of revisionists and orthodox Marxists, was losing its revolutionary potential and tending to adopt bourgeois values.

However, for Lenin this did not preclude the possibility of revolution. These facts dictated a new strategy for committed Marxists—they required a new conception of the role of a party structure in the movement as well as an analysis of the place of other dissatisfied groups in the revolution. In formulating a new strategy, Lenin began the process of materially altering classical Marxism to fit the new circumstances of the twentieth century. We will treat these Leninist contributions to the doctrine under three headings: the Communist party and its roles, state socialism and a socialist transfer culture, and the theory of imperialism. First, however, let us meet Lenin, the man and the revolutionary.

LENIN'S LIFE

Vladimir Ilich Ulyanov (1870–1924), who later adopted the "party" name Lenin, was born in Simbirsk (later renamed Ulyanovsky in his honor) on the Volga River, the son of a moderately prosperous director of provincial education for the Russian state. Vladimir was the third child in a family of seven and the second eldest son. He and his brother, Alexander, were rather close, the younger Vladimir always trying to emulate the intellectual and athletic feats of Alexander. Both were excellent in school, earning the highest marks throughout their academic careers. During this period, Russia was undergoing a severe political reaction to the assassination of the reformist Czar Alexander II, in 1881. His successor, Alexander III, proceeded systematically to repress dissent, discourage education, and make even more absolute the famed absolutism of Russian rulers.

The intelligentsia was understandably unhappy with this turn of events and prepared to make use of their favorite political weapon— another assassination. The Ulyanov family became intimately involved in these political affairs when Alexander, in St. Petersburg to continue his studies, was arrested by the police for plotting to bomb Alexander III. Because of his knowledge of chemistry he had been assigned to make the bomb. Following an eloquent defense at his trial of revolutionary action, Alexander was convicted. Refusing on principle to ask the czar for clemency, Alexander was executed. It was then that young Vladimir began, according to his sister, to think seriously about revolution.

The next several years saw the Ulyanov family move to the larger city of Kazan and then to the city of Samara on the Volga. The young Lenin completed his gymnasium (high school) education and briefly attended the University of Kazan only to be dismissed for being involved in protest activities. There is still a good deal of disagreement as to when Lenin began to study Marxism seriously. We have his sister Anna's statement that, while the ill-fated Alexander was reading Marx in 1886, the younger Vladimir was preoccupied with the works of Turgenev and had no real political views. The period in Kazan and in Samara undoubtedly provided him with the opportunity to read extensively and to think about his future since he did not have to work to maintain himself. He did, however, pursue a degree in law during this time and was admitted to the bar in 1892. Although he was permitted to practice law, Lenin spent much of his time at various radical meetings where he eventually developed a reputation for debating skills in defense of Marxist ideas.

Although we cannot pinpoint the exact time when he came to

accept the Marxian credo fully, by 1893 Lenin was an identifiable advocate of its doctrines. In 1895, he took what had by now become a customary trip for Russian radicals—a journey through Western Europe, meeting most of the leading Marxists of the time. Returning to St. Petersburg, he joined several other young radicals in the formation of a revolutionary action group designed to put some of the ideas of the radical "debating societies" into practice. The experience was short-lived: They were arrested by the police in December 1895. Lenin spent more than a year in prison in St. Petersburg, using the time to begin a major book, *The Development of Capitalism in Russia*, until the authorities decided he should spend three years in exile in Siberia. Ironically, the years of exile, near the river Lena from which he took the name Lenin, provided a rather pleasant interlude for the budding revolutionary. He had a good deal of freedom of movement, time to read and write as well as to plan strategy for his return.

His situation was further enhanced when he was joined by a young comrade, Nadezhda Krupskaya, whom he had met earlier in radical circles in St. Petersburg. She became his wife and lifelong collaborator. By the time he left Siberia in February 1900, Lenin was a dedicated revolutionary with a rather clear plan of how to accomplish his goals. This well-formulated strategy distinguished him from most other radicals, who tended to be vague regarding the methods of achieving their ideals.

Lenin's Years in Exile

With the exception of a brief return to Russia in the revolutionary period of 1905–1907, Lenin spent the entire time prior to 1917 in political exile. For a man of action, this was a particularly trying period: Cut off from events in Russia, he could only spend his time in forming a group of dedicated followers who would be ready to seize opportunities as they arose. It is a testament to Lenin's dedication to the cause of Russian Marxism that during all of this time, spent in a great number of European cities, he thought of nothing but the coming struggle. Lenin had by now become one of the major figures in the movement and the leading spokesman for its left wing.

At the Second Party Congress of Russian Marxists in 1903, Lenin led a fight to establish the party as a close-knit organization of dedicated revolutionaries, and he succeeded, after several splinter factions had withdrawn from the congress, in achieving a majority for his position. Because of this, Lenin was thereafter able to refer to his group as representing the majority (*bolshinstvo* in Russian) position even though it was actually one of many splinter factions warring for domination of the Russian Marxist movement. Such was the condition of Russian Marxism when, in reaction to an extremely unpopular and unsuccessful war with Japan, revolution broke out in St. Petersburg in 1905. Beginning with the massacre of peaceful demonstrators in February ("Bloody Sunday"), the revolt spread to most of European Russia, with councils ("soviets") of workers attaining a great deal of power in the major cities. During this time, Lenin and his followers attempted to turn the general discontent of the population toward Marxian ends, only to see the revolution brutally crushed by troops still loyal to the Czar and by the granting of numerous concessions, notably the October Manifesto of 1905, which established a parliament. Alternately impressed by the potential power of the discontented Russian masses and convinced that only through his tightly organized party could any revolution be a success, Lenin withdrew once again into exile.

The years after the abortive revolution of 1905 saw Lenin and his Bolshevik faction increasingly split off from the other more moderate Marxists in Russia. They held their own conferences, published their own newspaper (with the now familiar name of *Pravda* or "truth" in Russian), and in general took a standoffish attitude toward the international Marxist movement. Lenin's final break with the more moderate socialists of the international movement came with the start of World War I. Confirming his worst fears of the moderates and revisionists, he found most European socialists supporting their respective national governments in the war effort. Instead, Lenin advocated "turn the imperialist war into an international civil war" between classes. Castigating others for supporting a bourgeois war, Lenin, now in Switzerland, could only consolidate his Bolshevik faction even further and hope that the strain of a major war would finally topple the czarist regime. That hope (perhaps dream is a better word) was fulfilled in March 1917 when, with Russia completely out of control, the czar—the final vestige of Europe's *ancien regime*—at long last abdicated.

For Lenin, however, this was but the beginning. Learning of the Romanov abdication, he immediately made arrangements to leave Switzerland to return to Russia. The Germans, only too eager to have a revolutionary like Lenin causing further trouble in Russia, arranged the famous trip by sealed train through Germany and Finland. The exile returned to a triumphant celebration at the Finland Station in St. Petersburg, in April 1917.

The remaining events of that fateful year are far too complex to summarize here. Our intention has been to understand something of Lenin the person and to describe briefly the society with which he was dealing, rather than to attempt a history of the Russian revolution. Our prime interest is in Lenin the contributor to Marxist ideology; thus it is to his ideas that we must now turn.

THREE THEMES FROM LENINISM

Revolutionary Leadership and the Party

The history of all countries shows that the working class, exclusively by its own effort, is able to develop only trade union consciousness, i.e., the conviction that it is necessary to combine in unions, fight the employers, and strive to compel the government to pass necessary labour legislation, etc. The theory of socialism, however, grew out of the philosophic, historical, and economic theories elaborated by educated representatives of the propertied classes, by intellectuals.[3]

If there was one thing that made Lenin stand apart from his Marxist colleagues prior to 1917, it was his unique conception of a Communist party. Most commentators would rate the notion of the party as Lenin's foremost contribution to Marxist thought, if only because it turns highly abstract doctrine into a revolutionary movement. In another sense, Lenin's party provides an excellent example of the direction of all of his thought, which was to make Marxist doctrine compatible with the facts of the twentieth century and with the particular conditions in Russia.

Lenin's need to make Marxism applicable to specific situations makes it important *not* to treat the theme of any one era as if it were a timeless position; he, indeed, did alter the revolutionary theory to fit the constantly changing revolutionary context. Nevertheless, on the role of the party, his thought remained unchanging.

As we have seen, Karl Marx had at best a rather vague notion of a revolutionary party because of his belief that the contradictions of capitalism would produce a spontaneous revolution of the proletariat. His orthodox followers, still retaining the belief in spontaneity, believed that a workers' party operating within the bourgeois political system could provide material gains for the working class and develop in the proletariat a sense of its potential power. Although Lenin in his early days accepted this notion, he gradually came to the belief that such mass-based workers' organizations were ineffective and tended to impede the goal of revolution. Partially owing to the lack of a large proletariat in Russia and partially because the proletariat in more highly developed countries tended to adopt bourgeois values as it gained even limited political power, Lenin called for the establishment of a small, tightly organized band of dedicated Marxists whose task was to lead the alienated classes within a country to revolution. Here Lenin argues the need for a secret group of *professional revolutionaries* to bring about the revolution:

[3]V. I. Lenin, in *The Lenin Anthology*, Robert C. Tucker, ed. (New York: W. W. Norton & Company, 1975), p. 24.

I mean *professional revolutionaries,* irrespective of whether they have developed from among students or working men. I assert: (1) that no revolutionary movement can endure without a stable organisation of leaders
maintaining continuity; (2) that the broader the popular mass drawn spon-
taneously into the struggle, which forms the basis of the movement and
participates in it, the more urgent the need for such an organisation, and
the more solid this organisation must be (for it is much easier for all sorts
of demagogues to side-track the more backward sections of the masses);
(3) that such an organisation must consist chiefly of people professionally
engaged in revolutionary activity; (4) that in an autocratic state, the more
we *confine* the membership of such an organisation to people who are
professionally engaged in revolutionary activity and who have been professionally trained in the art of combating the political police, the more
difficult will it be to unearth the organisation; and (5) the *greater* will be
the number of people from the working class and from the other social
classes who will be able to join the movement and perform active work
in it.[4]

In adopting this position Lenin more or less stood alone. Rosa
Luxemburg, who shared many of his radical tendencies in interpreting
Marx's thought, retained her belief in a spontaneous revolution and,
therefore, did not see the need for a militant party. Even Leon Trotsky,
a trusted lieutenant of Lenin's during the revolution, did not come to
share Lenin's view until 1917. The reason for this lack of acceptance
was that Lenin, at least implicitly, was advocating a substantial alteration
in Marxian thought. Simply, he was saying that since it was impossible
for the proletariat to achieve class-consciousness by their own efforts,
it was also impossible to have a leaderless revolution.

However, in a country where there was a considerable amount of
discontent with the existing regime, it would be possible for a dedicated
band of revolutionaries to seize upon the people's "alienation" and
direct their energies toward Marxist ends. This is not to say that Lenin
believed in the possibility of a palace revolution engineered by a few
people in strategic places. He was firm in the belief that a revolutionary
movement had to have mass support, and he argued at great length
with those who advocated such a coup d'état strategy. Even so, the
important point here is that class-consciousness on the part of the
proletariat is not a prerequisite for revolution, provided that class-
consciousness exists in the revolutionary leadership. Given this addition
to Marxian thought, one can see all sorts of opportunities for revolutionary agitation opening up. If class-consciousness among the proletariat
is not necessary, the party could attempt to use any dissatisfied group
within society to further its ends. All kinds of alliances with different
groups would be possible, depending upon the degree of capitalistic
development in a particular country. If an alienated proletarian class,

[4]Ibid., pp. 76–77.

conscious of its own plight and potential power, is no longer a prerequisite for a Marxian revolution, then it is quite appropriate to advocate a revolution in countries that do not possess the characteristics of the classical Marxian model.

We have earlier spoken of Russia as a most unlikely place for a classical Marxist revolution because of its lack of economic development. While this remains true it must be noted that Russia had made very rapid strides toward industrialization during the latter part of the nineteenth century. The success of the workers' soviets in the revolution of 1905 indicated the presence of a growing proletariat in major Russian cities. Still, the country was primarily rural and the population mostly comprised of peasants. Most Marxians considered Russia a feudal society, where the economic substructure was beginning a rapid movement into industrial capitalism while the state superstructure lagged behind, retaining its feudal elements. In such a situation it would be necessary to have not one but two revolutions: the first bourgeois, the second proletarian.

The Doctrine of Permanent Revolution

Leon Trotsky had earlier advanced the doctrine of *permanent revolution,* which argued that in Russia the two revolutions could take place within a very short period of time. Even while the bourgeois revolution was occurring, Marxists should be organizing and agitating for the proletarian revolution—the two revolutions could be telescoped. In such a situation, the task of Marxist revolutionaries was to speed the success of the bourgeois revolution and then attempt to foment a proletarian one. Consistent with this principle, Lenin, prior to 1905, advocated an alliance between the proletariat and the liberal bourgeoisie, so that the aims of the bourgeois revolution might be accomplished. The proletariat's role was temporarily that of assisting the bourgeoisie in the overthrow of the autocracy of the czar. However, the revolution of 1905 changed all that.

The bourgeoisie, by accepting the czar's liberal October Manifesto, had, in Lenin's eyes, sold out to the forces of oppression; they had denied their own revolution. Moreover, the events of 1905 had produced a situation which must have wet the lips of a true revolutionary such as Lenin; there had been a temporary alliance between the small urban proletariat and the vast Russian peasantry. These events led Lenin to abandon the Russian bourgeois class and to rely increasingly upon an alliance between the peasants and the proletariat. Once again, we observe Lenin altering Marxian doctrine to suit the conditions of semifeudal Russia.

Karl Marx, who based his observations on the already developed capitalism of Western Europe, had concluded that the peasant class was one of the most conservative forces in society. However, the situation of the Russian peasantry was quite different, and Marx was aware of this fact. Achieving emancipation from serfdom only in 1861, the Russian peasants found their lot was unbearable and not at all dissimilar in revolutionary potential to that of Marx's alienated urban proletariat. After 1905 Lenin spoke with increasing frequency of a revolution of the *masses*, allying the proletariat with all dissatisfied classes in the society. It must be remembered, however, that Lenin retained a clear conception in his mind of the role of these groups: They were subservient to the class-conscious proletariat.

The task of Lenin's small, tightly disciplined party is now quite clear. Its function was to coordinate the actions of these various groups, always keeping control of the situation. When the revolution occurred, the party, because of its discipline and organization, would be in a position to assume overall leadership. To Lenin's thinking, one of the fundamental failures of the 1905 revolution was the lack of effective leadership and coordination, and he was determined not to let that happen again. To provide that leadership Lenin set up the decision-making process of the party to conform to the principles of a doctrine called *democratic centralism*. This doctrine presupposes that all the people involved in the process of making decisions for the party are committed to the Marxian goal culture. Given this, decisions still will have to be made regarding party tactics and there will undoubtedly be disagreements as to the right way of proceeding.

As the term implies, democratic centralism theoretically allows for a full democratic discussion of alternatives, but once a decision is made all members of the party must agree to abide by it. There are no minority reports in the party. This doctrine provided Lenin with precisely the tool he needed for revolutionary action: It is democratic by taking into account all positions, but it also provides for the unswerving allegiance necessary for swift action. Many people justifiably contend that the adoption of this decision-making process marks the beginning of a totalitarian party in communist thought, for the "democratic" of democratic centralism is so easily forgotten in the presence of a strong leader such as Lenin. Whatever the case, Lenin's Communist party, organized in this fashion, provided him with the means of taking control in the more chaotic days of the Russian revolution. While others debated, the Bolsheviks acted.

Despite all of Lenin's attempts to alter Marxian doctrine to suit the special situation in Russia, the fact remains that he succeeded in presiding over a revolution that appeared distinctly un-Marxian in nature. The first communist revolution in the world occurred in a country which, on a substructural level, was singularly unprepared for communism, and was a revolution via the political, or superstructure. As a dedicated Marxist, Lenin was aware of this. With his success in Russia he was now faced with the task of using the political structure of the society to develop the economic conditions that Marxism decreed necessary for a pure communist society. To revert to jargon, Lenin had to develop a "transfer culture" that would lead toward the "goal culture" of pure communism. The Communist party was to play a crucial role in this transfer period, but its activities after the revolution are best treated under the heading of the second of our "three themes of Leninism," namely, state socialism and the socialist transfer culture.

THE STATE AND REVOLUTION

Marx had taught that the workers' revolution, once begun, would eventually spread around the entire world until all capitalist regimes were overthrown. Therefore the immediate problem facing the Bolsheviks after their takeover in November 1917 concerned the relationship between the worldwide communist movement and the revolutionary regime in the Soviet Union. Many dedicated Bolsheviks wanted to carry the red flag of Marxism westward into the heart of Europe and at least partially fulfill Marx's prophecy. Initially Lenin agreed with this analysis, contending that the spark of the Bolshevik revolution could ignite the flames of revolution throughout Europe. The beachhead that had been established in Russia would be secured through the overthrow of other capitalist regimes.

In the euphoric days immediately following the Russian revolution, Lenin apparently saw the possibility of the rise of the proletariat throughout Europe, making the Soviet experience a sort of trigger for the revolt in more highly developed capitalist countries. However, such events did not occur, and it became increasingly obvious that some new analysis of the situation was needed. Characteristically, Lenin shifted ground and began to theorize that even though the Russian revolution was inextricably linked to the international movement there would probably be a lag in time between the initial success of the Bolsheviks and the revolution in other countries. Although he continued to believe that this lag would be of short duration, possibly a few years, admitting of its existence forced the young Soviet regime to develop policy for the interim period and to address itself at least tentatively to the question of the existence of a Soviet state surrounded by capitalism.

On a more practical level, the Bolsheviks were surrounded by chaos; the years of war and revolution had reduced the army to a disorganized mass, a civil war was raging, and the regime was in real danger of losing control completely. The optimism of the immediate postrevolutionary period, which saw a quick transition to economic socialism at home and the rapid spread of revolution abroad, was replaced by a grim struggle for existence. Whatever the ideological costs, the situation required that Russia get out of World War I, and after a good deal of argument this was accomplished through the Treaty of Brest-Litovsk (1918), which ceded large portions of European Russia to the conquering Germans.

Lenin was simply unwilling to sacrifice the Bolshevik success for the sake of a *potential* worldwide revolution. Still, consistent with the broad Marxian analysis, he similarly refused to abandon the international struggle for the sake of an independent Soviet nation-state. Confronted with the potentially conflicting goals of the Russian revolution and international Marxism, Lenin opted for both. The long-range goals of the international movement were not inconsistent with the idea of a Soviet state, for the latter would serve as an inspiration to proletarians the world over. Since the time lag between the Russian revolution and the world uprising would be of short duration, the Soviet Union could exist as an entity even though it was surrounded by hostile capitalist states. Marx's prophecy of an international movement was never in doubt; it was simply a question of time. While the international movement was by no means ignored, the Soviet leadership could now expend some energy in securing the gains of the revolution within Russia.

Dictatorship of the Proletariat

As we have said, the Russian revolution was of a political nature, accomplished by a small band of revolutionaries supported by a variety of discontented groups in the society. From the viewpoint of classical Marxism, the two things most conspicuously lacking in Russia were economic development and the presence of large-scale class-consciousness. Until these two goals were achieved it would be impossible to think of a truly communist society. Lenin's task inside the Soviet Union was to develop institutions and a value structure that would achieve these two goals; he had to develop a *transfer culture*. Because the people at large lacked true class-consciousness and had lived for so many years under the false value structures of feudalism and capitalism, it would be necessary to have a group of leaders to direct the economic development of the society and lead the people as a whole toward proletarianization. The Communist party would provide such leadership after the revolution in its role of vanguard of the proletariat by establishing a *proletarian dictatorship*. If the society as a whole was lacking in class-consciousness, it would be absurd, from the Leninist perspective, to give all people an equal say in the running of the country. Thus, it would be temporarily necessary for the party to act as the spearhead of the revolution and to assume a dictatorial role until the time when the last vestiges of capitalism and feudalism were removed.

In this type of environment Lenin argued for the temporary use of dictatorial state power to continue the class conflict; this time, however, it would be the instrument of the proletariat to be employed against all counterrevolutionary forces, especially the bourgeoisie. Lenin captured these ideas in his book *The State and Revolution:*

> The proletariat needs state power, a centralised organisation of force, an organisation of violence, both to crush the resistance of the exploiters and to *lead* the enormous mass of the population—the peasants, the petty bourgeoisie, and semi-proletarians—in the work of organising a socialist economy.
>
> By educating the workers' party, Marxism educates the vanguard of the proletariat, capable of assuming power and *leading the whole people* to socialism, of directing and organising the new system, of being the teacher, the guide, the leader of all the working and exploited people in organising their social life without the bourgeoisie and against the bourgeoisie.[5]

We must pause and note the enormity of the task confronting the Bolshevik leaders. If they were to remain true to their Marxian commitment they had to attempt to wipe out all of the institutions, values, and habit patterns acquired under generations of bourgeois and feudal rule. Consciously, they had to attempt to reeducate an entire people. This task was accomplished in industrialized Europe through the influence of Liberalism—over the course of centuries! The Bolsheviks' situation was completely different. They had to use education, propaganda, even coercion, to achieve their goals.

The same situation obtained in the economic realm. Despite the rapid growth of capitalism in Russia in the three decades before the revolution, Russia was appropriately called an underdeveloped country. Further, the revolution and civil war that followed it had destroyed much of the small industrial base which had existed in 1917. If extensive economic development was necessary to achieve the Marxian vision, the Soviet Union would have to go through a quasi-capitalistic phase, which would give to the society the technological expertise achieved elsewhere under capitalism. Recall Marx's observation in the *Communist Manifesto:*

> The bourgeoisie, during its rule of scarce one hundred years, has created more massive and more colossal productive forces than have all preceding generations together. Subjection of Nature's forces to man, machinery, application of chemistry to industry and agriculture, steam-navigation, railways, electric telegraphs, clearing of whole continents for cultivation, canalisation of rivers, whole populations conjured out of the ground—

---

[5]Ibid., p. 328.

what earlier century had even a presentiment that such productive forces slumbered in the lap of social labour?[6]

The country, under the leadership of the party and the state apparatus, must develop itself, but without the excesses of capitalism. To do this Lenin developed the notion generally called *state socialism*. Initially, this concept involved the appropriation of the means of production by the state as a whole so that the capital generated in the economy could be directed to ensure maximum economic growth. The word *capital* is appropriate here in that there was still exploitation of a sort under state socialism. Workers still labored longer than necessary to support themselves, and therefore generated a profit. Under socialism, however, this profit went to the state, which, acting as a trustee, used it for the benefit of the entire society, not for one particular class; similarly, Lenin hoped the society would acquire the technological expertise of capitalism without its class structure.

Thus, it is not surprising that there was very little by way of radical change in the economic structure in the immediate postrevolutionary period. Nor is it surprising to see policies promulgated that encouraged some individual competition, such as the New Economic Policy (NEP) of 1921. Under Lenin's *transfer culture*, "The socialist principle, 'He who does not work shall not eat,' is *already* realised; the other socialist principle, 'An equal amount of products for an equal amount of labour,' is also *already* realised."[7] Nevertheless, he knew this was not yet communism. The original Marxian principle—from each according to his ability, to each according to his needs—still remained the unfulfilled goal; and, until this was achieved, it was premature to expect the proletarian state to "wither away."

In summary, the objective of the Soviet transfer culture was the attainment of a highly developed economy similar to that in the West, which would provide the technology and expertise necessary for communism. In addition, because of the nature of the Bolshevik revolution, the entire value structure of the people must be changed so that they would possess the consciousness necessary for pure communism. It may well be that these two goals produced through Lenin's means become antithetical, that the achievement of one of them makes the other impossible. After all, Marx long ago recognized that the thing that made capitalism so successful was its emphasis on individual reward for increased effort, which eventually leads to some sort of class structure. Leninism requires the individual initiative of capitalism, yet must avoid its class divisions—a difficult thing indeed. We shall meet this problem

[6]Karl Marx, in *The Marx-Engels Reader*, 2nd ed., Robert C. Tucker, ed. (New York: W. W. Norton and Company, 1978), p. 477.
[7]*Lenin Anthology*, p. 378.

again in our discussions of Mao Zedong (Mao Tse-tung), Deng Xiaopeng, and Mikhail Gorbachev, but for the moment it is necessary to move to a discussion of the theory of imperialism, Lenin's third major contribution to Marxian doctrine.

THE THEORY OF IMPERIALISM

We have seen how Lenin and numerous other followers of Karl Marx attempted to make Marxist teaching more relevant to the twentieth century. In many respects this was not a difficult activity, for Marx had made some amazingly accurate predictions about the development of capitalism. His assertion that capitalism would spread around the world seemed confirmed in 1917; in accordance with his second law of capitalist development, the monopolistic nature of modern capitalism was increasing; various business crises with worldwide implications seemed to be occurring more frequently; and World War I seemed to confirm the hypothesis that capitalists would struggle mightily with each other for economic advantage.

Despite the apparent correctness of these predictions, a key hypothesis of Marx's entire analysis—that the material condition of the proletariat would become increasingly worse and inevitably lead to revolution—simply was not happening. Indeed, proletarians in highly developed capitalist countries seemed every year to grow more content with their lot as they shared in the benefits of the expanding economies. This fact led some Marxists to adopt the revisionist position of working within the system, and others such as Lenin to foment revolution in an underdeveloped country. But the fundamental question remained—why was the proletariat in developed capitalist systems becoming increasingly passive? Addressing himself to this question in 1916 Lenin published a book titled *Imperialism, the Highest Stage of Capitalism,* which set out the basic ideas of the theory of imperialism.

Before exploring these ideas it must be noted that the theory of imperialism was by no means original with Lenin. Many other Marxists, and some nonbelievers, had earlier advanced similar explanations for the decline in revolutionary activity by the proletariat, and Lenin borrowed freely from them. Still, Lenin's position as head of the only Marxist state in the world probably made it inevitable that his explanation would become *the* theory of imperialism.

At its broadest, the theory asserts that, despite the accuracy of his predictions concerning unmodified capitalism, Marx never fully developed his own theory of imperialism contained in the third volume of *Das Kapital.* Although he clearly saw the worldwide spread of capitalism, Marx did not foresee some of the implications this would have, particularly on the working class of the industrialized countries. As Marx noted, the dwindling number of capitalists would be forced into a mad scramble for new markets because of overproduction and diminishing profits at home. Saddled with great quantities of both nonexploitable *constant capital* (machinery) and *finance capital* (bank and industrial investment money), capitalists would seek out new sources of cheap raw materials and labor. In short, it was incumbent upon them to find and develop new markets, new sources of exploitation. They found what they were looking for in the underdeveloped countries of the world. In an attempt to show the incontrovertibility of this description of imperialism on these points, Lenin quoted the wealthy British industrialist Cecil Rhodes:

> I was in the East End of London [a working-class quarter] yesterday and attended a meeting of the unemployed. I listened to the wild speeches, which were just a cry for "bread! bread!" and on my way home I pondered over the scene and I became more than ever convinced of the importance of imperialism. . . . My cherished idea is a solution for the social problem, i.e., in order to save the 40,000,000 inhabitants of the United Kingdom from a bloody civil war, we colonial statesmen must acquire new lands to settle the surplus population, to provide new markets for the goods produced in the factories and mines. The Empire, as I have always said, is a bread and butter question. If you want to avoid civil war, you must become imperialists.[8]

With the armies of the capitalist states leading the way, capitalism would carve out specific spheres of influence and proceed to exploit the resources of these areas, both material and human, for all they were worth. With this seemingly inexhaustible labor supply, they could force the native population to work under deplorable conditions for tiny wages and extract tremendous profits. Some of the *super profit* derived in this manner could then be used to bribe their own internal proletariat with higher wages and better working conditions, thereby increasing consumption of the capitalists' products. Lenin wrote:

> Obviously, out of such enormous *superprofits* (since they are obtained over and above the profits which capitalists squeeze out of the workers of their "own" country) it is *possible to bribe* the labour leaders and the upper stratum of the labour aristocracy. And that is just what the capitalists of the "advanced" countries are doing: they are bribing them in a thousand different ways, direct and indirect, overt and covert.[9]

Therefore, the internal proletariat of highly developed capitalist countries was bought off with the profit from the exploitation of the under-

[8]Ibid., p. 236.
[9]Ibid., p. 209.

developed countries. Instead of the vast army of unemployed workers that Marx predicted, what resulted was an increasingly affluent middle class largely content with its lot and a firm defender of the bourgeois status quo. Here we see the major reason for the lack of revolutionary activity on the part of the proletariat in industrialized countries. Their condition was not growing worse but actually improving because of the material exploitation of underdeveloped countries. This results in a new exploiter-exploited relationship: It is no longer the bourgeois class versus the proletariat but highly developed capitalist *countries* pitted against underdeveloped ones. Marx's class analysis had changed under the imperialistic stage of capitalism to a situation in which "prenation" confronts nation.

This change to a nation-state orientation under the theory of imperialism cannot be overemphasized. Lenin had long ago recognized the revolutionary potential of nationalist slogans, and he had utilized all classes within Russia to achieve the revolution. Still, classical Marxism was avowedly internationalistic, and all good Marxists thought of nationalist ideology as nothing but another capitalist ploy to keep the workers in one country from allying with those in another.

Furthermore, the nation-state was a uniquely capitalist invention whose major purpose was to enhance the power position of the bourgeoisie; it would, after all, vanish under pure communism. The theory of imperialism united these seemingly contradictory goals of nationalism and internationalistic communism and in the process provided a completely new revolutionary strategy for modern communism.

Wars of National Liberation

With the internal proletariat in industrialized countries bribed by superprofits, Marxists now looked elsewhere for revolutionary groups. Under imperialism, revolutionary potential lay not with a particular class or alienated group within a society, but with entire exploited countries. Revolutionary activity would take place in the form of *wars of national liberation,* which would unite nationalistic groups and communists within underdeveloped countries to throw off the capitalist yoke. Once successful, these nationalist movements should be controlled by communists who would then lead the country into a socialist transfer culture, following the pattern of the Soviet Union. It is easy to read too many things into the theory of imperialism; the revolutions in China, Cuba, and Vietnam, for example, fit perhaps too neatly. Nevertheless, contained within this theory are all the implications of most of the communist revolutions that have since occurred. Lenin had turned backwardness into a virtue; underdevelopment was now almost a prerequisite for revolution.

What, we might now ask, of the old Marxian prophecy of an

international class-based revolution? Obviously Marx's predictions had been greatly changed under imperialism; class revolt had become national revolution, and underdevelopment was a virtue. Despite these changes Lenin, once again, remained true to the theoretical outlines of Marx's analysis. As we saw in our discussion of socialism in one country, Lenin both altered the time sequence of Marx's predictions and used somewhat different means. This is the *method of Marxism:* As history changes, so must the theory. Ultimately, however, the overall Marxian analysis remained unchanged.

Similarly, the wars of national liberation in underdeveloped countries were but the initial events that would eventually lead to worldwide communism. As these nationalist revolutions met with increasing success, they would cut off the source of cheap labor and raw materials from the capitalists. The superprofits that the capitalists formerly reaped from these countries would no longer be available to them, and in order to continue to make a profit, they would have to go back to exploiting their own internal proletariat. Once this occurred, all of Marx's predictions concerning highly developed capitalism would come to pass: overproduction, a vast army of unemployed, crises, and revolution. The worldwide revolution would occur, although in a way not envisioned by Marx; even so, his overall analysis would be vindicated.

The changes wrought in classical Marxism by Lenin's revolutionary experience are significant, so significant that it is appropriate now to speak of Marxism-Leninism. It should be emphasized that we have only skimmed the surface of Lenin's contributions and neglected many aspects of his thought that others might deem crucial. He was, for example, most interested in the concept of dialectical materialism and wrote a goodly amount on that subject. Yet in his thoughts on the party, a socialist transfer culture, and the theory of imperialism, we clearly see the tremendous impact this person had upon the development of the doctrine. In a sense, V. I. Lenin was a perfect Marxian man: a thinker and a revolutionary, a dedicated (almost doctrinaire) Marxist and an opportunist, unscrupulous yet idealistic. If, as Karl Marx said so many years ago, the point of philosophy was not to explain the world but to change it, Lenin surely was a success, for the world has not been the same since November 1917.

SUGGESTED READINGS

BERNSTEIN, EDUARD, *Evolutionary Socialism: A Criticism and Affirmation.* New York: Schocken Books, 1961.
DEUTSCHER, ISAAC, *The Prophet Armed, Trotsky, 1879–1921.* New York: Oxford University Press, 1954.

————, *The Prophet Unarmed: Trotsky, 1921–1929.* New York: Oxford University Press, 1959.

————, *The Prophet Outcast: Trotsky, 1929–1940.* New York: Oxford University Press, 1963.

FISCHER, LOUIS, *The Life of Lenin.* New York: Harper & Row Publishers, 1964.

GAY, PETER, *The Dilemma of Democratic Socialism: Eduard Bernstein's Challenge to Marx.* New York: Collier Books, 1962.

HOOK, SIDNEY, *Marx and the Marxists: The Ambiguous Legacy.* Princeton, N.J.: Van Nostrand Company, 1955.

KAUTSKY, KARL, *The Dictatorship of the Proletariat.* Ann Arbor: University of Michigan Press, 1964.

MAGDOFF, HARRY, *The Age of Imperialism.* New York: Monthly Review Press, 1969.

MEYER, ALFRED B., *Leninism.* New York: Frederick A. Praeger, 1963.

TUCKER ROBERT C., ed., *The Lenin Anthology.* New York: W. W. Norton & Company, 1975.

WILSON, EDMUND, *To the Finland Station: A Study in the Writing and Acting of History.* Garden City, N.Y.: Doubleday and Company, 1953.

WOLFE, BERTRAM D., *Three Who Made a Revolution: Lenin, Trotsky, and Stalin.* New York: Dell Publishing Co., 1948.

7

Soviet Marxism

I stress once again: perestroika *is not some kind of illumination or revelation. To restructure our life means to understand the objective necessity for renovation and acceleration. And that necessity emerged in the heart of our society.* The essence of perestroika *lies in the fact that* it unites socialism with democracy *and revives the Leninist concept of socialist construction both in theory and practice. Such is the essence of* perestroika, *which accounts for its genuine revolutionary spirit and its all-embracing scope.*

Mikhail Gorbachev

STALIN'S RISE TO POWER

After the successes of 1917, Lenin's position as the leader of Russian Marxism was virtually unchallenged. He was, after all, the "father" of the revolution and, in spite of the many difficulties which confronted the Bolshevik regime during its early days, Lenin's stature could only be enhanced. Indeed, his preeminence was such, particularly after the successful conclusion of the civil war in 1920, that the dictatorship of the proletariat became virtually the "dictatorship" of Lenin. While it is perfectly understandable that this would be the case, it provided a dangerous precedent for the development of Soviet Marxism; Lenin's tightly knit, highly centralized Bolshevik party provided all of the preconditions for the Stalinist totalitarianism that was to dominate the Soviet Union for well over twenty-five years. In fact, it can be argued that it is the ghost of Stalin, living inside the bureaucracies of the party and the State, that continues to haunt the Soviet Union today.

To understand Stalin and his place in Soviet history, it is helpful to remember Russian history and the role played by strong leaders throughout its past. Few nations have been invaded as often and as devastatingly as Russia. Not the least destructive of these invasions was conducted by thousands of troops from over a dozen foreign countries, including the United States and Great Britain, during the early revolutionary months of the Soviet Union. At this as well as other crucial moments in its history, the presence of a strong, often ruthless leader— the *vozhd*—seemed required. Ivan the Terrible, Peter the Great, and certainly Lenin, each was the *vozhd*. This concept has been translated as Leader, Duce, or Führer, carrying with it notions of infallibility and extraordinary power. Given this tradition, it is understandable indeed that during the initial months after the death of Lenin and during the bleaker months of the Great Patriotic War, the Soviet people needed and looked to a *vozhd* to succeed Lenin.

It may seem strange that Stalin, in spite of the indelible imprint he left on present-day Soviet life and despite his long tenure as supreme leader, made at most minor contributions to the development of Marxist-Leninist ideology. Yet from another perspective such a situation makes a good deal of sense. The broad, theoretical outlines of the Soviet transfer culture had been described by Lenin, and it can be argued that what was now required was a practitioner to transform those outlines into reality. Whether a Lenin would have had the determination, patience, or, for that matter, the stomach to pursue the type of policies that characterized Stalin's reign is, of course, a moot point. There is some evidence, which we shall explore later, that indicates that Lenin had real misgivings about the direction the regime was taking. Still, if a total transformation of the Soviet economy and the radical alteration of the beliefs of an entire people were the stated prerequisites of socialism, an argument can be made that some sort of Stalin-like era was a natural outgrowth of the Bolshevik revolution. If Lenin had provided all of the theoretical tools for the future development of Soviet Marxism, Stalin interpreted them to suit his purposes and used them with a vengeance.

Stalin's rise to the pinnacle of power in the Soviet Union is an extremely complex tale, one largely outside the confines of our concern. However, during his early life and his rise to power, he exhibited most of the personal traits that were to constitute his major contributions to the doctrine. For approximately twenty-five years Stalin *was* the Soviet Union; his personal whims governed the state, making it impossible to ignore Stalin, the man of steel.

Stalin's Life

Joseph Stalin was born to poor artisan parents in 1879 in a small village in the Caucasus Mountains of Georgia. His father, Vissarion Dzhugashvili, was apparently a rather bitter man who, it is sometimes said, took much of his frustration out on young Joseph (the pseudonym "Stalin" was adopted later in his life). His father died when Joseph was quite young, leaving his upbringing and schooling to his illiterate mother. Through tremendous personal sacrifice she was able to provide the means for her young son to study in Tiflis (now Tbilisi), the capitol of Georgia, where he received his education in a seminary. Whatever the quality of this education, Stalin was to be plagued throughout his life by his Georgian background, notably by his difficulties with the Russian language and by the generally "provincial" nature of his upbringing. In spite of its provincial setting, the seminary apparently was a center for the dissemination of liberal if not radical ideas, and the young Stalin gradually came under the sway of them. He got into increasing trouble with the school authorities and was finally dismissed for reading banned books.

By 1899, the year he was expelled from the seminary, he considered himself a committed Marxist, although many commentators doubt whether his knowledge of the doctrine was at all thorough. Stalin was to spend much of the time between 1900 and 1917 in prison, mostly in Siberia, a fact which surely indicates his dedication to the cause. With the split between Lenin's Bolsheviks and the Mensheviks occurring at the Second Party Congress in 1903, Stalin was increasingly drawn to the Leninist notion of a tightly organized, revolutionary action party. Some observers have noted that this was a perfectly natural development in that Stalin was always a man of action, a practitioner, and Lenin's call for agitation instead of discussion must have greatly appealed to him.

When he was not in prison Stalin was a major Bolshevik figure in the Caucasus, organizing strikes and leading raids against the Czarist establishment. His relationship with Lenin during this period was apparently that of a trusted functionary who could be counted on to carry out party directions to the letter. Certainly he was not well known, even in Russian Marxist circles. Writing theoretical treatises was the means by which young Marxists enhanced their reputations within the movement, and although Stalin had done some writing it was not of the sort to attract much attention. Leon Trotsky, while not the most objective of observers, later asserted that he hardly remembered Stalin's name in May 1917. He was, however, exactly the type of person that Lenin needed. He was tough, efficient, brave, and above all, loyal. It was not a coincidence that this was precisely the sort of person that Stalin himself found useful in his later rise to personal power.

Stalin's part in the revolution remains the subject of a good deal of interpretation—even today. Later Bolshevik accounts, written under the watchful eye of Stalin himself, place him at Lenin's side throughout the events of 1917. While this seems to be an obvious fabrication, Stalin was a member of the Central Committee during the revolutionary year and later played an important role during the civil war. Throughout this period he accumulated a variety of titles and posts, the most important being that of general secretary of the party in 1922. Most of these positions added to the personal power of Stalin, but as long as Lenin was alive it was he who dominated the revolution and its aftermath. When Lenin's health deteriorated further in 1922, however, these offices proved quite useful in Stalin's bid to be Lenin's successor.

Lenin's Distrust of Stalin

During the last several years of his life Lenin's relationship with Stalin began to sour. Lenin became increasingly distressed with the problems of overbureaucratization and the arbitrary use of power by some of his subordinates. Stalin, in particular, seemed guilty of these offenses. In an early indication of what was to become a persistent theme of Stalinism, he had rather ruthlessly removed some Georgian Bolsheviks who favored more local autonomy for Stalin's native land. Stalin, who one might think was ill suited at least by birth for the role, had become an advocate of *Russification*, that is, the spreading of Russian culture and language throughout the ethnically diverse country controlled by the Bolsheviks. Some commentators believe that the motivation behind such action was Stalin's mania for centralized bureaucratic control rather than any love of the Russian culture, but the results were the same. Stalin was accused of "Great Russian Chauvinism" and castigated by

Lenin for his high-handed tactics. These events in Georgia coupled with several others led Lenin to a growing distrust of Stalin, which culminated in his famous last testament to the party in which he criticized Stalin's actions and recommended that he be removed from his position as general secretary.

> Stalin is too excessively rude and this defect, although quite tolerable in our midst and in dealings among us Communists, becomes intolerable in a secretary-general. That is why I suggest that the comrades think about a way of removing Stalin from that post.[1]

This recommendation was never carried out. Stalin's position as general secretary had given him sufficient power to prevent widespread circulation of Lenin's views and the ailing leader could not summon the strength to implement them. With Lenin's death in January 1924 Stalin was very much in position to contend for power.

The period between 1924 and 1930, when Stalin achieved complete control, is marked by a tremendously complicated series of maneuvers by various aspirants to Lenin's mantle. While we cannot discuss these events in any detail, some mention of them is necessary if only to indicate how different Stalin was from the other major Bolshevik figures, for example, Leon Trotsky and Nikolai Bukharin. Stalin's primary rival, particularly during the early years, was Leon Trotsky, who probably had the best credentials to succeed Lenin. Although a late convert to Bolshevism, Trotsky had served admirably during the revolution and was everything Stalin was not: a highly respected Marxist intellectual, well known for his contributions to the doctrine, and steeped in the Western liberal traditions of the movement. Indeed, Stalin was easily distinguished from most of his Bolshevik colleagues: He was less educated, apparently dull witted, always somewhat provincial in his outlook, and, above all, untouched by the Western liberalism that was an important part of the Marxist heritage.

Despite the fact that Lenin had mentioned Stalin and Trotsky as his most likely successors, few people in leadership positions in the Bolshevik regime felt Stalin to be a genuine contender. In a sense this was a real asset for him since anyone with aspirations for power saw Leon Trotsky as their main obstacle, which led to numerous coalitions within the major decision-making organs designed to "stop Trotsky." This was not simply a matter of personal rivalry. Being schooled in history, the leadership feared *Bonapartism*—that Trotsky might be to the Russian revolution what Napoleon Bonaparte had been to the French

---

[1]Nikita S. Khrushchev, "Special Report to the Twentieth Congress of the CPSU," in *The Betrayal of Marx*, Frederick L. Bender, ed. (New York: Harper & Row, Publishers, 1975), p. 414.

revolution. Consequently, the period between 1924 and 1930 saw a constant shifting of alliances among the major figures of the party. Stalin's role in this maneuvering apparently was largely that of playing the moderate, all the while using his position as general secretary of the party to advance the careers of younger Bolsheviks who were loyal to him. By 1927 Stalin had amassed sufficient power to have Trotsky and his followers dismissed from the Politbureau, by then the central decision-making organ of the party, and by 1929 that group passed a resolution expelling Trotsky from the USSR. In the same year, Stalin began the process of collectivization and relocation of the Russian peasantry, a series of events that resulted in enormous loss of life and property. Thus began the Stalinist reign of terror, which, with varying intensity, was to last for almost twenty-five years. Stalin died at age 73, in March 1953.

After successfully orchestrating Trotsky's demise, Stalin set his sights on the next most powerful figure in the party, Nikolai Ivanovich Bukharin. An intellectual who wrote on a wide range of topics from economic theory to literary criticism and who was universally acknowledged as the party's leading theoretician, Bukharin served as editor of *Pravda* and *Izvestia* and was the author of numerous books and pamphlets, including *The ABC of Communism, The Economic Theory of the Leisure Class,* and *Imperialism and the World Economy.* Among his numerous theoretical contributions were his theory of imperialism, which Lenin drew upon, and "socialism in one country," which Stalin employed; he was also the chief supporter and principal architect of the New Economic Policy. Recall that the NEP was initiated by Lenin in 1921 as a reaction to the social unrest generated by the centralized state planning and forced collectivization of War Communism.

The NEP legalized private "profit" among the peasants and other workers as incentives to stimulate production. It created a somewhat mixed economy; it divided industry in two broad categories, private and socialist, but the State enterprises remained the most significant sector, employing over four-fifths of the workers and continuing to control all heavy industry and banking. In addition, the NEP reinstituted market relationships into the economy, with the State no longer enjoying a privileged position in terms of contracts, and it decentralized the administrative direction of state enterprises. The initial results from NEP were impressive; Bukharin argued that NEP must be allowed to continue for at least a generation as part of the transition to socialism. This liberalization of the economy had inevitable, corresponding consequences in the political and social arenas: Intraparty democracy and open debate existed among the party elite while artistic freedom flourished as intellectuals like Stanislavsky, Eisenstein, Shostakovich, Prokofiev, Chagall, Blok, and others enjoyed the false dawn which lasted from Lenin's final years until Stalin had gained a firm grip on the machinery of power. Nevertheless, the NEP was short lived, becoming but one of the victims of the power struggles that followed Lenin's death.

Labeled "soft wax" by Lenin, Bukharin shifted positions inside the party throughout his career. He was both ally and antagonist of Lenin, Trotsky, and Stalin at different historic moments. With Lenin's death, Bukharin initially sided with Stalin against Trotsky over the direction and control of the party. In 1928 Stalin destroyed the NEP with the implementation of his first five-year plan: It called for centralized planning and drastic measures to ensure the rapid collectivization of agriculture and the creation of the heavy industrial base prerequisite to socialism. The following year Stalin also implemented the unanimity principle, altering the concept of democratic centralism, wherein even members of the Politburo were forbidden to voice dissent inside the party. Thus Lenin's idea of democratic centralism became Stalin's notion of bureaucratic centralism, providing all the advantages of centralization without the "inefficiencies" of democracy. In 1936, after less than a decade of Stalin's economic policies, he declared that the foundations of socialism had been built. Ironically, if unsurprisingly, Bukharin eventually suffered a fate similar to Trotsky. In one of the great show trials of Soviet history, in the spring of 1938, Bukharin along with over a dozen other party officials was charged with treason, acts of diversion, terrorism, and numerous violations of the criminal code. Among the charges against Bukharin was that he attempted to assassinate Lenin. After a trial of approximately two weeks, on the ides of March the Soviet state announced that his execution had taken place. But the news of this event received scant international attention as it was overshadowed by Hitler's march into Austria three days earlier.

MARXISM-LENINISM-STALINISM

We have already noted that Stalin's theoretical contributions to the development of Marxism-Leninism were rather meager; indeed, it was Stalin who first used the term Marxism-Leninism, rather than Marxism *and* Leninism. The compound expression signifies the apparent unity of the two theories, while the latter wording implies two separate theories with separate views. Moreover, Marxism-Leninism symbolizes the correctness of this theory, implying that it would be impossible to have another Marxism coeval with Marxism-Leninism. As early as 1924, in *The Foundations of Leninism*, Stalin began the process of canonizing Marxism-Leninism: He, or writers using his name, authoritatively established what was, and what was not, Marxism-Leninism. At the height of Stalin's power in 1938, *History of the Communist Party of the Soviet Union*

(Bolsheviks): A Short Course was published, and Stalin was identified simply as the author of Chapter Four, "Dialectical and Historical Materialism." After World War II, Stalin was reported to be the author of the entire work, which was to be taught to the entire nation.

The *Short Course* reiterates the notion of socialism in one country and introduces the idea that class struggle will become fiercer as the building of socialism progresses. But the real addition to the history of Marxism was Stalin's attempt at the institutionalization of theory: Stalin wanted to codify Marxism-Leninism into a single authoritative and legitimate world view that would simultaneously provide him, as sole interpreter of the doctrine, with a potent instrument of power. Indeed, given the paucity of Stalin's contributions to theory, Stalinism is not so much a system of independent thought as it is a particular, highly rigid, and pedestrian interpretation of Marxism and Leninism.

At some risk of oversimplification, it could be said that all of Stalin's ideological contributions revolved around the intensification of the doctrine of *socialism in one country* and the resultant enhancement of the Soviet nation-state. Stalin had exhibited his penchant for Russification and centralized control in his dealings with Georgia in 1923, acts which evoked Lenin's displeasure. Now he was in a position to apply the same types of devices throughout the entire Soviet state. From the ideological point of view it was essential that the young Soviet state develop the industrial base necessary for socialism, as well as provide for the proletarianization of the people. Whether his motivation was born of a desire for a powerful Russian nation-state or from a commitment to Marxist ideas, Stalin was determined to industrialize the nation rapidly and was willing to inflict the costs that this action might entail upon the Russian people.

With a planned economy directed from Moscow, it was possible to reinvest the capital generated throughout the country in heavy industry at the expense of consumer goods and general creature comforts for the people. Those who dissented from such policies were easily dealt with through slave-labor camps and the secret police. Whether such policies were necessary and whether the industrialization of the country would have occurred as rapidly with other economic measures are questions we cannot answer here. It is enough to say that, while the cost in human lives was tremendous, with Stalin's death in 1953 the Soviet Union had emerged as a major industrial power.

The World's First Totalitarian State

Industrialization was, however, only one of the two goals of the Leninist transfer culture. Stalin was equally interested in proletarianizing the people. It would be necessary to eradicate all bourgeois values, to remove those people who continued to hold them, and to develop a new "Soviet man," loyal to the regime and dedicated to the advancement of the Soviet state. Utilizing the same sort of centralized control, with the Communist party and the secret police as the primary tools, Stalin produced what is generally recognized as the first truly totalitarian state the world had seen. The image the world had of the Soviet Union under Stalin was one in which everything became a political matter; the heretofore private affairs of individuals were now matters of state concern. An essential instrument for the destruction of social bonds was the universal system of spying on one's neighbors. Every citizen was under moral and legal obligation to do so. As a result, millions were arrested, and uncounted numbers executed. A gigantic propaganda machine, youth organizations, art, music—all were used to impose "proletarian" consciousness from above.

With the party as the vanguard of the proletariat leading the way, every aspect of human experience was examined for its political import. Schoolbooks were rewritten to reflect proletarian values and to correct bourgeois falsifications; socialist realism in art became the only permissible form; a rigorous system of censorship was instituted to ensure there was no deviation from the party line; and, after suppressing all university chairs in philosophy, Stalin expelled all non-Marxist philosophers from the country.

Capping this gigantic system of state control was Stalin himself, a kind of giant puppeteer, pulling the strings to manipulate every aspect of Soviet life. The worship of Stalin as a great man became an integral part of the ideology. Indeed, there is evidence to indicate that Stalin believed that this sort of dictator worship was to become a permanent part of the ideology, even after his death.

It is almost impossible to describe the impact of these policies on the Soviet citizenry, peasants and high-ranking party members alike. The policy of forced collectivization in agriculture radically altered the lives of millions of peasants, while purges, capped by obviously staged trials, systematically removed any potential dissenters from the society. By 1939 Stalin had achieved a true cultural revolution, forcing thousands of old Bolsheviks into slave-labor camps, retirement, or death. The effect of all this was to develop a mass of people conditioned to respond to Stalin's personal notion of the correct path to socialism and to endure any hardships that this journey might entail. At this time one was a Marxist not because of a commitment to any particular set of ideas or values as being true, but because one was prepared to accept whatever Stalin might proclaim. All of the horrors of Stalin's domestic policies were rationalized as being necessary to the development of a strong Soviet state. This enhancement of the Soviet nation-state dominated the

Stalinist ideology in other ways as well, notably in the area of foreign affairs.

Interests of the Soviet State Come First

We earlier noted some of the difficulties that Lenin faced in reconciling the goals of the Soviet nation-state with those of the international communist movement. After some equivocation, he opted for strengthening the socialist-safe area in the USSR while temporarily ignoring the worldwide revolution. Stalin, faced with the same set of problems, adopted a similar solution and expanded it to the extent that he is justifiably famed for his emphasis on the doctrine of socialism in one country. The implications of such a position in terms of both international communism and Soviet foreign policy are so vast that they constitute a genuine Stalinist contribution to the ideology and generate problems that remain to this very day.

Given what we know of Stalin's nationalist proclivities stemming from the early days of "great Russian chauvinism," it is perhaps not surprising to find that Stalin placed the interests of the Soviet nation-state above those of the international communist movement. Some of his earliest battles with Trotsky had resulted from Stalin's reluctance to involve the Soviet Union in "international adventurism." This does not mean that he doubted the eventual triumph of communism on a worldwide scale, but that he regarded the Soviet nation-state as being the prime vehicle for ensuring that eventual victory.

In its simplest terms, Stalin's policy was that the interests of the Soviet Union came first. When the base in the USSR was reasonably secure, more aggressive action in the international area was in order: But if Soviet national interests were threatened, the international activity was suspended. This policy, in effect, made the international movement (the formal body of which was called the Comintern) a tool of Soviet foreign policy and made Communist parties in other states agents of the Soviet Union. Stalin's penchant for centralized control, which was manifested in so many ways within the USSR, was applied to the international movement. Everything was directed from Moscow. While other Communist parties throughout the world were theoretically equal, Stalin made it quite clear that the Communist Party of the Soviet Union (CPSU) was first among equals. This situation posed some very interesting problems for the parties in other countries; they were accused not only of advocating the overthrow of legitimate capitalist regimes but also of being the active agents of a foreign power dedicated to that goal. Further, they were constantly subjected to rapid shifts in the party line when it suited Stalin's plans for Soviet foreign policy. The most notable of these shifts occurred in 1939 when, after years of active opposition to Adolf Hitler's regime in Germany, Stalin signed the Nazi-Soviet Pact making the USSR and, consequently, the international movement, a temporary ally of a doctrine dedicated to the destruction of Marxism. Strange bedfellows indeed, but a quite logical manifestation of Stalin's "Soviet Union First" foreign policy.

The Problems of Directing World Revolution

Even more interesting were the consequences of this policy in countries where indigenous communist movements were in open rebellion against existing regimes. We shall explore the somewhat special case of China more fully later, but a brief mention of Chinese difficulties will illustrate the problems of directing a world revolution from an apartment in the Kremlin. Following the current Moscow line of collaboration with other dissident groups within a society, the young Chinese communist movement had allied itself with the bourgeois nationalists of Jiang Jieshi (Chiang Kai-shek), only to have Jiang turn and slaughter thousands of communists. When the Chinese communists, led by Mao Zedong finally succeeded in 1949, it was largely without Soviet help and as the result of a strategy far removed from the model of the Bolshevik revolution. Owing little to the Soviet Union, it was perhaps inevitable that the Chinese would begin to think for themselves in matters of both doctrine and strategy.

Further evidence of cracks in the monolithic facade of the Moscow-controlled international movement was apparent during the 1940s. Joseph Broz Tito had succeeded in establishing a socialist regime in Yugoslavia through the use of a partisan army formed to combat the Nazi enemy. Tito simply refused to follow Moscow at every turn or to become a satellite of the USSR, and this led to his expulsion from the international movement by Stalin. All of these difficulties were to produce monumental problems for international communism after Stalin's death; in many ways the present warring factions within the movement can be seen as direct results of Stalin's conception of the role of the international movement. From the Stalinist perspective, the ideal situation was the general condition of Eastern Europe after the war, which was a fortuitous blend of expanding the international movement and serving Soviet national interests. The satellite states were creations of the Red Army and were clearly subservient to the USSR both materially and ideologically. They provided a buffer for the Soviet nation, ever fearful of German military might, while partially serving the ideological goal of spreading communism throughout the world.

From the ideological perspective perhaps the best word to use in summing up the career of Joseph Stalin is consistency. From his earliest days his vision of the path to pure communism required a Soviet nation-state, economically and militarily powerful, and he was prepared to sacrifice anything to achieve that goal. Internally, this resulted in the slaughter of thousands, perhaps millions, of people, many of them dedicated Bolsheviks. Externally, this vision reduced the once potent international communist movement to a puppet of the Soviet Union, a mere caricature of the movement of Lenin's time. It is quite tempting to see the mass horrors of the Stalinist era as a tragic mistake, the product of an insane mind bent on achieving tremendous personal power. Yet from an ideological perspective there was a cruel logic to Stalin's actions, a method to his madness. The "unity of theory and practice" ironically had been accomplished by Stalin, who effectively concentrated all doctrinal, political, and police power in his own person. It is imperative to remember that the USSR, symbol of the communist movement, was surrounded by openly hostile forces from fascism and capitalism—armies from both ideological systems had invaded and almost destroyed the revolution. Stalin's task, therefore, was to drag the young Soviet state into the twentieth century, to develop a strong economy, to eradicate any vestiges of bourgeois life, and to establish a military power which could guarantee the autonomy of communism. By the time of his death in 1953, he had in many respects succeeded.

SOVIET MARXISM AFTER STALIN

Common sense tells us that when a dictator dies the country he had ruled might fall into mass confusion. When the identifiable center of power ceases to exist, one could expect the people to feel a sense of great liberation and usher in an immediate and bloody struggle for power. While there was some of this type of reaction among the elite in the USSR at the death of Stalin, apparently the most general response was a feeling of grief, coupled with disbelief and disorientation. In a sense, the fact that there was no uprising and little chaos following his death is a tribute to the success of Stalin's policies, especially those that allowed the party to control virtually all information received by the people. Understandably, large numbers of people admired Stalin: He had, after all, successfully brought them through the Great Patriotic War. The rest of the populace, if not happy with the Soviet regime, was conditioned to accept its rule, and even the demise of the "master conditioner" was not enough to produce even the hint of outright rebellion. It is also a tribute to the rapid action and common sense of the remaining members of the ruling elite. The word "members" is appropriate, for Stalin had left no heir to his throne, and there was no one person with sufficient power to establish authority.

In many ways the situation was similar to that which occurred after Lenin's death, and the solution of the leadership elements within the state and party was much the same, with one major exception—at the top levels of the bureaucracies there existed an unspoken acceptance of the idea that a Stalin-like dictatorship could never again be allowed to develop. They reestablished the principle of collective leadership of the state and began an involved struggle for power that was to last ultimately until 1957. This leadership group, composed initially of Molotov, Voroshilov, Kaganovich, Mikoyan, Malenkov, Bulganin, Beria, and Khrushchev, was quick to realize that both their collective safety and any personal aspirations they might harbor depended on having Stalin quickly forgotten. Thus a process of "silent de-Stalinization," as Wolfgang Leonhard called it, began almost immediately. A new purge, which was begun by Stalin in his final years, was halted and the principal figures in this so-called doctors' plot were declared innocent. The number of members of the collective leadership was reduced by one when Lavrenti Beria, long hated as chief of Stalin's secret police, was declared an enemy of the state, removed from power, and executed.

These events are indicative of the general relaxation of totalitarian controls that followed Stalin's death. It can be argued that such a process was inevitable in order to secure support of party members and the people for the new regime. Nevertheless, few people in the Soviet Union or, for that matter, in the world were prepared for the wholesale rejection of the Stalinist years, which was to become the dominant theme of the latter 1950s. In pointing to these events and in marking their effect on Soviet ideology we have, for once, a rather clear benchmark—the Twentieth Party Congress of the CPSU held in February 1956.

If the period prior to the Twentieth Party Congress can be called the time of silent de-Stalinization, the congress marks the beginning of overt and vociferous de-Stalinization. The dominating theme of the entire congress was the errors of the former dictator. Beginning with speeches decrying Stalin's economic policies and censorship control, it culminated with Khrushchev's famous "secret speech" denouncing Stalin's cult in all of its manifestations. This congress has been called the most important one held since the time of Lenin, and from an ideological point of view that is correct. In the process of a wholesale renunciation of the Stalinist era, the collective leadership, dominated more and more by the figure of Nikita Khrushchev, adopted a series of policies which were, at least temporarily, to alter the face of modern communism. More important, Khrushchev's return to the principles of Leninism would establish a precedent for Mikhail Gorbachev's more contemporary attempts of defining the appropriate paths to achieving socialism. For our purposes we can once again summarize these changes using the categories of internal and external reforms.

Denunciation of Stalin

The most far-reaching alteration in internal policy was the rejection of the one-person leadership, which had been the cornerstone of Stalin's personal dictatorship. Khrushchev pictured Stalin to the party elite as a man with a mania for absolute control who presided over the slaughter of millions of loyal citizens only to gratify his desire for personal power.

> Lenin's traits—patient work with people; stubborn and painstaking education of them; the ability to induce people to follow him without compulsion, . . . were entirely foreign to Stalin. He [Stalin] discarded the Leninist method of convincing and educating; he abandoned the method of ideological struggle for that of administrative violence, mass repressions, and terror.[2]

Stalin was portrayed as the perverter of the Soviet state, an incompetent military strategist who refused to take seriously evidence of Hitler's plans to invade the Soviet Union, a butcher who forced the Soviet people to conform to his personal whims in matters as far ranging as architecture and economics. Quoting from Lenin's last testament, Khrushchev contrasted the democratic party of Lenin's day with the autocratic rule of Stalin, declaring the latter to have betrayed the goals of Bolshevism. Perhaps Khrushchev best captured the true horror of this era with this penetrating observation:

> This question is complicated by the fact that all this which we have just discussed was done during Stalin's life under his leadership and with his concurrence; here Stalin was convinced that this was necessary for the defense of the interests of the working classes against the plotting of the enemies and against the attack of the imperialist camp. He saw this from the position of the interest of the working class, of the interest of the laboring people, of the interest of the victory of socialism and Communism. We cannot say that these were the deeds of a giddy despot. He considered that this should be done in the interest of the Party; of the working masses, in the name of the defense of the revolution's gains. In this lies the whole tragedy![3]

One could go on, but it is enough to note here that this remarkable speech constituted a renunciation of the Stalinist regime and demanded a return to the true principles of Leninism. This separation of Stalin was symbolically represented some five years later when the party voted to remove Stalin's body from its hallowed burial place along side the still godlike Lenin in the Red Square mausoleum.

[2]English translation of Khrushchev speech to the 20th Party Congress on February 25, 1956, released by the U.S. State Department on June 4, 1956.
[3]Bender, ed., *The Betrayal of Marx*, p. 427.

All leaders of the Soviet Union, then and now, have been under considerable ideological pressure to demonstrate how the regime is progressing toward the goal of socialism. To this end the Soviet Union has published Lenin's official works in 55 volumes, Stalin's in 13, Khrushchev's in 8, and Leonid Brezhnev's in 9. In the 1930s Stalin declared that "the dictatorship of the proletariat," introduced by Lenin, had been surpassed. Like their predecessors, both Khrushchev and then Brezhnev felt the need to show their contribution to what Khrushchev called the "comprehensive building of communism." In the early 1960s Khrushchev declared exuberantly that "the present generation will live under communism!" With Khrushchev's political demise in 1964, the new leadership carefully retreated from this overly ambitious claim to a more modest one of achieving "developed socialism"—a "stage on the road to communism." Still, the Brezhnev leadership maintained its ties to Khrushchev, emphasizing the prolonged and gradual nature of the transition process: The goal was the same as Khrushchev's, only the pace of implementation was slowed considerably.

It also was Khrushchev who helped initiate the process of the gradual *democratization* of the political system by expanding the degree of participation in the state. From the late 1950s the soviet councils were revitalized in order to elevate their role in economic and cultural development. This, it was believed, would further demonstrate the progress toward communism, by beginning the process of the "withering away" of the state: The soviets would eventually cease to be organs of state power and would become organs of self-administration. While Brezhnev continued to pay lip service to the policy of revitalizing the soviets, change was—at best—of a more gradual, incremental manner. The current party leaders emphasized this gradualist perspective by quoting Lenin's warnings:

> We are not utopians. We know that an unskilled labourer or a cook cannot immediately get on with the job of state administration. . . . Politics is a science and an art that does not fall from the skies or come gratis. . . . A vast amount of educational, organizational and cultural work is required; this cannot be done rapidly by legislation but demands a vast amount of work over a long period.[4]

Further attempts at reform on the domestic front saw the cautious institution of some additional types of decentralization in decision making and a gradual movement away from Stalin's emphasis on heavy industry in the economy. Once the Stalinist censorship system was loosened, all types of criticisms of his regime began to appear in print. All of these

---

[4]A composite quote from D. A. Kerimov, ed., *Sovetskaya demokratiya v period razvitogo sotsializma*, 2nd ed. (Moscow: Mysl', 1979), pp. 138, 140, 142.

measures contributed to the period that is generally called the "thaw," a gradual movement away from the total political control of the previous era. We must note, however, that the type of criticism that emerged in the USSR after Stalin's death has to be taken in context. Stalin was condemned for denying the principles of Leninism and perverting the role of the party in building a socialist society. There was never any public doubt about those principles, or more important, about the ultimate control of the party as the carrier of revolutionary consciousness. However strange it may have seemed to Soviets who thought Stalin and the party were one, or wondered why other dedicated party members had not seen Stalin's perversions at an earlier date and removed him, such was the new party line. Indeed, the very leaders who condemned Stalinist practices had achieved their positions of leadership under Stalin. Needless to say, this produced some rather difficult moments for the post-Stalin leadership, to say nothing of problems in explaining their various roles under the dictator. Still, it was a liberalization of considerable magnitude when contrasted with the previous twenty-five years, and in a groping, limited way, it was a return to some of the principles of Leninism.

Changes in the International Movement

In the international sphere the same general relaxation of control occurred, but here it had much more far-reaching consequences for Marxist-Leninist theory. Almost immediately after Stalin's death the collective leadership began making overtures to Yugoslavia's Marshal Tito in an effort to bring his country back into the international movement. Tito had been expelled from that movement in 1948 for refusing to follow Moscow's line in international affairs and for numerous heresies on the economic front. Even during the last years of Stalin's reign it had become obvious that Tito was not going to knuckle under to Moscow, and that the only way the monolithic facade of international communism might be preserved would be by invading Yugoslavia. Short of this, Tito's brand of socialism might be seen as an attempt to apply the principles of Marx and Lenin under circumstances different from those in the Soviet Union and his experiment applauded as another way to build a socialist society.

Stalin could not possibly have taken such a position for at least two reasons. First, it would have denied Stalin's control of the international movement. Second, and perhaps more important, it would have challenged the Stalinist interpretation of Marxism-Leninism, which, as we saw earlier, held that while there could be a Marxist-Leninist-*Stalinist* view of the world there could not be, at the same point in history, an equally valid Marxist-Leninist-*Titoist* theory. Since Stalin could not control

Tito, the latter must be declared illegitimate! Stalin's successors had no such qualms and saw a rapprochement with Yugoslavia as one method of establishing their legitimacy as rulers of the international movement.

Thus, in May 1955, a high-level delegation headed by Khrushchev went to Belgrade in an attempt to patch over grievances between the two countries and discovered that Tito was as adamant as ever about pursuing his own course. All that could be done was to recognize Tito and the Yugoslavian Communist Party as legitimate socialists and declare that their regime was striving for the same basic goals as the USSR. Once it was admitted that there might be ways to achieve socialism that were different from the Soviet pattern, a host of possibilities presented themselves. At the Twentieth Party Congress, Khrushchev and several other speakers formally proclaimed the doctrine of *different paths to socialism*, which struck the final blow to Stalin's monolithic facade. Appealing with justification to the writings of Marx and Lenin, the speakers declared that there were numerous ways a socialist society might be achieved. At least three different paths were recognized: (1) the traditional Soviet Revolution model (by now idealized into an urban proletarian revolution), (2) a nationalist oriented partisan army type (like Tito's), and (3) a peaceful, electoral revolution. While the last might seem to be a vast departure from the Leninist approach to the doctrine, we must recall that Marx himself admitted of the possibility of a parliamentary revolution in a country like England. It appeared that Moscow had given up its monolithic control of the international movement; reactions to this new policy were almost immediate.

The combination of de-Stalinization and the rehabilitation of Marshal Tito's brand of socialism triggered revolutionary changes throughout the communist world. This was particularly the case in Stalinist satellite countries of Eastern Europe where reformist groups began clamoring for radical changes. The agitation culminated in the summer of 1956 when workers' strikes erupted in Poland and, with ominous overtones, a new government in Hungary proclaimed itself in favor of a whole series of reforms including free speech and a type of multiparty system. The reformers in Moscow were losing control: Prepared to make mild reforms in Stalin's policies, their actions had produced a revolutionary situation. Faced with the crumbling of empire in Eastern Europe and growing liberalization at home, they acted swiftly and decisively. The Hungarian regime was crushed by an invading Red Army, many Stalinist control devices were reinstituted, and reaction set in within the USSR itself.

The announcement of different paths to socialism and the renunciation of complete control of the international movement had beset the Soviet leadership with a dilemma. If complete control from Moscow was no longer possible, or perhaps even desirable, did that mean that the Soviet Union was giving up its role as the leader of world socialism? Obviously it did not, and the question now was *how much* deviation from Moscow's wishes was possible? How much independence could be tolerated? This remains one of the central problems for the USSR today and has resulted in a pendulum-like movement with respect to international communism—at one time the hard line, as in Hungary in 1956 or Czechoslovakia in 1968, at other times a toleration of experimentation or deviance within the movement, as in Eastern Europe in 1989.

Short of a new type of Stalinist control, which seems improbable, the problem of the relationship between the USSR and the international movement will remain, for it involves the conflicting aims of Soviet nationalism and international communism. A final ideological change to emerge from the Twentieth Party Congress exhibits the same general characteristics and has produced additional problems for modern Soviet communism. This is the doctrine of *peaceful coexistence.*

The Doctrine of Peaceful Coexistence

It was a long-established Marxist tenet that communism was locked in an unceasing battle with the capitalist forces of oppression throughout the world. While the doctrine of socialism in one country and the alliance with Western capitalist powers during World War II can be seen as deviations from this general policy, on the ideological level the doctrine remained firm: constant struggle and the eventual triumph of worldwide communism. Although many of the other ideological changes of the Twentieth Party Congress could be justified as a return to Leninism, any change in this doctrine would be counter to the words of both Lenin and Marx, who foresaw unceasing wars during the capitalist phase. Still, the reality of Soviet foreign policy for many years had been the tacit acceptance of coexistence, and at times cooperation with the enemy.

To justify these actions, the leadership group now proclaimed that socialism had achieved sufficient power that it was no longer threatened with annihilation by the capitalist powers or, if it were, the outcome would be mutual annihilation. Modern weaponry, particularly the development of nuclear devices, made the prospect of all-out war between the two camps less than desirable. Thus, cooperation with the enemy was seen as necessary in the second half of the twentieth century. This did not, however, alter the basic premise of Marxism-Leninism that communism would eventually triumph. Peaceful coexistence was described as a change in tactics in that competition with the capitalists would be carried on in other ways. Later Khrushchev would declare that socialism would beat capitalism at its own game by outproducing it and achieving world economic domination. Further, the Leninist doctrine of imperialism was given greater emphasis, and small wars of national liberation in the Third World were seen as sapping the strength of the major capitalist powers. Given these alterations in tactics, it became perfectly consistent for Khrushchev to proclaim coexistence and cooperation on the one hand and to declare that socialism would bury capitalism on the other.

Nonetheless, the elevation of peaceful coexistence to the level of dogma displeased many loyal Marxists throughout the world. Indeed, as we shall see in the following chapter, it constitutes one of the main ideological arguments between the Soviet Union and China. Many Western observers see the doctrine of peaceful coexistence as the major symbol of a general deradicalization of Soviet Marxism, and there is some basis for this view. As a large and powerful nation-state, the USSR is bound to have a stake in preserving the status quo, irrespective of its ideology. But before we accept a view of the Soviet Union as growing fat and complacent, willing to join hands with capitalist countries in preserving their positions of mutual power, we must remember that the Marxist-Leninist ideology has had a great effect on the actions of the leaders of the Soviet Union, and that this ideology requires further revolutionary changes in the world.

PERESTROIKA

If Khrushchev represented a liberalization of policy, the years of Leonid Brezhnev's leadership (1964–1982) were a conservative, bordering on reactionary, return to the slow-paced stability of the final Stalin years. Under Brezhnev a movement to rehabilitate Stalin made some progress, although it was blocked by many anti-Stalinists in power. Brezhnev returned the bureaucracy to its powerful position and attempted to transfer the concept of *vozhd* from the general secretary to the party itself. During his regime those individuals with *nomenklatura* status, that is, those holding important positions in the party or the state, or securing high-level party clearance for significant posts, comprised an elite who had access to special privileges and powers, including exclusive stores and spacious apartments. The daily lives of those with *nomenklatura* were so fundamentally different from the average soviet citizen that it could be said that it was as if they lived in a different country. Toward the end of Brezhnev's life, corruption and lethargy seemed to pervade many facets of society.

It has been well said that during the Stalin years the "state swelled up, the people grew lean." This was certainly true in the Brezhnev years as well: And on the ideological level Brezhnev's achievements are even more lean than Stalin's. Ironically, Brezhnev nevertheless did create a political situation that both demanded and permitted the emergence of a dynamic, almost puritanical leader whose first task became awakening the Soviet Union from its slumber in cynicism, corruption, alcoholism, and moral decay.

Following the death of Brezhnev in November 1982, the Soviet Union underwent two rapid changes in party leadership with the deaths of Yuri Andropov in February 1984, and thirteen months later, Konstantin Chernenko. In March of 1985, Mikhail Sergeyevich Gorbachev, a lawyer and agronomist, became the youngest general secretary of the party since Stalin. More significantly, he ushered in a new phase in Soviet ideology with his demands for *perestroika*.

Perestroika, usually translated simply as restructuring, was both the central theme in Gorbachev's plans for the necessary economic, political, and psychological changes in the Soviet Union and the title of his widely read book. To view *perestroika* as either a reform movement, a clever public relations trick of putting a new face on old policies, or as the Soviets finally adopting the methods of capitalism without calling it capitalism, is to miss the scope, dimensions, and essence of the idea. "*Perestroika* is a revolution," Gorbachev wrote, "and the most peaceful and democratic one at that."[5] In fact, it was a call for a total, cultural revolution that was to affect not only the economic and political structures but also the very individuals who comprised the Soviet Union; it was to affect not only the elites of the State and the party but also the entire population down to the lowest individual. Gorbachev explained that "The greatest difficulty in our restructuring effort lies in our thinking, which has been molded over the past years. Everyone, from general secretary to worker, has to alter this thinking. . . . We have to overcome our own conservatism." Clearly, this change in attitudes, in consciousness, must be total. It should start with *perestroika* of oneself. Economic and political structures must be *re*structured; so too must individuals: "I can see from my own experience that all of us are changing in the course of *perestroika*. It would be unfair to deny someone the right to experience their own *perestroika*."[6]

Gorbachev skillfully returned to the glorious moments in Soviet history, especially the NEP days of Bukharin and Lenin, to gain legitimacy for his own ideas. But even Stalin, subject publicly to vilification by Gorbachev, was carefully employed to marshal support for *perestroika* as Gorbachev explained its dialectical dynamics. Initially the need for *perestroika*, seen and developed by the party elite, took on the attributes of a "revolution from above," an image from Stalin's early days. How-

---

[5]Mikhail Gorbachev, *Perestroika: New Thinking for Our Country and the World* (New York: Harper & Row, Publishers, 1987), p. 74.
[6]Ibid., p. 65.

ever, *perestroika*'s success depends upon it ultimately becoming a "revolution from below." As *perestroika* gains energy from the "grass-roots" activity, it will take on a dynamic life of its own.[7] The extent to which Gorbachev can indeed accomplish this monumental task of gaining support for his policies among the masses—by drawing them into the decision-making processes of production and politics, by what he calls the "democratization of all aspects of society"—he will be successful in "guarantee[ing] that the current processes are irreversible."[8] In a very real sense, Gorbachev's own task as the leader of *perestroika* is to ensure that he, as leader, "withers away." If he accomplishes this feat, no amount of bureaucratic lethargy or outright opposition can halt the revolution.

While the subtitle of Gorbachev's treatise on *Perestroika—New Thinking for Our Country and the World*—emphasizes the subjective dimension to *perestroika*, there is little doubt that Gorbachev fails to appreciate the monumental objective factors standing in his way. While the Soviet Union's economic achievements since the end of its civil war are, in quantitative terms, impressive—creating a mode of production that in terms of GNP is second only to the United States—the quality, variety, and distribution of consumer goods are notoriously poor. The problem of goods and services is twofold: first, the average citizen may lack the money to purchase desired goods, and even more probably, when they have the money, the goods are simply not available for purchase.

Shortly after assuming the position of general secretary, Gorbachev addressed a large audience of local party officials in Leningrad. While criticizing the waste and inefficiency of the economy, he paused and told his audience, "You know what the trouble is? You don't feel it here [as he tapped his pockets and jangled his coins]. . . . And it's about time you did!"[9] Returning to many of the ideas behind the NEP programs of the now fully rehabilitated Bukharin, Gorbachev repealed many of the state regulations which prohibited individual economic initiative, created an enormous black market, and like prohibition in the United States turned millions of citizens into law breakers. To date, scores of different kinds of small, private enterprises have been legalized: of the two lawful categories, one is based on individuals, the other on cooperatives. While neither category are permitted to hire labor, they may employ family members, retired persons, housewives, students, and other citizens after they have performed their regular work. The cooperatives involve groups of individuals who share in the proceeds from

---

[7]Ibid., p. 56–57.

[8]Ibid., p. 32.

[9]Martin Walker, *The Waking Giant: Gorbachev's Russia* (New York: Pantheon Books, 1988), p. xvi.

the services provided, for example, restaurants and taxi services; it is the cooperatives, furthermore, that appear to be having the greater impact on the Soviet economy.

This utilization of positive incentives and market mechanisms have led some in the West to argue that the Soviets are finally recognizing that capitalism is a more efficient and dynamic mode of production and one that they too must adopt. This is wrong. It confuses incentives and markets with capitalism. It is also a bit of wishful thinking, not unlike those who mistakenly argue that a minimum wage in capitalist countries is the beginnings of socialism. To be sure, Gorbachev has promised an end to the authoritarian, bureaucratic system of strict planning through administrative edicts, but this is not synonymous with establishing capitalism. In *Perestroika* the historic goals of the USSR are reaffirmed: the Soviets are building to create a society based on the communist principle "From each according to his or her ability, to each according to his or her needs." Yet the leadership now acknowledge that they are generations away from that goal. In the transition period, the distribution principle of socialism, "From each according to his or her ability, to each according to his or her work," will be established, thereby allowing individuals to earn the extra income they desire. In contrast to capitalism, where small, private entrepreneurs are part of an overall system of exploitation and human degradation, under socialism individual private production is permissible—indeed it may be required—in that it meets the socialist distribution principle and helps build the economic base needed for the transition to communism.

To further ensure the opening, or liberalization of society, Gorbachev advocated an emphasis on the "rule of law," extending its protection of the individual against the state. In addition to initiating a discussion of the desirability of implementing the idea of the presumption of innocence until proven guilty into the criminal code, Gorbachev has already articulated the even more sweeping notion that "everything which is not prohibited by the law is allowed."[10] Under both Stalin and to a lesser degree Brezhnev, the obverse of this notion was the norm; that is, unless the law specifically permitted a particular behavior, the legality of the behavior was questionable. Obviously, this led to self-censorship and stifled individual creativity. It is precisely individualism, the "liberal" individualism of Marx and Engels, which Gorbachev argues has been one of the casualties of a misconceived collectivism. Gorbachev's position of valuing both individualism and freedom encouraged widespread and divergent approaches to all facets of life. (This approach, we shall momentarily see, has spilled over into the international arena.) It is small wonder that the intellectual, profes-

---

[10]Gorbachev, *Perestroika*, p. 108.

sional, and artistic sectors of society enthusiastically support his programs, hoping that this return to the *ethos* of Lenin's final weeks will this time become permanently entrenched into the nation's consciousness.

These new policies, if they are to succeed, must do more than put extra rubles in the pockets of the people; they must also create the consumer goods the citizenry want. Already there are signs that these types of goods are slowly entering the society as Soviet citizens take advantage of the new laws governing individual production and as Western merchants find Soviet consumers a rich new market to be exploited. Still, restructuring must be supported by at least one additional idea, that of openness or *glasnost.*

So crucial to the success of *perestroika* is the idea of openness that Gorbachev quickly adopted the concept of *glasnost* into his own policies: "We need *glasnost* as we need air." *Glasnost* can trace its most recent usage to the Soviet dissidents of the 1960s and 1970s, but it is also an idea that can be associated with Lenin. Like *perestroika, glasnost* is an attitude, a cultural norm, which must become internalized by the bureaucracy and the population. Not only will this further encourage individual initiative, but also encourage "criticism and self-criticism" of individuals, history, and the social system.[11] Even Lenin's thought, once considered sacred ground beyond questioning, has become the object of re-interpretation by Gorbachev. On several occasions, Gorbachev has explained that in spite of a common misunderstanding, Lenin never possessed a concrete, detailed, specific program of action to lead the Soviet Union from feudalism to socialism. Consequently, it is important to look to Lenin's writings as a guide, not a blueprint, to future action; it is the spirit, not the letter, of Lenin's ideas that provide fruitful insights to individuals and the party.

In this spirit of *glasnost,* Gorbachev has ordered the publication, without commentary, of the proceedings of the Central Committee immediately after each meeting. Criticism has also manifested itself in terms of Gorbachev's exposure, for perhaps the first time to the average Soviet citizen, of Stalin's crimes as well as criticizing some of the current Soviet leaders, among them Leonid Brezhnev and the once powerful Andre Gromyko, the last of the Soviet elite to have direct connections to Stalin's regime. In an economic and political milieu where corruption came dangerously close to being considered "standard operating procedure," encouraging the truth and exposing criminal corruption can certainly aid in weakening the bureaucracy and increasing the public perception that massive change is sweeping into all segments of the society, even into the party itself. Although the party must undergo *perestroika,* Gorbachev has made it equally clear that the revitalized party must remain the sole "political vanguard" of Soviet society.

---

[11]Ibid., pp. 78–79.

The multiple electoral processes—in the workplace, the party, and the state—are promising to open up politics by including choices among candidates in contested elections. In the first elections to the newly created Congress of People's Deputies several high-ranking party officials were defeated by alternative candidates. Among the most publicized of these defeats centered around former Moscow party boss Boris Yeltsin who ran on a platform calling for a more rapid pace to *perestroika*, an end to corruption, and elimination of the *nomenklatura* system. But not all party candidates were defeated by rival candidates; some, including an alternate member of the Politburo, were simply rejected by the voters who choose to cross the unopposed candidate's name off the ballot. This legal action on the part of Soviet voters is an interesting, and potentially very powerful, political option which liberal democratic governments do not normally provide to their citizens. When Soviet citizens strike the name of a candidate for office from the ballot, they are in effect voting for "none of the above"; this rejection—under the appropriate circumstances—could call in to question the legitimacy of the entire political system.

Gorbachev has also called for a two-term limit on all offices, including the general secretary of the party as well as the newly created state office of the "President" of the Supreme Soviet. Along these innovative lines, he argued for a clearer division between the party and the State and has attempted to create a strong, independent judiciary. Significantly, after initial discussions among some of the party elite had taken place on the possibility of an official multiparty system, Gorbachev specifically rejected this idea and endorsed the continuing necessity of a single party state. However, given the logic and dynamics of *perestroika*, the degree of pluralism and openness that had developed inside the Soviet Union and throughout much of Eastern Europe, and the political reality of *de facto* multiparty *politics*, it was inevitable that in time Gorbachev would eventually endorse the notion of a *de jure* multiparty *system*.

Glasnost has also improved the Soviet's standing in the international arena, a setting where any communist leader must have a political and moral concern. Here, too, Gorbachev revived some old themes and initiated a few new ones. He returned to Khrushchev's doctrine of peaceful coexistence and to Lenin's position that there is a "priority of interests common to all humanity over class interests" which, in a nuclear age, gains new meaning. "With the emergence of weapons of mass, that is, universal destruction," wrote Gorbachev, "there appeared an objective limit for class confrontation in the international arena: the threat of universal destruction."[12] Chemical, biological, and nuclear technologies of death make it clear that for the first time in history "mankind has

[12]Ibid., pp. 145–46.

lost its immortality."[13] To this end, Gorbachev has called for and initiated substantial cuts in the Soviet military.

Consequently, the Soviets have acknowledged that there are different paths to development, and "a nation may choose either capitalism or socialism. This is its sovereign right."[14] The theme of national self determination runs throughout Gorbachev's thought. Given recent past events in Afghanistan, Poland, and Czechoslovakia under Brezhnev, it has taken considerable courage for some of the so-called Soviet bloc nations to test the limits of this possibility even if Gorbachev appeared to be inviting it. Major political changes, however, have occurred—from the collapse of uncontested communist party control among Eastern European nations to the symbolically significant opening of the Berlin Wall. Gorbachev has, in general, endorsed and encouraged these changes. Indeed, Gorbachev has linked himself with the famous "Prague Spring" of 1968 by condemning the Soviet reaction to it and calling for "socialism with a human face" for the Soviet Union. However, in terms of the West, Gorbachev's position, "that we respect the right of the people of the U.S., as well as that of any other people, to live according to their own rules and laws, customs and tastes," must be appropriately understood.[15] Gorbachev still believes in Lenin's theory of imperialism. "Western states continue to collect neo-colonialist 'tribute.' Over the past decade alone, the profits U.S. corporations have siphoned off from the developing countries have quadrupled investments."[16] But confronted by the reality of the nuclear age, tragically felt by the Soviets at Chernobyl, where in Europe alone there exists hundreds of nuclear power plants and countless chemical manufacturers, the option of waging war—conventional or nuclear—remains out of the question for Gorbachev. While the Soviets will continue to support the liberation struggles of colonial peoples, these "wars of national liberation" will have to be fought out on the economic, political, and cultural levels. Moreover, Gorbachev assumes that the scientific basis of socialism still means that, in the long run, "if we adhere to its basic principles, if we take fully into consideration human interests and the use of benefits of a planned economy, socialism can achieve much more than capitalism."[17] And ultimately, capitalism will fall. Nevertheless, a class war between these two systems can only be fought out in nonmilitary ways: Nuclear war would truly be the end of history. Gorbachev furthermore understood that the potential for ecological disaster also links humanity in its common

[13]Ibid., p. 138.
[14]Ibid., p. 143.
[15]Ibid., p. 12.
[16]Ibid., p. 171.
[17]Ibid., p. 86.

threat to total extinction: "We are all passengers aboard one ship, the Earth, and we must not allow it to be wrecked. There will be no second Noah's Ark."[18]

Whether *perestroika* can become more than a set of ideas and actually becomes a concrete reality in terms of the daily lives of soviet citizens continues to be an open, and troubling, question. Gorbachev has inherited not only the lethargy and corruption of the Brezhnev era, but all the political problems confronting the leader of a vast country which spans five time zones and is comprised of different nationalities and ethnic groups, each with their own history and culture. In fact, *glasnost*— an ideal most Americans assume all individuals want—is a foreign notion to some of these groups who find it threatening to their very being; hence, it is probable that Gorbachev will encounter strong resistance to his revolution among ethnic and national groups inside his own country. Gorbachev has drawn a distinction, perfectly consistent with the notion of different paths to socialism, between what is appropriate behavior for foreign governments and what is permissible inside the Soviet Union. Indeed, there appears to be a split in the Soviet system between the center, where *glasnost* and *perestroika* are strong, and the periphery, where they have yet to penetrate and where conservatives can control the local machines for the near future. Nevertheless, it is clear that something fundamental has been initiated in the Soviet Union. *Perestroika* is a revolution whose significance has the potential of rivaling that of 1917 in terms of importance for both the Soviet Union and the world.

The more than sixty years of Soviet Marxism have produced numerous and far-reaching changes in Marxist-Leninist ideology. Still, one can argue that prior to Gorbachev the broad outlines of Marxism-Leninism remain fairly intact and that the alterations made by numerous leaders of the USSR have been merely tactical adaptations to fit changing circumstances. We have made only a small attempt to spell out the more recent twists and turns of Soviet policy, largely in the belief that without the perspective afforded by time it is difficult to know when such alterations are merely temporary. Nevertheless, it is clear that all Soviet leaders have felt the necessity of showing their personal allegiance to the ideological demands of progress: Lenin introduced "the dictatorship of the proletariat"; Stalin the "building of socialism"; Khrushchev the "comprehensive building of communism"; Brezhnev the more elegant "developed socialism"; and Gorbachev, *perestroika*.

Ideological considerations are, and will continue to be, of major importance to the Soviet Union. However, at least since the death of Stalin, the Soviet Union and its leaders have had no monopoly on interpretations of Marxism-Leninism. Other leaders, other countries,

---

[18]Ibid., p. 12.

have seen fit to interpret the doctrines differently. Thus, we will now turn our attention to a discussion of a central problem of modern communism—the existence of another major interpreter of Marxism-Leninism who claimed that much of the history of Soviet Marxism involved a perversion of the original doctrine. We will now examine the political thought of Mao Zedong.

SUGGESTED READINGS

BARRY, DONALD, AND CAROL BARNER-BARRY, *Contemporary Soviet Politics*, 4th ed. Englewood Cliffs, N.J.: Prentice Hall, 1992.

COHEN, STEPHEN, *Bukharin and the Bolshevik Revolution*. New York: Vintage Books, 1975.

———, *Rethinking the Soviet Experience*. New York: Oxford University Press, 1985.

DEUTSCHER, ISAAC, *Stalin: A Political Biography*. New York: Random House, 1960.

GORBACHEV, MIKHAIL, *Perestroika: New Thinking for Our Country and the World*. New York: Harper & Row, Publishers, 1987.

HILL, RONALD J., AND PETER FRANK, *The Soviet Communist Party*. Boston: Allen & Unwin, 1981.

HOUGH, JERRY, *The Soviet Prefects: The Local Party Organs in Industrial Decision-Making*. Cambridge, Mass.: Harvard University Press, 1969.

MARCUSE, HERBERT, *Soviet Marxism*. New York: Random House, 1961.

MENON, RAJAN, *Soviet Power and the Third World*. New Haven, Conn.: Yale University Press, 1986.

MERLEAU-PONTY, MAURICE, *Humanism and Terror: An Essay on the Communist Problem*, tr. John O'Neill. Boston: Beacon Press, 1969.

STALIN, JOSIF, "The Foundations of Leninism," in *Essential Works of Marxism*, Authur P. Mendel, ed. New York: Bantam Books, 1961.

TROTSKY, LEON, *The Revolution Betrayed*. New York: Merit Publications, 1937.

TUCKER, ROBERT, *Political Culture and Leadership in Soviet Russia*. New York: W. W. Norton & Company, 1987.

WALKER, MARTIN, *The Waking Giant: Gorbachev's Russia*. New York: Pantheon Books, 1986.

8

The Political Thought of Mao Zedong

. . . . a revolution is not a dinner party, or writing an essay, or painting a picture, or doing embroidery; it cannot be so refined, so leisurely and gentle, so temperate, kind, courteous, restrained and magnanimous. A revolution is an insurrection, an act of violence.

Mao Zedong

CHINESE MARXISM

Although Lenin's theory of imperialism prepared us for the phenomenon of a Marxist revolution in a Third World country, the notions of either Chinese Marxism or "socialism with Chinese characteristics" still seem a bit strange from a European perspective. Indeed, the transplanting of a technologically based Western European ideology in an agrarian-based Asian culture has produced some interesting and unique results, as should be expected. Certainly, if either the United States or Canada would become socialist, each nation would bring to socialism its own, *sui generis,* national characteristics. Having said this, one must still admit that the total impression of Chinese Marxism, at least while Mao lived, is quite consistent with the basic doctrine of classical Marxism-Leninism, and the political thought of Mao Zedong can be seen as a logical outgrowth of those classical doctrines. Indeed, even the recent reforms inside China have been carried out in the name of Marxism-Leninism and Mao Zedong Thought. Of course, China is not the only example of Marxism in an Asian setting—or for that matter—in a lesser developed country. It is, however, an early example of Marxism in a non-European culture. Moreover, in the figure and Thought of Mao Zedong we encounter a major contributor to the evolution of Marxism. In general, Mao's contribution to theory has come in the form of tactical application. Yet, given the Marxist notion of the unity of theory and action, it is easy to understand how Mao's innovations have had a profound effect on expanding the applicability of Marxism-Leninism.

The mere presence of a figure like Mao Zedong presents a host of difficulties. Much as in the case of Stalin, Mao's writings have been edited and changed at various times in order to establish his credentials as a major Marxist theoretician. As recently as 1977 the Chinese Communist Party (CCP) published the fifth, and perhaps final, volume of the *Selected Works of Mao;* this volume included only articles and speeches from 1949 to 1959, thus ignoring his more radical and politically threatening thoughts which led up to the now officially infamous Cultural Revolution. Nevertheless, his thoughts on even the most prosaic matters at times were treated by the Chinese as absolute dogma and elevated to the position of commands of God. To Western minds some of his thoughts seem silly, if not simply absurd. Still, there is little doubt that the figure of Mao Zedong loomed large not only in China but also on the international scene. During a time when the rising aspirations of the so-called Third World produced widespread instability and revolution, the Mao-led Chinese revolution became a major symbol of success.

To communists troubled by the apathy of the proletariat in highly developed capitalist countries, Mao's model of a successful revolution in an underdeveloped country was a source of hope for the future of international communism. To Western capitalists, the spread of Chinese influence under Mao appeared to be one of the major obstacles to world peace. Consequently, it is understandable that Westerners find the new Chinese leadership's more open-door policy toward capitalism to be a welcome change. Still, if assessments of Mao differ, all groups could agree on his importance, and on the details of his colorful life.

The Life of Mao Zedong

Born December 26, 1893, in Shaoshan, a village in the south China province of Hunan, Mao was the eldest child of a peasant family. He spent most of the first twenty-five years of his life in this area. Although his father was reported to be a demanding, authoritarian figure, his industriousness allowed Mao the freedom to pursue a classical education in a local village. From 1901 to 1906 Mao attended primary school in his district. At the age of 14, the family arranged Mao's marriage to a local girl; never living together, Mao repudiated the marriage. At the age of 17, Mao entered the Tungshan Higher Primary School. There he became interested in politics while participating in the Chinese Revolution of 1911. The revolution ended the Manchu dynasty, established the Republic of China under the short-lived, provisional government of Sun Zhongshan (Sun Yat-sen, 1866–1925), and initiated a prolonged period of political instability and warlordism. Following this initial brush with revolution, Mao returned to his studies, spending the next five years in the equivalent of a local college. In 1919 Mao took part in the May 4 Movement—an intellectually led reaction to the provisions of the Versailles Treaty, which left Japan in control of the former German concessions in Shandong; this developed into a boycott of Japanese goods when industrial and craft workers joined the scholarly community in political action. Shortly thereafter Mao embraced Marxism and participated in the First Congress of the CCP in 1921.

It was during the 1920s that Mao, on his own initiative, discovered, investigated, and helped develop the revolutionary potential of the peasants. The revolutionary potential of the peasants was so great that it is not too much to claim that they became the single most important force in altering China. As Mao put it in his famous 1927 *Report on an Investigation of the Peasant Movement in Hunan:*

> In a very short time, in China's central, southern and northern provinces, several hundred million peasants will rise like a mighty storm, like a hurricane, a force so swift and violent that no power, however great, will be able to hold it back.[1]

[1]Mao Zedong, *Selected Works of Mao Tse-tung*, 4 vols. (Peking: People's Publishing House, 1960), Vol. 1, p. 23.

The year 1927 witnessed two other crucial events in Mao's life. The disastrous Autumn Harvest Uprising in Hunan made Mao a wanted fugitive who was forced to seek refuge in the countryside. There he successfully established a revolutionary base in the Chingkang Mountains. These early years of struggle culminated in 1934–1935 when Mao, his movement facing imminent destruction, led the remaining 100,000 adherents of the Chinese Communist Party on the famous Long March some 6,000 miles north from Jiangxi to Yanan. Many of the leadership but less than 20,000 of the rank and file survived the arduous ordeal of the march. The Long March became a symbol of Mao's and the party's commitment to struggle against tremendous odds, and, as we shall see, that concept of struggle was to become one of the most important parts of Mao's later teachings.

Throughout China's war with Japan (1937–1945), Mao continued to struggle and build a support base in north China, this time against both the Kuomintang (KMT), under the leadership of Jiang Jieshi (Chiang Kai-shek), and the invading Japanese—even though the KMT was supposed to be in an alliance (called the United Front) with the CCP. Near the conclusion of the war, the Seventh Party Congress of the CCP in 1945 adopted the Thought of Mao Zedong as the official guide in all party work. The decade symbolically ended on October 1, 1949, when Mao, standing high atop Tiananmen, the Gate of Heavenly Peace in Beijung (Peking), proclaimed the founding of the People's Republic of China, which he would serve as the first chairman. Thus, like Lenin, Mao can be considered the father of the revolution as well as the founder of his nation's first united modern state. Until his death in 1976, Mao continued to act as a crucial force in the evolution of China. Indeed, few individuals have had as profound an impact, in both thought and deed, on the modern world. Mao's continuing influence on China's development will depend, as in the past, on the role played by his ideas—the Thought of Mao Zedong.

Mao's Rural Strategy

China's 600 million people have two remarkable peculiarities; they are, first of all, poor, and secondly, blank. That may seem like a bad thing, but it is really a good thing. Poor people want change, want to do things, want revolution. A clean sheet of paper has no blotches, and so the newest and most beautiful words can be written on it, the newest and most beautiful pictures can be painted on it.[2]

It has often been said that China provided a nearly perfect test

[2]Quoted in Stuart R. Schram, *The Political Thought of Mao Tse-tung*, rev. ed. (New York: Praeger Publishers, 1969), p. 352.

case for the Leninist theory of imperialism. Here was a country that had long dominated its neighbors, both militarily and culturally, only to succumb to the superior technology and military strength of colonial European powers. The beginning of the twentieth century saw China subservient in every sense of the word; the country had been carved up into spheres of interest by Western imperialists and subjected to the machinations of great-power politics. Faced with this condition of impotence, some Chinese saw a solution in the wholesale importation of Western technology and culture, others in the return to the basic strength of a superior Chinese culture. Given what we know of the process of cultural transformation and rejuvenation, it was perhaps inevitable that certain Western values were imported and altered to fit traditional Chinese patterns. Prime among those Western idea systems was Marxism.

Throughout its early days, the Chinese Communist Party operated as if the classical model of a Marxian revolution had a direct application to China. Efforts were largely concentrated on recruiting members of the proletariat, and organizational work was primarily in the larger cities. While Lenin's example in the Soviet revolution made the establishment of *peasant cadres* possible as well, there was no question in Lenin's mind that the proletariat retained its role as the leading element in revolutionary activity. Mao Zedong, although he was of peasant background, originally adhered rather strictly to the classical line advocating an urban-based, essentially proletarian revolution. Indeed, his peasant background initially made him quite skeptical of revolutionary action on the part of the Chinese peasantry, a position closer to Marx than Lenin. Further than that, the urban-based activities of the Chinese Communist Party were at odds with the revolutionary advice of the Comintern emanating from Moscow—advice which emphasized the central role of the peasant class in underdeveloped countries. Lenin and later Stalin both declared the peasantry to be a prime asset in revolutionary activity in China. Although it is difficult to date precisely, Mao's position on this matter apparently began to change during 1925, and the change became decisive in 1927 with his report on peasant activities in Hunan Province.

In his report on the Hunan peasants, Mao emphasized that most of the revolutionary activity in the province was being carried out by the poor peasants and that in the future they would play the major role in the Chinese revolution. So vast and mighty did Mao find the peasants as a revolutionary force, that he described to his party only three alternatives: the party could march at the head of the peasants and lead them, trail behind them, gesticulating and criticizing, or stand in their way and oppose them. Unequivocally, Mao advised his party, in the mold of a classical Marxist-Leninist, to organize them!

Although Mao may have been somewhat slow in initially discovering the peasants as a revolutionary vehicle, once that occurred he never abandoned them as the source of revolutionary power and theory. Indeed, Mao began to speak of the increasingly important role that the Chinese peasantry would play in *leading* the revolution, eventually coming to the position that some of the leadership elements of the party could be drawn from the peasantry. Whether or not such a position constitutes a genuine contribution to Marxism-Leninism, Mao had definitely altered the tactics of revolutionary activity. Even Lenin, who used the Russian peasantry extensively and emphasized their role in revolutionary activity, never granted them leadership status. To Lenin's mind the peasantry constituted an allied force that was always to be subservient to the control of the class-conscious proletariat. Given the leading role of the Chinese peasants it was a natural, if not logical, step for Mao to declare that the focus of revolutionary activity ought to be carried out on the peasant's home ground—in the countryside, rather than the cities. Here, then, are the three major elements of the rural strategy: (1) a revolution in which poor peasants could participate in leadership roles, (2) a base in the inaccessible countryside, and (3) the advocacy of guerilla warfare. These constitute genuine Maoist contributions to the doctrine.

It can be argued that Mao's entire rural strategy is but an extension of the doctrine of imperialism, but if that is so it is a most important extension. Under imperialism, the stronghold of the foreign capitalists is bound to be in urban areas where their monopoly on the use of force is most effective. If this is the case, the urban area is the least likely place for revolutionary activity to occur, and the small urban proletariat, whatever the extent of its consciousness, is easily suppressed. In much the same fashion as Lenin's imperialism, Mao advocated gradually gaining control of the countryside where the capitalist armies were most vulnerable, assaulting the capitalist citadels in the cities only at the end of the revolution, when success was guaranteed. Just as Lenin would have revolution in underdeveloped countries cut off the mother country's source of superprofit, depriving them of resources, so Mao would encircle the urban areas effecting the same result and thus ensuring the eventual capitulation of the imperialist dominated, bureaucratic, *compradore* regime in the cities.

Similarly, Mao looked on the backwardness of the peasants in the rural areas as a virtue. Since they lived in the countryside, removed from the destructive impact of imperialism, the peasants represented an unadulterated class, a class that had not been exposed to the embourgeoisement of capitalism. "Poor" and "blank," the countryside of China was the ideal area for basing a revolution. Mao summarized these tactics in four principles: when the enemy advances, we retreat; when the enemy camps, we harass; when the enemy tires, we attack; when the enemy retreats, we pursue. In support of this strategy, Mao urged the development of rural "safe areas," where peasant support was assured and supplies were plentiful, to which the revolutionary army could retreat in the face of concentrated opposition. The essential element in guerrilla warfare is the ability of the armed forces to live with the people and to be able to fade back into the mass of peasants when required. From this rural safe area, the guerrilla forces would launch periodic attacks on the enemy, avoiding major confrontations where the enemy's superior firepower would prevail, all the while expanding the area under their control.

From an international viewpoint, this meant that the underdeveloped countries of the world were like the countryside in China, and the imperialist nations were like China's cities; the international strategy, then, was for the international "countryside" to *encircle* the "cities" of the world. Naturally, China would serve as model and supporter of guerrilla wars around the globe. Guerrilla warfare against major Western powers has become common practice during the past several decades and, while there have been numerous refinements in the tactics of this type of military action, the basic strategy for this kind of communist revolution originated with Mao. From the theoretical perspective the entire rural strategy can be seen as an adaptation of the basic teachings of Marx and Lenin to Chinese circumstances. The leading role of the peasantry was undoubtedly dictated by the large number of peasants in China whose support was necessary for a successful revolution. In a sense, Mao was altering the doctrine to maximize his support, but the alteration in Marxist-Leninist theory nevertheless remains. Similarly, in an effort to gain further support from the Chinese people, Mao developed a concept of the advancement to and through socialism, which differs from the Soviet model and which may be seen as yet another contribution to the doctrine.

CHINA'S PATH TO SOCIALISM

Owing to the extremely backward state of the Chinese economic base, it was generally conceded that the country could not immediately move into a socialist phase after a successful revolution. Further, Mao realized that it would be necessary to retain the technical skills and the general support of many classes in order to develop the industrial base necessary for the march to socialism. We have seen that Lenin had similar problems in the USSR and tolerated a degree of bourgeois capitalism, particularly under the New Economic Policy. Still, Lenin was never very happy with the existence of a small bourgeois class, however weak, for he was sure that they would eventually try to subvert revolutionary goals; Stalin later solved this problem by eradicating most bourgeois elements in the society.

Because of the semifeudal nature of China, Mao contended that it would
be necessary to adopt a somewhat different solution. He proclaimed the
existence of a People's Democratic Dictatorship, which would unite all
anti-imperialist elements within the country in support of the revolutionary regime. Particularly noteworthy was his treatment of the
bourgeoisie in Chinese society. He made a distinction between the
national bourgeoisie, who were anti-imperialist, and the *compradore bourgeoisie* (also known as the *international bourgeoisie*), who were deemed lackeys
of the imperialist powers. The latter were intractable "enemies of the
people," while the former were considered to be part of the four-class
bloc called "the people." At that time, the four classes were the *proletariat,* the *peasantry,* the *petite bourgeoisie* (which included "rich peasants"), and the *national bourgeoisie.* Given the Marxist perspective, Mao
emphasized the point that even the term "the people" had different
meanings in different countries and in different historical periods within
each country. Consequently, nearly any group—if their thinking is
correct—can belong to the people. As Mao put it in 1957:

> At this stage of building socialism, all classes, strata, and social groups that
> approve, support, and work for the cause of a socialist construction belong
> to the category of the people, while those social forces and groups that
> resist the socialist revolution and are hostile to and try to wreck socialist
> construction are enemies of the people.[3]

Anyone, then, could be considered a legitimate member of the People's
Democratic Dictatorship provided that person was willing to help China
move through the presocialist phase into the establishment of a socialist
society. Here we see another attempt by a Marxist to integrate the
values of nationalism and communism for the purposes of revolution.
Mao was willing to tolerate the existence of bourgeois elements within
the society, even to declare them an integral part of the process of
developing socialism, if the historic conditions deemed it necessary. This
is not unlike the ideological logic employed by Deng Xiaoping in his
economic reform program initiated after Mao's death.

Although this is a significant departure from earlier thought, it
must not be overemphasized, for the national bourgeoisie must be
nationalist and ultimately will be assimilated into a single-class society,
which turns itself into a classless community. Indeed, the economic
developments within China from 1953 until Mao's death can be seen
as a continuing process in reducing the power of these bourgeois elements. The significant fact is that this will be accomplished through the
reeducation of the bourgeois group within the society. Articulating what

[3]Ibid., p. 305.

seems to be a recurring theme of Chinese communism, Mao declared that the bourgeoisie would be gradually reeducated so that they would gain the *people's perspective*, thus becoming full-fledged members of the socialist regime. In discussing this matter of the reeducation of the population Mao gave great emphasis to the process of proletarianization. Recall that the two major difficulties for any modern communist regime are the establishment of an industrial base and the development of a class-conscious proletariat. While Stalin's totalitarian state attempted to propagandize the entire population and was somewhat successful in that endeavor, there is little doubt that the Soviet Union had expended most of its effort on the development of an industrial base. On the contrary, throughout his writings Mao placed heavy emphasis on the human consciousness side of the coin. People of all classes were called upon to struggle with themselves to cast off old bourgeois values and to approach their everyday problems from the perspective of the new morality.

Emphasizing what Mao called the "red" side of the *red/expert* problem (that is, proletarianization/industrialization) does not mean that industrialization is to be ignored—no good Marxist could infer that. On the economic front the Chinese Communist regime has engaged in numerous experiments in an attempt to advance industrialization. Indeed, as we have already seen, Mao advanced the thesis that because China was so backward it could leap forward economically at a faster rate than even the Soviet Union, with the use of vast peasant communes and backyard industries. Still, Mao seemed above all concerned that the population should become, and remain, red; and if the industrialization of the country had to suffer slightly in order to ensure that goal, so be it. Nevertheless, proletarianization—properly united with consciousness—always remained Mao's goal. As we shall see in the forthcoming discussion of the Sino-Soviet rift, one of Mao's persistent criticisms of the leadership of the Soviet Union was that it had lost its touch with the people, becoming a bureaucratic class which advanced its own interests at the expense of the ongoing revolution. Such themes, somewhat ironically, have become central in Gorbachev's drive to "open" the USSR. This general theme of struggle, self-criticism, and interaction with the environment can also be seen as manifesting itself in another of Mao's developments in Marxism-Leninism: the notion of contradiction.

Mao on Contradiction

While Mao is generally given credit for his contribution on the question of a rural strategy for revolution in underdeveloped countries, the Chinese communists apparently stung by the charge that this was merely a tactical adaptation of Leninism, attempted to emphasize other more theoretical contributions of their famous leader. Following a long and distinguished line of Marxist thinkers, Mao is said to have made genuine theoretical breakthroughs in the study of dialectical materialism, notably through his ideas on contradiction in socialist societies.

In a 1937 essay on dialectical materialism, Mao explained the ubiquitous nature of contradiction, contending that everything contains contradiction and that without contradiction nothing would exist. Everything in the universe contains contradictions; from ideas, to matter, to social relationships, contradiction is the nature of reality. Given this position, Mao asserted that certain contradictions will continue to exist, even in communism.

In the discussion of the Chinese path to socialism, we examined Mao's argument that there would be different classes and groups in society who would unite, primarily through their opposition to imperialism. Naturally, Mao asserted that there would be conflict and struggle between these groups as they pursued their goal. This raised no real difficulty as long as these groups were united in moving toward a socialist society. However, Mao also argued that not all contradictions are the same. There are *antagonistic* and *nonantagonistic contradictions.* This doctrine of nonantagonistic contradictions constitutes a specific denial of the then-existing Soviet ideology and, despite some Leninist precedents, seems to be a genuine addition to the doctrine.

In classical Marxism the major source of conflict in the world was the struggle that was constantly occurring between classes. A basic Marxist teaching was that once the source of such conflict was eliminated through the institution of a classless society, peace and harmony would prevail throughout the world. In the final analysis, Mao reaffirmed the basically antagonistic nature of class conflict, or antagonistic contradictions; he asserted that this type of conflict can only be resolved through complete victory of the proletariat. There must be no compromise in the unending battle with capitalist powers.

There are, however, other types of contradictions present among the people that are nonantagonistic and that may be peacefully resolved. Perhaps we can characterize this type of conflict, as opposed to conflicts between the people and the enemies of the people, as resulting from a disagreement of the means to be pursued in achieving socialism. All agree on the goal but differ, and are in conflict, on how to get there. In a 1957 speech, Mao gave an example of contradictions worth examining:

> The contradiction between exploiter and exploited that exists between the national bourgeoisie and the working class is in itself an antagonistic one. But, in the concrete conditions existing in China, such an antagonistic contradiction, if properly handled, can be transformed into a nonantagonistic one and resolved in a peaceful way. But if it is not properly handled, if, say, we do not follow a policy of uniting with, criticizing, and

educating the national bourgeoisie, or if the national bourgeoisie does not accept this policy, then the contradiction between the working class and the national bourgeoisie can turn into an antagonistic contradiction as between ourselves and the enemy.[4]

This illustrates two important aspects to the issue of class antagonism. First, the antagonistic/nonantagonistic nature of a relationship varies with historic circumstances. Second, although violence may be necessary to halt counterrevolutionary forces, peaceful methods of criticism and education are preferable. As Mao explained, "A man's head is not like a scallion, which will grow again if you cut it off; if you cut it off wrongly, then even if you want to correct your error there is no way of doing it."[5]

Mao's theories on class conflict, then, put him at odds with the Soviet ideology of the time. The Soviets, adhering to the official line, had long ago asserted that conflict and contradiction had ceased to exist within its territory, and the Maoist notion of the necessity of nonantagonistic contradictions during the building of socialism was a direct refutation of that assertion. Further, Mao seemed to be saying that this contradiction was a rather desirable thing for it would produce, in proper dialectical fashion, a series of *qualitative changes* in the society, since the tension of the conflict would produce a synthesis that was notably better than that which preceded it. Thus a socialist society would be in a state of *permanent revolution*, with the results of these contradictions constituting qualitative changes or revolutions.

Even after the establishment of a communist society, the conflict between the forces of production and the relations of production will generate conflict and that, in turn, will produce conflict and resolution among the people. Echoing Heraclitus and Hegel, Mao emphasized the permanence of change through contradiction. To do otherwise would have denied one of the fundamentals of Marxism. Unsurprisingly, Mao believed Marxism also subject to these forces of change: "Marxism also has its birth, its development, and its death. . . . To say that it won't die is metaphysics. Naturally, the death of Marxism means that something higher than Marxism will come to replace it."[6]

What Mao had done was to reemphasize the dialectical basis of Marxism. Contradictions exist throughout reality. Although class conflict is still important, Mao believed other conflicts in a person's relationship to the world were also crucial. Mao's differences with the more dogmatic, Soviet view of dialectics was characteristic of the relationship between

[4]Ibid., p. 306.

[5]Ibid., p. 92.

[6]Quoted in John B. Starr, *Continuing the Revolution: The Political Thought of Mao* (Princeton, N.J.: Princeton University Press, 1979), p. 43.

the two nations, at least from the late 1950s until the 1980s. We have mentioned several points of ongoing disagreement between these two major socialist powers; now we must look more systematically at the Sino-Soviet split.

THE PRC AND THE USSR

The Sino-Soviet split must be called one of the most important events in the history of international communism. In spite of their historic, geopolitical relationship, the prospect of the world's two major socialist powers, supposedly friendly allies in the fight against capitalism, lashing out at one another on ideological grounds, even engaging in warfare on their common border, is rather difficult to understand. Marx or Lenin, to say nothing of Stalin, would have been horrified by this apparent breakup in the international communist movement. Given Mikhail Gorbachev's historic visit to China in the spring of 1989, it is questionable that the ideological and great-power difficulties between these two countries are a permanent facet of modern communism. We can say, however, that during Mao's reign, despite numerous attempts at accommodation, the disputes raged on with little hope for complete resolution. For the student of political ideologies this era presents a fascinating area for study because the battle for ideological supremacy brings out numerous contradictions and variations in the doctrine that might otherwise be papered over in the name of a united front. Once again, we shall emphasize the ideological nature of the conflict, largely ignoring the very real interests of the two nation-states in competition for territorial and economic domination. Although there are commentators who will defend the proposition that differences between China and the Soviet Union began as early as 1949, with the success of the Chinese Communist Party, a far more concrete benchmark appears to be the death of Stalin and the emergence of de-Stalinization in the Soviet Union.

The Chinese response to the de-Stalinization policies of the Twentieth Party Congress of the CPSU was ambivalent. Reacting to the wholesale denunciation of the Stalinist era by Stalin's successors, Mao agreed that the Soviet leader had made some errors; in particular he denounced the Stalinist cult of the hero. Still, the tone of Chinese de-Stalinization was far more muted than the same process within the USSR. Despite Stalin's errors, Mao asserted that Stalin was a great leader of Marxism-Leninism and had performed a most valuable role in developing the Soviet Union economically. In retrospect it is obvious that the tone of the Chinese response to Stalin's death was far more laudatory than that of the USSR, undoubtedly presaging the much more acrimonious ideological splits that were to follow.

In a sense, however, one could argue that some sort of contest for ideological supremacy was inevitable from the beginning. As far back as 1936, Mao declared that he was not fighting a revolution in China only to turn the country over to Moscow. Moreover, the Chinese revolution was successful without a great deal of Soviet support and it evolved a strategy for revolution far different from the classic Soviet model. This being the case, it was perhaps only natural for Mao to declare that his revolutionary model was more appropriate for Marxists in the less developed world, and that the winds of revolution would blow much more strongly from the East during the imperialist phase of capitalism.

Implicitly, then, merely by existing as an alternative to the Soviet model, the Chinese revolution offered a different way. It is, of course, a long way from the establishment of an alternative revolutionary model to the acrimonious exchanges that marked relations between the two socialist powers in the 1960s and 1970s, but in a sense it all revolves around Stalin's figure and his policies.

Faced with increasing denunciation of Stalin by the USSR, Mao found himself in a difficult position. He believed that strong party leadership was necessary in order to achieve the goals of a socialist state and he knew that a good deal of suffering on the part of the Chinese people would be part of that process. One can argue that under such circumstances it was necessary to invent an almost superhuman leader who could act as a unifying symbol for the struggle of all the people and serve as a source of inspiration. Briefly, Mao created a different "cult of the hero" in order to speed the development of China, yet he was faced with constant denunciation of that very concept from the Soviet Union. This, as much as anything, seems to be the reason for the Chinese emphasis on Stalin as a hero of Marxism-Leninism. They were going through a process similar to that of the Soviet Union in the period from 1930 to 1953, a period which necessitated tremendous sacrifice and iron-handed control.

Thus, although Stalin could be condemned for certain excesses, a wholesale denunciation of his type of regime might lead to an undermining of Mao's position. Much of this is, of course, in the realm of speculation, and there are other ideological points where the split between the two powers was more obvious. Using one of the nastiest words in Marxist-Leninist jargon, the Chinese accused the Soviet Union of a general policy of *revisionism*.

Revisionists and "Paper Tigers"

There are many facets to this particular charge, but the most general statement that can be made is that the USSR was seen as pursuing a policy of conciliation with capitalism and denying the goals of Marxism-Leninism. Specifically, the Chinese simply refused to accept the Soviet doctrine of peaceful coexistence with capitalism. In response, the CCP issued their own "five principles of peaceful coexistence" emphasizing that, unlike the Soviets, they would not *capitulate* to capitalism. We have seen that Khrushchev's (and more recently Gorbachev's) notion of peaceful coexistence did not deny the ongoing struggle with capitalism but affirmed that all-out war would be mutually destructive and must be avoided. Adopting a pugnacious stance, at least ideologically, Mao declared that Khrushchev was selling out to capitalism, denounced the West as a "paper tiger," and asserted that China with her vast population would survive a nuclear war if the imperialists elected to employ their nuclear superiority to attempt to save their decaying system. This is a particularly difficult notion to understand, for we are forced to compare public statements with actual practice.

Despite his denunciation of the capitalist powers as "paper tigers" and however often he called for an all-out, protracted war hitting the imperialists powers at the weakest link in the system, Mao's actions were not much more bellicose than those of the USSR. We cannot go into the various armed conflicts that the Chinese have had with the West, nor can we examine the Chinese role in formenting revolutionary movements in other underdeveloped countries. What Mao seemed to be trying to achieve by denouncing peaceful coexistence and adopting this belligerent stance was the unification of the Chinese people in the face of outside enemies. Furthermore, such a position placed Mao in the forefront of revolutionary ideology in modern times and permitted him to call the Chinese the true bearers of the revolutionary idealism of Marx and Lenin. Perhaps he was only scoring some ideological points at the expense of the Soviet Union, but the image of Mao, the eternal revolutionary, has had great attraction for dissatisfied people throughout the world, and continues after his death.

Peaceful coexistence/capitulation was not the only manifestation of Soviet revisionism condemned by the Chinese. They saw the USSR illicitly experimenting with various economic reforms at home and attempting to advance Soviet national interests abroad at the expense of world revolution. Most important from the ideological perspective, they accused the leadership elements of the USSR of divorcing themselves from their own people and of constituting a leadership elite that advanced its interests at the expense of the Soviet people.

We noted earlier that Mao viewed classes and nonantagonistic class conflict as part of the process of building socialism in China. From his point of view, the Soviet Union, while declaring that it had achieved a single-class society, was actually covering over the existence of a vast bureaucratic class that was so eager to preserve its position of privilege that it had become counterrevolutionary. This is, of course, a most serious charge. Ironically, as we noted earlier, it is similar to one of the recent charges made by General Secretary Gorbachev, justifying his demands for *perestroika*. But, if the Soviet Union after more than fifty years of building socialism had succeeded only in producing a society based upon a different class relationship, there must have been something wrong with the Soviet model. In criticizing the class-based nature of the Soviet Union, Mao exhibited two additional traits that seem to be persistent in his thought: dislike for formal education that leads to elitism and emphasis on the innate wisdom of the common people.

In summary, let us stray briefly from the ideological plane to say that much of the Sino-Soviet conflict seemed to be the result of the differing perspectives of an almost developed nation-state and one that is still in the early stages of economic development. From the Chinese perspective the Soviet Union had become antirevolutionary because it was basically satisfied with its position in the world. As a major power, the USSR seemed to support the maintenance of the status quo, both by accommodating competing capitalist powers and by supporting existing regimes irrespective of their ideology. Insofar as support of the status quo meant keeping China in a relatively powerless position, the USSR was bound to be condemned by Mao as reactionary. It is in this sense that Mao could speak, as he did, of the possibility of an alliance between the USSR and the United States designed to keep China in a condition of relative impotence.

From their "have-not" perspective, the Chinese under Mao demanded change and revolution throughout the world and condemned their fraternal socialists in the Soviet Union for collaborating with reactionary capitalists. Here, for the final time, we observe the difficulty of reconciling the aspirations of nation-states with the internationalism of Marxism-Leninism. This is a persistent problem of modern communism, one that shows no signs of being resolved in the near future.

MAO ZEDONG AS A SYMBOL

Throughout Mao's life many endearing labels were associated with him: Great Leader, Great Supreme Commander, Great Teacher, and Great Helmsman, to name a few. Nevertheless, Mao considered these titles to be a nuisance; he claimed that his desire was to be remembered simply as "teacher." This, it seems, is consistent with Mao's thoughts. Although he played the roles of leader, commander, and helmsman, they were not what he considered to be his greatest contribution to the revolution. At times he even seemed to disdain his exalted position, as in 1966 when he denounced the "superhuman power" attributed to his writings: "When tigers are absent from the mountain the monkey then becomes king. I have become such a king."[7] Still, his role as teacher is of tremendous importance not only to the Chinese experience, but also— as Paulo Freire has made evident in his influential *Pedagogy of the Oppressed*—to the exploited throughout the Third and Fourth Worlds; therefore, it should be discussed in some detail.

Despite repeated exhortations to the Chinese people to reeducate themselves, Mao had considerable dislike for formal education. Numerous references abound in his writings to the basic wisdom of the uneducated masses. In a discussion of education, Mao articulated his basic epistemological position: "You know I've proclaimed for a long time: we must teach the masses clearly what we have received from them confusedly."[8] Here Mao demonstrates that if it is appropriate to conceive of "truth" residing anywhere, it is with the people, not with an educated elite. He consequently warned against producing a technologically sophisticated elite that is divorced from that wisdom. Related to this was his fear of producing a Soviet-like managerial class that advanced the economy at the expense of proletarianization, or redness. Evidence now shows that the Cultural Revolution of 1966–1969 was in part instituted in an effort to break down what Mao perceived as growing class stratification in China. By sending the most radical elements in the population—the students—out to destroy pockets of embourgeoisement throughout the country, Mao was giving an object lesson to those who might stray from his model. Furthermore, by insisting that these student groups then retire to rural areas to work with their hands among the peasants he was again emphasizing the innate wisdom of the masses.

During the Cultural Revolution, countless copies of the then famous "little Red Book"—*Quotations from Chairman Mao Zedong*—were distributed by the People's Liberation Army (PLA) to help in the reeducation of China. Coming on the heels of the Vietnam war, the Cultural Revolution was yet another attempt by Mao to bring about what can be called a spiritual transformation of humanity. It was designed to shake China to its very core in hope of creating the consciousness needed for the years of struggle ahead: a China that appeared increasingly isolated and a China that soon would be without the example of Mao. Thus Mao returned to his essential belief in the desirability of struggling through contradictions, and he produced his final revolution.

Quotations from Chairman Mao Zedong was to be used as a personal guide to achieve *correct thinking*. Although the book contains numerous "inspirational" thoughts, it does not contain one practical, operational

---

[7] Ibid., p. 96.

[8] Cited in Paulo Freire, *Pedagogy of the Oppressed* (New York: Continuum, 1970), p. 82.

prescription. Hence, individuals are forced, by reading Mao, to struggle with, and incorporate into their own existence, the appropriate manner of life. During the more hectic, final months of the Cultural Revolution, it was reported that roving army medical teams were on rare occasion able, by thinking and correctly applying the chairman's thoughts, to raise the dead. Clearly, blind obedience was not the goal. Rather, the creation of hundreds of thousands of "Mao-like," dedicated revolutionaries is what was desired. The Cultural Revolution also reflected Mao's faith in the human (existential or subjective) element in history. Mao told the following story:

> There is an ancient Chinese fable called "The Foolish Old Man Who Removed the Mountains." It tells of an old man who lived in northern China long, long ago and was known as the Foolish Old Man of North Mountain. His house faced south and beyond his doorway stood the two great peaks, Taihang and Wangwu, obstructing the way. With great determination, he led his sons in digging up these mountains hoe in hand. Another graybeard, known as the Wise Old Man, saw them and said derisively, "How silly of you to do this! It is quite impossible for you few to dig up these two huge mountains." The Foolish Old Man replied, "When I die, my sons will carry on; when they die, there will be my grandsons, and then their sons and grandsons, and so to infinity. High as they are, the mountains cannot grow any higher and with every bit we dig, they will be that much lower. Why can't we clear them away?" Having refuted the Wise Old Man's wrong view, he went on digging every day, unshaken in his conviction. God was moved by this, and he sent down two angels, who carried the mountains away on their backs. Today, two big mountains lie like a dead weight on the Chinese people. One is imperialism, the other is feudalism. The Chinese Communist Party has long made up its mind to dig them up. We must persevere and work unceasingly, and we, too, will touch God's heart. Our God is none other than the masses of the Chinese people. If they stand up and dig together with us, why can't these two mountains be cleared away?[9]

If the necessary will and consciousness could be created and sustained, nothing could stand in the way of the revolution. And, from the perspective of a man who rose from the ranks of the peasantry, who spent over two decades in armed conflict, including a 6,000-mile forced march, who saw his country emerge from the crippling effects of abject poverty to the status of a strong, economically self-reliant nation, this was understandable indeed.

Thus Mao's thought could become a perpetual, ongoing guide for revolutionary action. And Mao, even after his death, could continue his cherished role as teacher.

[9]Mao Zedong, *Selected Works*, Vol. 3, p. 272.

CHINA AFTER MAO

With the death of Mao in 1976, China began the process of continuing the revolution without his physical presence. After the initial power vacuum was filled by the silencing of Mao's widow as part of the "gang of four" and the eventual emergence of Deng Xiaoping as undisputed leader of the party, Deng astutely moved to solidify his position by coming to terms with Mao's legacy, carefully using his name and memory to legitimize efforts at reform. The term de-Maoification is used by some Western scholars to describe the process employed by the new leadership of slowly separating themselves from Mao. To be sure, it is important for today's leaders to establish their own credibility as they emphasize the industrial/technological side of the red/expert debate; however, to claim that they want to disassociate themselves totally from Mao seems excessive.

De-sacralization, rather than de-Maoification, seems the more appropriate term to explain Deng's usage of the image of Mao. Deng openly criticized errors made by Mao, calling the Cultural Revolution an "appalling mistake." He also silently rebuked Mao by rehabilitating the good name of, and if possible reappointing to positions of power, many of Mao's former enemies. Deng himself was twice purged, first during the Cultural Revolution and then immediately following Mao's demise. Perhaps the most significant change, at least symbolically, was the omission of the reverential title "Chairman" before invoking Mao's name; indeed, even the head of the CCP is no longer called chairman but simply general secretary to emphasize further the point that no person should ever again have as much power as Mao. Since Deng's third coming to power, Mao's humanity and revolutionary vision was to be celebrated, but his godlike, infallible status was to be destroyed. All of this being said, Deng willingly and skillfully invoked the specific language and images of Mao most supportive of Deng's position, especially those reflecting Mao's undogmatic and realistic approach known as the "Yanan Heritage." Mao thus became a legitimizing tool for Deng's own policies and programs. And in point of fact, none of the new vocabulary and symbols employed to implement China's economic reform programs were antithetical to Mao Zedong Thought. It appears, then, that Deng preferred to use Mao as a symbol of the revolutionary past to assist in the dual policies of reaching out to the West and initiating economic development at home. In terms of both of these policies, Deng adroitly shifted Mao's notion of "self-reliance" to fit China's new needs: China must take technological and scientific advancements from the West in order to become self-reliant; at the same time China must remain independent of, not isolated from, capitalism. Nevertheless, this ongoing attachment to Mao is inherently risky: Like the angels in "The

Foolish Old Man Who Removed the Mountains," the spirit of Mao the revolutionary instigator of the Cultural Revolution remains present, albeit officially repudiated, for the more red, existentially oriented of China's leaders. And in light of the public squashing of the student led Pro-Democracy movement in the spring of 1989, it appears inevitable that the next leadership should be more red. Before attempting to assess both Deng's ability to carve his own path with Mao's image and his handling of the Pro-Democracy movement, it is necessary to examine briefly the significant changes in China since Deng's reemergence.

The Rise of Deng Xiaoping

Deng Xiaoping represented the expert/bureaucratic side in the red/expert debate. A rugged survivor of the Long March and years of struggle inside the CCP, his rise to leadership after Mao's death represented a clear signal that a majority of the elite inside the party recognized the need for a substantive change in the direction of China. While Deng was critical of the "whatever faction"—those who argued that *whatever* policies and directives Chairman Mao articulated before his death should be carried out—he also wanted to have the prestige of Mao's legacy on his side. His strategy seemed to be one of declaring the Mao of the Cultural Revolution *persona non grata*, except to criticize and humanize him. Mao's thoughts and writings independent of the Cultural Revolution, especially the early Mao, were to be read, analyzed, and applied as a guide to current practice.

Almost a decade before Gorbachev's calls for *perestroika* in the Soviet Union, China launched its own program for rational, systematic development under the "four modernizations" campaign and the "new open-door" policy: The former was to modernize agriculture, industry, national defense, and science and technology; the latter to open China to Western ideas and markets. Proclaiming itself in the "primary," or underdeveloped, stage of socialism, China recognized the need for major economic reform. Even with massive reform, China could not "leap" over this primary stage and would remain in it until sometime around the middle of the next century, and the attainment of communism remained many generations away. Unlike Mao who emphasized the subjective over the economic element, Deng argued for vast substructural changes. With a population of over 1 billion, 800 million of whom lived in rural areas and used hand tools to scratch out an existence, Deng proclaimed the urgent need to modernize China while remaining consistent with the goals and values of socialism. Material, not spiritual, incentives were deemed essential to developing socialism. Consequently, China's economic policies were to be redesigned to achieve industrialization and to commercialize, socialize, and modernize production. A kind of "commodity socialism" or market socialism was needed at that present historic moment to modernize China. The party attempted to blend planning with market mechanisms, where the state regulates the markets and the markets guide enterprises. This did not mean that China must go through a period of capitalism in order to develop the economic base to sustain developed socialism: This type of argument was labeled "mechanistic" by the CCP who believed, in Mao-like fashion, that subjective forces remain crucial to history. While supporting the development of the forces of production, Deng adamantly opposed the "*bourgeois* liberalization" of China. To assist in the guidance and limitation of this modernization process, Deng proclaimed allegiance to "Four Cardinal Principles": (1) keeping to the socialist road, (2) upholding the people's democratic dictatorship, (3) following the leadership of the communist party, and (4) applying Marxism-Leninism and Mao-Zedong Thought as the defining and limiting factor in the reform programs.

While Deng strove to revitalize China by opening up its economic and political system to new and younger voices, a clear notion of *continuity* with its revolutionary past was also apparent. He instituted a Central Advisory Committee as part of the upper levels of the CCP. Formally only a consultative body, membership on this prestigious committee required at least forty years of service in the party. Its role was to provide an institutionalized memory of China's past as a generation was coming to power who had no firsthand experience with the party's founding era. The committee's first chair, Deng Xiaoping helped establish the committee's position inside the party structure where it could shape and mold party programs.

Deng's economic policies included NEP style programs which linked financial rewards to profits earned. The term "entrepreneurship" was now officially used in English language publications. And intellectuals and experts who assist in the development of science and technology were to be materially rewarded. Of course, agriculture remained a, perhaps *the*, major economic problem facing China. Again, NEP-like programs were developed, emphasizing decentralization and individual initiative. "Peasants who get rich first" were no longer proclaimed enemies of the people, but rather were held out as role models in an attempt to encourage productivity. The rationale behind the peasants getting rich *first* campaign was that once China had developed economically, became "rich," then—but only then—could questions of socialist distribution be dealt with. "Chinese socialism" or "socialism with Chinese characteristics" became the hallmark of Deng's economic reforms.

On the political front, Deng was less successful in carrying out widespread reforms in spite of calling for "democratization" of the system. Some minor political reforms were instituted. For example, at the lower levels of the political system, the electoral machinery mandated secret ballots, open nominations, more candidates than positions, and direct elections up to the county level. Deng also took some measures to create an independent judiciary and a new legal code, to separate along functional lines the party from the state, and to improve the oversight role of legislative bodies. Finally, the party itself was to undergo reform; while still playing the leadership role, it was to be subject to the law. Nevertheless, corruption and nepotism continued to be major problems throughout the political system. The net result of the economic and political alterations remained the creation of de facto pluralism in the economic arena combined with deepening, widespread resentment over both the rampant political corruption and the failure to institutionalize the promised liberalization of the political arena.

Deng's advanced age made it imperative that he move swiftly if he was to make a lasting impression. He solidified his own power base by replacing reds with experts in positions of power. This alteration in economics had given China a decade of its most rapid economic progress ever; yet tied to this development came a nearly 30 percent rate of inflation, rampant and open corruption, and all the problems associated with the rising expectations of the masses. He opened China to Western ideas and culture, scholars and tourists, inviting cultural exchange programs varying in diversity—rock groups, the Boston Symphony, Western literature, philosophy, and films. Reciprocally, large numbers of Chinese students were permitted to study abroad. While Deng was anxious to open China to Western science, technology, and economic innovation, he failed to realize that liberal political ideals would also penetrate the system and take on a life of their own. There can be little doubt that China experienced a relatively significant degree of liberalization during this period. But this served only to whet the appetite of the students and intellectuals; for some, the pace of liberalization was too slow, for others it appeared to be coming to a stop. Although Deng, the expert, was willing to tolerate economic reform, he was opposed to the necessary corresponding political alterations. The consequences were predictable: As Marx had discovered, when the substructure and superstructure fall out of harmony, conflict results. In what has been called "four days that shook the world," in the spring of 1989, forty years after Mao first seized control over China, the world watched in disbelief as the People's Liberation Army openly fired upon students and workers in Tiananmen (which ironically means Gate of Heavenly Peace) Square. Even though it is far too early from an ideological perspective to draw conclusions from these dramatic events, a few comments seem in order.

The Fall of Deng Xiaoping

Since 1949, every decade has witnessed a major, dramatic "revolution" inside of China: the Hundred Flowers campaign and Great Leap Forward (1957–58), the Cultural Revolution (1966–69), the Democratic Wall campaign (1979–80), and the 1989 Pro-democracy movement. The most recent events were sparked by the death of Hu Yaobang, the once hand-picked successor of Deng. Hu, one of the remaining survivors of the Long March, was credited with opening China to the West and as the first of the old guard elite to adopt Western dress. In fact, he was buried in a Western-style suit and tie while Deng, dressed in the traditional Zhongshan ("Mao") jacket, looked on at the man he had sacked from head of the party months earlier. Shortly after Hu's funeral, Mikhail Gorbachev visited China: As if following Mao's advice to "Seize the day, seize the hour!" thousands of students, later joined by more students and workers, the combined forces numbering in the hundreds of thousands, jammed central Beijing and occupied Tiananmen Square; they embarrassed the party and caused Deng the loss of face by making it impossible for them to meet Gorbachev in the Great Hall of the People. Gorbachev's reforms, especially *glasnost,* had captured the imagination and support of the students. The students chanted "Dialogue, Dialogue, We must have Dialogue!" and demanded a free press, publication of the finances of state leaders to help end corruption and nepotism, self-criticism for mistakes in education policy, and a fair assessment of Hu's career. Students and workers called for an end to corruption and nepotism, a chilling reminder to Deng of strikingly similar demands made during the high point of the Cultural Revolution.

Events between the party and the Pro-Democracy movement quickly escalated. Zhao Ziyang, second of Deng's hand-picked successors, refused to carry out orders to suppress the demonstrators. Instead, he elected to visit the hunger-strikers among them and was reported to have said: "We have come too late. We are sorry. And it is right for you to criticize us." While this helped solidify his position of champion of the students, it also signaled that his reign as general secretary of the CCP was over: Deng did not want a replay of the Cultural Revolution. Deng, who had maintained his position as head of the Central Military Commission, ordered the PLA to restore order and control over the capital. Realizing the fragility of their position as troops encircled the city, the students rapidly constructed the famous Goddess of Democracy statue. The students sang the *Internationale* as they assembled the statue and finally placed it facing a giant portrait of Mao—all three of these symbols representing what the students ultimately wanted. The rest of the events are well known. After some initial reluctance, the PLA stormed the protestors killing hundreds, and perhaps thousands; workers and students by the hundreds who participated in the demonstrations were rounded up, put on trial, and punished—a few losing their lives. The crackdown was swift, brutal, and very public, to make sure all Chinese received the unambiguous, official message: "Counterrevolutionary activities" and "*bourgeois* liberalization" would not be tolerated. Although this was the official party line, creating the face-saving illusion that Deng's desperate actions saved the revolution, the students had a different response. Rhetorically they asked: "What color is Deng now?" And sarcastically they answered, "Red, with the blood of Tiananmen."

What, then, becomes of Mao? While the Western world seems anxious to bury Mao, as well as communism itself, the death of each is greatly exaggerated. In spite of much of the American press's coverage of these recent events in Tiananmen Square, the students were *not* calling for either capitalism or liberal-style democracy. Rather, they wanted to begin to create a socialism that tolerated free expression but not corruption. As for Mao, even if it is appropriate to narrow Mao Zedong Thought to being nothing more than his ideas during the Cultural Revolution, then obviously many of the elite in the CCP have turned their backs, at least for the present, on China's Maoist heritage. But the student protestors of the spring of 1989 must have found something of value in even this narrow slice of Mao Zedong Thought, as some of their demands clearly rekindled memories of the earliest months of the Cultural Revolution. On the other, more realistic, hand when Mao Zedong Thought represents the entire corpus of his work, spanning well over half a century, then Mao lives—continuing to color China's future red. Indeed, given Mao's writings "On Contradiction," it seems dialectically appropriate that an expert like Deng, who failed to appreciate the subjective side to reform movements, should have tragically failed. There can be little doubt that Deng's own, harsh judgment on the Cultural Revolution as an "appalling mistake" will be history's judgment of his handling of Tiananmen.

This is no place for a summary of the teachings of Marx and Engels as they have been developed and applied over the past century. In a very real way the four previous chapters provide only the bare outlines of the development of Marxist-Leninist ideology, thereby in themselves constituting a summary. Neither is this the place for an attempt at an extended critique of those doctrines. As we stated in the introductory discussion, the major aim is an understanding of the ideology as a prelude to evaluation. Still, there are numerous problems of communism that have entered the discussion, ranging from the lack of a truly classical communist revolution anywhere in the world to the difficulties of integrating nationalist values with Marxist internationalism. These problems surely are the beginning of a critique for anyone who feels the need to attempt one. Indeed, if there is one thing we possess in abundance in the West it is authoritative and, in many instances, well-reasoned criticisms of communist thought. Finally, before we move on to the third of the three idea systems under consideration, it will be helpful to examine briefly some of the continuing issues in communism.

SUGGESTED READINGS

FREIRE, PAULO, *Pedagogy of the Oppressed.* New York: Continuum, 1970.

LIFTON, ROBERT J., *Thought Reform and the Psychology of Totalism.* New York: W. W. Norton & Company, 1961.

————, *Revolutionary Immortality: Mao Tse-tung and the Chinese Cultural Revolution.* New York: W. W. Norton & Company, 1976.

MOODY, PETER R., *Chinese Politics After Mao.* New York: Praeger Publishers, 1983.

SCHRAM, STUART R., ed., *The Political Thought of Mao Tse-tung.* New York: Frederick A. Praeger, 1963.

————, *Chairman Mao Talks to the People.* New York: Pantheon Books, 1974.

SCHURMANN, FRANZ, *Ideology and Organization in Communist China.* Berkeley: University of California Press, 1966.

SNOW, EDGAR, *Red Star over China.* New York: Modern Library, 1944.

STARR, JOHN BRYANN, *Continuing the Revolution: The Political Thought of Mao.* Princeton, N.J.: Princeton University Press, 1979.

TOWNSEND, JAMES R., and BRANTLY WOMACK, *Politics in China,* 3rd ed. Boston: Little, Brown and Co., 1986.

WAKEMAN, FREDERIC, JR., *History and Will.* Berkeley: University of California Press, 1973.

9

Continuing Issues
in Communism

*. . . democracy certainly has a future. But in my view it certainly
does not have a present.*

Herbert Marcuse

Ever since the deaths of Marx and Lenin, the ideology of communism has continued to change in accordance with both local and global political realities. Although Marx and Lenin established the broad foundations of this ideology, it is still necessary to discuss some of the more recent developments in communism, not in the hope of presenting a detailed analysis of these additions but to show the continuing ideological debate within Marxism over many of the central ideas already presented in terms of our discussion of Marx, Lenin, and even Mao. Specifically, this chapter will briefly look at Antonio Gramsci, Eurocommunism, and Herbert Marcuse as examples of the ongoing evolution of communist ideology.

ANTONIO GRAMSCI: THE PHILOSOPHY OF PRAXIS

One of the most original political theorists of the post-Lenin generation, Antonio Gramsci (1891–1937) is often looked upon by those contemporary European communists who desire a more "open" democratic Marxism and who believe that the working class must be an active participant in its own emancipation. Head of the Italian Communist party from 1924 until his imprisonment by Benito Mussolini in 1926, Gramsci spent his next seven years in jail writing nearly three thousand pages of notes, essays, and letters. Although he died in 1937, his literary life belongs to post-Stalinist Marxism as it was only in the 1950s and 1960s that his six-volume *Prison Notebooks* were published.

Gramsci's notebooks reveal an attempt to develop a comprehensive Marxist philosophy of culture. Based on Marx's early writings, Gramsci argued against historical inevitability and economic determinism. There is, moreover, in his view no such thing as an unchanging human nature; there are only historically variable human relationships. Human beings are the center of Gramsci's universe. All human behavior and all products of human action are "true" only in relation to the universal historical processes of which they are a part. In this view, truth is always socially pragmatic; that is, an idea is true because it expresses the historical reality of the time. Gramsci's view contradicts the normal, commonsense view that truth is truth regardless of whether or not it is known, or when and by whom it is known.

In Gramsci's view even science and philosophy—as well as Marxism itself—is subject to this historical relativism. Marxism's success is due to the fact that it expressed the truth of its time better than any of the other competing theories. To Gramsci an "objective" science independent of human conception is impossible. Everything in the universe— including ideas—is a product of historical, human relationships. This was Gramsci's *theory of praxis*—the unity of theory (ideas) and human action. He wrote that, "Matter is thus not to be considered in itself but as it is socially and historically organized for production; in the same way, natural science is to be regarded essentially as an historical category, a human relationship."[1] Nothing exists independent of human action; all is praxis. "According to the theory of praxis it is clear that human history is not explained by the atomistic theory, but that the reverse is the case: the atomistic theory, like all other scientific hypotheses and opinions, is part of the superstructure."[2]

Since Gramsci's theories placed considerable weight on the role of humanity in comprehending the world, it is logical that he, like Rosa Luxemburg at an earlier time, should also have believed that the working class must play an important role in its own liberation. As we saw in our discussion of Lenin, the question of the relationship of elites and masses is an old one in Marxism. Where Lenin believed that an active, professional vanguard was needed to lead the revolution, Gramsci's philosophy of praxis involved an attempt to bring intellectuals and masses together in a cooperative effort at revolution. Gramsci believed that "all men are intellectual . . . but not all men have in society the function of intellectuals." Consequently, it was the task of what he called "organic" intellectuals to mobilize and draw out the inherent intellectual inside of each person. "Each man, finally, outside his professional activity, carries on some form of intellectual activity, that is, he is a 'philosopher,' an artist, a man of taste, he participates in a particular conception of the world, has a conscious line of moral conduct, and therefore contributes to sustain a conception of the world or to modify it, that is, to bring into being new modes of thought."[3]

Since every person is an "intellectual" in some respect, it is important for organic intellectuals to function in conjunction with the masses to raise the latter to higher levels of culture and ultimately to assist them in the development of their own culture. The organic intellectual is to express critically, in the language of culture, what the masses can only feel. From this perspective it is clear that "truth" resides neither in intellectuals nor in the masses, but develops out of the combined efforts of both. The organic intellectual, then, is to articulate in a coherent fashion the alienation and frustration the masses feel but cannot yet express.

The concept of *hegemony*, which is crucial to Gramsci, fits in at this point. At times he appeared to identify hegemony with coercive power, but usually it refers to control of the intellectual life of society by cultural

---

[1]Antonio Gramsci, quoted in *Main Currents in Marxism,* 3 vols., ed. Leszek Kolakowski (Oxford: Oxford University Press, 1978), Vol. 2, p. 160.

[2]Ibid.

[3]Antonio Gramsci, *Selections from the Prison Notebooks* (New York: International Publishers, 1971), p. 9.

means. If the working class is to rule it must first replace the old bourgeois norms, opinions, and ideas with its own cultural values. To Gramsci, intellectual supremacy is a precondition for political rule. Again, cultural hegemony, in his view, required the united efforts of intellectuals and masses.

Gramsci also argued that new political institutions would have to be developed to replace the outmoded ones. In particular, labor unions, which cared only for higher wages and better working conditions, and parliamentary parties, which were preoccupied with their own power and self-interest, had to be replaced. The workers' councils coming into existence during the Turin strikes of 1919–1920 were to be the model for the future. Workers' councils were to direct and organize all facets of production as well as become the hub of cultural development. All wage earners were to vote for the workers' councils, which were to rule every part of society. Like Lenin in *State and Revolution*, Gramsci believed in "all power to the soviets" and "government by council" rather than government by party. And like Lenin, he argued that while there could be some strategic value in participating in parliamentary government prior to the revolution, the revolution could not come about through an outmoded parliamentary system.

In Antonio Gramsci, then, can be found the rudiments of a *critical theory*, which built on the early writings of Marx and called for a more "open" and democratic communism. Although the Italian Communist party was the first to use his ideas in separating themselves from the ideological control of the Soviet Union, more recently other European communist parties have found Gramsci's thoughts helpful in developing a critical theory tailored to the unique needs of their particular countries. It is undoubtedly this linkage that has caused some scholars to claim that Gramsci is the intellectual fountainhead of Eurocommunism.

EUROCOMMUNISM: REVOLUTION
THROUGH THE BALLOT?

In the mid-1970s, a phenomenon which has come to be called *Eurocommunism* developed in continental Europe. Originally the term was employed by the critics of communism, but now the label has been embraced openly by many of the communist parties of Western Europe. Although the Italian Communist party (which Gramsci headed from 1924–1926) was the first publicly to call itself Eurocommunist, the Spanish and French parties quickly followed suit. From an ideological viewpoint Eurocommunism is important because it again raises the twin questions of whether or not the transition to socialism can be achieved peaceably through contemporary political institutions, and assuming an affirmative response to this question, what is the role of the state in this process? Both of these issues have been central to communism since the time of Marx and both have been answered in different ways by different individuals in different historical contexts. Prior to examining the Eurocommunist response, we must attempt to understand why it developed and the basic issues it emphasized.

Probably the single most important factor leading to the development of Eurocommunism has been the gradual lessening of the Soviet Union's control over international communism. From the days of Marshal Tito's confrontation with Stalin, to the death of Stalin and Khrushchev's secret report, through the open split with Mao, and the rise of Gorbachev, it has become increasingly clear that the Soviet Union does not control the other communist parties throughout the world. Still, the erosion of Soviet hegemony is only one factor. In addition, there is a growing suspicion among many communists that in the nuclear age a class war of the type Marx envisioned could just as likely lead to a nuclear holocaust as to world communism. Consequently, finding peaceful mechanisms to alter society has become crucial.

Finally, if the policy of detente between the United States and the USSR is to be successful, an autonomous Europe dependent upon neither of the superpowers seems to many to be imperative. Although each of these factors undoubtedly contributed to the recent creation of Eurocommunism, from a larger ideological perspective Eurocommunism is simply the logical and rather unsurprising outgrowth of Marx's theoretical understanding of the necessity of applying the method of Marxism to individual nations, each at a particular stage of development, and each with its own unique culture and heritage.

The word Eurocommunism itself is meaningful for it emphasizes several important dimensions: It identifies the European geographic base of the movement and with it a historic commitment to democratic values and traditions; it reaffirms the long-term commitment of these political parties to the goal of achieving communism rather than merely assuming the management of a capitalist society as has occurred in Sweden and England. An ongoing effort to adapt communism to changes in advanced capitalism, Eurocommunism demonstrates the growing tendency of each individual nation attempting to create its own strategy in order to fit into, and ultimately change, the mores, customs, and traditions of the home nation. In this sense, Eurocommunism is as varied as the nations in which it exists. Given the national autonomy built into this mass-based movement, it is still possible to talk of several common elements.

To begin, each of the Communist parties is struggling to create an ever-broader system of alliances among the traditional working class and other alienated groups, for example, women, youth, and intellectuals. Second, each has a commitment to the importance of democracy and democratic procedures at every stage of the transition to socialism. Third, each believes in the full autonomy and independence of its respective parties while simultaneously recognizing the transitory nature of the nation-state in terms of the long-range goal of world communism. Finally, each is committed to the construction of internal party organizations characterized by a free, more open politics within the framework of democratic centralism.

This much having been said about Eurocommunism, several things should be evident. Eurocommunism is both a rejection of Stalinist Marxism and an attempt to build indigenous communist movements structured to the needs of each particular nation. And in Gorbachev they should find an ally. Insofar as the Communist parties appear to be willing to employ and abide by the parliamentary procedures of Western Europe, they do not view the state as an inevitable tool of the capitalist class. However, even given this position of believing the state can be an instrument of socialist transition, the question of how the capitalists will react to a real threat of revolution remains unanswered. For instance, will capitalism allow a peaceful transition to communism? Will capitalists look for strong measures to save the free-enterprise system? From the perspective of ideology, finally, there is not much new in Eurocommunism. Rather, it is the continuation of a tradition in Marxism of trying dialectically to find historically and culturally appropriate responses to some central questions in revolutionary theory. This last observation cannot be said of Herbert Marcuse, who has attempted to make an important new addition to Marxian analysis.

HERBERT MARCUSE:
"... THAT WHICH IS CANNOT BE TRUE"

Born in Berlin in 1898 and emigrating to the United States after Adolf Hitler's rise to power, Herbert Marcuse was a relatively unknown figure outside of academic circles until the late 1960s when student activists in Germany, France, and America proclaimed him to be one of their intellectual leaders. Since Marcuse did little to court directly the attention of these groups, part of his attraction may well have been the result of his belief that in advanced industrialized societies the working class is no longer a revolutionary force and that the revolutionary future resides among students, women, blacks, and other alienated groups. Although his first writings concerned G. W. F. Hegel, his major contribution to Marxism came in his second period of development; in his book *Eros and Civilization* he attempted to blend the psychological theories of Sigmund Freud with the political theories of Karl Marx.

Marcuse began the development of his own theory by accepting most of Freud's philosophy of civilization. Freud, the founder of psychoanalysis, discovered that an individual's behavior is the result of both conscious and unconscious factors. These conscious and unconscious human drives are often conflicting in nature and consequently can be the source of considerable human discontent. Freud often discussed the conflict in terms of the *pleasure principle* and the *reality principle.* The pleasure principle demands immediate gratification for the individual; it cares little or nothing for others. However, if the individual always received immediate gratification, the person would not develop and would perish. Consequently, reality intervenes and teaches the human organism that if it can learn to postpone gratification, it can eventually achieve fulfillment and simultaneously reduce personal risks. Still, individuals prefer immediate need satisfaction and only reluctantly do they give in to the superior force of external factors: mother, father, nature.

While Freud saw the conflict between the pleasure principle and the reality principle going on inside every individual, it also goes on between the individual and society: "What decides the purpose of life is simply the programme of the pleasure principle . . . yet its programme is at loggerheads with the whole world, with the macrocosm as much as the microcosm. . . . One feels inclined to say that the intention that man should be 'happy' is not included in the plan of Creation."[4]

In order to accomplish the tasks necessary to run and maintain society, individuals must learn to postpone pleasure and to work, which is an activity that gives the individual little immediate gratification. As civilization develops it requires increasing amounts of labor, which requires increasing renunciation of pleasure by individuals. The history of civilization, then, can be viewed as an ongoing progression of increasing repression of, and unhappiness obtaining for, individuals. Freud believed this situation was inevitable and would probably conclude in the death of the human race. Marcuse, on the other hand, held out the possibility of an end to the escalating unhappiness and repression, opening up the chance for humans to create a (sexually) free society.

Marcuse supported Freud's assertion that repression is necessary for both the individual and society. However, Marcuse drew an analytical distinction and divided repression in two: *basic* and *surplus* repression. Basic repression is "the 'modifications' of the instincts for the preservation of the human race." Surplus repression is "the restrictions necessitated by social domination"; it is the "instinctual" renunciation demanded by *particular types* of societies in the service of that society and at the expense of the individuals who comprise it.

Like Marx, who viewed human history in terms of ever-increasing—

---

[4]Sigmund Freud, *Civilization and Its Discontents* (New York: W. W. Norton & Company, 1962), p. 23.

and unnecessary—levels of economic alienation, Marcuse through Freud viewed history as a chronicle of increasing sexual alienation. Western civilization's glorification of science, technology, and efficiency along with its celebration of the twin "virtues" of hard work and self-denial have resulted in a form of social organization called *mass industrial society*, which is making unbearable demands upon the individual. Ever-new amounts of sexual energy must be renounced in order to provide the energy needed to work and maintain the way of life associated with this society. Although advanced monopoly capitalism was the most obvious target of Marcuse's analysis, his social critique can be applied to all mass industrial societies including the Soviet Union. To Freud, unhappiness and discontent were part of the human condition; to Marcuse, advancements in science and technology have created a situation where the possibility exists for humanity to free itself not only from the economic alienation of Marx but also the sexual alienation of Freud—if both surplus labor and surplus repression can be overcome.

It is so difficult for humans even to imagine what such a sexually unalienated life would be like that Marcuse had to rely on poetic metaphors and ancient myths to convey his meaning. Prometheus, who stole fire from the gods, represents Western civilization's (including Marx's) culture hero; he symbolizes human productiveness and suffering as the price extracted for civilization. In contrast to this culture hero of "toil, productivity, and progress through repression," Marcuse placed Orpheus and Narcissus. "They have not become the culture heroes of the Western world: theirs is the image of joy and fulfillment; the voice which does not command but sings; the gesture which offers and receives; the deed which is peace and ends with the labor of conquest; the liberation from time which unites man with god, man with nature."[5] In this countercultural vision, play and joyful fulfillment replace toil and self-denial. Given Marcuse's goal culture it is quite understandable that it found many advocates among the student population of Western societies.

In his book *One-Dimensional Man*, Marcuse further analyzed civilization and concluded that both the so-called free world and the totalitarian world are one-dimensional in all facets: science, economics, art, technology, and politics. Civilization has become stagnant; it has lost the second dynamic—negative dimension. Returning to his Hegelian roots, Marcuse argued that the world that is (the world of appearance) must be understood in contrast to the world that could, and ought to, be. This contrasting world of how humans ought to live is imaginatively constructed by normative philosophy and art; it is, Marcuse argued, a

[5]Herbert Marcuse, *Eros and Civilization: A Philosophical Inquiry Into Freud* (New York: Beacon Press, 1962), pp. 146–47.

world of joy, beauty, freedom, reason, and peace. In Marcuse's theory it is the historic role of philosophy and art to compare critically the apparent "reality" (that which is) to the ideal reality (that which ought to be, given the current level of civilization) so that humanity can try to achieve it. Thus, it is the "power of the negative," the ability to conceive of historically feasible, alternative realities that are freer and more beautiful, that allows history to progress. If this negative moment is lost, so too is the possibility of movement toward the goal culture.

Satisfying Human Needs

One of the unique attributes of mass industrialized society is its ability to absorb and neutralize all opposition through its capacity to satisfy the human "needs" which it creates. Marcuse argued that these "needs" are false in that they perpetuate injustice, poverty, imperialism, alienation, and the continuing threat of nuclear war. He wrote: "Most of the prevailing needs to relax, to have fun, to behave and consume in accordance with advertisements, to love and hate what others love and hate, belong to this category of false needs."[6] Ultimately, only individuals can decide what are true and what are false needs. But this decision can be made only after the individual is freed from manipulation and alienation.

An old question again arises: How can individuals who have been the object of effective and productive domination free themselves? Marcuse believed that the working class in advanced industrialized societies had been absorbed and neutralized; contented in false consciousness, the workers would not be the leading force in the revolution. In the revolutionary role of the working class, Marcuse placed students, women, blacks, the permanently unemployed, and other alienated groups, believing that the growing consciousness of their own enslavement made them candidates for revolutionary action.

By combining the ideas of Freud with those of Marx, Marcuse extended both the method of social analysis and the vision of a goal culture. Although the legitimacy of this Marcusean approach to Marxism has been the focus of heated debate among leftists, it is still too early to tell if his ideas will remain more than an historical curiosity. Gramsci and Eurocommunism do not attempt to alter Marxian theory and as a result do little to change the ideological content of the doctrine. This could be said as well about other leftist groups in the contemporary world; for example, the New Left, the "Greens," and the radical feminists. Nevertheless, what is demonstrated by the proliferation of new

---

[6]Herbert Marcuse, *One-Dimensional Man: Studies in the Ideology of Advanced Industrial Society* (Boston: Beacon Press, 1964), p. 5.

groups is the reopening of Marxism into perhaps a second age of creative development as well as demonstrating the continuing attempts of Marxism to capture the imagination of alienated groups. If these plural elements ever succeed in joining forces there can be little doubt that they will be a force with which to be reckoned. As they stand now, loosely connected groups with their own perspective, they are little more than a novelty—demonstrating both the adaptability of Marxian analysis and reemphasizing the importance of theories of action.

From these discussions of communism, beginning in its early days with Marx and Engels through Lenin and Gorbachev, Mao and Deng, and now Gramsci and Marcuse, it becomes clear that communism is an ideology with a rich, colorful history containing many different philosophic points of view. It is important to remember that many of the questions raised by Marx and Lenin continue through to the present. Can revolutions in advanced capitalist countries be peaceful? Must they be violent? Is trade union consciousness the highest level of awareness that the workers can achieve without leadership? When will the state wither away? What can be done to halt the ongoing exploitation of the less developed world by capitalism? Can capitalism and communism peacefully coexist? Must they inevitably collide?

All of these questions and issues demonstrate the continuing dialogues inside of Marxism. Ultimately, if Marxism is correct, it is the dialectic between humanity and history that will resolve these issues. For the moment, suffice it to say that communism is, in many ways, a "pluralist" ideology that encourages—within the confines of its frame of reference—discussion, criticism, and innovation.

With the presentations of liberalism and communism completed, it is appropriate to move on to a discussion of our last ideology, fascism, which claims to be a response to the errors of both.

SUGGESTED READINGS

CARRILLO, SANTIAGO, *Eurocommunism and the State.* New York: Lawrence Hill, 1978.

GRAMSCI, ANTONIO, *Selections from the Prison Notebook,* Quinton Hogre and Geoffrey Nowell-Smith, eds. New York: International Publishers, 1971.

GRIFFITH, WILLIAM E., ed., *Communism in Europe,* 2 vols. Cambridge, Mass.: M.I.T. Press, 1967.

HABERMAS, JURGEN, *Legitimation Crises.* Boston: Beacon Press, 1973.

JACOBS, DAN N., ed., *From Marx to Mao and Marchais.* New York: Longman, 1979.

MARCUSE, HERBERT, *Eros and Civilization.* Boston: Beacon Press, 1974.

———, *One-Dimensional Man.* Boston: Beacon Press, 1966.

New Left Review, *Western Marxism: A Critical Reader.* London: Verso, 1978.

10

Fascism

Fascism is therefore opposed to that form of democracy which equates a nation to the majority, lowering it to the level of the largest number; but it is the purest form of democracy if the nation be considered—as it should be—from the point of view of quality rather than quantity, as an idea, the mightiest because the most ethical, the most coherent, the truest, expressing itself in a people as the conscience and will of the few, if not, indeed, of one, and tending to express itself in the conscience and the will of the mass, of the whole group ethnically moulded by natural and historical conditions into a nation, advancing, as one conscience and one will, along the self-same line of development and spiritual formation. Not a race, nor a geographically defined region; but a people, historically perpetuating itself; a multitude unified by an idea and imbued with the will to live, the will to power, self-consciousness, personality.

Mussolini

How does one begin to write about a set of ideas as apparently varied as fascism? To people who lived through World War II, the term itself is almost a synonym for evil, for the "war to defeat fascism" contains many bitter memories. Even those who had no firsthand experience with the fascist regimes of Italy and Germany invariably use the word with a bad connotation. When the police are thought to be overzealous in performing their duty they are called fascist; sometimes people who deem themselves to be good conservatives are referred to as fascists by other ideologists; and we speak darkly of fascist tendencies in the modern nation-state. It is probably inevitable that any word which is frequently used in common language will lose some of its initial meaning and be employed in a vague or general way, but that phenomenon seems compounded in the case of fascism. Sometimes it seems that almost anything a person dislikes is arbitrarily labeled "fascist." There are some reasons for such a situation.

Fascism as a set of ideas was never as clearly formulated as Marxism-Leninism or liberalism, although we believe that there is more coherence among the ideas than is frequently supposed. Further, people speak of fascism as a rather peculiar phenomenon, existing only during a particular period in history and largely confined to the two nation-states of Italy and Germany. Because of this identification with historical nation-states there is a tendency to refer to all of the actions of those states as somehow expressive of the phenomenon of fascism. It is as though every action of the Soviet Union or of China were to be seen as expressive of the doctrine of Marxism-Leninism or every American policy a manifestation of the liberal tradition when we know that the actions of these countries are best seen as attempts to apply certain ideas that exist independently of their application. There is a relatively coherent set of ideas called Marxism-Leninism and there have been numerous attempts to apply those ideas, but that is not to say that the ideas are to be equated with every practical policy of a particular nation. The same thing obtains with liberalism and, we believe, with fascism. Fascism can be viewed as a set of ideas that attempts to say something about human beings, their society, and their future development, and that set of ideas can be analyzed separately from attempts to apply it to particular nations.

The difficulty of understanding fascism is compounded by the fact that we have surprisingly little scholarship that has concerned itself with fascism as a set of ideas. There are numerous books on Mussolini's Italy or biographical studies of Hitler, or discussions of fascism in other countries, but there have been few attempts to look at the ideology per se. As A. James Gregor has noted, "We have been studying fascism for half a century and the number of competent works devoted to the ideology of Mussolini's Fascism could be counted on one hand."[1] While recent scholarship has remedied the situation somewhat, the contrast between the number of studies of fascist ideology and liberalism or Marxism-Leninism remains quite striking. Again, there are reasons for this. Drawing support from the statements of prominent fascists, many commentators have concluded that there is no ideology of fascism, that it is a doctrine lacking in principles, that it celebrates violent, irrational action for its own sake, and that to look at it as though it were a relatively coherent set of ideas is simply to distort it. Such interpretations of fascism see it as a highly pragmatic form of extreme nationalism and view any attempt to examine it through intellectual categories as doomed to failure. Other interpretations place great emphasis on the leadership element in fascist doctrine and assert that leadership is so fundamental to the phenomenon that a study of fascism ought to consist of a series of political biographies.

There is a degree of truth in both of these positions. The role of the leader in fascist regimes is crucial, so much so that Mussolini could declare late in life, "What would Fascism be, if I had not been." Furthermore, there is little doubt that fascism appeared to celebrate a form of irrationalism and that its doctrines changed considerably with the passage of time, making it difficult to apply tests of traditional logic to the doctrines. Despite these difficulties we contend that it is possible both to discover among fascist ideologists certain shared characteristics and values, and to develop an ideology that is appropriately coherent, given the premises of fascism. Stanley G. Payne, summarizing the more recent view of Italian fascism, has noted: "Though an exact and elaborate codification of doctrine was never achieved, it is now becoming recognized that Italian Fascism did function on the basis of a reasonably coherent set of ideas."[2]

A glance at the table of contents of this book reveals an additional point concerning our treatment of fascism: the discussion is confined to only three, relatively short chapters. Such a structure indicates that fascism will be viewed largely in the reflected light of communism and liberalism; that is, fascism will provide us with a critical perspective of the other two idea systems. This relatively brief treatment should not, however, be taken as an indication that we regard fascism as less important than the other two ideologies, or that we view it as a "dead" phenomenon. As Mussolini put it:

[1]A. James Gregor, *Interpretations of Fascism* (Morristown, N.J.: General Learning Press, 1974), p. 244–45.

[2]Stanley G. Payne, *Fascism: Comparison and Definition* (Madison: University of Wisconsin Press, 1980), p. 42.

Given that the nineteenth century was the century of Socialism, of Liberalism, and of Democracy, it does not necessarily follow that the twentieth century must also be a century of Socialism, Liberalism, and Democracy; political doctrines pass, but humanity remains; and it may rather be expected that this will be a century of authority, a century of the Right, a century of Fascism.[3]

An excellent although controversial case can be made for the position that fascism, in its various manifestations, has had at least as much impact—perhaps more—during the twentieth century as either of the other two ideologies. A. James Gregor, for example, argues, "However one chooses to characterize 'fascism,' it is clear that modern revolutions share more affinities with the fascism of Benito Mussolini than they do with the Marxism of Karl Marx or Friedrich Engels."[4] Mussolini's observation may be as accurate today as it was in 1932 when he stated that every age has its own characteristic doctrine and that there were a thousand signs that point to Fascism as the characteristic doctrine of his time. In addition, as to fascism being a dead phenomenon, Anthony Joes argues: "The fascist solution to the problem of economic frustration and political instability seems to 'fit' in many cases. A formula of nationalism, corporatism, and elitism, originally concocted in a European 'great power' environment, has been adapted at various times from Lima to Accra, and from Cairo to Tokyo."[5]

As a final introductory point, mention must be made of the rather strict separation herein made between fascism and National-Socialism. In common language, fascism is often used to refer to the particular political structures in both Italy and Germany. As previously noted, such use is inappropriate in that a set of fascist ideas can be seen as existing independent of those two particular nation-states, something that could be called *generic fascism*. Further complicating this matter is that the founding father of the movement, Benito Mussolini, served as the leader of Italy during its fascist period. Hence, it becomes quite difficult to separate the doctrine from its applications in Italy. While we should not see every action of Mussolini as head of the Italian state as an expression of fascist doctrine, in many ways Mussolini's Italy can provide us with an ideal model of a fascist regime. If this is the case, the actions and doctrines of other so-called fascist leaders can be evaluated in terms of the degree to which they conform or deviate from the Italian archetype. From this perspective, Adolf Hitler cannot appropriately be called a fascist even though his regime expressed many fascist traits. We should

[3]Benito Mussolini, "The Political and Social Doctrine of Fascism," in *Fascism: An Anthology*, Nathanael Greene, ed. (New York: Thomas Y. Crowell, 1968), p. 43.

[4]A. James Gregor, in *Fascism in the Contemporary World* by Anthony Joes (Boulder, Colo.: Westview Press, 1978), p. xii.

[5]Joes, *Fascism in the Contemporary World*, p. 199.

note that taking such a position is somewhat controversial. As Anthony Joes explains:

> In any case, it is not legitimate to equate all fascism with Nazism. Some scholars . . . deny that Nazism is an example of fascism at all. Others argue that fascism includes regimes remarkably different from Hitler's Germany in many important ways. It is our position [Joes] that the Nazis were one manifestation, and not a typical one, of a general fascist phenomenon.[6]

We concur with Joes: In our view, at best, National-Socialist Germany can be seen as an extreme form of fascism, but it can more appropriately be characterized as the worst form of biological racism the modern world has ever seen.

We conclude our attempt to deal with this difficult phenomenon with a discussion of "continuing issues in fascism." There, through a short presentation of Islamic thought, we attempt to provide the reader not only with some understanding of that very important contemporary movement, but also to determine whether, as is often contended, contemporary fundamentalist Islamic thought can appropriately be considered a type of fascism. These definitional distinctions will become clearer as we pursue the subject matter, but for the moment the term "fascism" is restricted to the ideas of Benito Mussolini and their application in Italy.

EVOLUTION OF THE DOCTRINE

While it is certainly true that Marxism did not emerge full blown from the pen of Karl Marx at any particular date, we have argued that the development of Marxist doctrine followed a rather consistent pattern at least from 1844. Such is not the case with fascism. There is a parallel between the two doctrines in that they were both articulated largely by one person; thus we can speak of a founding father or at least a group of founding fathers—in many ways, this distinguishes them from the liberal tradition. At first glance, however, Mussolini's ideas seem to have undergone a considerable change during his lifetime. He began his political career as a confirmed Marxist socialist, added some rather vague voluntarist and elitist elements at an early date, took a seemingly abrupt turn from international socialism to Italian nationalism during World War I and emerged from that war proclaiming the existence of something called Fascism—an Italian word referring to a tightly knit political group. Even then the doctrine was only beginning.

[6]Ibid, p. 4.

Further developments included the emergence of an ethical dimension to the conception of the state, the creation of the idea of corporativism, and the insertion of social Darwinism, and a form of racism. What, then, are we to do with such a grab bag of ideas? To most commentators the critical change in Mussolini's intellectual development occurred in 1914 when, as editor of the major socialist paper *Avanti!,* he abandoned the socialist line of international class war and called for the intervention of Italy in the "bourgeois" world war. Whatever the reasons for this change, or however great a change it actually was, it provides us with an excellent vantage point for viewing the evolution of his ideas. Let us, then, look at the socialism of Mussolini prior to 1914 and then attempt to determine how orthodox a Marxist he was with an eye toward partially explaining his radical change during World War I. First, however, a brief look at the man and his historic age.

Benito Mussolini

Benito Mussolini was born in 1883 in the Italian town of Predappio. His father, who the young Benito much admired, was a blacksmith whose political views can best be described as radical: socialist, anticlerical, republican. Most scholars of Mussolini believe that Benito's early home environment, coupled with local customs and traditions, had a profound and lasting effect on him. Whatever his basic character, the young Mussolini's early life was beset with rebellion. His formal education was interrupted several times because of acts against authority figures; nevertheless, he did graduate in 1902 certified as an elementary school teacher. He pursued that career off and on, but it seemed to be somewhat of a sidelight to his growing political involvement. The first decade of the twentieth century saw Mussolini becoming more and more prominent in socialist circles, culminating—after several terms in prison for revolutionary agitation—in his 1912 election as editor of the socialist paper *Avanti!* This brief sketch of the man gives an indication of some of his personality traits. But what of Mussolini's ideas?

Even today, after years of scholarship on the man, one still can evoke cries of surprise or at least raised eyebrows by calling Mussolini a *Marxist,* yet of this there is no doubt. Indeed, it can be argued that his early Marxism was in many ways similar to that of Lenin. The intellectual battle against the revisionist tendencies within the international communist movement found Mussolini and Lenin on the same side. They were uncompromising in their advocacy of the necessity of violent class warfare. Both were disgusted by the nationalist sentiments that seemed to be undermining the internationalism of classical Marxism, and both thought the adventurism of capitalist armies to be but a device for delaying the revolution. One could go on, but the significant point is that during the period between 1902 and 1914 Mussolini constantly used Marxist terms, cited Marx as an authority for his actions, and thought in categories that can only be called Marxist. Having said this, however, we must recall that there were many different schools of Marxism existing during the first decade of the twentieth century. Ranging from the outright revisionism of Bernstein to the radical revolutionary position of Lenin, Marxism was many things to many people. Where did Mussolini fit in this ideological spectrum? As mentioned earlier, his position was rather close to that of Lenin; he too opposed revisionism and called for revolutionary agitation but, most important, he also shared Lenin's distrust of a mass spontaneous revolution.

Recall that Lenin advanced the conception of a small, tightly knit revolutionary party as a solution to proletarian apathy and as a device for fomenting revolution in a largely underdeveloped country. While we have not emphasized the term *elitist* in the prior discussion, there is little doubt that Lenin's party was an explicitly elitist organization. Its purpose was to utilize the latent energy of the masses of people and direct it toward appropriate Marxian ends. Mussolini shared this skepticism concerning the revolutionary potential of the masses, and he argued with increasing frequency for the need for a force to guide the supposedly spontaneous revolution. Numerous times during this early period of development Mussolini spoke with a good deal of contempt for the apathetic masses and he emphasized the need for *elite leadership.* In doing this he was reflecting the current thinking in Italian intellectual circles.

Two of the most prominent advocates of elitist theories of the state, Gaetano Mosca and Vilfredo Pareto, had advanced theories of political participation that denied any important role for the masses in politics and thought government was best seen as the rule of successive elite groups. Pareto, in particular, had a direct influence on Mussolini, for the latter enrolled in two of his courses at the University of Lausanne and later called Pareto's theory of elites "the most ingenious sociological conception of modern times." Although this reliance on elite leadership was by no means uncommon with Marxists of this period, it does provide us with an early indication of a doctrine that later became central in fascist thought. If mass participation in political life was to become a fact of the twentieth century, there must be an elite leadership group to mobilize and guide. Here, then, is an initial deviation from classical Marxism in Mussolini's thought.

Another facet of Mussolini's early thought, which was to have important consequences in the development of fascism, was his emphasis on *human will.* This is a difficult concept to describe in that it is more of a way of approaching reality and an affirmation of action rather than an intellectual category. Mussolini was desperately concerned with creative action and firm in his belief that it was well within the power of properly directed human beings to create their own history. Rather than being mere pawns in the hands of some superhuman Hegelian historical process or limited in their power by an economic system, human beings were capable of reshaping the world to fit their image of what it ought to be. Looked at from a Marxist-Leninist perspective, this can be seen as a major deviation from the doctrine. By asserting that human will is capable of altering the environment by sheer determination to change it, Mussolini was implicitly undermining Marx's "scientific" laws of development. After all, for Marxism-Leninism, human consciousness and will are largely determined by the objective economic conditions obtaining at any time; the individual human being is generally limited by the class circumstances in a particular period in history. In implying that the creative actions of human beings could radically alter history, Mussolini was saying that human will was independent of economic conditions. There is then an extreme emphasis on *voluntarism* in the young Mussolini, which is distinctly un-Marxian and emerges full blown in later fascism. Perhaps this reliance on will can be attributed to Mussolini's interest in the writings of Friedrich Nietzsche who believed that a truly human person could transcend his or her environment, throw off one's chains, and reconstruct the world according to that person's own image of what it should be.

Whatever the case, this voluntarism led Mussolini to an interest in the role of myth in human affairs, and specifically to the question of how myths could be used to mobilize masses to engage in acts of change and creation. Here Mussolini could rely on the authority of the French philosopher Georges Sorel who in investigating human motivation came to the conclusion that myths were the prime force in human affairs and that violent activity in pursuit of the fulfillment of a myth is not to be feared. Whether Sorel had any direct influence on the development of Mussolini's ideas is a matter of conjecture, but we do know that Mussolini claimed he was influenced by him. These difficult notions of will and myth are more fully explored later in this chapter; for the moment it is sufficient to note their presence in Mussolini's early thinking.

CHARACTERISTICS OF FASCISM:
THE NATION-STATE, ANTILIBERALISM,
ANTIBOLSHEVISM, CORPORATIVISM

Despite being bound by treaty to Germany, Italy remained neutral during the early stages of World War I. Socialists in Italy were in many ways more consistent than their counterparts in other countries, for they agitated in behalf of neutrality and continued to proclaim the international solidarity of the working class. While the German proletariat and many of its leaders were rallying around the banner of nationalism, Italian socialists remained firmly neutralist. Given this, imagine the surprise when *Avanti!*, under Mussolini's editorship, appeared in October 1914 and called for the abandonment of neutralism and the entry of Italy in the war on the side of the Allies. It was to be Mussolini's last editorial: He was forced from his position as managing editor and eventually drummed out of the party.

How can we explain such an action—the public flouting of a basic tenet of Marxism by a dedicated Marxist? Before leaping to the conclusion that Mussolini was simply jumping aboard the bandwagon of growing nationalist sentiment in Italy, we must recall the dilemma that World War I caused dedicated socialists throughout Europe. The war provided the first real test of Marxism's internationalism, and in general the doctrine failed to pass the test. There were exceptions such as Rosa Luxemberg and Lenin, but for the most part European socialists supported their respective countries in the "bourgeois" war. In a sense, then, Mussolini was in the mainstream of socialist action. Further, we have already noted some early tendencies toward voluntarism and violence in Mussolini's thinking, where the human will is seen capable of performing tremendously heroic actions, even remaking history. Given this, it must have been extremely difficult for a man of Mussolini's temperament to sit back calmly and assume a neutralist posture while the world-shaking events of the war were occurring all around him. Listen, for example, to the tone of that famous editorial in *Avanti!*:

> We enjoy the extraordinary privilege of living at the most tragic hour of the world's history. Do we wish to be—as men and Socialists—inert spectators of this grandoise drama? Or would we prefer to be, in some way, its protagonists?[7]

The Nation-State

Whatever the reasons for this change, the idea that forms the keystone of fascist ideology was gradually being established, and this concept of the nation-state was to dominate Italian political thinking for the next thirty years.

We must now leave the historical development of Mussolini's intellectual and political career to concentrate on the major doctrines that comprise the ideology of fascism, remembering that these doctrines emerged only gradually. It is also important to remember the political

---

[7]Benito Mussolini, in *Fascist Italy*, by Alan Cassels (New York: Thomas Y. Crowell, 1968), p. 19.

context of Italy in the first quarter of the twentieth century. World War I was an exceptionally bitter experience for most Italians. In addition to the economic problems of acute inflation and high unemployment, there was considerable social dislocation as a result of the war. As if this was not enough, the Versailles Treaty failed to grant Italy her share—as co-victor—of the spoils of war. Years of strikes and violence along with an ineffective parliamentary system created a general mood of disillusionment and discontent. When the government failed to act on the social problems, Mussolini emerged with promises and plans for a glorious Italian future. If there is one single authoritative statement of fascist ideology it in all probability is Mussolini's *The Doctrine of Fascism*, published in 1932, and that document appropriately emphasizes the notion of the *nation-state.*

The change from the concept of class to the concept of nation involves a major change in conceptual framework. In Marxism, the fundamental unit of analysis is class. Everything is defined in terms of its class base: With the qualifications noted earlier, one is either proletarian or bourgeois; institutions are bourgeois; consciousness is defined largely by class. In fascism the fundamental unit of analysis is the nation: One is either a member of it or one is not; values are national values; one achieves realization of human potential only in and through the nation. Moreover, the nation is not simply the numerical summation of the individuals comprising it, but it possesses a history, a cohesiveness, and a destiny of its own. The nation is thus an entity that is both real and ideal; it can be physically defined in terms of national boundaries and size of population, but it is more than these two features. It has a past that differentiates it from other nations and a future potential that may or may not be achieved.

Fascist speakers constantly used an organic metaphor in referring to the relationship of the nation to the individuals who comprise it. The nation was seen as a biological organism that lives, breathes, grows, and, presumably, dies, while individuals are seen as cells that perform their function and achieve fulfillment only insofar as the entire organism is healthy. The individual simply does not exist without the nation, for humans are by nature social animals and can realize themselves as individuals only as members of a collectivity. If the nation thus constitutes the highest ethical entity, the state becomes its political manifestation, the expression of its will and power. Here is how Mussolini explained it:

> The State, as conceived of and as created by Fascism, is a spiritual and moral fact in itself, since its political, juridical, and economic organization of the nation is a concrete thing; and such an organization must be in its origins and development a manifestation of the spirit. The State is the guarantor of security both internal and external, but it is also the custodian and transmitter of the spirit of the people, as it has grown up through

the centuries in language, in customs, and in faith. And the State is not only a living reality of the present, it is also linked with the past and above all with the future, and thus transcending the brief limits of individual life, it represents the immanent spirit of the nation.[8]

Perhaps this conception of the nation-state can be more completely explained by briefly examining fascist arguments against liberal democratic thinking.

Antiliberalism

We have discussed the intellectual origins of liberal democratic thought at length in the earlier chapters, but we must briefly restate some of its basic assumptions at this point so that we may understand fascist opposition to it, for *antiliberalism* is an important fascist value. In general, as we have seen, the liberal democratic tradition saw people existing as individuals prior to the establishment of political institutions. Further, they possessed certain rights—as individuals—granted to them by God or nature. Because of certain inconveniences of this presocial, prepolitical situation (recall the state of nature), individuals banded together and gave up certain of their natural rights to a collectivity so that they could, as individuals, live a more comfortable existence. State and society are thus established for specific purposes, have limited powers and functions, and may be abolished if they exceed their granted powers. The state and society are, in short, artificial creations of sovereign individuals. Democratic representative institutions (parliaments, congresses, and so forth) are generally designed to translate the desires of individuals in the society, normally on a majority rule basis, into public policy. Representative institutions are, by their very nature, intended to express the *particular wills* of individuals within the society. The preferences of a majority of individuals on any issue are simply that—a summation of individual preferences totaling more than 50 percent. Finally, liberal democratic thought is quite clear about the locus of sovereignty in the society: Ultimately it lies with each individual, and the actions of the state must be with the consent of those individuals.

To the fascist this is all simply absurd. The mainstream liberal tradition defines freedom as an absence of restraint on individual action, yet it requires humans to give up some freedom (for example, relinquish natural rights) in order to attain freedom. How, fascism asks, does one become free by giving up freedom? Indeed, a fascist would argue, in talking about giving up natural rights so as to achieve a more convenient situation, the individualistic liberal exposed the fallacy of the entire

---

[8]Benito Mussolini, "The Doctrine of Fascism," in *Social and Political Philsoophy*, John Somerville and Ronald E. Santoni, eds. (Garden City, N.Y.: Doubleday and Company, 1963), p. 44.

enterprise. As fascists view it, liberal democrats are saying that freedom cannot exist without a stable body of laws and political institutions, and the only way true freedom can exist is through obedience to those laws. It is *law* and a framework of *order* that ensures freedom. The myth of the isolated sovereign individual is thus destroyed and we come to understand that the individual can exist only in and through the state. As Mussolini stated:

> Anti-individualistic, the Fascist conception of life stresses the importance of the State and accepts the individual only insofar as his interests coincide with those of the State, which stands for the conscience and the universal will of man as a historic entity. It is opposed to classical liberalism which arose as a reaction to absolutism and exhausted its historical functions when the State became the expression of the conscience and will of the people. Liberalism denied the State in the name of the individual; Fascism reasserts the rights of the State as expressing the real essence of the individual. And if Liberty is to be the attribute of living men and not of abstract dummies invented by individualistic liberalism, then Fascism stands for liberty, and for the only liberty worth having, the liberty of the State and of the individual within the State.[9]

Any rights that individuals may possess are granted and may be removed by the state; similarly, the private interests of individuals must be subordinated to the general interests of the collectivity. Insofar as representative institutions, political parties, and all of the other trappings of parliamentary democracy are designed to reflect the interests of individuals (particular wills), they must be discarded and replaced by institutions that will determine the *general will* of the nation. The properly constituted state thus becomes the articulator of the general will of the nation.

One of the more commonly used modern attempts to describe the function of political institutions refers to them as authoritative allocators of value for the society as a whole, meaning that states can, within certain limits, control what is done by other institutions and individuals within the society. Fascist ideology takes this type of descriptive statement, expands it, and adds an ethical dimension. The nation is the source of ultimate values for all members of the community and the political arm of the nation—the state—gives articulation to those values. There is, simply, no higher ethical authority. If this is the case, individual human beings fulfill themselves by assuring that the goals of the collectivity are achieved. Indeed, the terms *individual* and *state* are incorrect abstractions insofar as they indicate separate entities—in fascism they are but two sides of the same coin. The nation is struggling to achieve actuality, to fulfill its potential; individuals are human when they con-

[9]Benito Mussolini, in Ibid., p. 426.

tribute to that quest. Given this, it is obvious why fascism was opposed to liberal democratic thought: The latter's assumption is that the state is ultimately the creation of and subservient to the individual. Fascism contended that such thinking had led to conflict, disunity, even chaos in society and afforded no notion of national cohesiveness. Liberal democratic thought was in the end predicated upon assumptions of selfishness and conflict and as such prevented human beings from living in moral association with one another. As Mussolini declared in 1929, "When the conception of the State declines, and disunifying and centrifugal tendencies prevail, whether of individuals or particular groups, the nations where such phenomena appear are in their decline."[10]

Antibolshevism

If the basic fascist premise is that the nation-state is the ultimate authority in all matters, it must, of necessity, be in direct opposition to Marxism-Leninism, providing us with another basic fascist value—*antibolshevism*. To the Marxist, nationalism is but another capitalist trick designed to prevent the formation of an international proletarian movement. From the fascist point of view, communism is one of the prime sources of disunity in the state for it preaches unending class conflict and therefore divides the people. Further, communism is particularly dangerous in that it asserts that nation-states are but passing phenomena on the path toward a world society. It was thus almost inevitable that fascism would adopt a radically anti-Marxist stance, whatever the intellectual origins of its founding father. Indeed, the anti-Bolshevism of fascism was so vehement that it has been seen by some as the central trait of the ideology.

While fascism had little use for the excessive individualism of liberal democratic theory, it was especially polemical about Bolshevism. Indeed, at many points fascists thought of themselves, or at least let it be thought, that they were improving on the liberal democratic form of governance in order to combat more effectively the Bolshevik menace. This is one of the reasons why many people continue to believe that fascism was a conservative or reactionary movement. If Marxism is on the radical left of the political spectrum, it is assumed that any movement violently opposed to it must be on the right wing. As we shall see, however, fascism was in many ways as revolutionary as Marxism ever hoped to be, and to dismiss it as simply a right-wing reaction to communism is to deny its complexity and power as an ideology.

Any attempt at comparison between fascism and the state socialism of a Lenin or a Stalin reveals a tangled web, but also may afford some

---

[10]Benito Mussolini, in *Anthology*, Greene, ed., p. 44.

insights into fascist ideas. At the same time Mussolini was calling for national strength to resist the "red menace" of Bolshevism and his fascist squads were violently attacking Italian socialist groups, he was adopting many policies in the economic realm that can clearly be called socialist. From his early appeals for the destruction of the monarchy and his battles with the Catholic Church, to the nationalization of many sectors of the economy, there was a definite socialist thread in his thought. But to call the mature Mussolini a socialist would certainly be a mistake, for he was quite tolerant of particular aspects of capitalism as an economic system, and the fascist movement received considerable support from big industry. Indeed, it is still quite common to hear that it was Mussolini who not only "made the trains run on time" (no doubt a major accomplishment in strike-prone Italy) but who also saved Italian capitalism from the Bolsheviks. Moreover, Mussolini eventually reached accommodation with both the Catholic Church and the monarchy. On the other hand, frequent references were made to a "national-socialist" state. The fascist regime often intervened in economic affairs, and the authority of the state to totally control all aspects of life was constantly emphasized. How, then, is one to understand fascist economics?

We can, it seems, make sense of this only by reemphasizing the prime goal of fascism—*autarky:* the creation of a more productive, powerful, and autonomous nation. Private property and the accumulation of capital were certainly acceptable—sometimes highly desirable—insofar as they contributed to that goal. Similarly, socialist economic policies (planning, collectivization, and nationalization) were to be utilized where they seemed best suited for the pursuit of economic productivity. It is here that the comparison with the state socialism of Soviet Marxism, particularly that of Lenin, may prove useful.

Corporativism

We have seen that in the transfer culture of Soviet Marxism the state and party are viewed as temporarily assuming control of all facets of national life for the purpose of building a strong Soviet state. When Mussolini stated that the goal of fascism was to create a greater and more powerful nation and that the state must have total power to pursue that end, he was articulating a not dissimilar doctrine. Indeed, in 1925 Mussolini and the Italian philosopher Giovanni Gentile began describing the state as a totalitarian entity, which in Stanley G. Payne's words was "aspiring to an organic unity of Italian society, economic activity, and government . . . [exercising] total guidance of national goals."[11] Of course, for a Marxist-Leninist such a concept of the nation-state was to

---

[11]Payne, *Fascism: Comparison*, p. 73.

be a temporary measure, necessitated by the special circumstances of the Russian revolution and an exceptionally hostile, capitalist world—the goal remained international communism. For Mussolini's fascism the powerful nation was the ultimate goal, and in pursuit of it a policy of *corporativism*, or corporatism, was adopted. In Mussolini's words:

> The Corporation is established to develop the wealth, political power and welfare of the Italian people. Corporativism means a disciplined, and therefore a controlled, economy, since there can be no discipline which is not controlled. Corporativism overcomes Socialism as well as it does Liberalism: it creates a new synthesis.[12]

How does the corporate state work? What kind of "synthesis" does it provide? Herman Finer, writing in 1935, concluded that there was "considerable mystification" about these ideas of ". . . The Corporation, and State tonics for private enterprise," not only abroad but in Italy itself.[13] Much of that "mystification" remains. But insofar as Mussolini declared the notion of the corporate state to be the "keystone of fascist doctrine" we must try to understand at least what it was designed to accomplish.

The idea is relatively simple. If liberal capitalism produces class conflict and controlled competition in the economy because of its excessive individualism, and if Marxism supports class warfare between workers and owners, corporativism is designed to remove all conflict in the economic sector. Labor and management rather than attempting to win gains for their respective groups are to achieve a unity of purpose in pursuit of the goal of greater productivity. To this end the state will set up various corporations representative of different segments of the economy (for example, the steel industry, the transportation industry) which will contain representatives from both workers and management. These will be organized vertically, that is, representing the whole industry, rather than the more familiar horizontal organization wherein a group or class of workers confronts a group or class of owners. These corporations will be empowered to make decisions on wages and production quotas on an industrywide basis. All of this, of course, will be under the watchful eye of the party and the state. A corporative chamber, designed to replace parliament, would contain representatives from the various corporations, and this chamber would aid in making economic decisions for the entire nation. We cannot go into the institutional details of this conception of the corporate state—indeed, they were never really very clear; for our purposes it is primarily important as a device to

---

[12]Herman Finer, *Mussolini's Italy* (New York: Grosset & Dunlop, 1935, 1965), p. 502.

[13]Ibid., p. 492.

eradicate the influence of selfish interests, whether expressed by a single capitalist or by an entire working class.

Finally, two things one must note with respect to fascist economic policies. It must be emphasized that corporativism is not necessarily synonymous with fascism, although many people tend to think so. There are numerous examples of the operation of aspects of corporativism in nonfascist societies. In Great Britain, Sweden, Japan, and even to a lesser extent the United States, industrywide decisions concerning wages and profits are made in many sectors of the economy—all under state supervision.

Looked at from another perspective, the corporate state was Mussolini's answer to the five-year plans in the Soviet Union, which attempted to set production goals, centralized economic decisions, and rationalized the allocation of resources for the entire country. Second, it must be emphasized that the goal of all this is increased productivity, social unity, and collective strength, not necessarily greater redistribution to the people. But, given the logic of fascism, as the productivity of the nation rises through cooperative action, all Italians, whatever their status, will benefit. Given this argument, the "socialist" in Mussolini could accommodate his support of Italian capitalist elements in the name of making things better for everyone. From the ideological perspective one thing stands out: Institutional arrangements are carefully constructed by the state and the party to achieve the goals of national unity and strength. Those aspects of capitalism and socialism that support these goals are maintained; those that detract are discarded. In clear control of all aspects of the economy, the state and the party construct a "third way," an alternative economic system that utilizes the best components of the other two economic systems. Still, it seems Stanley Payne is correct when he states, "No point remained less clear in the doctrines of most fascist movements than economic structure and goals."[14]

NATIONAL GOALS, ELITISM, AND LEADERSHIP

We have seen that one of the major goals of fascism is to supplant the selfish individualism of liberal democracy with national solidarity expressed in the form of the will of all of the people. We must now inquire as to the source of that will, what it is and how it is to be found. Asking such questions immediately involves us in *voluntarism, anti-intellectualism,* and *elite leadership,* three additional doctrines in the constellation of fascist ideas.

If the nation is to be seen as a type of organism, it must possess

---

[14]Payne, *Fascism: Comparison,* p. 9.

certain functions, a purpose, and have goals which it is to accomplish. While it is true that Italian fascists constantly spoke of the spirit of the nation and invoked the concept of a will that was general in nature, there was little in the way of systematic articulation of the goals of the Italian nation. Vague references abounded to the glories of ancient Rome and the potential greatness of the Italian people, as well as aspirations to Empire, but nothing as specific as the goal culture which we shall find in Nazi Germany. Perhaps it was inevitable that the concrete form of these vague references to Italian power resulted in various attempts to expand the influence of the nation-state in foreign affairs. Italian adventurism in Ethiopia and, for that matter, in World War II can be seen as an attempt to provide the material resources and physical boundaries necessary for national greatness. We should not, however, be surprised by the lack of specificity of goals to be reached by a great Italy, for Mussolini's celebration of action for its own sake is an important element here.

> Fascism was not the nursling of a doctrine worked out beforehand with detailed elaboration; it was born of the need for action and it was itself from the beginning practical rather than theoretical; it was not merely another political party but, even in the first two years, in opposition to all political parties as such, and itself a living movement.[15]

He later declared that the fascist movement of the early 1920s had no specific goals, and surely did not possess a well-formulated program for political action. *Social Darwinism*, a general name given to describe social theories that view life as a struggle for survival between groups, is also very much part of fascism. In an almost Hegelian fashion, the nation and its people come to know what they can be only by constantly testing themselves through ceaseless action. The exercise of national will is as important, perhaps more important, than the fulfillment of any set of goals; action and violence are celebrated almost for their own sake. Emphasizing what we might today call a "macho syndrome," fascism viewed forceful and violent actions as indicators of a strong and healthy movement. Only by continually testing itself through struggle with other countries can the nation find its limits. The advocacy of what Mussolini called "controlled violence" and the seemingly unnecessarily violent actions of fascist groups against perceived enemies seem to support this conclusion. However, in attempting to describe this, there is no substitute for Mussolini's own words:

> The years which preceded the march on Rome were years of great difficulty, during which the necessity for action did not permit of research or any

---

[15]Benito Mussolini, in *Anthology*, Greene, ed., p. 40.

complete elaboration of doctrine. There was much discussion, but what was more important and more sacred—men died. They knew how to die. Doctrine, beautifully defined and carefully elucidated, with headlines and paragraphs, might be lacking; but there was to take its place something more decisive—faith.[16]

It should be apparent from the above that fascism has little use for the "rational" quibbling of intellectuals. If action is what is desired there is little point in spending a great amount of time debating or spelling out logical systems of ideas. There is a very distinct and deep strand of anti-intellectualism in fascism, accompanied by the belief that human emotions provide the true seat of wisdom and truth. Human beings, while they are thinking animals, find true wisdom in their emotional responses to words and actions and show that wisdom through committing their collective will to further activity. As such, speeches and written statements are not used to communicate information so much as to induce certain emotional responses in the audience, to stir them to action.

To a cynical observer, this means that the speaker or writer is merely using symbols for their propaganda effect. There is, however, evidence to indicate that both Mussolini and Hitler believed that the interchange of emotion that occurred during their speeches and at mass rallies was actually a fundamental method of communicating with the people. Here again we encounter the elitist element in fascist doctrine, for if the spoken word is seen as a device for inducing emotional response and is a fundamental method of communication between people, the person who is speaking those words becomes most important indeed. Hence, to appreciate fully the notions of emotionalism, will, and mass action we must look at the person who is to be the source of all these— *the leader.*

The fascist leader is the person who discovers the general will of the nation, interprets it, and communicates it to the people in a way that will lead them to fulfill its commands. As such, the leader is in many ways the key to all fascism. To return to the organic analogy, the leader is literally the personification of the nation; the leader's body and will express the will of all of the people. We must emphasize that fascist doctrine asserts that the leader does not act out of personal interest; that is, all of the leader's words and actions are supposedly dictated by the general will. In a sense the leader is a captive of that will and could not act arbitrarily or on the basis of personal whim. Benito Mussolini is unimportant; *Il Duce* is everything.

We have already noted that the spirit of the people exists through-

---

[16]Benito Mussolini, in *Sources in Twentieth Century Political Thought*, Henry S. Kariel, ed. (Glencoe, Ill.: The Free Press of Glencoe, 1964), p. 89.

out time independent of any person, so the leader is really discovering and being led by a national will which already exists. Thus, we must ask how a particular person such as the leader comes to know what that will is. Fascist doctrine provides us little in the way of an explanation of this discovery process. The leader's communication with the general will is shrouded in mystery; the leader simply knows it and is chosen by history to be the one person who gives verbal form to the national spirit. That will always existed in potential, but it required a great person to know it, translate it for the rest of the nation, and mobilize the people to ensure that the potential is fulfilled.

How do people know when a particular person such as Mussolini or Hitler is the authentic manifestation of the general will? Fascists assert that the true greatness of the people and the leader is manifested when the people simply recognize the leader when the leader emerges from the struggle for political power and they agree to follow all of the leader's commands. Again we see the emotional, irrational, social Darwinist base of fascism. How does the leader know that he (or she) is chosen to articulate the will of the people? The leader simply knows it! How do the people recognize the leader when he (or she) appears? They simply do and thereafter follow the leader's commands! There just is no rational explanation for these phenomena for they arise from the will and emotions of the people or, as Mussolini said in the passage just quoted, the process is based on faith.

From another vantage point one can see the tremendous power that fascism gives to the leader, particularly when this concept is combined with other doctrines. If, as we stated earlier, the nation is the final authority in all matters and the leader is the personification of the nation, that person's commands are by definition law. Ultimately, the leader is accountable only to the will of the nation. The masses show both their wisdom and demonstrate their greatness by acknowledging and following the leader. Here we can see with greater clarity the elite-mass distinction observed in the thought of the young Mussolini. The leader possesses the truth, and it is the leader's historical duty to communicate that truth to the masses and to ensure that the nation fulfills its destiny. Fascism sees the masses as possessed of great potential energy; the problem is to mobilize them toward the proper goals. Thus, the question of the method of communication between the leader and the masses is of great importance. Here the elite finds the use of myth and propaganda extremely useful. Much as the "noble lie" of Plato, myths are used to communicate to the people a simplified version of the general will, and propaganda is used to direct their energies. Note that according to the doctrine this does not mean that the leader is manipulating the masses for the leader's own personal power. Rather, what the leader is doing is leading them on the proper path to personal and national fulfillment. If successful, the entire nation will be mobilized in pursuit of national glory, and the will of the people, however vaguely defined, will be achieved. What could be more democratic?

Here, then, are some of the central traits of Mussolini's fascism: corporativism, irrationalism, emotionalism, will, leadership, action for its own sake—all within the confines of that supreme value of national greatness. Before moving to a more explicit summary of the ideas of Benito Mussolini, we must talk briefly about the role of racial doctrines in Italian fascism, for it provides one of the major distinctions between fascism and National Socialism.

Fascism and Race

It is difficult to encapsulate the racial doctrines of Fascist Italy, for the issue is clouded by confusion, lack of consistency, and most important, the alliance with Nazi Germany. Even after 1936, when Italy officially referred to itself as a racist society, there was a good deal of confusion as to what the term meant. Further, several of the major theoreticians of the fascist movement, notably Giovanni Gentile, explicitly denounced German national-socialist racial doctrines as simplistic and unproved. Finally, despite the eventual existence of anti-Semitic legislation in Italy, there is a good deal of evidence to indicate that its application was half-hearted and that many major fascist figures gave covert assistance to Jews escaping the expanding German empire.

The confusion surrounding these doctrines revolves around the concepts of *race* and *nation*. Early in the 1920s, Mussolini had spoken of the superiority of the Italian race and its potential for greatness. Yet it is quite clear from the context of his speeches that he used the word almost as a synonym for nation. The notion of an Italian race was simply impossible, for Italy was a country made up of individuals of myriad racial backgrounds—more of a cosmopolitan melting pot than a homogeneous body. Furthermore, while Hitler and the Nazis were proclaiming the existence of one particular race (variously referred to as Aryan, Nordic, and sometimes even German) as physically and culturally superior to all others, Italy was in the position of having very few so-called Nordics in its population. How can one refer to Italy as a superior nation if superiority is defined in terms of the prevalence of Nordics? This is but a more complex way of saying that Italian racism was constantly associated with Italian nationalism and that references to an Italian race generally included all Italians irrespective of their racial background. "There were few epithets used by Western liberals against Nazis that were not applied by Fascists, who also coined special slurs of their own, denouncing the Nazis, for example, as a 'political movement of pederasts.' "[17] Even after the alliance with Germany was concluded and a policy of racism was officially announced, Mussolini, speaking in defense of that policy, could say:

> Jews possessing Italian citizenship who have unquestionable military or civil merit in the eyes of Italy and the regime will find understanding and justice.[18]

This is not to deny that there are theoretical bases in fascist doctrine for some sort of racial and cultural separatism. The concept of a people, or a *Volk*, immediately asserts that there is something distinctive and usually superior about a particular group of people. If that group can be seen as "chosen," as separate and superior, it is but a short step to assert that they should somehow dominate other groups who are less fortunate. Further, fascism contained a distinct strain of anti-Zionism, opposing it largely on grounds similar to its opposition to Marxism; Zionism preached a doctrine which placed the values of international Jewry higher than those of the nation-state. Given fascism's opposition to any doctrine challenging the ultimate authority of the nation it is obvious why such sentiments had to be countered. Having said all that, what is apparent, once again, is that the central conceptual category of Italian fascism was the nation, and that any racism involved was usually defined in terms of the nation. Such, as we shall see, was not the case with German National Socialism.

Perhaps the single most correct statement one can make concerning racism in Mussolini's doctrine is that it was part of an attempt to cement relations between Fascist Italy and Nazi Germany. How else can one interpret Mussolini's early attempts to dissuade Hitler from his racial policies? How else can one explain the prominence of people like Giovanni Gentile in the fascist state, whose opposition to Hitler's racial policies was well documented? On balance, racism in Italy is best seen as an ad hoc addition to the doctrine, instituted for strategic purposes and never made fully compatible with the far more basic value of Italian nationalism.

Fascist Traits

Before moving to a discussion of German National Socialism it seems worth attempting a summary of the major themes of Italian fascism, if only to serve as a source of comparison and contrast for

[17]Payne, *Fascism: Comparison*, p. 79.
[18]Benito Mussolini, in *Mussolini and Italian Fascism*, by S. William Halperin (New York: Van Nostrand Reinhold, 1964), p. 175.

further discussion. Little more need be said of the doctrine of the nation-state, for it has dominated our discussion throughout the chapter. Much like the notion of "class" in Marxism-Leninism, the "nation" forms the fundamental unit of analysis in fascist doctrine. One is tempted to dismiss fascism by simply asserting that anything that is good for the nation-state is, by definition, part of the doctrine. Yet we have seen that there were several general themes used to enhance that goal of national greatness, certain traits and values that are appropriately associated with the term fascism, even if they do not constitute a precise definition. Let us attempt to summarize and clarify those themes and traits by looking at some attempts at systematic definition of the fascist phenomenon. For example, a dictionary definition reads:

> Any authoritarian, anti-democratic, anti-socialistic system of government in which economic control by the state, militaristic nationalism, propaganda, and the crushing of opposition by means of secret police, emphasize the supremacy of the state over the individual.[19]

This definition is accurate in many respects, containing many of the themes we have associated with fascism, but it suffers, perhaps inevitably, from superficiality. Moreover, it is in the complex interrelation of traits that fascism achieves its power as an ideology. For example, fascism is "antidemocratic" if by that we mean that it opposes the excessive individualism of classical liberalism and the representative institutions associated with it. But we know that fascism was fully willing to borrow from that tradition, or leave it undisturbed, when it suited its purpose as in the case of capitalism.

Further, fascism is indeed "antisocialistic" if that means violent opposition to the internationalism and class analysis of socialism. However, it did rely on many socialist measures in the economic realm and had its intellectual origins in the mind of a confirmed Marxist. What about "the supremacy of the state over the individual"? Is this good fascism? Yes, if by that phrase we mean the nation-state defines the norms for action for all people and admits of no higher authority. Still, a good fascist would declare that the implied opposition of the terms *state* and *individual* in the definition is but another example of excessive democratic individualism. Being social animals, humans can fulfill themselves as individuals only in and through the nation; to imply that there is some sort of opposition between the two is to distort human nature. Finally, the dictionary definition suffers by ignoring other aspects that seem central to fascism: Where, for example, are elitism, leadership, activism, and corporativism?

---

[19]Charles Earle Funk, ed., *New Practical Standard Dictionary of the English Language.* Vol. 1 (New York: Funk & Wagnalls Company, 1954), p. 481.

Another attempt at a "first definition" of fascism is offered by Ernst Nolte in his *Three Faces of Fascism:*

> Fascism is anti-Marxism which seeks to destroy the enemy by the evolvement of a radically opposed and yet related ideology and by the use of almost identical and yet typically modified methods, always, however, within the unyielding framework of national self-assertion and autonomy.[20]

The major virtue of this definition is that it correctly points out the centrality of anti-Marxism and nationalism while attempting to show the complexity of the doctrine through the use of qualifying phrases. Still, it seems incomplete and surely suffers from vagueness. More helpful, it would seem, is the summary of fascist concepts offered by Anthony Joes: nationalism, explicit repudiation of parliamentary liberalism, statism, productionism, corporativism, authoritarianism, and elitism. Perhaps this, or something like it, is the best we can hope for in trying to come to grips with the phenomenon of fascism—a list of traits, tendencies, and values. As A. James Gregor has stated:

> There is little prospect that the near future will deliver a fully competent theory of Fascism. We will have to be content with plausibilities and detailed historical accounts. The best efforts will be "eclectic," attempting to weave together the most defensible of plausibilities into a narrative in which we can invest some confidence.[21]

All this is but to underscore the emotionalism and anti-intellectualism of the fascist movement, for its repudiation of rational argument makes systematic exposition of the doctrine most difficult. Such is not the case, however, with our next subject for discussion: Adolf Hitler was all too explicit about what he intended. The problem was both too few and too many people believed him.

SUGGESTED READINGS

FINER, HERMAN, *Mussolini's Italy.* New York: Grosset & Dunlap, 1965.
GREENE, NATHANAEL, ed., *Fascism: An Anthology.* New York: Thomas Y. Crowell Co., 1969.
GREGOR, A. JAMES, *The Ideology of Fascism.* New York: The Free Press, 1969.
LAQUEUR, WALTER, ed., *Fascism: A Reader's Guide.* Berkeley: University of California Press, 1976.
LEWIS, SINCLAIR, *It Can't Happen Here.* New York: New American Library, 1963.

[20]Ernst Nolte, *Three Faces of Fascism*, (New York: Holt, Rinehart and Winston, 1966), pp. 20–21.

[21]A. James Gregor, in Joes, *Fascism in the Contemporary World*, p. 261.

MUSSOLINI, B., "The Doctrine of Fascism," in *Social and Political Philosophy*, John Somerville and Ronald E. Stantoni, eds., Garden City, N.Y.: Doubleday and Company, 1963.

NOLTE, ERNST, *Three Faces of Fascism*. New York: Holt, Rinehart and Winston, 1966.

O'SULLIVAN, NOËL, *Fascism*. London: J. M. Dent & Sons Ltd., 1983.

PAYNE, STANLEY G., *Fascism: Comparison and Definition*. Madison, University of Wisconsin Press, 1980.

SCHNEIDER, HERBERT W., *Making the Fascist State*. New York: Oxford University Press, 1928.

WEBER, EUGEN, ed., *Varieties of Fascism*. Princeton, N.J.: Van Nostrand Company, 1964.

WOOLF, S.J., ed., *The Nature of Fascism*. New York: Random House, 1969.

11

National Socialism

All who are not of good race in this world are chaff.

Adolf Hitler

With the foregoing words in *Mein Kampf (My Struggle)*, Adolf Hitler pointed at once to the prime difference between Italian fascism and German National Socialism as well as to the major category of national-socialist thought. We have stated in the preceding chapter that the idea of the nation provided the fundamental building block in Italian fascist thinking and that despite some rather awkward attempts to speak of an Italian race, Mussolini's doctrines remained fundamentally nationalist. While it is a subject by no means free from controversy, it is here submitted that almost the opposite situation obtained in Hitler's doctrines of National Socialism. Despite his appeals to German nationalism and his constant references to German history and greatness, Hitler was primarily the champion of a particular racial group, and the fruition of his plans would have led to the supersession of the German nation-state. To support such a conclusion we must once again enter into that murky area of the relationship between nation and race, or better, between the *Volk* (people) and the racial group.

In discussing these ideas with respect to Italian fascism we found that Mussolini was rather obscure as to the history and composition of the Italian people, preferring to make vague references to the glories of ancient Rome and the future potential of the nation. In the case of Germany we are dealing with a different situation, for the celebration of uniquely Germanic myths, culture, and history was very much part of both popular and intellectual traditions. Tracing their roots back to the Germanic tribes who conquered mighty Rome, an entire line of writers was able to refer to an idealized German *Volk* that was unique insofar as it possessed characteristics which separated it from—and made it superior to—all other peoples.

In our discussion of Italian fascism we emphasized that the concept of a people does not merely refer to the individuals populating a given geographic area at a particular period of time. Rather, the *Volk* consists of an entire tradition, possesses a will of its own, and has a destiny which is unique to it. In Germany of the nineteenth and early twentieth centuries these vague and essentially mystical ideas were given specific content through reference to a whole host of events in the history of the region. As such, the notion of a German *Volk* received a far more concrete manifestation and provides us with a much better example of this type of *volkish* thinking than its Italian counterpart.

GERMAN ROMANTICISM

The *volkish* or romantic tradition as it is sometimes called was in many respects a reaction to the complexities produced by a rapidly developing industrial economy. The relative security and stability of the feudal era were being replaced by rapid change and apparent instability. The urban areas that grew up around varying industrial complexes attracted un- counted numbers of people with promises of greater rewards and a new life. While the opportunity to "better themselves" undoubtedly existed, in many cases people encountered the type of conditions that so repelled Karl Marx. Torn by impersonal forces from the familiar surroundings of the rural village and performing the seemingly meaningless tasks of modern industry, the alienation of which the young Marx spoke was a very real thing in Germany, even for those who did not share his specific definition of the term or his vision of the future. This condition of perceived alienation or "rootlessness" was, as we have noted, a general phenomenon throughout industrializing Europe, and a common response was a desire to revert to an idealized past. In Germanic areas, this response was advocated most vociferously by a diverse group of social critics, artists, and intellectuals generally placed under a rather large umbrella called German *romanticism*. One of their responses to this situation was an attempt to construct an idealized past, where life was simple and a person had historic and cultural roots. If there was one central idea in the diversity of notions that characterized German ro- manticism it was that humans had somehow lost their bearings in modern civilization and had to return to a more natural, simple setting in order to cure their sickness. Romantics of all stripes stressed the necessity of restoring a harmonious interrelationship between the human animal and the forces of nature. As George Mosse described it:

> The genuineness of the natural environment was held up to praise and credited with engendering in the population such qualities as sincerity, integrity, and simplicity. The culture of a Volk rooted in nature was posited as the very opposite of a mechanical and materialistic civilization. . . . Only nature was genuine, since it was infused with both the life force and historical meaning for the Volk.[1]

Moreover, this was seen as particularly true for the German *Volk* whose strength and wisdom lay in natural settings and whose grandeur could only be achieved by remaining true to those origins. The *volkish* spirit was believed manifesting itself in the physical environment—indeed, in the very landscape populated by Germans. In particular, the Germany of mists, hills, and dark forests was seen as being something uniquely German and an appropriate manifestation of the *volkish* spirit. Despite its veneer of Christianity, there was a good deal of pagan pantheism in much of the romantic tradition. The spirit of the Germanic people was to be found in the forests and streams which made up its ancestral

[1]George L. Mosse, *The Crisis of German Ideology* (New York: Grosset & Dunlap, 1964), p. 19.

home, and it communicated with members of the *Volk* through those natural objects. The image of the sun, for example, played a very important role in popular *volkish* literature as the symbol of the strength and power of the German spirit. Germans were seen as looking up from their dark and mysterious forests to the sun for guidance and strength in achieving their unique goals as a people. This contrasted with the experience of other peoples whose existence was arid and devoid of mystery because of their origins in flat, treeless regions. The development of this form of stereotype and determinism by the natural environment was to play an equally important role in later racist literature, but it is important to note that it already was an essential part of the *volkish* tradition prior to the development of the racial doctrine.

Such an image of the true German provided a stark contrast with the modern rootless laborer whose spirit had been corrupted by the supposed sophistication of civilization. The modern German was a sick animal whose life was devoid of meaning. If the greatness of the German spirit lay in the mystery and simplicity of the natural setting, the metropolis could only be viewed as an artificial thing—a corruptor of nature, culture, and the *Volk*. This juxtaposition of urban dominated *civilization* with true *volkish culture* produced a bevy of interesting contrasts as well as some real problems for the romanticists. Civilized people were seen as preoccupied with the superficialities of life such as clothing styles, whereas the true German was content with simple functional dress— protection from the elements and little more.

Typical of this desire for simplicity was the advocacy by one Father Jahn—an early romantic spokesman—of a sort of "cult of the body," which included a celebration of the virtues of nude bathing. Urban dwellers were caught up in the marketplace, necessitating the constant pursuit of material objects and the money necessary for their purchase, whereas true members of the *Volk* worked the soil for their everyday necessities and harmoniously interacted with nature.

Many writers contrasted their stereotyped German with an equally fictionalized French citizen, the latter being materialistic, shallow, and lacking in the virtues of true humanity. A good expression of the antimodern stance of German romanticism can be seen in some of the proposals that were made for economic reform, for, as we have noted, a major cause of all of the difficulties of modernity was to be found in economic growth. There were numerous proposals to return to the equivalent of the guild system of the Middle Ages and to break up industrial complexes and move them to rural areas. Here again we can observe both the desire for simple solutions to complex problems that was characteristic of romanticism as well as a willingness to renounce the materialistic rewards of economic progress in the name of reuniting humans with their natural environment. Some of the later literature of this tradition managed to accommodate itself to the necessity of large-scale industry and modernization in order to produce a strong nation-state, but the deepest roots of German romanticism rejected the notion.

Emotionalism Versus Rationalism

It should not be surprising that a movement that placed tremendous emphasis on reuniting humans with nature also tended to celebrate human emotions and to deprecate rationality. Indeed, the mystical communication that occurs between the individual will and the *volkish* spirit cannot really be described with words; it is something that must be felt. Many of the problems of modernity could be directly attributed to the overdevelopment of human rational capacities. As such, there was a need to return to the soil (mother earth), thereby resurrecting the emotional side of the human animal so that it might once again become whole. Much as in the case of Mussolini's fascism, a person's immediate emotional responses were considered more correct guides to truth and action than lengthy deliberation and intellectualizing. Or as Hitler, echoing this romantic theme, was to put it in 1923: "The Movement must not rust away in Parliament, it must not spend itself in superfluous battles of words, but the banner with the white circle and the black Swastika will be hoisted over the whole of Germany on the day which shall mark the liberation of our whole people."[2] In the process of denying validity to the trappings of rationality, some of the writers in the romantic tradition went so far as to celebrate violence for its own sake, seeing the desire to inflict punishment on others as a natural expression of human emotion. Thus, if intellect and excessive rationality were the cause of most human problems, the simple solution was to resurrect the will as the prime vehicle for directing thought and action.

A final example of the romantic effort to place myth and mystery at the center of human nature can be found in the attempts that were made to transform Christianity in such a manner as to make it more compatible with *volkish* ideas. From the romantic perspective, Christianity through its long history had become institutionalized to such an extent that it was dominated by sterile dogma—mere form with little substance. Living doctrines had been rationalized, intellectualized, drained of their spiritual and mystical origins. In the view of romanticists, Christ was as much a symbol of the divine spirit as an originator of a body of doctrine; furthermore, His religious experience exemplified precisely the sort of mystical communication that German romanticists envisioned existing between the *volkish* spirit and the people. To put it all too simply, the

[2]Adolf Hitler, *My New Order*, Raoul de Roussy de Sales, ed. (New York: Reynal & Hitchcock, 1941), p. 49.

tradition placed a great emphasis on the irrational and mystical side of Christianity, thereby making it quite compatible with their *volkish* themes. Finally, in a manner later to be copied by Nazism, several efforts were made to "Germanize" Christianity, to make it a national religion by deemphasizing the more internationalistic aspects of the Christian tradition.

Here, then, is the romantic view of the human condition as well as an ideal type to which all members of the *Volk* ought to aspire. There is a great danger in reading too much into this tradition, despite the apparently widespread dissemination of *volkish* ideas in both popular literature and in intellectual circles. To imply that the romantic tradition was the only strain of thought present in nineteenth and early twentieth-century Germany and that somehow its existence caused the later developments of National Socialism would be to distort reality. After all, the same region that produced *volkish* thinkers also generated the highly rationalistic G. W. F. Hegel as well as the scientific and materialistic Karl Marx.

Having dismissed the notion that romanticism and *volkishness* were somehow uniquely characteristic of a monolithic German mind, we must note, however, that the existence of this type of tradition provided fertile soil for the growth of National Socialism. With such ideas as part of the popular and intellectual marketplace it was possible for national-socialists to pick and choose ideas from the tradition to suit their purposes and build their own mythology.

On the other side of the coin, then, it would also be a distortion of reality to deny that romanticism and *volkish* thinking contributed significantly to German National Socialism. But one crucial element was necessary before this volatile mixture of ideas that characterized Nazism was possible—the factor of racism.

RACISM

The notion that a particular racial group is somehow culturally and spiritually superior to all others is surely not German in origin. Minimally, the distinction is as old as that between Greeks and barbarians, the latter being regarded in ancient times as literally subhuman. One is tempted to say that some form of racism is as old as humanity. Similarly, the singling out of a particular racial group for censure, or as a scapegoat for all human ills, was not unique to Germany, whether that group was designated as Jews or nonwhites. Indeed, a rather convincing argument can be made that during the nineteenth and early twentieth centuries, France and Russia, rather than Germany, were the real hotbeds of anti-Semitism. Racism, it seems, knows no national boundaries nor is it new in human affairs. Yet it was in Nazi Germany that ideas of racial superiority and anti-Semitism became the official policies of the state and resulted in the slaughter of uncounted numbers of innocent people.

Why in Germany? Obviously that question cannot be answered within the brief confines of this discussion; perhaps the final answer can only be found in the mind of Adolf Hitler. Nevertheless, that would be too easy an answer: There already existed a distinct tradition of racist ideas of which Hitler was an adherent, and Nazi policies, however horrible, cannot simply be dismissed as manifestations of a disturbed mind. Nor can one, as some have suggested, simply be silent in the face of the Holocaust, somehow allowing the horror to speak for itself. It demands explanation, or at least the attempt at explanation.

One might consider it ironic—if irony is possible in this discussion—that the person whose racist ideas had the greatest impact on late nineteenth-century German thought was French, the people so derided by the romantic tradition. Despite the existence of numerous racial theories throughout Europe it was the publication of Count Joseph Arthur de Gobineau's *Essay on the Inequality of Human Races* in 1854 that gave the "scientific" study of race its most coherent form. While Gobineau's work achieved fame in Germany only at a somewhat later date, it is generally recognized that his theories had a great influence on most of the Nazi racial theorists and that his ideas provided much of the framework for later racist thought. Gobineau asserted that race was the only significant variable that could be used to explain human progress and decline. Ideas, institutions, culture, and freedom were, to borrow the Marxian phrase, mere superstructural elements that were reflections of the more basic category of race. Gobineau divided the human species into three basic racial groups—white, yellow, and black— and gave each certain dominant characteristics. The black race possessed little intelligence but was endowed with a very powerful type of primitive sensuality; the yellow race was stereotyped as lacking in imagination and creativity, being prone toward excessive materialism. It was the white race that was endowed with all of the virtues of humanity—nobility, freedom, honor, and spirituality. Once understood, these basic racial characteristics provided the key to the understanding of all of human history. As Gobineau put it, "The basic organization and character of all civilizations are equal to the traits and spirit of the dominant race."[3] All too simply, where the white race (increasingly coming to be called *Aryan*) dominated, people and culture flourished; where other races were in ascendancy, degeneration occurred.

Gobineau was, however, generally pessimistic about the future of

[3]Joseph Arthur de Gobineau, quoted in George Mosse, *Toward the Final Solution* (New York: Howard Fertig, 1978), p. 52.

humanity, for he saw that the Aryan race (which, by the way, was seen to have its origins in India) tended to "intermingle" with inferior races, thus diluting its superior characteristics. Europe, for example, was initially populated by the "yellow" race, its greatness as a region only occurring when the Aryan strain of blood was superimposed as the result of migration. But Aryans intermarried with their inferiors, thus diluting the pure strain and ensuring decline.

What are we to make of this? While it is difficult to regard such thinking seriously, it must be emphasized that Gobineau was laying the groundwork for a body of ideas that in varying forms would be accepted by untold numbers of people as fundamental truth. Again, in terms of emphasis, Gobineau and other racial thinkers asserted that this is not merely one way of looking at human history, but the only way—it was scientifically provable. However crude or simplistic this may appear, it must be regarded seriously. Finally, it must be noted that Gobineau was no anti-Semite. He viewed Jews as a strong and intelligent people. Their fate, moreover, was the same as that of Aryans, for they too tended to mix their blood with the lesser races. It is only with the importation of Gobineau's basic ideas into Germany that his view of Jews was altered to produce anti-Semitism.

Influence of Richard Wagner

As mentioned earlier, Gobineau's work lay dormant in Germany for a period of time but eventually became to be accepted and popularized by a group of intellectuals and artists who formed a group centered in the small Bavarian town of Bayreuth. During the last decades of the nineteenth century, Bayreuth became the principal center for the dissemination and popularization of racist doctrines for the entire region. Most of the individuals who later served as intellectual apologists for Hitler's regime had some connection with the Bayreuth Circle, so much so that the town became a religious shrine for the Nazi movement. The originator and major light of Bayreuth until his death in 1883 was the composer Richard Wagner, who gathered around him a cluster of people whose purpose was the celebration of the *volkish* tradition. Wagner's influence is somewhat difficult to assess and his works, both musically and politically, remain even today the subject of a good deal of controversy. His operas served as vehicles for popularizing German mythology; the image of a Teutonic Siegfried—a primitive German beyond the petty conventions of good and evil—became a central symbol of the Third Reich. There is little doubt of Wagner's influence on Hitler; Wagner was his favorite composer, and Hitler himself asserted that his early life was greatly influenced by the composer's operas.

Thus, it was from Bayreuth that the clearest popular formulation of racial doctrines emanated, particularly after Wagner's death. Toward the end of his life the composer had befriended Gobineau and that relationship apparently solidified some of the racist themes that were present in Wagner's earlier political writings. It was, however, his widow, Cosima, son Siegfried, and son-in-law Houston Stewart Chamberlain who expanded on those themes and made Bayreuth a magnet for anyone with racist inclinations.

It is in the work of the Bayreuth Circle that we can see the blending of German romanticism with doctrines of racial purity in their clearest fashion. Wagner himself asserted that the source of German woes was race-mingling and that the sole hope for the future was the resurrection of the pure Aryan strain. To accomplish this a leader would emerge, dedicated to German greatness and determined to purify the race—in particular to eradicate French and Jewish elements. That Wagner himself would have approved of Hitler's final solution to the "Jewish problem" is doubtful in light of the many liberal themes in both his writings and his music. Still, he did lend his famous name to the anti-Semitism that culminated in the Holocaust.

It is extremely difficult, if not impossible, to assess the influence of the Bayreuth Circle either in the popularizing of racist doctrines or in the thinking of the young Hitler. We know, for instance, that Hitler met and talked with Houston Stewart Chamberlain shortly before the latter's death, but many of the racial doctrines Hitler adopted were at odds with Chamberlain's teaching. Some commentators assert that Hitler's ideas crystalized in conversations with Dietrich Eckhart while others contend that his ideas about race derived from Ludwig Woltmann and Hans F. K. Guenther. While we can make no attempt to show a causal relationship between the ideas of any of these men and later Nazi doctrines, we can spell out several additional aspects of the amorphous body of racist ideas that later influenced Nazi policies.

Emphasis on Aryan Leadership

The Aryan race, however it was defined, was seen as the sole source of all of the positive achievements of humanity. The existence of sophisticated civilizations in other parts of the world was explained by the aforementioned migration of Aryan elements to those areas. Using the argument familiar to racists of all stripes, its theorists explained the existence of superior achievements in non-Aryan regions by attempting to prove that Aryan blood flowed through the veins of their leaders. Italy, Spain, and France were, as nations, capable of greatness only because of the existence of Aryan leadership. The worldwide spread of Aryans, while providing truly human values for other less fortunate races, did, however, tend to produce the blood-mingling that caused Gobineau to despair. The pure Aryan strain was gradually being lost.

In modern times, one of the remaining groups of Aryans was found in northern Europe, particularly in Germany; here the destiny of the German nation and all humanity resided. These Aryans had to be identified and elevated to positions of leadership so that they could lead humanity to further glories. The problem, then, became the identification of those persons possessing the purest quality and largest quantities of Aryan blood—surely all Germans did not possess it!

To aid in this identification process a list of typically Aryan traits was drawn up; these physical characteristics gave evidence of an indwelling Aryan spirit. These characteristics included a general lightness of skin color (further indication of the tendency to identify Aryanism with the "white" race), blonde hair, blue eyes, a long narrow skull, and a perfect proportion between head size and body length. Common to these attempts was a reliance on the authority of a crude "science" of anthropology, later, as we shall see, to be buttressed by a similarly superficial reliance on the theories of Charles Darwin. This attempt to determine traits of Aryanism scientifically through external observation was later to cause the Nazis some minor difficulty because of the obvious fact that many of their leaders, including the Führer himself, did not seem to have such bodily attributes. This was circumvented by saying that physical traits were not the only way of identifying an indwelling Aryan spirit, but simply a good rule of thumb. The introduction of this type of "scientific" facade to racial doctrine provided additional means by which the "chosen people" could be identified, and it lent a form of scientific credibility to the doctrine.

We must emphasize here how the traditions of German romanticism and nationalism were rapidly becoming merged with racial doctrines. The Siegfried of the German romantic tradition had become the blonde, blue-eyed bearer of the Aryan strain of blood. Germany, although long dormant as a nation-state, was destined for glory because the fatherland possessed people with a significant amount of the primal strain of Aryan blood. Indeed, Germany would fulfill its destiny as a nation through the leadership of the master race. Typical of this blending of German romanticism, nationalism, and Aryan racism was a speech by Hitler in 1922:

> They [conservative politicians] ought day by day to din into the ears of the masses: "We want to bury all the petty differences and to bring out into the light the big things, the things we have in common which bind us to one another." That should weld and fuse together those who still have a German heart and a love for their people in the fight against the common heredity foe of all Aryans.[4]

In much the same fashion, several other elements of the romantic

[4]Hitler, *Order*, p. 20.

tradition were amalgamated with racial dogma and transformed to produce a more dynamic synthesis. The traditional romantic fear of industrialization and the evils inherent in it was overcome by noting that non-Aryans had presided over past economic development. Industrialization, by itself, was not an evil as some romantics had argued; it had resulted in alienating conditions only because inferior people were in positions of power. Rapid economic growth and the development of an industrial base could now be seen as positive benefits in the assertion of German greatness, provided, of course, that Aryans were supreme in the economic sphere.

Similarly, the pessimism that had pervaded much of the earlier racial literature was circumvented. It was argued that although blood-mixing had led to a decline in the human condition, this did not necessarily have to continue. Rather than pointing to a glorious but long-lost past, people of will and energy could work to resurrect the Aryan strain, which would provide the precondition of an era of even greater human progress. In buttressing this argument, racial theorists appealed to the authority of a crude social Darwinism, which held that the human race was in a constant struggle in which only the fittest survived. If this were the case, Aryans, who were by definition the most fit, needed only to assert their natural superiority and the future of humanity would be assured. This lent a type of scientific credibility and historical inevitability to the doctrine. In effect, it became a crude syllogism: Aryans are most fit; the fittest will survive; therefore, Aryan culture will triumph over the forces of evil!

The Struggle between Aryans and Jews

One final aspect of this general grab bag of ideas of racism in the early twentieth century must be emphasized before we move on to a discussion of the young Hitler. This was a change in the stereotype of the Jew. Anti-Semitism, of course, existed in the world for a long period prior to the nineteenth century; it varied in intensity, one could argue, with the power Jews possessed in particular countries. Despite the Jewish people's ability to attain political and economic power, most early anti-Semitic doctrines pictured Jews as inferior beings who through some mysterious craft and cunning were able to succeed in spite of their innate failings. As we have noted, there were exceptions to this general picture—Gobineau is an example—but the general view, particularly in popular literature, was that Jews were inferior. However, the difficult question of how a supposedly inferior race could achieve power at the expense of a superior race was seldom directly addressed in racist literature. A rather ambivalent attitude developed toward Jews whereby, on the one hand, they were viewed as inferior objects of ridicule and, on the other, as a potent force to be feared and demolished. Indeed, it was noted that Jews seemed to possess the solidarity as a racial group that the supposedly superior Aryans lacked. Viewed in this fashion, history could be seen as a perpetual struggle between Aryans and Jews: one group representing culture and progress, the other evil and decay. Jews were seen not merely as parasites and debasers of culture but as a formidable foe to be treated most seriously. In Hitler's words:

> The Jew is not only a foreign element differing in his essential character, which is utterly harmful to the nature of the Aryan, but the Jewish people in itself stands against us as our deadly foe and so will stand against us always and for all time.[5]

It is in this context that we meet full-blown the notion of a Jewish conspiracy against mankind, whereby Jews, through cunning and treachery, seek to control the world. The infamous *The Protocols of the Elders of Zion*, which was purportedly the outline of the Jewish plan for world domination, was a clear forgery, yet it fed popular belief in the myth of a Jewish conspiracy. Inferior though they be, Jews represented a threat to all that is truly human, so the doctrine preached.

It was from this inconsistent mixing of racial ideas that the Nazis fashioned their racial *myths.* The fact that such doctrines were common currency around the turn of the twentieth century is surely more important than the writings of any one racist thinker. Whether the young Hitler ever read Houston Chamberlain or Ludwig Woltmann or any other treatise on the subject is somewhat immaterial. These thinkers provided a respectable, pseudoscientific overlay for very deep-seated human prejudices, and they permitted a person like Hitler an appeal to authority in support of his own emotional prejudices. In Nazi hands these myths became reality, with genocidal consequences.

ADOLF HITLER: RACE, LEADERSHIP, AND THE NATIONAL SOCIALIST STATE

The life and personality of Adolf Hitler have in all probability been subjected to more detailed analysis than any other figure in the twentieth century. Confronted with the enormity of the evil committed by Nazi Germany under his leadership, untold numbers of scholars and laypersons have attempted to find an explanation for—and too often to explain away—Nazism in Hitler's personality. We make no attempt to summarize that scholarship or to add to it, but brief mention of Hitler's life and

[5]Ibid, p. 32.

the circumstances in Germany that permitted his rise to power seem necessary to any understanding of Nazi ideology.

Adolf Hitler was born in 1889 in the small town of Braunau on the border between Austria and Bavaria. Hitler was later to describe his early life as one of poverty and suffering, although the evidence indicates that his father, who was a minor civil servant, provided adequately for the family. The young Hitler was not a success in formal education; his grades were poor, he was a disruptive influence, and he seemed to lack the discipline necessary for concentrated study. Some have argued that these early experiences led to Hitler's lifelong contempt for formal education and those who possessed it. In any case, his dream was to be an artist or an architect. After his father's death, his mother moved to Linz, in Upper Austria, where the young Hitler pursued that dream doing sketches and drawings in an effort to sustain himself. In 1907, after two years in Linz, Hitler journeyed to Vienna to further his artistic ambitions by attempting to enroll in the Academy of Fine Arts. He was denied admission on the grounds that he lacked artistic talent. In spite of this, he remained in Vienna until 1913. By his own account, these years were crucial to the development of both his personality and his ideas.

He lived an essentially solitary existence, barely sustaining himself through sketching and architectural drawing. He was described by contemporaries as moody, incapable of finding a job, and possessing a passion for politics and opera (particularly Wagner). Alan Bullock characterized the young Hitler as possessing the artist's temperament without talent, training, or creative energy.[6] In 1913 Hitler left Vienna for Munich, where he led basically the same type of existence, until the outbreak of World War I.

There is little doubt that the war gave direction to Hitler's life and provided an outlet for his energies. He volunteered for and was accepted into a Bavarian regiment that saw considerable action throughout the war. Although he was decorated several times for his actions, he was only able to achieve the rank of corporal, whether through lack of ability or lack of ambition. He was gassed, temporarily blinded, and in the hospital recovering from his wound when the war ended.

We cannot attempt to chronicle the events that led to Hitler's rise in 1933 to the position of Chancellor of Germany. Our concern must remain with Hitler's ideas. Before exploring them, however, we need to sketch briefly the social and political environment within Germany after the war, particularly since many commentators believe that these circumstances were crucial to the eventual success of Nazism.

Germany at that time presented a general picture of political and

[6]Alan Bullock, *Hitler: A Study in Tyranny* (New York: Bantam Books, 1961), p. 8.

economic chaos, interrupted only briefly by periods of relative stability. The nation had been defeated on the battlefield, although the myth that the German army had been "stabbed in the back" by leftist politicians rather than defeated militarily was to grow in strength in the coming years. The country was saddled with an economy in shambles and a large debt for war reparations imposed by the Treaty of Versailles. Further, the economic depressions that swept all of Europe throughout the 1920s had particularly severe effects in Germany, producing rapid inflation and dislocations throughout the economy.

On the political front, there existed very strong socialist and communist parties, paralleled on the right by an established conservative movement as well as a new grouping of "radical rightists" from which the Nazi party was eventually to emerge dominant. Street violence and political assassination, particularly in the early 1920s and 1930s, were common occurrences. As economic conditions worsened in the early 1930s, the Nazi party, heretofore a somewhat obscure regional group, rose to a position of national prominence, winning, for example, 107 seats in the Reichstag elections of 1930. By early 1932, the Nazis controlled 230 seats out of 608 in the Reichstag as nearly 14 million Germans voted for Hitler and his Nazi party. Taking into account the fact that Germany had many political parties, this represented an unprecedented success accomplished in a very short period of time. It should also be noted, however, that the parties of the left remained quite strong even as the Nazis grew in power. The German political arena was polarizing on the left and right. Finally, on January 30, 1933, Hitler was appointed Chancellor and the Nazi era began.

With this brief background completed, let us return to our major concern and summarize the ideas of the young Hitler to see how they incorporated the various intellectual traditions we have been describing, and to provide points of comparison with Italian fascism. It is appropriate to speak of the *young* Hitler because in large measure the ideology of National Socialism was firmly set in his mind by the time he was 24. Ernst Nolte in a deft phrase refers to National Socialism as "practice as fulfillment," asserting that the ideology was "preformed" in Hitler's mind and that all that was necessary was its "fulfillment." As such, the ideas of Hitler's youth can be used as keys to understanding not only the ideology of National Socialism but also the entire Nazi movement. Once again, we must point to the centrality of racist ideas, for in Hitler's mind race explained everything.

Hitler's own description in *Mein Kampf* of his conversion to anti-Semitism perhaps will help us to understand this point:

> Once, when I was walking through the inner city, I suddenly came across a being in a long caftan with black sidelocks. My first thought was: Is that a Jew? In Linz, they did not look like that. I watched the man stealthily

and cautiously, but the longer I stared at the strange countenance and studied it feature by feature, the more the question in a different form turned in my brain: Is that a German?[7]

From this early experience on the streets of Vienna, Hitler moved to the position of finding race at the core of all human affairs. In particular, it was the existence and widespread influence of Jews that served both as an explanation for the sorry condition of Germany and a rationalization for Hitler's personal lack of early success in life.

It is true that Hitler went on in *Mein Kampf* to spell out most of the major themes that we have associated with Italian fascism. He condemned Bolshevism, class, democratic institutions, the liberal press, and spoke in glowing terms of national unity, organicism, duty, and a vaguely socialistic economy. What differentiated Hitler from Mussolini, however, was that blood-mixing and Jews were seen as the basic cause of all of the problems of modern life contained in the fascist litany. Marxism, for example, was viewed by both men as a dire threat to national unity and as a revolutionary doctrine that competed with fascism for recruits. But for Hitler, Marxism was a doctrine invented by a Jew (Marx's father was a convert to Christianity) and used by international Jewry to prevent the German working class from realizing its prime allegiance to *Volk* and state. "And so the Jewish leaders succeeded in hammering into the minds of the masses the Marxist propaganda: 'Your deadly foe is the bourgeoisie; if he were not there, you would be free!' "[8] Similarly, democracy, and all of the so-called freedoms associated with it, was a doctrine designed and dominated by Jews. By asserting that political equality was a basic presupposition in governing, Jews had tricked people into believing that they were equal to legitimate members of the *Volk*. Thus, democracy as a political form ensured the debasement of the *Volk* while at the same time permitting Jews to rise to positions of power.

Finally, free speech and press, two of the cornerstones of a liberal democratic society, were seen as vehicles of international Jewry in that they spread equalitarian falsehoods or, at the least, prevented a united *Volk* by fostering differences among the people. Behind all of these evils of modernity was the Jew, a member of a lesser race, a parasite living off the body politic, yet a clever and dangerous adversary. Perhaps one can fully appreciate the depth of Hitler's racism by reading his own words—presented here at length—from a 1922 speech in Munich:

the Jews are a people of robbers. He has never founded any civilization, though he has destroyed civilizations by the hundred. He possesses nothing

[7]Adolf Hitler, *My Battle,* abridged ed. trans. E. T. S. Dugdale (Boston: Houghton-Mifflin Company, 1933), p. 19.
[8]Hitler, *Order,* p. 57.

of his own creation to which he can point. Everything that he has is stolen. . . . He has no art of his own: bit by bit he has stolen it all from the other peoples or has watched them at work and then made his copy. He does not even know how merely to preserve the precious things which others have created: as he turns the treasures over in his hand they are transformed into dirt and dung. He knows that he cannot maintain any state for long. This is one of the differences between him and the Aryan. True, the Aryan also has dominated other peoples. But how? He entered on the land, he cleared the forests; out of wilderness he created civilizations, and he has not used the others for his own interests, he has, so far as their capacities permitted, incorporated them into his State and through him art and science were brought to flower. In the last resort it was the Aryan and the Aryan alone who could form States and could set them on their path to future greatness.[9]

Having discovered his truth—that is, that Jews *destroy* and Aryans *create* civilization—it became Hitler's self-appointed task to communicate it to the German masses so that the evils of Jewish control could be eradicated and a new Aryan culture established. Sure of his truth, Hitler's main difficulty was in conveying it to masses conditioned by false values; nevertheless, it was in this area, perhaps more than anywhere else, that his particular genius lay. While we have discussed the notions of leadership, emotion, and mass psychology in connection with Italian fascism, Hitler's development of these doctrines are of such proportion that they merit additional attention.

Mystical Exchange of Spiritual Energy

He, at one with Mussolini, had considerable contempt for masses of people; at the same time he believed that they possessed tremendous potential energy. They needed, therefore, leadership by an elite. This leadership was to be achieved largely through emotional communications between elite and mass and, in particular, through the spoken word. Mass rallies and emotion-laden speeches designed to achieve a religious-like catharsis for both speaker and audience were Hitler's major devices for ensuring the success of the Nazi movement. In his words: "if a people is to become free it needs pride and will power, defiance, hate, hate, and once again hate."[10]

There is a good deal of evidence that shows Hitler regarded his speeches as the fundamental means of communication between the leader and the followers. They were designed not primarily to communicate ideas or to convey information but to provide for a mystical exchange of spiritual energy. As Alan Bullock observed:

[9]Ibid, p. 35.
[10]Ibid, p. 49.

Speech was the essential medium of his power, not only over his audiences but over his own temperament. Hitler talked incessantly, often using words less to communicate his thoughts than to release the hidden spring of his own and others' emotions, whipping himself and his audience into anger or exaltation by the sound of his voice.[11]

In even bolder terms, Joachim C. Fest describes a speech by Hitler at Hamburg:

There, amid the cheers of thousands, he delivered one of his passionate speeches that whipped the audience into a kind of collective orgy, all waiting tensely for the moment of release, the orgasm that manifested itself in a wild outcry. . . . No doubt there was a deeper meaning to Hitler's frequent comparison of the masses to "woman." And we need only look at the corresponding pages in *Mein Kampf*, at the wholly erotic fervor that the idea and the image of the masses aroused in him, to see what he sought and found as he stood on the platform high above the masses filling the arena—his masses. Solitary, unable to make contact, he more and more craved such collective unions. In a revealing turn of phrase (if we may believe the source) he once called the masses his "only bride." His oratorical discharges were largely instinctual, and his audience, unnerved by prolonged distress and reduced to a few elemental needs, reacted on the same instinctual wave length. The sound recordings of the period clearly convey the peculiarly obscene, copulatory character of mass meetings: the silence at the beginning, as of a whole multitude holding its breath; the short, shrill yappings; the minor climaxes and first sounds of liberation on the part of the crowd; finally the frenzy, more climaxes, and then the ecstasies released by the finally unblocked oratorical orgasms.[12]

This is, of course, thoroughly consistent with the antirationalism and emphasis on mystery and emotion that we have noted before. Hitler saw himself as the reincarnation of ancient German rulers, returned by history to lead the people in fulfilling their destiny. In asserting these ties to historical Germany, Hitler was able to draw on large portions of the romantic tradition that had become so much a part of everyday culture. Ancient symbols were resurrected to assert these historical ties; the simple strong man of the soil became an ideal German; even architectural styles copying the designs of the Middle Ages were in vogue. These symbols of the romantic tradition were, as we have noted earlier, combined with those of racism to produce a view of the forthcoming Third Reich that was simultaneously German and Aryan. All this is but another way of saying that Hitler was an instinctive master of the new art (science?) of propaganda and mass psychology.

---

[11]Bullock, *Hitler*, pp. 323–24.
[12]Joachim C. Fest, *Hitler* (New York: Harcourt Brace Jovanovich, 1973), pp. 323–24.

Use of Propaganda

Early in life he was greatly impressed with British efforts at propaganda during World War I, and he realized the potential of mass communication. All of the media were used to emphasize the Aryan ideal and to condemn the Jewish influence in German life. The motion picture art form was perfected by the Nazis even though the use of films for political purposes had only been recently recognized. Hitler's personal taste in art and architecture dictated aesthetic values for the entire society, while the whole cultural and educational structure was revamped to wipe out liberal values and Jewish influences.

> This cleansing of our culture must be extended to nearly all fields. Theater, art, literature, cinema, press, posters, and window displays must be cleansed of all manifestations of our rotting world and placed in the service of a moral, political and cultural idea. . . . The right of personal freedom recedes before the duty to preserve the race.[13]

Typical of such movements, particular emphasis was placed upon ensuring that the *youth* of Germany—the next generation—would grow up uncontaminated by foreign influences. Führer worship became an integral part of the socialization of the youth of Germany. For example, the following is a prayer that was to be said before meals by children in Cologne:

> Führer, my Führer, bequeathed to me by the Lord, Protect and preserve me as long as I live! Thou hast rescued Germany from deepest distress, I thank thee for my daily bread. Abideth thou long with me, forsaketh me not, Führer, my Führer, my faith and my light!
>
> *Heil, mein Führer!*[14]

Similarly, Christianity was "Germanized" and "Aryanized" to lend the weight of religion to the movement:

> As with every people, the eternal God also created a Law for our people especially suited to its racial character. It acquired form in the Führer Adolf Hitler and in the National-Socialist state that he formed. . . . One People!—One Reich!—One Church![15]

Such examples could be duplicated endlessly.

[13]Adolf Hitler, *The Speeches of Adolf Hitler*, Norman H. Baynes, ed. (London: Oxford University Press, 1942), p. 568.

[14]George L. Mosse, ed., *Nazi Culture* (New York: Grosset & Dunlap, 1966), p. 241.

[15]Ibid, p. 242.

Racist Internationalism

It is in this attempt to develop what George Mosse has called a "Nazi culture" that we can see the genuinely revolutionary nature of Hitler's enterprise. He was attempting to change the values of an entire population and point them toward a new society, composed partially of elements of an idealized historical Germany but dominated by a vision of a new Reich. Finally, we must underscore the fact that such an attempt at producing a total culture was only possible because of the existence of a modern bureaucratic state. The rise of a rationalized *bureaucratic class* whose purpose was the effective implementation of orders given to it provided a mechanism for putting Nazi culture in place. The bureaucrat's purpose was not to question the orders given, but to implement them efficiently, without bias or scorn, regardless of how absurd or inhuman they appeared to be.

We cannot enter into a detailed discussion of the economic policies of Nazi Germany. It can be argued that none is necessary for Nazi economic policies in general exhibited the same type of eclectic accommodation to varying groups in the society that we have observed in Mussolini's Italy. At an early date, Hitler had proclaimed socialism to be a doctrine only possible within the confines of the nation-state; international socialism, particularly Marxism, was declared to be a perversion of the fundamental doctrine—a central element in the "international Jewish conspiracy."

After their assumption of power the Nazis were able to blend this vague socialism with the existing corporate interests in Germany to produce economic policies whose goals were easily stated—power and greatness. Such practical accommodation was not, however, a distinguishing trait of National Socialism, nor was it characteristic of Hitler. We noted earlier the fascism of Benito Mussolini possessed no clear conception of a goal culture and tended to emphasize action and involvement almost for its own sake. Such was not the case with Hitler; he had an all too clear conception of his new society and the actions that would be necessary to achieve it.

At the beginning of this discussion of National Socialism it was asserted that Hitler was fundamentally an Aryan racist and that the fruition of his plans would have led to the destruction of the German nation-state. By now we believe we have established the importance that race played in Hitler's mind, but the full import of those doctrines can be seen only by examining his plans for the future society. Once again, perhaps it is better to let Hitler speak for himself:

> The main principle which we must observe is that the State is not an end, but a means. It is the foundation on which higher human culture is to

rest, but it does not originate it. It is rather the presence of a race endowed with the capabilities for civilization which is able to do this.[16]

Hitler asserted clearly that the state serves as a vehicle for the elevation of the Aryan race to a position of power where the race can create higher human culture and civilization. That is the state's prime purpose. Surely, one might ask: But doesn't that mean greater power and glory for all Germans? By no means. It must be remembered that the existing German nation had been corrupted by blood-mixing and therefore contained impurities that had to be eradicated.

> In its capacity as a State, the German Reich must gather all Germans to itself; it must not only select out of the German nation *only the best of the original racial elements* and conserve them, but must slowly and surely raise them to a position of dominance.[17]

Not merely the state, but the existing German *Volk* itself is a device for resurrecting the pure Aryan strain. In effect, a German whose blood is not pure is at best a culture sustainer, at worst a destroyer of culture and civilization. The only true human is an Aryan, and anyone existing within the state who has mixed blood must either be a slave to the Aryan or be eliminated. While Jews are both the most obvious and dangerous of culture destroyers, they are not alone.

Here we see Hitler's racism in full-bloom. The thousand-year Reich will not be a German nation-state, but an Aryan state in which any non-Aryans exist only to serve the interests of the culture creator. Extermination became Hitler's final solution to the Jewish menace, but it must be remembered that Auschwitz and Buchenwald were also slave-labor camps whose bureaucratically calculated goal was working "people" to death—a world, in Richard Rubenstein's words, "of the living dead." In addition, the expansionist military policies of Nazi Germany against other non-Aryan nations were not simply designed to provide "living space" for the German nation as Hitler frequently stated. Their ultimate objective was the subjugation of all non-Aryan peoples to the master race. And all destroyers of culture would have to be themselves destroyed.

This, then, is not German nationalism but *racist internationalism.* Given that, many of Hitler's actions and Nazi policies fall into a pattern. The "scientific" efforts to determine Aryan blood, and programs formulated literally to breed people possessing Aryan characteristics, can be seen as direct means for achieving the goal culture. Further, during the latter days of World War II, Hitler could declare that Germany had failed him without destroying the basic premise of his racism. That

[16]Hitler, *My Battle*, p. 158.
[17]Ibid, p. 161 (emphasis added).

is, the fact that Germany was losing the war had nothing to do with the innate superiority of Aryans but showed that Germans of mixed blood had not been strong enough to fulfill their task of achieving Aryan supremacy. Finally, with retreating armies on all sides, Hitler could declare that he had been successful, because his extermination camps and breeding policies would ensure that from the ashes of a defeated Germany would inevitably arise a new Aryan-dominated society, one free of Jews. His racial doctrines, with all of their horrifying consequences, remained with him to the end.

The results of Hitler's racist policies defy comprehension. One searches in vain for words to describe the horror of Auschwitz and the other concentration camps. In a fundamental way, Nazism denies the basic purpose of this entire book, which is an attempt to understand—rationally—competing ideologies, as alien as they may seem to be. But if comprehension is beyond our reach, silence is not the answer. We must continue to try to understand, for like Marxism, fascism, and liberal democracy, racism is not a dead doctrine.

SUGGESTED READINGS

ADORNO, THEODOR W., et al., *The Authoritarian Personality.* New York: Harper & Row, Publishers, 1960.

BULLOCK, ALAN, *Hitler: A Study in Tyranny.* New York: Bantam Books, 1961.

HITLER, ADOLF, *Mein Kampf,* tr. Ralph Manheim. Boston: Houghton Mifflin Company, 1971.

_____, *The Speeches of Adolf Hitler,* 1922–1939, Norman H. Baynes, ed., 2 vols. Oxford: Oxford University Press, 1942.

MOSSE, GEORGE L., ed., *Nazi Culture.* New York: Grosset and Dunlap, 1966.

_____, *Nazism: A History and Comparative Analysis of National Socialism.* New Brunswick, N.J.: Rutgers University Press, 1978.

_____, *The Crisis of German Ideology: Intellectual Origins of the Third Reich.* New York: Universal Library, 1964.

RUBENSTEIN, RICHARD L., *The Cunning of History.* New York: Harper & Row, Publishers, 1978.

SHIRER, WILLIAM L., *The Rise and Fall of the Third Reich.* New York: Crest Books, 1962.

12

Continuing Issues— Resurgent Islam

[Islam] is a religion that provides guidance for conducting the affairs of state and a guide to the straight path, which is neither Eastern nor Western. It is a religion where worship is joined to politics and political activity is a form of worship.

Imam Ayatollah Khomeini

We have stated in the last two chapters that we believe Adolf Hitler's racism eventually transformed the fascist categories that he adopted from Mussolini into a fundamentally different ideology. As we also noted, many commentators recognize major differences between Italian Fascism and German National Socialism, but stop short of our conclusion that they are, in the end, very different belief systems.

This is but to underscore, once again, the difficulty with defining the phenomenon commonly called "fascism." Perhaps scholars should simply refuse to use the word, referring instead to a body of contemporary, change-oriented ideological thinking that denies any distinction between public and private, views the individual as indistinguishable from the social whole, uses extreme emotional appeal in pursuing converts to its doctrines, is antimodern in perspective, and, above all, believes that some entity—the nation-state in generic fascism, the Aryan race in German National Socialism—is the ultimate authority in all human affairs. If we were to adopt that position, it would afford us at least a vague category and a reason for speaking briefly of an additional system of belief—a change-oriented, revolutionary ideology—that has recently reemerged as a major political force in contemporary world affairs. We could, in the phrase of John L. Esposito, speak of "resurgent Islam." Even so, it would be important to keep in mind that "resurgent Islam" comprises but a portion of Islam.

But why single out Islam for treatment in this context? The latter half of the twentieth century has witnessed the birth or revitalization of numerous movements whose doctrines and actions might well fit our loose definition just outlined. Various forms of fundamentalist Christianity might well fall within that rubric, and some would argue that forms of Judaism would fit as well. Yet we believe Islam, in particular, deserves discussion in a book on ideologies for several reasons.

Initially, in terms of sheer numbers, Islam in various forms claims the allegiance of fully one-fifth of the world's population. While usually associated exclusively with the Middle East, Islam has followers around the world; in the Soviet Union, after slavic groups, Muslims comprise the largest ethnic and cultural group, consisting of approximately 20 percent of the population. Moreover, Islam is and has been a belief system containing a built-in command to spread its truth. At various points in its long history, that command has produced events of history altering proportions, and, in the minds of many, we appear to be entering such a period today. Unlike other religious movements, resurgent Islam is unequivocally political and international in its orientation. While particular nations have attempted to establish Islamic states, Islam—as a body of ideas—remains independent of the authority of any particular State since God alone is considered the sole authority. Finally, recalling one of our earlier comments on Marxism-Leninism, we suspect that the potential reader of this book will have scant knowledge of Islam, "sharing the general . . . public's perceptions of Islam [that] have tended to be characterized by ignorance, confusion, and misinformation."[1] All of this being said, a word of caution is in order. Islam is an incredibly complex religious, cultural, and political phenomenon. It contains a rich and extensive history and is hardly a monolithic entity: it too has subdivisions and differing schools of thought. Given the prominence of the late Ayatollah Khomeini's role in Iran and world politics, it is inevitable that a book on ideologies should address him and his interpretation of Shi'ah Islam. It is necessary to remember, nevertheless, that Islam remains independent of any particular human. As authors, we are again in the uncomfortable position of trying to make simple albeit meaningful statements, in a brief chapter, about a vast, complicated subject matter. The attempt will inevitably fall short of an adequate treatment, since exceptions to almost any generalization about Islam can be found; yet we remain committed to our pedagogical position that a little bit of knowledge about a subject matter is better than none.

ISLAM: BASIC BELIEFS AND VALUES

Islam is based upon the belief in a single, all-powerful, all-knowing God, *Allah*, which is arabic for God. This is the same God as Christianity's Jehovah and Judaism's Yahweh. Islam believes that human beings are the special creation of God, and exist for the purpose of fulfilling His will, and are held responsible for their actions on earth at the Day of Judgment. God's will has been revealed through a series of prophets—Adam, Abraham, Moses, and Christ—whose words and actions provide the standards for human conduct. Muslims believe, however, that the will of God as revealed to Moses and later Jesus had become distorted by Jews and Christians, particularly as their teachings became embodied in formal religious institutions. Because of this corruption, there arose the need for a final prophet to whom God revealed His will in total form. That prophet was Muhammad.

Muhammad ibn Abdullah was born in Mecca in 570 C.E. (Christian Era) and spent most of his early life engaged in the commercial life of that prosperous city. At the age of 40 this introspective and contemplative man received the first of a series of revelations from God and was to continue to do so for a period of more than twenty years. As the final chosen messenger of God, Muhammad was to spend the rest of his life spreading God's word and exhorting humans to return to righteousness.

[1]Fred R. Von Der Mehden, "American Perceptions of Islam," in John L. Esposito, ed., *Voices of Resurgent Islam* (New York: Oxford University Press, 1983), p. 18.

It is important to note that in spite of Muhammad's centrality to Islam, he is considered a mortal human who, although chosen by God to bring His word to humanity, is neither to be worshiped nor thought of as the founder of Islam. Indeed, Allah alone is to be worshiped; He alone the creator of Islam.

Muhammad serves at least two important purposes in the Muslim faith. First, as the recipient of the word of God, Muhammad recorded— one verse at a time—His messages in a book called the *Qur'an* (Koran). It is the sacred scripture for all Muslims. Second, Muhammad's exemplary life of piety and perfection provides Muslims with a role model of the type of life all true believers ought to lead. Therefore, the early history of Islam under Muhammad's leadership becomes extremely important in understanding its current thinking and practices.

The early days of Muhammad's prophecy were difficult ones wherein he preached the will of God to a small but ever-expanding body of followers in the city of Mecca in present-day Saudi Arabia. It was his movement from Mecca to the city of Medina that provided more fertile ground for what was to become an extremely dynamic religious and political movement. At Medina, Muhammad legislated and preached a doctrine that by his death in 632 had spread to the entire Arabian peninsula. More significant for our purposes, this initial Islamic state established precedents and exhibited values that demonstrated the proper application of the will of God in the temporal world. As such, it became, and remains, an ideal for practitioners of Islam to this day.

THE IDEAL ISLAMIC STATE

The conception of the Muslim *community*, following the word of God as recorded in the *Qur'an* is one of the central conceptions of Islam. Both as individuals and as members of the community, Muslims are obligated to follow the specific strictures of the *Qur'an*, for the book is viewed not as a human interpretation of God's will but rather as containing the literal words of God. There are five demonstrations of faith incumbent upon all Muslims: profession of faith, prayer, almsgiving, fasting, and the pilgrimage to Mecca. Islam possesses no abstract conception of the individual independent of society such as we have encountered in liberalism. Even though there have been powerful, existentialist approaches to Islam, there remains no separation between the individual and the Muslim community. Humans fulfill themselves as individuals only in and through the community of Islam whose laws and practices must follow God's will. The word "Islam" derives from the Arabic root *salima*, which can be interpreted to mean peace, obedience, and submission; indeed, the term "Muslim" means one who submits to God.

Other distinctions familiar to followers of the liberal tradition such as that between religion and politics, or public and private, simply do not exist in their liberal form in Islam. Recall that it was John Locke, who in his 1689 *Letter Concerning Toleration,* was among the first liberals to call for this separation. However, the very ideal of the separation of church and state was considered by the Ayatollah Khomeini to be a critical part of imperialist propaganda designed to keep Islam weak. "This slogan of the separation of religion and politics and the demand that Islamic scholars not intervene in social and political affairs have been formulated and propagated by the imperialists . . . and their political agents in order to prevent religion from ordering the affairs of this world and shaping Muslim society."[2] The public and private viewed as part of God's dominion—the twin guideposts of the *Qur'an* and the model of Muhammad—govern every aspect of the life of all believers. It may well be the *totality* of Islam's influence into virtually every facet of a person's life that is most striking to North Americans: It contains "laws and practices for all human affairs . . . extending from even before the embryo is formed until after he is placed in the tomb."[3]

One should not, however, interpret the aforementioned "submissiveness" to God to mean a type of quiet acceptance of His will, for Muslims are morally obligated to spread the word of God. This does not mean, however, that all nonbelievers should be converted to Islam. For example, Christians and Jews—"people of the book"—are permitted to practice their religion without interference. Muslims are required to attempt to convert only pagans and polytheists to the true path. While the modern-day Sunni branch of Islam has avoided the messianism that has recently attracted the attention of the West, it too has had its militant moments. Shi'ah remains more action oriented; the power of its messianic mission has been demonstrated through its history, most recently in reaction to the political policies of the last Iranian monarch, Mohammad Reza Pahlavi, better known as the shah of Iran. As Imam Khomeini, leader of the Shi'ah opposition to the Shah, put it: "Islam is the religion of militant individuals who are committed to truth and justice. It is a religion of those who desire freedom and independence. It is the school of those who struggle against imperialism."[4] The extremely rapid early successes in spreading the faith under Muhammad's leadership, and the continued worldwide spread of Islam after his death, serve but to demonstrate the correctness of their vision. Indeed, to many modern Muslims the relative lack of success of Islam in more

---

[2]Imam Khomeini, *Islam and Revolution: Writings and Declarations of Imam Khomeini* (Berkeley: Mizan Press, 1981), p. 38.

[3]Ibid., p. 30.

[4]Ibid., p. 28.

contemporary times is the direct result of straying from the righteous path, and their remedy lies in a return to the origins. In much the same way as they view Christians and Jews, modern fundamentalist Muslims view many of their brethren as having been seduced by the false values of the modern world—and its false ideologies—and see salvation only in a return to the ideal Islamic state. Part of the power of this ideal state derives from the blending of memory and imagination. As Fouad Ajami explains it:

> The Islamic state that tantalizes true believers and frightens those in the West who worry about the receding of civilization is a memory that makes the present order look hopelessly compromising. No one knows what an Islamic state would or would not do, would or would not look like. Memory may imagine and resurrect—on paper, in sermons, in the tracts of the true believers—a world that was once whole and autonomous.[5]

This *reactive* element in the Islamic faith will be examined more fully at a later point in our discussion. For the moment we must briefly attempt to explain the evolution of Islam, particularly in terms of its leadership, after the death of Muhammad.

LEADERSHIP AND AUTHORITY AFTER MUHAMMAD

Islam contains several interpretative schools of thought, but the most basic and fundamental division is between the Sunni and the Shi'ah. So deep is this division that each group will not recognize the other as legitimate Muslims. Given the disproportionate numbers of Sunni compare to Shi'ah, it is understandable how the Shi'ah feel like a conquered people, even in the Middle East. The vast majority of Muslims, around 80 percent, are Sunni; they identify with not only the *Qur'an* but also the *sunna*—a body of legal and moral principles that predate the Islamic era. Inside the Sunni there are at least four jurisprudential schools: *Hanbali, Hanafi, Shafi'i,* and *Maliki.* The Sunni believe that Muhammad left no specific provision for leadership of the greatly expanded Muslim community after his death. However, the principle of submission to the authority of God and His Prophet was well established. There could be no prophetic successor to Muhammad for he was the final prophet, but the *Qur'an* and the model of Islamic behavior exemplified by Muhammad's life would serve to guide the future of Islam. To direct that effort the position of caliph, meaning representative or agent, was established in 632, whereby one elder of the community was designated as ruler.

[5]Fouad Ajami, *The Arab Predicament: Arab Political Thought and Practice Since 1967* (New York: Cambridge University Press, 1981), p. 192.

Abu Bakr was the initial caliph. The institution of the caliphate was to exist well into the thirteenth century, although the designation of individual caliphs often produced considerable turmoil. Of particular note is the reign of the fourth caliph, Ali, who was the cousin and son-in-law of Muhammad. Ali's followers—later to be called Shi'ah (meaning "faction" or "political party") Muslims—were of the belief that the only true caliphs were to be the direct descendants of Muhammad or, following Ali's reign, his descendants. When Ali was killed in 662 another caliph was appointed, leading Ali's followers under the leadership of his son, Husain, to rebel. The rebellion was quickly crushed, and Husain was killed, but the basis for the contemporary splitting of Islam into the two major groups—Sunni and Shi'ah—was established.

Shi'ah Muslims believe that the leadership of Islam can only come from certain lineage descended from Muhammad through Husain, and the martyrdom of Ali and Husain continues to color their world view. Whereas the Sunni institution of the caliphate was achieved through selection of a leader by the community, Shi'ah believe that the only legitimate leaders of Islam are the *Imam*—direct descendants of Muhammad and the first Imam, Ali. The Imam was considered an *ayatollah,* meaning "emanation of God" or a "sign from God." Consequently, he is of higher authority than either a prophet or a caliph; this results in differing political organizations and differing political terminology between the two divisions. Where the Sunni employed the title caliph (in the twentieth century the title was discontinued), the Shi'ah continue to use the titles Imam and Ayatollah. While the fundamental split in Islam revolves around the issue of who are the legitimate successors to Muhammad, given the power of Islam's religious leaders and the leaders' relationship to sacred law, the rift created doctrinal disputes. And, as has been the history of all such internal disputes among devoted followers of an ideology, the internal clashes have been particularly emotional and bloody. Hard as it is for North Americans to believe, the passion of the Arab-Israel conflicts pales in comparison to the religious fervor—underpinned by international, regional, and domestic political issues—released in Muslim civil wars as recently witnessed in the Iraq-Iran war.

Shi'ah view the Imam as the sole interpreter of God's will, whose authority in all matters—social, economic, political, and religious—is absolute. While he is not a prophet, he is divinely inspired. The Sunni caliph, by contrast, is elected by the community and possesses much authority in all matters, but does not necessarily possess divine inspiration or infallibility. Simply, the Shi'ah conception of the Imam is much more authoritarian. Shi'ah disagreements as to precisely which descendants of Ali were legitimate Imams led to the development of numerous splits and sects within this branch of Islam, some of which continue to this day. However, the general contemporary belief is that the line of direct descendants of Ali has been terminated, hence there is no identifiable Imam. Nevertheless, according to Shi'ah theology, the Twelfth Imam, although born in 869, is not dead, but is absent or "in hiding," waiting to return in the future. Until that day, when the Twelfth Imam as the *mahdi* (divinely guided messiah) returns, all political authority is fundamentally illegitimate, even though the mullahs and ayatollahs serve in the *mahdi's* place. For our purposes the absence of an identifiable Imam means that it is necessary to have others—legal scholars and religious leaders—interpret God's will for the community. We will return to this Shi'ah conception of leadership in the following discussion of contemporary Islam. For the moment, however, brief mention of the amazing successes of Islam in politics, scholarship, and culture throughout its history seems necessary so that we may understand the contemporary view that Islam must return to the practices that made it so successful in the past.

THE GROWTH OF ISLAM

We have already alluded to the fact that the early growth of the Islamic movement under Muhammad was extraordinarily rapid. That growth process was to continue after his death well into the sixteenth century. Armed with the *Qur'an's* teaching that the will of God is not abstract doctrine requiring simple belief, but a set of commands requiring action, Muslims under various leaders engaged in the practice called *jihad*. The word means "an exertion for a pious purpose" and can specifically mean "holy war," but it should not necessarily be interpreted to mean armed struggle. Those who fight in the name of Islam are called *mujahiddin*, the most famous of which are the so-called freedom fighters in Afghanistan. It is the obligation incumbent on all Muslims to spread God's will through preaching, teaching, and, if it seems necessary, armed struggle. The borders of the Islamic community expanded to include the entire Middle East, considerable portions of southern Europe, and were moved eastward to include parts of India and modern-day Indonesia. In battle, a mythology developed around Muslims who became known for their tenacity and willingness to sacrifice their lives for the cause, a sacrifice that would guarantee them eternal reward. Their military successes paved the way for tremendous achievements in culture. With Christian Europe in the throes of what is commonly called the Dark Ages, Muslim scholars established centers of learning which preserved, added to, and disseminated the cultural traditions of Ancient Greece and Rome. These religious scholars, the *ulama*, eventually came to form a sort of international Islamic intelligensia, and their scholarly achievements, particularly in the elaboration of Islamic law (*Sharia*), gave them special status within Islam.

The scope and power of the international Muslim community in the later Middle Ages was unparalleled. Under the leadership of religious-political leaders called sultans, numerous Muslim empires were established throughout the world (Persian, Ottoman, Mughal in India, to name a few). While they were all united under the banner of Islam, much of their success was due to the fact that these empires were able to accommodate themselves to many varied local practices in the areas under their rule. While the Islamic faith provided a set of core beliefs and practices for all Muslims, its application to specific settings was quite varied. Such adaptation to the practices and customs of varying conquered areas resulted, in the eyes of some, in a tendency to dilute the message of God and would make Islam too susceptible to "foreign" and "modern" ideas in the future. Such deviations from "the straight path"—particularly in the minds of contemporary fundamentalist Muslims—has been responsible for the relative decline in power and international influence Islam has experienced since the sixteenth century.

ISLAM AND THE MODERN WORLD

In a fundamental way, many of the values and practices commonly associated with the modern western world are, in principle, alien to the beliefs of Islam. Or, if they are not totally alien, can only be assimilated with tremendous difficulty. Hence, we should not be surprised by the fact that attempts by the Muslim world to adopt—and in some instances absorb—Western values and institutions were, and continue to be, quite varied.

The rise of the modern nation-state, the Western emphasis on individualism, secularism and the increasing tendency to separate religion and politics, Western concepts of rationalized bureaucracy, and the overall emphasis on materialism and technological development—all can, in varying degrees, be seen as developments that are difficult to integrate with traditional Muslim values. Certainly, the last of these items—the emphasis on materialism and technology—has been the most difficult for many Muslims to accept since, among other things, it tends to detract from a spiritualized understanding of the world. Remember also, while there are a few minor Islamic movements that claim to be communist in perspective, from the mainstream Islamic perspectives both liberalism and communism—while different in many ways—are both Western value systems that contain elements unacceptable to Islam.

Some Muslim countries—Egypt, Turkey, and initially Iran, for example—were rather quick to adopt many of the innovative ideas of modern civilization. Other nations were more wary of these "foreign" influences, less sure that Western-style development and modernization were unmixed blessings. Simply, it is difficult to summarize the responses of Islamic countries to the importation of Western culture and values, particularly given the brevity of our discussion. Suffice it to say that traditional Muslim culture, habits, and behavior patterns have been severely challenged by those foreign influences during the colonial and neo-colonial periods, and that the adoption of many of these influences by Muslim countries prepared the groundwork for contemporary fundamentalist attempts to preach a return to "the straight path" of Islam.

In our earlier discussion we used the term "reaction" to indicate one of the more fundamental characteristics of the Islamic faith. In this more contemporary context, the use of that word is even more appropriate in that much of the basis for the recent fundamentalist Islamic movement can be seen, from a liberal perspective, as a *reaction* to the aforementioned Western values. In the eyes of some commentators, resurgent Islamic fundamentalism is intimately tied to the more general question of lesser developed countries and their experiences with Western colonialism. In this view, "modernization" and "development" along Western lines had served not only to undermine traditional Muslim values, but had produced a new, highly Westernized elite class who were totally cut off from the masses. With the gap between rich and poor growing in many Muslim countries, the rallying cry of *anti-colonialism* could be used not only to combat "Westernization" but as a device to attack the class discrepancies and redress the economic imbalances produced by colonialism. Insofar as resurgent Islam helps individuals overcome the psychological self-contempt of colonialism, it must be seen as a positive development. Furthermore, this anticolonialism is not merely a reaction to existing circumstances—a purposeless lashing out—for the Islamic model of an alternative society (a true society) was readily available in the twin guideposts of the *Qur'an* and the teachings of the Prophet Muhammad.

At the risk of gross oversimplification, it may be stated that the modern resurgence of Islam has taken two paths, distinguished largely by the degree of their commitment to return to the basic teachings of the doctrine and their willingness to accept Western models of modernization. The more radical of the two paths believes that Western ideas of modernization and development have totally corrupted Islam and calls for a complete transformation of contemporary Muslim states—a return to the traditional ideal Islamic community. This return, called *reactionary* in the West, is considered *progressive* from this Muslim point of view. Perhaps Imam Khomeini's view of western wealth and technology is illustrative:

> As the imperialist countries attained a high degree of wealth and afflu-ence—the result both of scientific and technical progress and of their plunder of the nations of Asia and Africa—these [Iranians] lost all self-confidence and imagined that the only way to achieve technical progress was to abandon their own laws and beliefs. When the moon landings took place, for instance, they concluded that Muslims should jettison their laws! . . . Let them go all the way to Mars or beyond the Milky Way; they will still be deprived of true happiness, moral virtue, and spiritual advancement and be unable to solve their own social problems. For the solution of social problems and the relief of human misery require foundations in faith and morals; merely acquiring material power and wealth, conquering nature and space, have no effect in this regard.[6]

The best example of this type of resurgent Islam is to be found in the Iranian Islamic Republic established by Ayatollah Ruhollah Khomeini in 1979. While we can make no attempt here to assess the lasting impact of the Iranian revolution, from the ideological perspective it is clear that it preached a total revolutionary transformation of Iranian society— a cultural revolution—guided by the goal culture of traditional Islam. Steps were taken to transform education and legal codes, strict censorship was established, traditional Muslim customs including appropriate cloth-ing styles were reintroduced, political decision making and administration was placed in the hands of the clergy, and, in general, everything "Western," or influenced by Western values, was to be abolished— including members of the socialist, Muslim opposition, which had helped overthrow the shah. What must be emphasized in all of this is the charismatic leadership role of the Ayatollah Khomeini and the profound and widespread devotion he received from the masses of people. The similarity between Khomeini and other twentieth-century revolutionary leaders is striking: like Lenin, he started a revolution in exile and returned to lead it; like Gandhi, he mobilized spiritual forces for political ends; and like Mao, he pushed beyond nationalism to international ideological and cultural revolution.

As Iran is an almost totally Shi'ah country, Khomeini's authority in all matters was derived from the Shi'ah conception of a divinely inspired Imam discussed earlier. To highlight his position, he created the post of *wali fagih,* ruling theologian, who is superior to any political leader. Hence, his authority was seen as absolute and his word was law. Nevertheless, the Imam's rule was subordinate to God's:

[6]Ibid., pp. 35–36.

The fundamental difference between Islamic government . . . and constitutional monarchies and republics . . . is this: whereas the representatives of the people or monarch in such regimes engage in legislation, in Islam the legislative power and competence to establish laws belongs exclusively to God Almighty. The sacred Legislator of Islam is the sole legislative power.[7]

With the death of the Ayatollah Khomeini in 1989 the future direction of the Iranian revolution remains in doubt, and, as mentioned, the lasting impact of the changes initiated during his period of leadership remains to be assessed. What is clear, however, is the great symbolic effect that the Iranian revolution has had on Muslims and Muslim countries throughout the world—including those less fervently committed to the total transformation of their societies.

In a sense, the Ayatollah Khomeini's Islamic Republic provides a vague standard against which one might judge the second path to resurgent Islam mentioned earlier. This second type of Muslim state also exhibits the fundamentalist desire to reinfuse their countries with traditional Islamic values and practices, but they seek to do so without the total rejection of the Westernizing influences they have adopted during the twentieth century. While a "ranking" of various Muslim countries in terms of the degree to which they have attempted to reestablish traditional values in their societies would hardly be appropriate here, several examples of their efforts might give us a better indication of their intent.

A typical symbol in the more moderate countries of the reemergence of the Islamic values is the adoption of traditional personal habits—Muslim dress for women (head scarves; loose, body covering clothing) and the growing of beards by men. In some countries, however, such change in demeanor, while it might be encouraged by authorities, is not made a matter of law. Additionally, where the *Qur'an* (not unlike the *Bible*) explicitly prohibits usury and requires a religious tithe from the rich for the benefit of the poor, several experiments with interest-free banks have been attempted in Pakistan, for example, and ostentatious displays of wealth have been discouraged. The modern Western conception of women as full and equal competitors with men—particularly in the work force—has been seriously reexamined in many Muslim countries, in light of the *Qur'an's* teaching that the primary role of women is to be found in the family. Finally, there has been an increased emphasis placed on prayer and Mosque attendance throughout the Muslim world.

Such practices have, however, not been instituted in an effort to replace Western concepts of development and modernization totally in

[7]Ibid., p. 55.

the case of the more moderate Muslim countries, but to transform those Western ideas so as to make them more compatible with traditional Muslim values.

ISLAM AND FASCISM

In the earlier discussion we argued that in spite of the difficulty involved in defining fascism, there were certain tendencies or characteristics that were identifiable in generic fascism. We spoke of an organic community; authoritarianism; leadership; a general reactive tendency; an emphasis on belief, emotion, activity; certain economic tendencies; and the totalizing impact of its values into all facets of life.

It should be obvious from our brief discussion of Islam that it shares many of these "traits," although perhaps not all of them. Be that as it may, there is one central—indeed crucial—characteristic of generic fascism that is not present in Muslim thought—the nation-state. In fascism, the "people," a clearly definable entity possessing a past, present, and a future, was the central analytical category. All other fascist activities were seen as processes designed to enhance the power and realize the potential of the nation-state. In contrast, the Islamic faith is international in scope and potential. Converts to Islam are to be sought irrespective of nationality. And Muhammad was prophet for all people, not for any particular national group. As Hassan al-Turabi has said, "an Islamic state is not a nationalist state because ultimate allegiance is owed to God and thereby to the community of all believers—the *ummah*. One can never stop at any national frontier and say the nation is absolute, an ultimate end in itself."[8] Clearly, given this unique perspective toward nation-states, Islam presents an enormous political problem for the traditional nation-states, be they liberal or communist as both the United States' experience in Iran and the Soviet Union's experience in Afghanistan proved.

SUGGESTED READINGS

AJAMI, FOUAD, *The Arab Predicament: Arab Political Thought and Practice Since 1967.* New York: Cambridge University Press, 1981.

BILL, JAMES A., *The Eagle and the Lion: The Tragedy of American-Iranian Relations.* New Haven, Conn.: Yale University Press, 1988.

DONOHUE, JOHN, ed., *Islam in Transition: Muslim Perspectives.* New York: Oxford University Press, 1982.

[8]Hassan al-Turabi, "The Islamic State," in *Voices of Resurgent Islam*, p. 242.

ESPOSITO, JOHN L., ed., *Voices of Resurgent Islam.* New York: Oxford University Press, 1983.

————, *Islam: The Straight Path.* New York: Oxford University Press, 1988.

GOLDZIHER, IGNAC, *Introduction to Islamic Theology and Law.* Princeton, N.J.: Princeton University Press, 1981.

KHOMEINI, IMAM, *Islam and Revolution: Writings and Declarations of Imam Khomeini.* Berkeley, Calif.: Mizan Press, 1981.

INAYAT, HAMID, *Modern Islamic Political Thought.* Austin: University of Texas Press, 1982.

RODINSON, MAXIME, *Islam and Capitalism.* New York: Pantheon Books, 1973.

13

Ideological Conflict in the Nuclear Age

> History [is] the slaughter bench at which the happiness of peoples, the wisdom of states, and the virtue of individuals have been sacrificed.
>
> Hegel

The twentieth century has been, and in all likelihood will continue to be, a time of tremendous ideological conflict—a competition for the hearts and minds of people. Recent events such as *perestroika*, the opening of China to the West, efforts at self-determination in Eastern European countries, the collapse of the Berlin Wall, and a general "liberalization" occurring in the communist world have led some to proclaim an "end to history" because the ideological conflict between two of the idea systems we have discussed is over. That is, these events "prove" that liberalism and capitalism have triumphed over socialism and communism. We do not think that is correct. To be sure, communist nations have turned to capitalist nations for technology, scientific information, consumer goods, and money. These same countries, however, have shown little interest in capitalism as a mode of production or as an ethical system: They want capital, not capitalism! There have often been periods when ideological conflict between these two idea systems has been temporarily muted, leading some to proclaim a termination of the struggle—an "end of ideology." But the conflict between them and their respective visions of the ideal human society seems always to reemerge. Perhaps that is inevitable. As the memories of the Vietnam war begin to fade from the collective consciousness and a new generation comes to adulthood ignorant of all but the cinematic horrors of war, it becomes increasingly important to recall all the people—over 100 million—who have died during this century at the hands of their fellow beings, the result of well-intentioned efforts to make the world safe for their particular vision of the good life.

Although individuals may kill for a variety of reasons—passion, self-defense, jealousy, revenge—it has only been groups of individuals (sects, classes, factions, nations) who kill other groups of individuals over questions of philosophy. Quite often it seems to be words and ideological visions, neither territory nor economic power, that are the dynamic, motivating force behind groups attacking other groups. In order to begin to understand why this occurs, it is important to remember our assertion in the introduction that each of the ideologies studied adamantly believes (1) that it alone knows what the human essence is, (2) that it alone knows how humans can reach their full potential, and (3) that it alone possesses the appropriate vision of "the beautiful."

At a general, ethical level, then, each idea system believes that it contains the seeds that will allow for or ensure the full flowering of humanity. Small wonder that so many have willingly fought, suffered, and died in these modern crusades to establish the City of God on earth. Arthur Koestler, examining pathological trends in human history, appropriately argued that "we are thus driven to the unfashionable conclusion that the trouble with our species is not an excess of *aggression,* but an excess capacity for fanatical *devotion*. Even a cursory glance at history should convince one that individual crimes committed for selfish motives play a quite insignificant part in the human tragedy, compared to the numbers massacred in unselfish loyalty to one's tribe, nation, dynasty, church, or political ideology, *ad majorem gloriam dei.*"[1]

There is at least one additional feature of our century that makes it unique: This is the nuclear age. Since August 6, 1945, humanity has tried to adapt itself to the horrific reality that it now possesses the capacity to commit *species* suicide. This is both ironic and tragic: The same species that so often appears desperately to want to build appropriate societies where all people can freely develop their humanity is also quite capable of completely obliterating itself in the process. Perhaps it is humanity's tragic fate simply to bring an end to its suffering rather than continue to struggle for the creation of the beautiful. As Nietzsche asked, "How much did this people have to suffer in order to become so beautiful?" Or perhaps we will remember Aristotle and *logos*, reasoned speech, and elect to begin a *dialogue* with others over the meaning of freedom, the essence of humanity, and the nature of the beautiful.

SOME THOUGHTS RECONSIDERED: COMMUNISM AND LIBERALISM

One of the questions left unanswered in the introduction to this book asked about the relationship between idea systems and political action. There it was asserted that although no causal relationship between ideologies and political acts could be proven, common sense seemed to indicate that they were indeed connected. The debate over the question of ideology and action has intensified in recent years, in proportion to the waves of political activism that have swept through the world. The student radicals of the 1960s and early 1970s in North America, the Chinese students in the 1980s, and the average citizens throughout Eastern Europe in 1989 demonstrate clearly that few periods in recent history have witnessed a greater concern with political ideas and their implementation. Diverse groups in the United States today cry out that the traditional values of freedom, equality, and self-determination have been used by politicians as camouflage to disguise a society that is racist, imperialist, sexist, and elitist. Citizens in Warsaw and Washington condemn their respective governments on grounds that are surprisingly

---

[1] Arthur Koestler, *Janus: A Summing Up* (London: Pan Books Ltd., 1978), p. 14.

similar. The cry of "power to the people" rings out in countries through-out the world. The ideological battles of the cold war, with the "free world" and "fraternal socialist states" in constant competition for con-verts, seem to many to pale in an era in which the United States and the Soviet Union are deemed equally culpable of imperialism and racism.

In spite of such feelings, this is not the place to attempt system-atically to relate the propaganda slogans of modern revolutionaries to the idea systems we have discussed. Such a project would require another book. Rather, in support of our earlier contention that these three ideologies form the theoretical base for many of the criticisms being leveled at as well as the aspirations being sought by modern societies, let us simply indicate a few areas where a knowledge of these more basic idea systems can help in illuminating contemporary affairs.

The United States and the Soviet Union stand today as the major representatives of two of the idea systems we have studied. We noted earlier that liberal democracy and communism, as bodies of ideas, can be separated from the imperfect attempts of various states to put those ideas into practice. However, in modern times the prime charge against both America and the Soviet Union was that they continued to talk as though they had achieved a liberal democratic and socialist society, respectively, while in fact they were a long way from realizing those goal cultures.

Indeed, some would contend that each nation was so far from the fulfillment of its ideal that the best solution was to scrap completely the existing society and start all over again—a communist revolution in the USSR, a democratic one in the United States. Whether we call it a performance gap or studied hypocrisy, each of these states was accused of denying, or at least being far from fulfilling, its own set of ideals. In the past the Soviet Union, while declaring itself to be a democratic socialist society, systematically repressed dissent and refused to acknowl-edge legitimate claims of its citizens. As the self-acknowledged leader of the socialist world and in spite of the doctrine of different paths to socialism, it saw fit to intervene in the internal affairs of fraternal socialist countries that strayed from the prescribed path as envisioned by Moscow. It stood condemned from within its own ideological camp by Mao Zedong and numerous others for subverting the goals of the revolution through the development of a new bureaucratic class structure, which makes a mockery of the socialist norm of equality, and surely prohibits the development of a communist society.

To be sure, the unexpected emergence of Mikhail Gorbachev and his programs of *perestroika* and *glasnost* have already had a dramatic impact on Soviet praxis. He has publicly acknowledged the serious economic and political shortcomings of the Soviet Union, recognizing that they are generations away from achieving their stated goals. He has taken steps to liberalize the Soviet state's treatment of its citizens and has urged his allies to explore their own paths to economic development—so long as they remain consistent with the values of socialism. While it might appear that Gorbachev's revolution would be applauded in the West, since many of the changes go a long way toward meeting past American criticisms of the USSR, politics is rarely that simple. Indeed, it may be the case that *perestroika* is the last thing that the United States wishes for the Soviet Union. After all, if Gorbachev successfully revives the economy and eliminates the human rights violations, what will the United States have to criticize? Moreover, will not a more open, flexible Soviet Union be more appealing to other nations, including those in the nonaligned world? In terms of ideological conflict, therefore, the net effect of Gorbachev's leadership may be an intensification, rather than relaxation, of the tensions between the superpowers.

To its critics, the crusade by the United States to maintain the security of the free world has foisted upon a considerable portion of the globe an economic system that serves only to fill the pockets of a small group of capitalists. Proclaiming itself a free and equal society, it has denied blacks, Hispanics, and women a fair place in its economic system and has developed a body of customs and laws that ensures that they can be neither free nor equal. America is, it is argued, imperialist, racist, and sexist. From within its own camp, democratic elitists and advocates of "alternative liberalism" accuse the United States of having a rigid class structure that benefits the few at the expense of the many, precluding once again the possibility of achieving the espoused ideals of liberal democracy. Despite proclamations to the contrary, America has undergone neither a revolution nor its own *perestroika* as the never-ending body count from homelessness, substance abuse, social diseases, environmental pollution, and urban life-styles reminds us. Two critical questions surface: Is it possible to have capitalism with a human face? Do not widespread poverty and homelessness in an affluent land of plenty equally constitute violations of human rights?

This raises another issue: Careful readers of this book will note that the sections on communism and fascism contained separate chapters on continuing issues inside their respective ideologies. This is not the case with liberalism. Although it too has major ideological problems to be confronted, it has remained remarkably silent in terms of ideological development. In part, this is understandable since it remains *the dominant* ideology, exercising its hegemonic influence over the entire globe. Exhibiting all the dynamic traits of the status quo ideology, it is logical to ask: If liberalism continues to fail to respond substantively to changes in the other ideologies, how long will its reign continue?

Competing Ideological Claims

The American political scientist Robert Dahl has observed: "There is no Democratic theory, only democratic theories."[2] In at least an historical sense this is accurate. Democracy has meant different things to different individuals at different times in history. For Plato and Aristotle, democracy was considered a political option, albeit a highly undesirable one, for a type of rule—rule by the *demos,* the people. Although neither philosopher thought very highly of the idea of democracy, both thought of it as not merely a type of government but also a *type of society* with a certain quality of life associated with it. Indeed, it was because democracy could not, in their view, provide the *good life* for all of its citizens that both philosophers opposed it.

Still, in its earliest foundation democracy was conceived as class rule and this, as we have shown, is also how Marx thought of both liberal democracy and the transition to communism. To Marx, the bourgeois would be overthrown by the proletariat, who would temporarily govern in the objectively best interest of all. Once the transition from capitalism to communism was completed, all members of the community would be able to reach their particular fulfillment as species beings. It is communism's quest, therefore, to free humanity from the irrational capitalist economic system, which structurally denies the majority of humanity the real chance to reach its potential. In recent times, the Soviets have taken measures which in effect bring liberal elements into their society: for example, the rule of law, the notion of innocent until proven guilty, open speech, and easier emigration. To be sure, the Soviets (and, for that matter, the Chinese) still do not completely meet the standards of liberal democracy in terms of civil and political rights. But then, they do not want to! They do not want to be a liberal— that is, bourgeois—democracy. That, through their ideological eyes, would be a reactionary movement. Instead, they concentrate efforts on social and economic reform.

Liberal democracy, like communism and fascism, also claims a monopoly on understanding humanity. Originally the democratic franchise was tacked onto liberalism to meet the pressing demands of the working class. Today, the dominant school of liberal democratic theory— pluralism—continues to view democracy primarily as an electoral mechanism for choosing between political leaders. Contemporary political scientists who subscribe to this view do not consider democracy as a type of society with a certain quality of life associated with it. Rather, democracy is seen as a question concerning who rules and how these

---

[2]Robert Dahl, *Preface to Democratic Theory* (Chicago: The University of Chicago Press, 1956), p. 1.

rulers are selected. In this conception, to be a democratic nation means to have relatively open elections between two (or more) political parties where no single party has a disproportionate chance of winning. The Soviets scoff at this limited notion of democracy. After all, what difference does it make if you choose among candidates X, Y, or Z if each is a capitalist? How significant, then, is the difference between the electoral systems of the United States and the USSR since the latter also has a reasonable degree of competition among its political elites? From the Soviet perspective both political systems are, in effect, single-party systems. Moreover, in their view at least the Soviets are actively striving to create economic democracy while the Americans are actively striving to perpetuate and expand the wage slavery inherent in capitalism.

Within the liberal democratic tradition there continues to exist a small but tenacious movement that argues that liberal democracy is more than a question of governmental rule—it is a matter of quality of life. We have referred to this movement as possessing an "alternative vision" of a liberal democratic society. This scholarly community argues that if liberal democracy could be extricated from the capitalist market system, and if its theorists could restore their early commitment to a notion of democracy as a type of society that values political and civil liberties while striving to end economic exploitation, then liberal democracy can meet the major communist criticism of it.

Communism and liberalism are the ideological systems of the world's superpowers. As the communist system continues to show that it too can deliver the military goods while it tries to create the economic infrastructure necessary to produce the desired consumer goods, it becomes increasingly clear that the superpower confrontation will be taking place in a war of words, of ideologies, particularly since neither power has a monopoly on the ability to survive a nuclear holocaust. And, here, Gorbachev's presence has already had a profound impact, for he clearly appreciates the power of words and images. Indeed, with his unilateral initiatives in nuclear arms reduction, Gorbachev upstaged and replaced former President Reagan if not as the moral leader of the world, then at least as the "great communicator" of the 1980s. The question then becomes: Which of the two superpower systems can change more readily. Can the Soviets continue to permit political and cultural freedom—a brief moment in their Leninist past? Or can Americans begin to abandon their attachment to the market and terminate its system of economic exploitation? The system which adapts itself to these issues will become relatively more appealing to supporters around the world.

Still, much of the nonaligned world, remains reluctant to adopt either communism or liberal democracy. These ideologies seem inappropriate to the particular cultural and historical needs of the nonaligned nations. Rejecting what they view to be the crass materialism and excessive competitiveness of capitalism as well as the ideas of atheism and class struggle behind official Marxism, these nations find more appealing the example of Italian (or generic) fascism and Islamic fundamentalism.

With the notions of corporativism, leadership, will, emotion, and organic national community, fascism has proven itself a powerful ideology for pulling together a collection of diverse groups and individuals even if the term *fascism*—for obvious political reasons—is used by few people today. Moreover, the continuing importance of the nation-state and nationalism in general gives at least partial support to Benito Mussolini's early contention that nationalism and collectivism would be dominant themes of the twentieth century. While both liberalism and communism utilize nationalism and the state for the achievement of their goals, it is only in fascism that the nation-state is central and all-embracing. Hence, in spite of the lack of individuals willing to proclaim themselves "fascists," the doctrine is alive and well as a competing ideology.

Finally, we have all too briefly introduced the phenomenon of resurgent Islam into the ideological debates of the latter twentieth century. While noting the similiarities between Islamic and fascist thought, we concluded that Islam could not be properly called "fascist" in that it is international in its scope and universal in its appeal, finding ultimate authority not in the nation-state but in the word of God. Whatever label one chooses to attach to it, it seems obvious that Islam—particularly in its fundamentalist posture—is and will continue to be a powerful competitor for the hearts and minds of people, for it too believes that it possesses the truth.

SHADOWS OF THINGS THAT WILL (OR COULD) BE: SOME FINAL THOUGHTS

Recall Plato's Cave. Perhaps we are still prisoners in it. However, you have now been exposed to the "puppet shows" that each ideology claims mirrors reality. Each ideology purports to know the good, the beautiful, and the truly human. Each is convinced that it—and it alone—is best for humanity. Which one is true? Which an illusion? Which one has the answers to the important questions of the human condition? What visions of the future are correct? The answer: They all are—or at least they all believe they are. But which is right?

As we said at the outset of this presentation of ideologies, we recognize the human longing for the comfort and security of a world with few questions and readily comprehensible, easily accepted values— the original fool's paradise of Plato's Cave where individuals believe they are free because they remain ignorant of their own enslavement. As Dostoevsky's cardinal in *The Grand Inquisitor on the Nature of Man* demonstrates, little has changed since the time of Plato.

> Today, people are more persuaded than ever that they have perfect freedom, yet they have brought their freedom to us and laid it humbly at our feet.[3]

It is now your chance—and your responsibility—to try to carry on your own dialogue with the shadows on the wall in hopes of better understanding them and perhaps finding a way to live a more fully human life inside of, if not out of, the cave. If you recall our introductory discussion, it was precisely at this point that we parted company with Plato and looked to John Stuart Mill for further inspiration for our investigations. Plato was sure that the path to the sun lay open to at least a few human beings if they were willing to engage in the extraordinarily difficult process of education that he prescribed. Plato was sure, in other words, that at least some members of the species were capable of achieving absolute knowledge about reality. We are less sure.

Perhaps in the final analysis no one can offer you, or any other person, ultimate answers to the important questions that have been raised throughout this book. We can, however, tell you that we believe that only after you are able to understand *critically* your own belief system and, as Mill would have it, *empathetically* see the world through the eyes of other belief systems can you even begin to develop grounds for judgments—both empirical and moral—on how humans do, and ought to, live. As Immanuel Kant so eloquently put it, "The death of dogma is the beginning of morality." We also know that *action* based on informed judgment is necessary. This book has attempted to present three, perhaps four, ideologies in a relatively sympathetic manner in an effort to understand whatever truth each possesses. As such, we have tried temporarily to suspend judgment concerning each of them while engaging in this "academic" exercise. But the hour of value judgments inevitably does, and must, return. Human beings, particularly in an age of ideology, must constantly make choices among competing values— they must act in the real world even if it is a world of shadows. And at a time when humanity seems perched precariously on the edge of self-destruction from nuclear, chemical, or ecological sources of its own creation, such choices and action are even more important.

Human beings are, after all, purposive creatures. We are capable of directing our thoughts and actions toward the achievement of the

---

[3]Fyodor Dostoevski, *The Grand Inquisitor on the Nature of Man* (Indianapolis: Bobbs-Merrill, 1978), p. 26.

goals we desire. In the twentieth century we have become extraordinarily adept at inventing countless and miraculous *techniques*—nuclear energy being perhaps the ultimate ironic statement of that capability. However, we have, in our judgment, been far less successful in the creative construction of our *goals*. We continue to resist the critical examination of our belief systems, forgetting Mill's warning that such a practice not only robs us of the chance to learn from other alternative visions and to substitute truth for error, but also turns what we think we believe into dead dogma. It seems we still prefer to hug our comfortable chains of enslavement rather than face the responsibility and uncertainty of freedom. While this behavior may be all too human, it is a denial of our humanity nevertheless. And, as Nietzsche reminds and encourages:

> A very popular error: having the courage of one's convictions; rather it is a matter of having the courage for an *attack* on one's convictions!!![4]

SUGGESTED READINGS

DOSTOEVSKI, FYODOR, *The Grand Inquisitor on the Nature of Man*, tr. Constance Garnett. Indianapolis: Bobbs-Merrill, 1978.

DÜRRENMATT, FRIEDRICH, *The Visit*, tr. Patrick Bowles. New York: Grove Press, 1979.

FREUD, SIGMUND, *Civilization and Its Discontents*, tr. James Strachey. New York: W. W. Norton & Company, 1962.

KARIEL, HENRY S., *Beyond Liberalism*. New York: Harper & Row, Publishers, 1978.

KOESTLER, ARTHUR, *Janus: A Summing Up*. London: Pan Books, Ltd., 1979.

MACPHERSON, C.B., *The Real World of Democracy*. New York: Oxford University Press, 1975.

THOMPSON, E.P. and DAN SMITH, eds., *Protest and Survive*. New York: Monthly Review Press, 1981.

TRUMBO, DALTON, *Johnny Got His Gun*. New York: Bantam Books, 1970.

[4]Friedrich Nietzsche, quoted in *Nietzsche: Philosopher, Psychologist, Antichrist* by Walter Kaufman (Princeton, N.J.: Princeton University Press, 1974), p. 19.

Index